Locus of Authority

Locus of Authority

The Evolution of Faculty Roles
in the Governance of Higher Education

WILLIAM G. BOWEN
and EUGENE M. TOBIN

ITHAKA
New York, Princeton, Ann Arbor

PRINCETON UNIVERSITY PRESS
Princeton and Oxford

Requests for permission to reproduce material from this work should
be sent to Permissions, Princeton University Press

Published by Princeton University Press, 41 William Street, Princeton,
New Jersey 08540

In the United Kingdom: Princeton University Press, 6 Oxford Street,
Woodstock, Oxfordshire OX20 1TW

press.princeton.edu

ISBN 978-0-691-16642-1

British Library Cataloging-in-Publication Data is available

This book has been composed in Sabon with Gotham display by
Princeton Editorial Associates Inc., Scottsdale, Arizona.

Printed on acid-free paper. ∞

Printed in the United States of America

10 9 8 7 6 5 4 3 2 1

To the memories of
Robert F. Goheen and Clark Kerr,
who did so much to support evolutionary
changes in faculty roles, and who were
exemplars of the values for which
higher education must continue to stand

CONTENTS

PREFACE AND ACKNOWLEDGMENTS

WHEN WE AND OUR COLLEAGUES began this project, we assumed that questions of governance would be critical in shaping the ability of colleges and universities to adapt to a new world. We feel this even more strongly today. From the outset we were struck by three facts. The first is that recent scholarship on American higher education pays scant attention to the role of faculty in governance; second, many intelligent people in the academy know very little about governance; and third, governance must always be understood in the context of the times as institutions confront different challenges and opportunities. In short, "governance" (by which we mean simply the location and exercise of authority) is far from a static concept.

We made early decisions to focus on the evolution of faculty roles in decision-making over a long period of time and to take advantage of a small number of case studies that track changes in specific settings. Others will have to judge whether these were good decisions, but we believe this approach has been valuable in enriching our perspectives. Walter Reuther, legendary head of the United Automobile Workers, once described the contracts he negotiated as "living documents" because their language had to be constantly re-interpreted and re-imagined as circumstances changed. We have the same view of faculty roles in governance. They continue to be shaped, as they should be, by the needs of the society that higher education exists to serve, as well as by new opportunities to improve teaching and research. This is not to say that there are not some "immutable" principles—with the lasting value of a carefully defined sense of academic freedom first among them—but they are relatively few. In many other areas, modifications, small and large, are, in our view, required.

It is also true, as one faculty reader pointed out, that an understanding of faculty roles in governance requires an appreciation of the roles of other principal actors, including especially presidents, provosts, and deans, as well as trustees/regents. One faculty reader suggested that this study is really about leadership, and how it is both constrained and exercised in the modern college or university. We agree. Faculty are not generally in a position, nor are they responsible, for providing institution-wide leadership on their own. That is what presidents and their key colleagues, in consultation with the faculty and trustees, are expected to provide. But one of the main themes of this study is that faculty can either encourage (and facilitate) the wise exercise of leadership by others or, conversely, throw limitless amounts of sand in the wheels. This simple proposition is why, in the concluding chapter, we argue for re-thinking the concept of "shared governance" and putting more emphasis on genuine collaboration.

* * * * *

This book is a member of a rapidly growing family of ITHAKA projects and publications having to do with ways that advances in information technologies might assist institutions of higher education in contributing to the solution of vexing national problems. We should explain that ITHAKA is an independent not-for-profit organization founded by the Hewlett, Mellon, and Niarchos Foundations to help the academic community use digital technologies to preserve the scholarly record and to advance research and teaching in sustainable ways. Led by its president, Kevin M. Guthrie, ITHAKA is the parent organization of JSTOR, the globally recognized searchable database of scholarly literature that recently enrolled its 9,000th institutional subscriber—a museum in Japan. The astonishing success of JSTOR is an example of what technology can make possible when embedded in a clear understanding of the needs of faculty, students, and institutions. In addition to continuing to develop the capacities of JSTOR and its partner operating entity Portico (which preserves born-electronic content), ITHAKA's activities include the work of an expanding unit devoted to research and strategic advising called Ithaka S+R, led by Deanna Marcum.

Ithaka S+R's research is motivated by three propositions: first, that this country's system of higher education faces daunting challenges to improve educational outcomes and address "equity" concerns without commensurate increases in cost (see the introduction for an elaboration of this point); second, that advances in technology offer opportunities to address some of these issues; and third, that progress in this area depends on a mix of strategies that have to include some significant modifications in the way colleges and universities operate, including the nature of the roles played by faculty and university leaders.

The best short description of the research agenda of Ithaka S+R is to be found in the foreword, by Kevin Guthrie, of the recently released paperback edition of *Higher Education in the Digital Age*, a book providing an updated version of the Tanner lectures given by one of us (Bowen) at Stanford in the fall of 2012. Recent companion projects, most of them ongoing, include:

- A study at the University System of Maryland of efforts to employ online technologies (including massive online open courses, or MOOCs) to address the needs of large public systems of higher education.
- An attempt to identify, for consideration by various types of institutions, new protocols for "ownership," "licensing," and "sustainability" of platforms and course content in a digital age; this is truly uncharted territory.
- A study of the evolution of staffing patterns, including questions concerning the treatment of the growing numbers of non-tenure-track faculty.
- An attempt to estimate, using simulation strategies, potential cost savings that could be realized in various institutional settings if it were possible to relax constraints on not only deployment of "hybrid" teaching methods (which utilize a blend of face-to-face and online approaches), but also new modes of scheduling.
- An assessment of the initial effects of significant modifications in state support of public universities in Virginia—with a focus on what happens to the enrollment and persistence of students above the Pell-grant cut-off (the "near poor").
- An interview-based study of public university collaborations in developing and using technology.

All of us involved in this family of ITHAKA-sponsored projects continue to be delighted (and amazed) by the synergies among them, and it is clear to us that the present study of evolving faculty roles will lead to other research projects. The Spencer Foundation, led by Michael S. McPherson, is our institutional partner in these undertakings, and we also continue to benefit from the active involvement of Lawrence S. Bacow, president emeritus of Tufts University and leader-in-residence at the Harvard Kennedy School's Center for Public Leadership. There are a great many others who contribute mightily to this set of

ITHAKA projects, and we list immediately below those who have been especially helpful in our work on this study.

* * * * *

In writing this book we have adopted an informal conversational mode of presentation. We are well aware of the limitations of our direct experiences, which consisted of serving as faculty members and administrators at leading selective colleges and universities, even as we are grateful for the opportunities we have been given to learn about the circumstances of a great many other, very different, institutions through our work in the foundation world, and from conversations with many participants actively involved in the work of a highly diverse set of colleges and universities. In any case, we have tried to encourage readers to add (in their minds at least) their own vignettes to those we present and to correct our misimpressions and enlarge on what we think we have learned. We have also included a large number of footnotes, both to avoid encumbering the text with too much detail and to provide a place for identifying dissenting views and suggesting other approaches.

In an effort to "put some flesh on the bones," we have included at the end of the book four case studies of how faculty roles in governance have evolved at particular institutions (the University of California, Princeton University, Macalester College, and The City University of New York). As we are all too well aware, there are approximately four thousand nonprofit degree-granting colleges and universities in the United States, and each zealously embraces a degree of exceptionalism, especially in its governance processes and experience. We make no claim that these four case studies capture the individual campus or system-wide nuances and particularities of such a heterogeneous, decentralized, and diverse educational enterprise. Indeed, our reading of the historical scholarship on higher education and the more contemporary literature convinces us that to seek to construct a "representative sample" would be a fool's errand. There is no point in pursuing an illusive "will-o'-the-wisp."

At the proverbial eleventh hour, two of our ITHAKA colleagues, Kevin Guthrie and Christine Mulhern, spent three full days at Arizona State University, reviewing relevant documents and interviewing President Michael M. Crow, senior administrators, deans, and faculty in an effort to understand and assess the university's exceptionally determined efforts to redesign its offerings to increase enrollment, improve completion rates, and control costs. We considered transforming their extensive report into a fifth case study, but decided that it was wiser to present the report in its extant form on the ITHAKA website. We have cited the report a number of places in the book in order to capture the main features of the Arizona State experience, which is quite different from the experiences of our four case-study institutions and, for that matter, from the experiences of most of the rest of higher education. At various other times in working on this study, we did preliminary work on the histories of other institutions (including Towson University, the University of Maryland–College Park, the California State University system, DePaul University, San Diego State University, and the University of Wisconsin–Madison), but we lacked the time and capacity to produce full case studies. We have, however, learned from these efforts as well as from the ITHAKA study of public university collaborations in developing and using technology (mentioned earlier).[1]

1. Among the many people who helped with these explorations, we express our deep appreciation to Provost and Vice President for Academic Affairs Timothy Chandler and Dean of University Libraries Deborah Nolan at Towson University; President Reverend Dennis Holtschneider and Secretary of the University Reverend Edward Udovic of DePaul University; President Elliot Hirshman and Andrea Rollins of San Diego State University; and Chancellor Rebecca Blank, Chief of Staff Becci Menghini, and Secretary of the Faculty Andrea Poehling at the University of Wisconsin–Madison.

A further word on the value of the four case studies is in order. Anyone who has read, much less tried to write, a standard college or university history soon realizes the limits of public sources, including those stored within an institution's archives and special collections. Faculty handbooks, minutes of boards of trustees, faculty task force reports, and even oral histories have often been sanitized for the protection of both people and places. This imperfectly understood fact of life has placed a premium on selecting institutions with unusually strong and credible historical resources and with knowledgeable participant observers on whom we could rely. From the beginning of this project we recognized that our personal connections with some of the case-study institutions provided valuable entrées to sources and eyewitnesses, and we have taken full advantage of privileged channels of access. At the same time, we have made every effort to verify our conclusions and to test our hypotheses against other sources and documentary evidence. And we have not spared our case-study institutions criticism when that seemed warranted.

We should acknowledge that there is repetition (considerable in some places) between material presented in the text and discussions in the four case studies. The reason is that some readers will, we suspect, be interested in reading one or more of the case studies as stand-alone contributions. (The CUNY case study, prepared by Martin A. Kurzweil, is a particularly valuable account of events in a major public-urban university system not currently available, to the best of our knowledge, any other place.) To truncate the case studies by editing out material presented in the text would be a disservice to these readers. We rely on the capacity of other readers to skim the case studies or simply to rely solely on the text if they choose to do so.

As a final alert (really, we confess, an admonition), we want to encourage readers to resist any temptation they may have to "skip to the end" and look first at the broad conclusions we state in Chapters 4 and 5. We would be disappointed if interest in the proverbial bottom line deprived readers of the pleasures, as well as the insights, we have gained from tracking changes over time, and rooting changes in specific historical events. As the Greek poet Cavafy urged in the poem from which ITHAKA takes its name, please enjoy the journey, trying always to learn from "harbors entered for the first time."

* * * * *

It is with great pleasure that we acknowledge the help we have received from a legion of colleagues and friends. We have already mentioned the special roles played by Lawrence S. Bacow, Kevin M. Guthrie, and Michael S. McPherson—whom we regard as genuine collaborators in every sense of the word. In addition, we have received valuable comments on drafts of the manuscript from Norman Augustine, Henry Bienen, Derek Bok, Gordon Gee, Hanna Holborn Gray, William ("Brit") Kirwan, Earl Lewis, Philip Lewis, Pat McPherson, Jo Ellen Parker, Taylor Reveley, Brian Rosenberg, Harold Shapiro, Judith Shapiro, Sarah E. Turner, Daniel Weiss, and Mariët Westermann.

At the Spencer Foundation, Charles Kurose has been a steadfast assembler of key data, including figures on expenditures by various sets of colleges and universities. At the Andrew W. Mellon Foundation, Susanne Pichler, the librarian, has been an unfailing source for references and other material; she also prepared updated versions of Figures 1 and 2. Members of the ITHAKA team, in addition to President Kevin Guthrie, who have been especially helpful are Johanna Brownell, Martin Kurzweil, Deanna Marcum, Christine Mulhern, Clara Samayoa, Richard Spies, and Derek Wu. Ms. Brownell took full responsibility for checking references, editing the manuscript, and putting all of its parts in order for Princeton University Press.

The creators of the case studies, and some of their colleagues, are identified (along with the content they have provided) in the latter part of the book. We owe particular thanks to C. Judson King at the University of California, David Dobkin and Robert K. Durkee at Princeton University, Jack E. Rossman at Macalester College, and Alexandra Logue at CUNY—all of whom worked to ensure that the accounts of developments at their colleges and universities were as accurate as possible.

As always, our wives, Mary Ellen and Beverly, have been thoughtful critics, empathetic supporters, and exceptionally patient partners.

Finally, we thank Peter Dougherty and his colleagues at Princeton University Press for their unfailing support, good ideas, and professional expertise. We could not have had a better publishing partner. Peter Strupp and his team at Princeton Editorial Associates have also been valuable contributors in producing the book.

If errors, omissions, and confusions remain, as surely they do, we take full responsibility for them.

Locus of Authority

It certainly needs
desperately new,
modification, but
not any more
along
corporate
lines.
technological
lines!!

1

Introduction

AMERICAN HIGHER EDUCATION is widely praised for its accessibility, scale, and diversity. In recent years this acclaim has been tempered by concerns over rising costs, cutbacks in support of public education, low degree completion rates, and skepticism about higher education's ability to contribute to the clear need for upward mobility in America, all of which raise troubling questions about the nation's capacity to lead a global economy. Almost every contemporary issue facing higher education—from broadening student access, to achieving better learning outcomes (especially higher completion rates and reduced time-to-degree), to increasing productivity and lowering costs—is impeded and frustrated by a hundred-year-old system of governance practices that desperately needs modification. Perhaps most worrisome is the uncertainty one senses about higher education's resolve to reform from within.

The question of why anyone should care about a subject as arcane as the practices governing colleges and universities is a reasonable one. Contrary to the adage that academic politics is so vicious because the stakes are so low, today there is little doubt that the societal consequences of not addressing college and university governance are greater and more serious than

yes, but not for the reasons they both is likely to suggest (tandose!)

they have ever been. Our country faces the transcendent challenges of raising the overall level of educational attainment and reestablishing the principle that higher education is the pathway to social mobility. This latter principle, which began to be enunciated forcefully only in the postwar years, is much more fragile and impermanent than we care to admit. If we are going to increase the fraction of the population with college degrees to as much as 60 or 70 percent (as President Obama has urged us to do), and provide meaningful opportunities for upward mobility, the heaviest lifting will have to be done by the less privileged and less well-resourced institutions that serve so many of our students.

Obviously, the *quality* of the education delivered is of great importance, but we do not deal with that tricky issue in this study because of its complexity. We concentrate instead on three other crucial aspects of educational outcomes— attainment, degree completion, and disparities in outcomes related to socioeconomic status—that are, in at least some respects, more amenable to analysis.[1]

First, as is well known, overall completion rates (measured for present purposes by the percentage of 25- to 29-year-olds with BAs) had been stuck on a plateau since the late 1970s.[2] More recently, there has been an uptick in educa-

[1] For a fuller discussion of the current "state of play" in each of these areas, complete with figures, data sources, and references, see William G. Bowen, "Technology: Its Potential Impact on the National Need to Improve Educational Outcomes and Control Costs," talk given at Rice University, October 13, 2014, available at the ITHAKA website, www.ithaka.org.

[2] The start of this plateau followed a long period of steady increases in attainment dating back to the "high school movement" of the early 1900s, which was responsible for producing the base of college-ready students that made possible this country's remarkably high level of degree completion at the college level. See figure 1.2 and associated commentary in William G. Bowen, Matthew M. Chingos, and Michael S. McPherson, *Crossing the Finish Line* (Princeton, NJ: Princeton University Press, 2009). Goldin and Katz deserve the credit for explicating both the long record of increasing educational attainment in the United States and the subsequent plateau (Claudia Goldin and Lawrence F. Katz, *The*

misguided emphases on completion rate! — esp. in a climate of diminished standards of achievement.

tional attainment, with the percentage of 25- to 29-year-olds holding BAs or higher degrees increasing from 30 percent in 2007 to 34 percent in 2013. But the changing demographics of America warn us that elements of the population with below-average attainment rates (especially Hispanics) are growing relative to the main group with above-average rates (the white population). A second reason for caution in extrapolating progress is that we do not know how much of the recent uptick in attainment rates is due to the timing of the 2007 recession—or to what extent more recent improvements in labor markets will lead to decreases in enrollment and attainment (full-time undergraduate enrollment was 3 percent lower in 2012 than in 2010).[3] Moreover, the absolute level of the current educational attainment rate remains unacceptably low if the United States is to compete effectively in an increasingly knowledge-driven world—a world in which other countries have been improving their attainment rates much more rapidly than we have.

Second, overall time-to-degree is long and has increased rapidly. The percentage of students completing their studies in four years fell from 58 percent for the National Education Longitudinal Study of 1972 (NELS-72) cohort to 44 percent for the NELS-88 cohort—the putative high school class of 1992.

Third, another very troubling "fact of life" is that in America today there are serious disparities in both completion rates and time-to-degree associated with socioeconomic status—and that, once again, the problem appears to be getting worse.

Race between Education and Technology [Cambridge, MA: Harvard University Press, 2008]).

3. U.S. Department of Education, National Center for Education Statistics, Integrated Postsecondary Education Data System (IPEDS), "Fall Enrollment Survey" (IPEDS-EF:90–99); IPEDS Spring 2001–Spring 2013, enrollment component. See *Digest of Education Statistics 2013*, tables 105.20 and 303.70. See also Bowen (2014).

Disparities in completion rates between those in the top and bottom income quintiles are appreciably greater in the 1979–83 birth cohort than they were in the 1961–64 birth cohort.[4] Compounding the problem of growing differences in graduation rates are increased disparities in time-to-degree.[5]

Fourth, there is widespread concern about the affordability of higher education (some of it exaggerated and misplaced, to be sure, but these concerns are real, and perceptions matter almost as much as realities). Worries about the rising net costs of higher education for many students and their families are exacerbated by what David Leonhardt calls "the great wage slowdown of the 21st century"—the fact that "the typical American family [today] makes less than the typical family did 15 years ago, a statement that hadn't been true since the Great Depression."[6]

We must ask whether it is reasonable to expect a century-old structure of faculty governance to enable colleges and universities of all kinds to respond to new demands for more cost-effective student learning. Will institutions that educate growing numbers of students from first-generation, under-represented, and disadvantaged backgrounds be able to make the organizational and pedagogical changes that preserve higher education as an engine of social progress? And can those institutions regarded as pacesetters in both the public and private sectors do more than maintain their positions in the higher education hierarchy? Can they provide both examples

4. Martha J. Bailey and Susan M. Dynarski, "Gains and Gaps: Changing Inequality in U.S. College Entry and Completion," National Bureau of Economic Research Working Paper 17633, December 2011, figure 3.

5. See John Bound, Michael F. Lovenheim, and Sarah Turner, "Why Have College Completion Rates Declined? An Analysis of Changing Student Preparation and Collegiate Resources," *American Economic Journal: Applied Economics* 2, no. 3 (July 2010): 129–57.

6. David Leonhardt, "The Great Wage Slowdown of the 21st Century," "The Upshot," *New York Times*, October 7, 2014.

of successful uses of new approaches and leadership for higher education generally?

We believe it would be wise to heed the cautions of Clark Kerr, one of the twentieth century's wisest, most thoughtful, and innovative higher education leaders:

> The professoriate is not well organized to consider issues of efficient use of resources. Many decisions with heavy cost consequences, including faculty teaching loads and size of classes, are made at levels far removed from direct contact with the necessity to secure resources. Departments usually operate on the basis of consensus and it is difficult to get a consensus to cut costs.[7]

At this point in time, we are dealing with deeply entrenched cultural expectations that are a century old and system-wide and cannot be changed easily. As Kerr presciently observed in 1963:

> Faculty members are properly partners in the [higher education] enterprise with areas reserved for their exclusive control. Yet when change comes it is rarely at the instigation of this group of partners as a collective body. The group is more likely to accept or reject or comment, than to devise and propose.[8]

Both of these observations by Kerr were made years ago, but they certainly continue to ring true—perhaps more so today than even Kerr could have anticipated. Most college and university presidents would probably agree that governance falls near the bottom of an imposing list of financial, demographic, technological, and cultural concerns that occupy their

---

7. Clark Kerr, *The Uses of the University*, 5th ed. (the Godkin Lectures on the Essentials of Free Government and the Duties of the Citizen) (Cambridge, MA: Harvard University Press, 2001), p. 180.

8. Ibid., p. 75.

days. In private moments, however, we suspect that many presidents recognize that the unpredictable pace and nature of change repeatedly expose longstanding flaws in institutional governance. A growing number of trustees are frustrated by the slow, deliberative nature of institutional decision-making. They want clearer boundaries between decisions that affect the curriculum (narrowly defined) and those that involve the institutional mission and budget. Many faculty members categorically reject the values, vocabulary, theories, and methods of "corporate" approaches. Faculty nominally endorse the concept of "shared governance," a concept we interpret as presuming the absence of an inherently adversarial relationship between faculty and administrators/trustees and the embrace of a collaborative approach to achieving common goals. But even within the faculty ranks, cherished traditions of debate, consultation, deliberation, and the search for consensus have been diminished by the compartmentalized nature of the academy and by faculty members' loyalties to their disciplines rather than to their institutions.[9]

Yet, as our colleague Lawrence Bacow astutely observes, context is important: "People assume that the way things are

9. Recent publications suggest a growing interest in college and university governance. Larry Gerber, a historian and longtime national leader of the American Association of University Professors, provides an elegant historical overview (*The Rise and Decline of Faculty Governance: Professionalization and the Modern American University* [Baltimore: Johns Hopkins University Press, 2014]). Unfortunately, in our opinion, his argument that corporate-driven market practices have eroded the faculty's historic role as professionals and as equal participants in shared governance is oversimplified and a misreading of his own scholarly analysis. We sense an equally narrow and polarizing perspective in an August 2014 report issued by the American Council of Trustees and Alumni. This report ("Governance for a New Era: A Blueprint for Higher Education Trustees") identifies several contemporary challenges that deserve consideration, but we are skeptical of the wisdom of recommendations that encourage trustees to involve themselves in curricular decisions and in acting to protect the academic freedom of students by redefining the boundaries of dissent. See www.goacta.org/publications/governance_for_a_new_era and Scott Jaschik, "Call for Trustee Activism," *Inside Higher Ed*, August 19, 2014.

today is the way they have always been and will always be [even though] things have evolved over time as institutions have confronted different challenges and opportunities."[10] "Governance" (by which we mean, as we have already said in the preface, "where authority is located and how it is exercised") is far from any pre-ordained set of abstract concepts, much less an established set of rules and regulations—and far from the static creature that some may assume it to be. Governance has always been a product of the times, and it has evolved in response to the pressing needs of new days. The current governance system needs to continue to evolve, we believe, and perhaps to change in quite fundamental ways. Accordingly, we think it is important to track historically the evolution of governance practices—and especially to identify the forces that have driven changes in the authority granted to faculty in different areas and within different sectors.

Although we hope that this volume will be informative across a wide range of higher education institutions, our focus is primarily on faculties of arts and science at four-year colleges and universities. This focus reflects the limits of our personal and professional experiences, the constraints of time, and an overriding interest in improving the overall level of the nation's educational attainment, which will be determined in no small part by what happens in BA-granting programs. We recognize that both professional schools and community colleges serve absolutely essential purposes in the structure of higher education. Moreover, these institutions represent a valuable source of insights about governance policies, functions, and cultures. Certainly the experiences of schools of law, medicine, and business differ markedly from those of schools focused on the arts and sciences, particularly in terms of autonomy, dependency,

10. Lawrence S. Bacow to William G. Bowen, March 17, 2014, private correspondence.

and responsiveness to demands for university-wide centralization. Community colleges also function in distinctive ways. We trust that other scholars will complement what we have done by examining closely these other sets of institutions, and the roles of their faculties in shaping policies and practices. We are also conscious of the fact that we do not deal with the for-profit sector of higher education, which provides yet another set of governance issues.

Studies of governance in higher education often focus on boards of trustees and presidents. Both are important actors in the governance drama, and there is no lack of books about them.[11] Legislators, alumni, and students matter, too. But, of course, so do faculty, especially when it comes to decisions about staffing, curricula, and teaching methods, all areas of growing concern.

We certainly do not believe that governance is ever an end in itself. In colleges and universities it is a means to the fundamental educational ends of teaching, learning, scholarship, and service. An institution can have an impeccable governing structure and still do badly in serving its core mission. Errors of judgment, and errors of both commission and omission, can have harmful consequences even when all processes are in excellent order. A good governance structure is no substitute for having excellent leadership in key positions—and at least a modicum of good luck! It is also true, however, that even the best leadership can be thwarted by poor governance.

For reasons mentioned earlier and explained in some detail later in this study, we are persuaded that faculty roles are of prime importance at this juncture—both positively, in terms of the ability of faculty to drive badly needed substantive change, and negatively, in terms of the ability of fac-

11. Bowen has written about both presidents (in *Lessons Learned: Reflections of a University President* [Princeton, NJ: Princeton University Press, 2011]) and boards (in *The Board Book* [New York: W. W. Norton, 1994, 2008]).

Faculty will not + does not stand in the way [of] changes [they] demand, request, it, based on academic values!!

ulty to stand in the way of that change. We start, then, with the twin premises (1) that the governance challenges facing American higher education today—as it copes with pressures to adapt to a new world marked by a lethal combination of high expectations concerning educational outcomes, severe fiscal constraints, and rapid technological change—are of absolutely central importance, and (2) that these challenges have to be addressed on the basis of a deep understanding of faculty roles, and how they have evolved over time. In our view, the ability of American higher education to take full advantage of, among other things, the opportunities that emerging technologies offer, depends critically on the continuing adaptation of governance structures to new circumstances. Successful adaptation requires a clear understanding of faculty roles today—how we got where we are and what we must preserve—and of why a more capacious interpretation of *shared* governance need not be either solely consensual or adversarial.[12]

[margin: Jove draws out a potential—istic]

[margin: Blather broad! ? empty lang.]

This study has five chapters and a separate section containing the full versions of our case studies:

- This introduction is chapter 1.
- Chapter 2 sketches in broad strokes the major factors that have shaped American higher education from its colonial origins to the end of World War II. Our big-picture account is, we recognize, a highly impressionistic one, and a "high-light" film at that. It is in no sense original work, and we want to record our debt to major scholars of the unfolding panorama, including Richard Hofstadter, Walter Metzger,

12. For a thoughtful reminder of the faculty's central role in any future reform of American higher education, see Norman M. Bradburn and Robert Townsend, "Higher Education's Missing Faculty Voices," *Chronicle of Higher Education,* June 2, 2014, available at http://chronicle.com/article/Higher -Educations-Missing/146871/?cid=at&utm_source=at&utm_medium=en.

Wards
Deany, party Herbert et al

Lawrence Cremin, Laurence Veysey, Frederick Rudolph, Jurgen Herbst, Roger Geiger, John Thelin, and John Aubrey Douglass, among many others.[13]

- Chapter 3 takes this story forward from the end of World War II to the present day. In this more contemporaneous presentation of a historical overview, we have supplemented rich secondary sources by preparing four case studies of the evolution of faculty roles. This effort has focused on the experiences of several specific educational institutions that, taken together, provide insights into how at least some present-day features have developed in response to changing circumstances. In seeking in this way to "put some flesh on the bones," we have worked especially closely with colleagues from The City University of New York (CUNY), Princeton University, the University of California, and Macalester College. The highly varied experiences of these quite different institutions are referenced in chapter 3 (and, to a more limited extent, in chapter 2).

- Chapter 4 is a topical analysis of how governance practices are and are not effective in addressing specific challenges facing higher education today, including who makes

13. See Richard Hofstadter and Walter P. Metzger, *The Development of Academic Freedom in the United States* (New York: Columbia University Press, 1955); Lawrence A. Cremin, *American Education*, vols. 1–3 (New York: Harper and Row, 1970–88); Laurence R. Veysey, *The Emergence of the American University* (Chicago: University of Chicago Press, 1970); Frederick Rudolph, *The American College and University: A History* (Athens, GA: University of Georgia Press, 1990; reprint of 1962 ed.); Jurgen Herbst, *From Crisis to Crisis: American College Government, 1636–1819* (Cambridge, MA: Harvard University Press, 1982); Roger L. Geiger, *The History of American Higher Education: Learning and Culture from the Founding to World War II* (Princeton, NJ: Princeton University Press, 2015); John R. Thelin, *A History of American Higher Education* (Baltimore: Johns Hopkins University Press, 2004); and John Aubrey Douglass, *The California Idea and American Higher Education: 1850 to the 1960 Master Plan* (Stanford, CA: Stanford University Press, 2000) and *The Conditions for Admission: Access, Equity, and the Social Contract of Public Universities* (Stanford, CA: Stanford University Press, 2007).

faculty *faculty*

staffing decisions and the locus of authority over online learning.

- Chapter 5 is an avowedly normative discussion of what needs to stay as it is, and what needs to change. Key overarching questions include whether departments are the right way to organize some kinds of decision-making. Is there a need for more horizontal and less vertical organization of efforts to address certain questions, but not others? A closely related issue is whether the core concepts of "academic freedom" and "shared governance" need to be sharpened and even redefined. Our overriding objective, we should make clear, is (not to diminish faculty roles but rather to facilitate the most effective contribution of faculty to university life in a new day.

vague

But this is really the result of the revisions endorsed by these writers, I am willing to bet!

At the back of the book are our four case studies. These constitute a kind of appendix, but they are really more than that because they contain some original material that we reference in the main text. As we have explained in the preface, we make no claim that our case studies are "representative" of the large and incredibly varied set of institutions that comprise higher education in this country. Even so, we believe that these studies, along with the special report on Arizona State University that we reference in the preface, provide powerful illustrative examples ("teaching moments") that might otherwise remain abstract and difficult to communicate. We acknowledge that ultimately this study relies on our own considered judgments, and we do not claim anything like scientific validity for our claims and assertions. Our views are influenced by our own experiences in ways we understand and surely in ways we do not. We have tried to propose a useful set of "opinions" for our readers to ponder and, we hope, take to another level. Others will have to judge how well we have succeeded in meeting this objective.

? Huch?
opinions are cheap.
i.e. to carry about,

Most changes will undoubtedly contribute to the deprofessionalization of the faculty + the reduction of faculty control of matters significant within the scope of their expertise & knowledge!!

2

Historical Overview, Part 1— From the Beginnings to World War II

A NUMBER OF THE KEY organizational features of American universities today date back only a hundred years or so to a time when, in the decades after the Civil War, "the academic profession took on, for the first time in a full measure, the character, aspirations, and standards of a *learn*ed profession."[1] In the late 1890s and the early 1900s, "captains of industry and erudition," "university builders," state legislatures, and boards of trustees negotiated the terms of organization and management that, in the main (with some perturbations), continue to govern much of American higher education.[2] But in considering the history of governance arrangements, we should not just jump to the beginnings of the modern era.

1. Richard Hofstadter and Walter P. Metzger, *The Development of Academic Freedom in the United States* (New York: Columbia University Press, 1955), p. xii, authors' emphasis. All subsequent references use the Transaction and Columbia University Press paperback editions: Richard Hofstadter, *Academic Freedom in the Age of the College* (New Brunswick, NJ: Transaction Publishers, 1996), and Walter P. Metzger, *Academic Freedom in the Age of the University* (New York: Columbia University Press, 1961).

2. The quoted phraseology belongs to the historian John R. Thelin (*A History of American Higher Education* [Baltimore: Johns Hopkins University Press, 2004], p. 110).

Antecedents in Europe and Colonial America

There are some large lessons to learn from the very earliest days of American colleges, and from their ancestral origins in Europe. They are few, albeit very basic, and they emerge from both English and European traditions. The first major takeaway is that faculty in America had little if any influence on governance in the earliest days of American higher education—and the reason was that there was no established base of faculty on whom anyone could rely.

In tracing the origins of America's earliest colleges, Richard Hofstadter surveyed the long sweep of medieval history. He described the archetypal universities of Paris and Bologna with their contrasting master- and student-led guilds and attributed the evolution of German and British universities to the model developed at Paris. According to Hofstadter, "Cambridge was modeled in a broad sense on Oxford; and Cambridge, together with the English dissenting academies, was the primary formative influence on Harvard and most of the American colonial colleges."[3]

Though recent scholarship emphasizes a multifaceted lineage encompassing the influence of the Reformation and Scottish practices, Hofstadter's focus on the insecurity and vicissitudes of daily life in America led him to conclude that European models were no match for the raw uncertainties of a wilderness environment that greatly inhibited the emergence of a teaching profession.[4] The governance structures of European and English

3. Hofstadter, pp. 3–5, quote on p. 5.
4. In his study of nineteenth-century college government, Jurgen Herbst demonstrates that colonial colleges were greatly influenced by the experience of educational institutions created during the European Reformation. These "territorial" universities were secular, not ecclesiastical, corporations and represented "a form of academic government practiced . . . among Calvinist–Reformed groups . . . from Switzerland to the Netherlands and Scotland." Jurgen Herbst, *From Crisis to Crisis: American College Government, 1636–1819* (Cambridge, MA: Harvard University Press, 1982), pp. 2–3. Rather than continue the medi-

universities differ substantially with respect to their religious, ecclesiastical, and governmental origins, particularly the degree to which civil and church officials exercised influence. But in all cases the faculties exercised real control. The relatively weak authority of rectors and the absence of strong external boards reflected the senior faculty's extraordinary influence and status.[5] These European and English models would have been entirely impractical in the structuring of the colonial colleges because there was no tradition of guilds and, in reality, no faculty on whom anyone could rely.

[handwritten marginalia: "rightly so!", "not extra-ordinary rather just appropriate", "?", "But there were good writing models !!"]

Whether the founders of Harvard College (1636) and the College of William & Mary (1696) initially intended to follow the English tradition of faculty control is a matter of conjecture, but there is little doubt as to the outcome.[6] There was

---

eval model of self-governing groups of students or masters, Reformation colleges and their colonial American counterparts adopted an alternative model of state–church control. As Douglas Sloan persuasively argues in *The Scottish Enlightenment and the American College Ideal* (New York: Teachers College Press, Columbia University, 1971), the founding of colleges at Edinburgh and Aberdeen (with close connections to their respective town governments) created a model that would take root with the establishment of America's earliest colleges. Edinburgh's first charter placed the college, known as the "Town College," under the complete control of the Town Council, and a subsequent act (1621) confirmed the council's authority "to appoint and dismiss faculty members and to set regulations for the course of study and for the granting of degrees" (pp. 18–19). In a graceful extended footnote that includes a quotation from Samuel Eliot Morison warning against the exaltation of "what is at best a remote cousinage into direct parentage," Sloan makes a powerful case for Scottish influences, particularly the "similarity between the control of the College of Edinburgh by the Town Council and the control of Harvard by the Board of Overseers, consisting of ministers and magistrates" (pp. 20–21 n). See Samuel Eliot Morison, *The Founding of Harvard University* (Cambridge, MA: Harvard University Press, 1935), pp. 126–39.

5. Larry G. Gerber, *The Rise and Decline of Faculty Governance: Professionalization and the Modern American University* (Baltimore: Johns Hopkins University Press, 2014), pp. 12–13.

6. The most vexing constitutional struggles were not between "faculty" and "trustees" but rather between boards of trustees and governmental authorities. According to historian Hugh Hawkins, the first century of debates revolved around two questions: "Should the ruling body be the masters or some external board?" and "Should the civil government or the church be assigned the

no faculty presence strong enough to offset the overwhelming influence and authority of the Board of Overseers at Harvard and the Board of Visitors at William & Mary. Although faculty at Harvard in the 1720s and at William & Mary in the 1750s tried to combine external lay boards with internal academic bodies of fellows or masters, this was not an option during the earliest years. At both institutions lay boards ultimately assumed dominant control because colonial communities found the teachers "inadequate to the demands of self-government."[7]

"The first compromise with English practice," as Frederick Rudolph notes, "was necessitated by the fact that a company of scholars could not assemble in the woods of Massachusetts without being called together by someone."[8] In 1636, when Harvard was founded, "it seemed impossible to commit to a group of men as yet unknown and unchosen the full powers of management."[9] Apart from its first president, Henry Dunster, a graduate of Magdalene College, Cambridge, the teaching staff was bereft of mature, continuing faculty and consisted (well into the early 1720s) of transient, underpaid tutors biding their time while awaiting a call to the ministry. Barely older than their students, tutors rarely stayed long enough to become proficient in anything more than dodging bottles and stones

---

principal external governing power?" Specific outcomes reflected the variety of colonial conditions and the still developing distinction between public and private. There was, in any case, an explicit general understanding that educational institutions had an obligation to contribute to provincial society by training an elite for leadership in church and state. See Hugh Hawkins, "Foundations of Academic Pluralism," *Reviews in American History* 10, no. 3 (September 1982): 341–42.

7. Herbst, p. 61.

8. Frederick Rudolph, *The American College and University: A History* (Athens, GA: University of Georgia Press, 1990; reprint of 1962 ed.), p. 166. In making this same point, Hofstadter is less categorical and says simply that he finds "no evidence that the founders of Harvard College at first intended to depart from familiar and respected practices of academic governance" (p. xx).

9. Hofstadter, p. 127.

thrown by unappreciative students. "In the power structure of the American College," as one scholar observes, "the tutor represented cheap labor" and "was perhaps one answer to inadequate collegiate financial resources."[10] This feature of the colonial colleges is critical in explaining why, from the earliest days, faculty were not front and center in the governance of American colleges as they were in some European universities, where many had enjoyed the prerogative of self-government. "So long as the bulk of college teaching was in the hands of youngsters for whom teaching was only a by-path to more desired careers, faculty self-government was bound," as Hofstadter observes, "to seem less acceptable, indeed less meaningful, than . . . in European universities."[11]

The Harvard experience is particularly instructive. Within a year of its founding, the Massachusetts Bay General Court delegated governing responsibility to a committee of magistrates, ministers, and the college president that soon evolved into the Board of Overseers. This largely absentee body found it difficult to fulfill its managerial responsibilities, which may have been a source of friction with President Dunster. In 1650, he obtained a charter of incorporation from the General Court establishing the (Harvard) Corporation, a separate governing body consisting of the president, treasurer, and five fellows, empowered with the authority to make the rules, manage the finances, and elect their successors—subject to a veto by the Board of Overseers.[12] In practice, authority remained firmly with the Overseers until the late eighteenth century, when the Corporation, except

10. Rudolph, p. 164.
11. Hofstadter, p. 124.
12. In 1654, after fourteen years in office, Dunster resigned the Harvard presidency under pressure following a long-simmering dispute over what he considered to be the General Court's excessive scrutiny and tightfisted control over college finances and his very public heretical objection to infant baptism. See Hofstadter, pp. 86–91, including the reminder that Dunster's resignation "bears only the remotest resemblance to a modern academic freedom case" (p. 86).

for the president, became a predominantly nonresident body. "With only minor qualifications," Hofstadter observed tongue-in-cheek, "it can thus be said of the Harvard Corporation that while it was in any serious measure a resident body of teachers it did not govern, and that when it finally took on the functions of government, it was a group of nonresident men who were not teachers."[13]

This historical insight about the importance of practical realities is relevant to present-day discussions of governance because of evidence that many faculty are now less committed to their institutions than once was the case. Forces driving this still-evolving pattern include (among other things) greater disciplinary specialization, online collaborations at a distance, the marked increase in the use of adjunct (or contingent) faculty, and the greater fragmentation of faculty as market pressures lead to ever more pronounced differences in salaries, workloads, and support at many institutions. As we suggest in chapter 5, hard thought should be given to the question of how these modern-day pressures toward fragmentation and lack of cohesiveness affect (and should affect) faculty roles in governance, and specifically the authority delegated to faculty on a de facto if not a de jure basis. The answer is likely to vary, of course, by institutional type and mission. It is often noted, for example, that many liberal arts colleges (and not just the most selective ones) differ in this respect from the "multiversities" that Clark Kerr made famous. This is true, but the trend toward ever greater specialization, as well as some of the same factors at work at the Berkeleys of the academic world, can also be seen at much smaller colleges such as Macalester—though in muted form.[14]

Historically, a practical consequence of the lack of an established faculty in the earliest days of American colleges was that

13. Hofstadter, p. 130.
14. See the Macalester College case study in the final section of this book.

these colleges had to be placed under the control of some other group. By the early eighteenth century, the representatives of civil society were fully in charge of America's colleges. As Jurgen Herbst notes, "In Massachusetts, the magistrates among the Overseers gained the upper hand over the ministers of the Corporation . . . [and] in Virginia the Visitors of the gentry ruled over the Oxford-trained clerical masters." The faculties at Harvard and William & Mary attempted "to reintroduce corporate faculty government on the model of the medieval universities or of the English colleges," but "it proved impossible to . . . revitalize the medieval corporations of masters and scholars."[15]

The implications for faculty governance (or, really, for the lack of faculty governance) in these formative years are obvious: "The essence of lay government," as Richard Hofstadter observed, "is that the trustees, not the faculties, *are*, in law, the college or university, and legally they can hire and fire faculty members and make almost all the decisions governing the institution."[16] While the formal locus of authority has remained much the same, the de facto distribution of authority has changed greatly over the years in response to changing circumstances. But it is well to remember this starting point.

The lack of an established faculty not only led to vesting full corporate authority in a lay board; it also led to a second lasting feature of American higher education that, like lay boards, dates back to the earliest days: the appointment of a strong president. For the Harvard Overseers, *the* highest priority was to recruit a good president, who at that time had to be a learned clergyman. The president was a teaching officer and, indeed, for many years was the only experienced person with instructional responsibility. Because of the young and transient character of

15. Herbst, pp. 48–49.
16. Hofstadter, p. 120, author's emphasis.

the tutors in those days, he was the only figure of continuing importance among the instructional personnel. "The development of nonresident control [in a lay board]," as one scholar observes, "helped to change the president from being either first among equals or spokesman or leader of the faculty into something far greater—representative of the governing board and a significant power in his own right."[17] The vesting of administrative authority in a president who reported directly to a lay board—and not to the faculty—represented a radical departure from the English experience. Historian John Thelin argues that the combination of an external board and a strong president is "a legacy of the colonial colleges that has defined and shaped higher education in the United States to this day."[18]

As Hofstadter explains:

> The only secure and sustained professional office in American collegiate education was that of the college president himself. He alone among the working teachers of the early colleges had, in the community and before the governing boards, the full stature of an independent man of learning. To this situation can be traced the singular role and importance of the American college or university president. . . . Between the trustees, who had the legal capacity but not the time or energy to govern, and the teachers, who were considered too young and too transient to govern, there was created a power vacuum. This vacuum the presidents quickly began to fill.[19]

17. Rudolph, p. 167.
18. Thelin, p. 12.
19. Hofstadter, pp. 124–25. We reference Hofstadter frequently in this discussion of the earliest years for American higher education because he was such an astute observer and, unlike many other historians, shared our interest in understanding faculty roles, seen in conjunction with the roles of other actors. We are also aware that, as Roger Geiger points out in his *Introduction to the Transaction Edition* (of Hofstadter's book [1996]), later historians have criticized Hofstadter's treatment of the period between 1820 and the Civil War. A more recent generation of scholars has agreed with Hofstadter that conditions (vis-à-vis academic freedom) changed for the worst at the start of the nineteenth

Some members of boards of trustees ("Overseers," in the case of Harvard) worked closely with the president in managing the colonial colleges. These boards were invariably products of religious denominations. American colleges, like their European counterparts, were wards of religion, but the pattern in this country of essentially private denominational sponsorship with only a modest admixture of state supervision was different. This characteristic of the founding of American colleges was responsible in no small measure for both the continuing importance of the private sector in this country's system of higher education and the extraordinary diversity of our educational landscape—a characteristic that has been widely noted and generally acclaimed.

An obvious but important lesson to be learned from experience in even the earliest colonial years is that shifting constituencies and financial realities often drive the distribution of authority. Once again, Harvard's history is instructive. Whereas "Harvard began its existence at a time when one theology and one religious group held sway in the colony, . . . by the beginning of the eighteenth century that sect split into two factions and students from both wings attended the college. . . .

---

century, but they disagree with him as to why conditions changed. Hofstadter emphasized the proliferation of colleges, which he regarded as the result of "intense rivalry among denominations" to supply every locality with a cheap and indigenous institution. Later historians have put less emphasis on denominational rivalries and instead stressed other factors driving the proliferation of colleges that were rooted in the society of the time. Hofstadter also was wrong in suggesting that resources devoted to these colleges could have been pooled to form large centers of learning; the resources were very local in their origins. According to Geiger, the emergence of Jacksonian democracy had a greater impact on the colleges. There was a general hostility to any institution that might confer social distinction. The growth of small colleges was mainly the result of efforts to meet the practical needs of local communities. Hofstadter gave too little weight to the power of local conditions—to the fact that they reflected local society. But Hofstadter was not wrong in pointing out that, for whatever combination of reasons, these ante-bellum colleges were relatively unconcerned about generating new knowledge.

The College was well advanced in the transition from the Puritan age to the age of the Enlightenment."[20]

The broadening of the base of support for Harvard mirrored trends in society at large and reflected the needs of colleges for ever more inclusive constituencies that could provide both students and direct financial support. These forces are evident in the histories of many early colleges.[21] The dominance of clergymen on boards declined, and businessmen and lawyers began to be elected. One broad finding in our review of this history is that market pressures and "business needs" are consequential in shaping trends in governance. We see here a relatively early example of this proposition. To survive, colleges needed to attract both students from varied backgrounds and financial support from a range of patrons. The process of private college formation in the ante-bellum period extended from the Northeast and the South throughout much of the country, and continued for well over a hundred years. However, as Stinchcombe and other students of organizational life cycles have taught us, formation of institutions of a particular type tends to occur in "spurts" or "waves" in response to particular needs and opportunities.[22] Organizational voids tend to get filled by replication of effective models and then, after some time, another type has its

20. Hofstadter, p. 99. Hofstadter goes on to observe, in this wise and witty comment, "The advance in tolerance [under the presidency of John Leverett] was another index of the decline of the religious scruples of the pristine Puritan age; for tolerance is, unfortunately, too often the virtue only of those who do not care excessively" (p. 112).

21. See David B. Potts, *Wesleyan University, 1831–1910: Collegiate Enterprise in New England* (New Haven, CT: Yale University Press, 1992). For an analysis of denominational fundraising strategies, see James Findlay, "Agency, Denominations, and the Western Colleges, 1830–1860," in Roger L. Geiger, ed., *The American College in the Nineteenth Century* (Nashville, TN: Vanderbilt University Press, 2000), pp. 115–26.

22. See Arthur Stinchcombe's classic contribution, "Social Structure and Organizations," in J. G. March, ed., *Handbook of Organizations* (Chicago: Rand McNally, 1965).

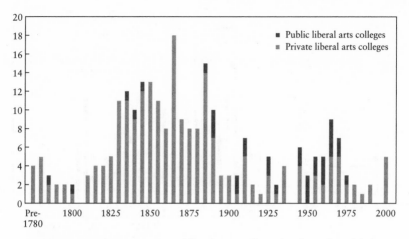

FIGURE 1 Trends in entrants to liberal arts colleges by date of establishment, 1990–2010

Source: Data, for surviving institutions, supplied in July 2014 by Higher Education Publications, publishers of the *Higher Education Directory*.

Notes: The bars represent five-year intervals (for example, 1900 represents 1900–1904). The colleges represented in this figure are those with the 2010 Carnegie Classification "Baccalaureate Colleges—Arts & Sciences."

own spurt. Thus the selective liberal arts colleges in existence today were largely established in the nineteenth century, primarily between the 1820s and the 1880s (see figure 1), and the public land-grant universities (see figure 2) emerged after the Civil War, spurred by the passage of the two Morrill Acts in 1862 and 1890.[23] These institutions often evolved from still smaller organizations (often "literary colleges") and served a

23. The analysis underlying figures 1 and 2 is explained in William G. Bowen, Thomas I. Nygren, Sarah E. Turner, and Elizabeth A. Duffy, *The Charitable Nonprofits* (San Francisco: Jossey-Bass, 1994), chapter 5. Our colleague Susanne Pichler has updated the data shown in our earlier study, again relying on the *Higher Education Directory*. These data must be interpreted with one large caveat in mind: institutions founded as one type not infrequently morph into another type. Early colonial colleges such as Harvard and Columbia are now research universities and appear in that category (see figure 2). Thus the bars on figure 1 understate the number of (then) liberal arts colleges established before, say, 1820.

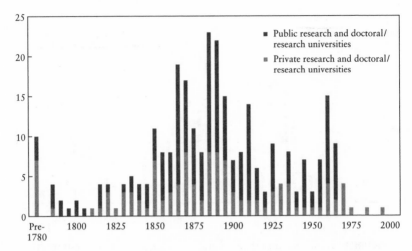

FIGURE 2 Trends in entrants to research and doctoral/research universities by date of establishment, 1990–2010

Source: Data, for surviving institutions, supplied in July 2014 by Higher Education Publications, publishers of the *Higher Education Directory*.

Notes: The bars represent five-year intervals (for example, 1900 represents 1900–1904). The research and doctoral universities represented in this chart are those with the 2010 Carnegie Classifications "Research Universities (very high research activity)," "Research Universities (high research activity)," and "Doctoral/Research Universities."

wide variety of religious, social, and economic purposes. Their small scale was appropriate to their times and circumstances, because they served primarily local and regional needs.[24]

24. As we noted previously in citing Geiger's commentary on Hofstadter's work, Rudolph is the best-known account of this period. But see also C. B. Burke, *American Collegiate Populations: A Test of the Traditional View* (New York: New York University Press, 1982), for an even stronger emphasis on the capacity of the "literary colleges" to adapt to local needs. In the South, the second Morrill Act stimulated the creation of a network of under-funded black land-grant institutions that more closely resembled secondary schools than colleges. See John R. Wennerstein, "The Travail of Black Land-Grant Schools in the South, 1890–1917," *Agricultural History* 67, no. 2 (Spring 1991): 54–62. For a provocative analysis of the myriad political and economic challenges facing historically black colleges and universities, from the Civil War through the mid-1930s, see James Anderson, *The Education of Blacks in the South* (Chapel Hill: University of North Carolina Press, 1988).

Walter Metzger provides this succinct summary of the factors driving a not-so-subtle shift in the locus of decision-making authority in the first half of the nineteenth century:

> The denominational college in the period between 1800 and 1860 faced two commonplace problems with which it could not cope—the problem of internal discipline and the problem of financial insolvency. . . . The need to check constant student disorder led to the growth of faculty (as opposed to trustee) control over discipline and instruction. [This was not a problem that presidents, alone, could handle.] The effort to offset mounting deficits resulted in the organization of the alumni into collegiate philanthropic associations. . . . [Both remedies] proved harmful to the regime which they were intended to fortify.[25]

That is, trustees had no choice but to cede power to faculty and to alumni. We see, once again, the irresistible need to respond to the realities of the day.

From a broad governance perspective, there was over these years a "dispersal of authority" across institutions and across the country. Faculty influence no doubt varied widely, depending on the power/attitudes of church leaders, the inclinations of presidents, and a wide variety of local (chance) circumstances. There was no institutionalization of faculty control over any major aspect of college affairs—with the possible exception of student discipline.[26] Even in this area, faculty exercised authority that was delegated and could be taken back. Our University of California case study illustrates dramatically how one

25. Metzger, p. 4.
26. See Steven J. Novak, *The Rights of Youth: American Colleges and Student Revolt, 1798–1815* (Cambridge, MA: Harvard University Press, 1977); David Allmendinger, *Paupers and Scholars: The Transformation of Student Life in Nineteenth-Century New England* (New York: St. Martin's, 1975); and Roger L. Geiger with Julie Ann Bubolz, "College as It Was in the Mid-Nineteenth Century," in Geiger (2000), pp. 80–90.

board, acting through its president, exercised high-level control over discipline even in the mid-twentieth century (during the turmoil of the 1960s at Berkeley).[27]

It is also important to note another formative development that dates from the ante-bellum years. In the late 1700s and in the first half of the new century, there was a consequential change in the numbers of faculty members (as we understand the term today). By the 1840s, the paucity of regular faculty, which had had such a powerful effect in limiting the faculty role in the colleges of colonial America, had changed. Faculty ("professors") increased in numbers. Early nineteenth-century colleges had been fortunate if they had two professors, one in Latin and Greek, and a second in mathematics and natural philosophy, to supplement the instruction of the president (usually in divinity and moral philosophy) and the tutors. By 1840, as Roger Geiger observes, respectable eastern colleges needed at least six faculty to cover science (including mathematics), the classics, literature, history, and rhetoric.[28]

One consequence of the growth in the size of the faculty was that presidents increasingly played the role of intermediary between faculty and the board.[29] As the nineteenth century progressed, the growing influence of alumni representation on college boards further increased the distance between trustees and faculty. As Frederick Rudolph notes, governing boards "would suffer the professors to attend to those matters of curriculum and college management for which they, as busy men of affairs, had no time, but they would not permit the professors to for-

27. In *The Gold and the Blue: A Personal Memoir of the University of California, 1949–1967,* Clark Kerr provides a characteristically thoughtful and precise accounting of the steps he recommended to the Board of Regents regarding "disciplinary matters in the area of political activity." See vol. 2, *Political Turmoil* (Berkeley: University of California Press, 2003), pp. 230–36.

28. Roger L. Geiger, "Introduction: New Themes in the History of Nineteenth-Century Colleges," in Geiger (2000), p. 17.

29. Hofstadter, p. 233.

get that the definition and public image of the institution itself were peculiarly matters for trustee decision."[30]

Thus we see signs of a gradually emerging change in the role of the faculty.[31] As colleges and universities became more complex, it would have been surprising indeed if the truly "simple" (one might even say "simplistic") model of strong trustee/presidential oversight of matters of all kinds had remained untouched by the march of time. It did not. But it was only with the emergence of the research universities, after the Civil War and especially at the end of the nineteenth century, that a markedly different organizational model began to take hold. And even then, as we will see when we discuss academic freedom issues in the late 1890s and the early part of the twentieth century and examine carefully the histories of our two oldest case-study institutions (Princeton and the University of California), it was difficult for some institutions to give up old ways of handling sensitive faculty personnel matters.

The Emergence of the Research University

First, however, we must pay close attention to a tremendously important development: the relatively sudden, and transformational, appearance on the educational scene of the research university. We will try to pluck the key lessons germane to our interest in governance from the mass of rich detail on the period from roughly 1876 (the founding of Johns Hopkins) to

30. Rudolph, p. 161. See also Geiger (2000), p. 32.
31. The Yale case is instructive. Hofstadter notes "the transition toward faculty participation at Yale under the regime of Jeremiah Day (1817–46)" (p. 235). "Day adopted the practice of discussing and deciding all questions connected with college policy in a meeting of the assembled faculty. By the end of his regime, a strong precedent had been established that even the Corporation should not take action without the recommendation or assent of the instructors. The principle that a new professor or other officer connected with instruction should not be appointed without the consent of his future colleagues seems to have been observed with particular scrupulousness" (p. 235).

the at first halting development of the American Association of
University Professors (AAUP) in 1915.[32]

A key feature of the research university, which distinguished it
sharply from the denominational colleges, was the presence and
growing importance of graduate and professional programs. The
underlying forces responsible for this "revolution" (as it has aptly
been called by one of its main chroniclers, Bernard Berelson, and
by other authors) include the fact that the denominational colleges could not meet the needs of an increasingly complex, indus-
trialized society. The claims of science, and of applied studies
of all kinds, became more and more insistent at the same time
that the hold of religion on higher education weakened. There
was increasing dissatisfaction with the classical curriculum and
with the passive "recitation" mode of instruction. There was
also patriotic competition with the acclaimed German system, as
well as the intrinsic attractions of advanced study. In addition,
there appeared on the scene both wealthy philanthropists and
ambitious university presidents interested in either creating new
universities de novo or building new structures on existing foundations. And then, of course, the passage in 1862 of the Land
Grant College Act (the Morrill Act) stimulated the establishment
of what became great state universities. The profound impact of
this combination of forces can be seen in figure 2, which shows
graphically the remarkable number of today's research/doctorate
universities established over the span of a relatively few years.[33]

32. The best-known, most nuanced, and most widely quoted study of this
period is Laurence R. Veysey, *The Emergence of the American University* (Chicago: University of Chicago Press, 1970). Thelin also covers this period in *A History of American Higher Education.* We have found particularly helpful a third
(under-appreciated) source: Bernard Berelson, *Graduate Education in the United
States* (New York: McGraw-Hill, 1960), especially pp. 9–16.

33. Moreover, the convention used by the *Higher Education Directory* in
providing the underlying data leads us to understate the pace of change by locat-
ing the founding of many private research universities, such as Harvard, Columbia, and the University of Pennsylvania, in the colonial period—when these
universities were first created as colleges. (See note 23 accompanying figure 1.)

Especially noteworthy from a governance perspective are these features of the rapidly evolving university landscape:[34]

- The founding presidents and principal architects—some might say, autocrats—of the nation's modern research universities, including such legendary figures as Andrew Dickson White (Cornell), Charles W. Eliot (Harvard), William Rainey Harper (University of Chicago), Daniel Coit Gilman (Johns Hopkins), and David Starr Jordan (Stanford), among others, used their authority to recruit faculty, shape the curriculum, and establish professional schools. It is not surprising that their successors found themselves responding to their faculties' demands for greater consultation and the formal delegation of authority.
- Proponents of exclusively graduate institutions lost out to those who favored, in effect, superimposing a German-like program of graduate study on top of an undergraduate college on the English model; the related practice of intermingling graduate and undergraduate faculties (and teaching) quickly became widely established.
- The faculty, including the graduate faculty, generally followed the German model of a single faculty rather than the French model of division by broad fields.
- Research and the earned PhD were central to the very idea of the research university, which from the beginning gave a high priority to science.

Berelson gives us this succinct account of what transpired between the founding of Johns Hopkins in 1876 and the establishment in 1900 of the Association of American Universities (the AAU) as the prestigious "club" of leading research universities. His summary deserves to be quoted in its entirety:

34. Berelson, pp. 9–15.

It is by no means hyperbole to call this period one of educational revolution. In 1876 the college was at the top of the educational program with a largely ministerial faculty, a classical and tradition-centered curriculum, a recitative class session, a small student body highly selected for gentility and social status, an unearned Master's given to alumni for good behavior after graduation; and serious advanced students went abroad. By 1900, in a short twenty-five years, the university was firmly established in America and was leading the educational parade with its professional character, its utilitarianism and community-centered programs, its stress on advanced learning, its new subjects of study, its seminars and laboratories and dissertations, its growing attraction for a new class of students—all capped by the earned PhD. Graduate education was on the road of growth and of increasing importance in American education: it was institutionalized in the graduate schools of the important universities, it had dedicated faculties, it had ambitious students, it had adequate funds, and it had an important mission. The face of American education would never be the same again.[35]

We are aware of Roger Geiger's reminder that as late as 1890 the vast majority of students still attended denominational colleges. These "multipurpose" institutions were growing. Many had introduced new programs in science, engineering, business, and agriculture. Some had forged partnerships with professional schools of theology, law, and medicine, and a few others had created ill-conceived PhD programs. By 1900, when the AAU was created to safeguard the standards and prerogatives of the emerging research universities, the denominational and multipurpose colleges acknowledged that they could not compete at the same scale

35. Ibid., p. 16.

and wisely reaffirmed their commitment to undergraduate education.[36] The old order had indeed changed.[37]

One direct consequence of this huge "spurt" in the founding of new research universities, as well as the transformation of some existing colleges into research universities, with a concomitant increase in resources, was a strong expansion in the demand for professors in the late 1890s and early 1900s.[38] As we will see when we discuss changes in the status of the professoriate, including the creation of tenure, the growing market power of faculty had a pronounced impact on their role in governance—and especially on their role in the faculty appointment/advancement process. But this did not happen right away.

The same expansionary factors, as Laurence Veysey notes, led to "increasing presidential authority, bureaucratic procedures of many sorts, the new functions of the deanship, the appearance of the academic department with its recognized chairman, and the creation of a calculated scale of faculty rank." This elaborate (for its times), and by now familiar, form of organization came into being without deliberate debate; it

36. See Geiger (2000), "The Era of Multipurpose Colleges in American Higher Education, 1850–1890," p. 128, and "The Crisis of the Old Order: The Colleges in the 1890s," p. 270. James McLachlan's essay, "The American College in the Nineteenth Century: Toward a Reappraisal," *Teachers College Record* 80, no. 2 (1978): 287–306, argues that "the American university did not emerge de novo toward the end of the nineteenth century" and that "it was not the simple result of the grafting of the German university to the English college" (p. 294). Summarizing the early work of revisionist scholars (such as Colin Burke and David Potts), McLachlan points to the continued vitality of nineteenth-century colleges that neither faded away nor tried to emulate the university model.

37. For a persuasive defense of the "college's" continued vitality in the late nineteenth and early twentieth centuries, see W. Bruce Leslie's superb monograph *Gentlemen and Scholars: College and Community in the "Age of the University," 1865–1917* (University Park: Pennsylvania State University Press, 1992).

38. Veysey, p. 264. After 1885, enrollment began climbing upward. Also, there was a flow of large private gifts. Veysey observes: "The basic climate of growth would never again be in doubt. The University had achieved a stable place among American institutions" (p. 265).

became taken for granted.[39] Veysey goes on to describe the role of the president as follows:

> Routinely the president wielded pre-eminent power at most of the major universities. . . . At the end of the nineteenth century, university heads often personally selected the faculty, though in consultation with deans and department chairmen. . . . Faculty government, where it formally existed, served much the same function as student government. It was a useful device whereby administrative leaders could sound out opinion, detect discontent so as to better cope with it, and further the posture of official solidarity by giving everyone parliamentary "rights."[40]

Our principal interest is not in student life, but it is necessary to recognize that in the latter part of the nineteenth century, unruly students were a significant problem and had real effects on faculty roles and the distribution of authority within the college/university. This is an area in which Veysey's careful attention to detail, and his sense of nuance, makes a real contribution. He writes: "Between undergraduates and their professors at the end of the nineteenth century, a gulf yawned so deep that it could appropriately be called 'the awful chasm.'" Students were not very interested in academic pursuits (had strong social interests), and disciplinary problems abounded.[41]

There was, at the same time, a gulf between professors and administrators. Veysey is unequivocal in telling us: "From the

39. Veysey, p. 268.
40. Ibid., p. 305. This is a good warning not to assume that "form" necessarily translates into real power. Later, in *The Academic Revolution* (Garden City, NY: Doubleday, 1968; reprinted by Transaction Publishers, 2002), Christopher Jencks and David Riesman commented: "What Veysey found after exhaustive study of late nineteenth-century academic life confirmed our own conclusions, based on more superficial inquiries into many other periods and problems, about the limits of documentary research. Like him we have therefore had to look at what happened and have then tried to reason backward to find out why it happened" (p. xxi).
41. Veysey, p. 294.

administration, the professor was often to feel as isolated as he did from his undergraduates."[42] This combination of "divides" contributed, along with the rapid growth of institutions, to the introduction of many of the bureaucratic controls with which we are familiar today. As John Thelin tells us: "One development that was probably unavoidable was that growth and specialization created a need for an academic bureaucracy—a structure characterized by departments and deans. . . . It is hard to avoid the conclusion that bureaucratic procedures became essential to continuity of effort, once one grants that American universities should be of generous size."[43] Here is Veysey's formulation:

> By 1910 the structure of the American university had assumed its stable twentieth century form. . . . Looking back, it could be seen that the decade of the nineties witnessed the firm development of the American academic model in almost every crucial respect. . . . With a board of trustees containing men enjoying the confidence of the respectable elements of the community; with a well-defined system of academic rank; with a president, department chairmen, athletic program, transcripts [et al.].[44]

These statements, however, correct as they are, should not lead us to make the false assumption that important issues of governance were hereby settled for all time. They were not, as we explain in some detail in succeeding chapters. Moreover, even the most fundamental of faculty prerogatives—strong influence over, if not outright control of, decisions concerning faculty appointments and tenure—was still very much in a "state of play." The now established formal structures, described so well by Veysey and others, tell us only so much about the real locus of decision-making power.

42. Ibid., p. 302.
43. Thelin, p. 316. More recently, Kingman Brewster, president of Yale University (1963–77), said, in effect, "bureaucracy is the price of size."
44. Veysey, p. 340.

Control of Faculty Personnel Decisions—
and Issues of Academic Freedom

We begin this section by recounting in some detail the evolution of the locus of authority for faculty personnel decisions at Princeton—one of our case-study institutions—during the period in the late nineteenth and early twentieth centuries when it was becoming a research university.[45] We intersperse comments on parallel, contemporaneous developments we observed in our case study of the University of California, the second of the two "old" universities we studied in detail. We then broaden the discussion to examine the process nationwide that led eventually to the wide adoption of the AAUP's 1940 *Statement of Principles on Academic Freedom and Tenure.*[46]

At Princeton today, the president, senior deans, and a powerful elected faculty committee (the so-called Committee of Three) are clearly in charge when it comes to making faculty personnel decisions of all kinds. These actors operate, to be sure, within budget and staffing parameters determined through an elaborate process that ends up, after much faculty consultation and strong leadership by the president/provost, with decisions by the board of trustees. But the location of authority for making personnel decisions is well understood to rest with the faculty and the president. This has not always been the case—a gross understatement! The processes whereby change occurred are both revealing and relevant to present-day issues.

45. See the Princeton case study. We are fortunate to have at our disposal a detailed examination of Princeton's history by a distinguished historian, James Axtell, who has perused the relevant documents and conducted numerous interviews. See James Axtell, *The Making of Princeton University: From Woodrow Wilson to the Present* (Princeton, NJ: Princeton University Press, 2006). The quotations that follow are all from the Axtell book, pp. 38, 40–47, and 48–58. They are intended to give a textured flavor of his findings.

46. See AAUP, www.aaup.org/AAUP/pubsres/policydocs/contents/1940statement.htm, accessed April 11, 2014.

X Trustees played a major role in faculty appointments at Princeton prior to Woodrow Wilson's presidency (1902–10). In trying to deal with the "inadequate faculty" of his time, James Axtell tells us that President James McCosh [1868–88] had to contend X with the fact that "the Trustees jealously guarded their prerogative of appointing faculty members. At best, McCosh could send them two or three nominations . . . but they chose in the end."

The election of Francis Patton to succeed McCosh in 1888 was a hopeful sign to the younger faculty who wanted to transform Princeton into a true university. Patton said all the right things but turned out to be lazy and unwilling to do what needed to be done to change things. Patton characterized college administration as "a business in which Trustees are partners, professors the salesmen, and students the customers." The appointment process was inconsistent and often marked by favoritism and "outrageous nepotism." Retiring chairs often selected their own successors. In the end, "particularly with the president's abdication in faculty development, the trustees were responsible for all appointments in fact as well as in law." Dissatisfaction with Patton mounted, and he was persuaded to retire in June 1902. √ Woodrow Wilson was elected to succeed him.[47]

In the early 1900s, Wilson took power from the trustees. He prepared the way for major reform by "reordering key faculty committees, making important administrative appointments, and receiving—and taking—from the trustees effective authority over academic and faculty affairs." Wilson simply went ahead ?? and made key faculty appointments ahead of trustee approval. Trustees had to approve as a matter of law, but de facto authority was exercised by the president. Wilson shared power with faculty—when he chose to do so. In spite of his autocratic tendencies, he opted to delegate considerable authority to his chosen department heads, and he counted on them to "enforce the

47. Quotations from Axtell, pp. 40–47.

higher new standards." Wilson nonetheless kept real control in the president's office until his resignation in 1910. As one of his young faculty supporters put it, Wilson became "an autocrat up to the limit. In [appointments] he hardly left anything to the faculty." "The trustees acceded to Wilson's request for unpublicized power to fire faculty, even tenured and chaired professors." Wilson then asked for the resignations of three key faculty members whom he regarded as "dead wood." Axtell tells the full story of these "resignations" in gory detail.[48]

It is instructive to interject here the amazingly parallel history of the University of California at essentially the same time.[49] In 1899, just three years before Wilson was elected president of Princeton, Benjamin Ide Wheeler accepted the presidency of the University of California. Wheeler faced both serious financial problems (declining state appropriations) and the aftereffects of unsuccessful experiences with a series of short-lived predecessors. His acceptance of the presidency depended in no small measure on the regents' readiness to give him an unusually free hand in all areas of university governance. The regents agreed to stop micromanaging and gave the new president complete authority over faculty appointments, dismissals, compensation, and educational policy. Under Wheeler's nearly autocratic control, which allowed for neither consultation nor negotiation, specific responsibilities were delegated to the faculty. The curriculum was reorganized. Twenty new academic departments were created. Articulation agreements were negotiated with the state's normal schools and emerging two-year colleges. Admission standards were raised, and the first system of peer review was introduced for faculty appointments and promotion.[50]

48. Ibid., pp. 48–58.
49. See the University of California case study.
50. John Aubrey Douglass, "Shared Governance at the University of California: An Historical Review," Research and Occasional Paper Series, Center for Studies in Higher Education, 1 (March 1998), pp. 3–5.

Although many faculty objected to Wheeler's autocratic methods, they respected his academic judgment, enjoyed a measure of control over the curriculum, and admired his success in garnering resources that materially strengthened the university and attracted scholars with national reputations.[51]

Back to the Princeton story. According to Axtell: "The abrupt and acrimonious end of Wilson's presidency in 1910—his forced resignation by the Trustees as he ran for the governorship of New Jersey—could easily have slowed or reversed his curricular reforms and faculty development." However, John Grier "Jack" Hibben was elected Wilson's successor, and Hibben saw that progress was not interrupted. "According to Wilson's key lieutenant, Dean Henry Fine, Hibben upon election called a meeting of Wilson's faculty leaders and begged them to join him in 'continuing and furthering the great instructional and University work that Wilson had begun.'" The transition was seamless.[52]

The same cannot be said of the only slightly later events that accompanied the end of Wheeler's tenure as president of the University of California. At the end of Wheeler's second decade in office, an increasingly disgruntled faculty used the president's pro-German sympathies (one respect in which the experiences of Wilson and Wheeler are entirely divergent), which had become a political embarrassment during the First World War, to precipitate a crisis of confidence that led to his forced retirement in July 1919. During Wheeler's last year in office, the Board of Regents created a Council of Deans to exercise presidential responsibilities, but this misguided experiment occurred at a

51. See Roger L. Geiger, *The History of American Higher Education: Learning and Culture from the Founding to World War II,* chapter 8, "The Creation of American Universities" (Princeton, NJ: Princeton University Press, 2015), and an earlier work by Verne A. Stadtman, *The University of California, 1868–1968* (New York: McGraw-Hill, 1970), pp. 179–201.

52. Axtell, pp. 72–73.

time of institutional instability and proved to be a disaster. Emboldened by the Regents' action (and by the lack of presidential leadership), the Academic Senate asked for Board approval to play an advisory role in the selection of the next president and for formal powers to choose their own leaders and make decisions regarding educational policy. In June 1920, the Regents approved a series of Standing Orders that codified the senate's authority, subject to the Board's approval, over the conditions of admission, degree requirements, and educational policy. These new arrangements gave the senate an advisory role to the president on faculty personnel policy, budget issues, and the appointment and dismissal of deans; it also gave the senate the right to choose its own committees and to determine its own rules and organization.[53] This evolution of faculty authority, known as the

53. Readers interested in the history of faculty governance at the University of California should consult Angus E. Taylor, *The Academic Senate of the University of California: Its Role in the Shared Governance and Operation of the University of California* (Berkeley: Institute of Governmental Studies Press, University of California, 1998). As part of the Standing Orders adopted by the Board of Regents in 1920, Taylor notes that membership in the Academic Senate was defined as consisting of "the president, deans, directors recorder, librarian and all professors and instructors giving instruction . . . but instructors of less than two years' service" were not entitled to vote. At its inception, the senate was authorized to choose its own chairman, but beginning in 1933 President Robert Sproul served as chair ex officio of the entire senate and the Northern and Southern Sections had a faculty member as vice chair (p. 3). Individual faculty began serving as chairs of the Academic Senate in the early 1960s. Today, Academic Council chairs are chosen by the Assembly, the university-wide legislative body of the Academic Senate. As a result of the 1919 Berkeley Revolution, the senate was authorized to choose its own committees. As Taylor notes, this was "the basis for the senate's early establishment of a Committee on Committees . . . [which] is, arguably, the cornerstone of the senate's power to act independently of the administration" (p. 3, n 3). But in the senate's formative years, the president exercised some influence through the Dean of Faculties, who chaired the Committee on Committees. In the words of President David Barrows (1919–22), "this arrangement would seem to assure a proper consideration of the President's desires in the composition of committees" (Taylor, p. 7). Today, members of the Committee on Committees on each university campus are elected by the senate members on that campus, and the Committee on Committees determines its own chair.

"Berkeley Revolution of 1919–1920," has been called a "watershed moment" in the history of shared governance.[54]

At Princeton, the election of Hibben led to what might be called the second phase of the devolution of power over faculty personnel matters from the trustees to the president, and then to the faculty. "Local conditions," as is so often the case, played an important role in precipitating changes in governance. The increasing curricular demands resulting from Wilson's introduction of his preceptorial system put extraordinary pressures on the Princeton faculty. "To enable them to perform and compensate them for these heavy duties, Hibben (and his successors) sought to give them maximum autonomy and competitive economic rewards. . . . Hibben believed that the time was right to fully enfranchise the faculty. At the first faculty meeting after he assumed office, Hibben 'turned over to the Faculty the appointment of all its committees.'" Dean Fine applauded this step and called it "a thing wholly unprecedented and of the first importance."[55]

Hibben did more. "He created a faculty-elected advisory committee to meet regularly with the trustees' curriculum committee. . . . He appointed three faculty each year to the trustees' honorary degrees committee. . . . And most important of all, he established a Faculty Advisory Committee on Appointments and Advancements, whose three elected members, all full professors and often department chairmen, met with the president to decide all nominations for tenure, retention, and promotion. This hardworking, powerful 'Committee of Three' [as it is still known informally] gave the faculty major authority over its own development as it dealt with departmental recommendations." Hibben also put in place new safeguards to protect the rights of individual faculty who were

54. Taylor, pp. 2–5, and Douglass, p. 5.
55. Axtell, pp. 76–77.

dismissed. On Hibben's retirement, the faculty recognized that "'from the first, he chose [unlike his predecessor . . .] to be primus inter pares, taking the faculty into his confidence, entrusting to it a full measure of responsibility, steadily safeguarding its privileges and dignity.' In short, he had completed the foundation of the modern Princeton faculty."[56] As the Princeton case study shows, the new faculty personnel structures put in place in Hibben's time have had amazing longevity; in their key features, they exist today.

There are many lessons to be gleaned from these two histories, some noted here and some reserved for later chapters. Lesson one is that what needs to be done in a particular university setting clearly has a significant impact on the power the president has to exert. In the cases of both Princeton and the University of California, a major upgrading of the faculty was needed when Wilson and Wheeler took office. A second lesson is that when the faculty are more established and simply "better," it is easier to give them authority. We should note particularly the steps that Hibben took after Wilson's upgrading process had had some real success; in California, too, presidential success in strengthening the faculty created an environment in which the faculty naturally expected a larger role in governance and were capable of exercising more authority. A third lesson, especially evident in the Princeton history, is that the timing of grants of authority to the faculty is often closely related to the need to alleviate pressures on them, and to the need to recruit able faculty. That is, timing is related to the market power of the faculty, as can be seen clearly from events during the early years of Hibben's presidency (from 1912 on). This was a period when many of the emerging research universities were strengthening their faculties and Hibben could not afford to disrespect his faculty in any way; it is hardly a coincidence that this was the

56. Ibid., pp. 77–78.

time when three of the key faculty committees that give faculty important roles in governance at Princeton today were established (the Committee on Committees, the Committee of Three, and the Conference Committee).

During these same decades, there were any number of controversies at colleges and universities nationwide that forcefully joined the issue of control over faculty personnel decisions to the issue of academic freedom—issues that were not really joined in those years at either Princeton or California. (The University of California's turn would come, with a vengeance, during the highly contentious loyalty oath controversy of the 1950s.) Perhaps the most famous case at the start of the twentieth century was that of Stanford University economist Edward A. Ross, who was fired in 1900 for having expressed unpopular opinions and criticized Mrs. Leland Stanford. Scholars have chronicled many other widely discussed controversies, some of them earlier. To cite only a few examples to illustrate the wide range of disputes: Alexander Winchell at Vanderbilt was dismissed because of his views on evolution (1878); William Graham Sumner at Yale had a famous dispute with President Noah Porter over his use of Herbert Spencer's *The Study of Sociology* (1880); Richard T. Ely was attacked for "teaching socialism" at the University of Wisconsin (1894); Edward W. Bemis at the University of Chicago was terminated, presumably because of his critique of railroads as corrupting the political process (1894); John M. Mecklin at Lafayette was forced by the president to resign because of his views as an outspoken liberal philosopher (1913).[57]

These cases and others provoked much debate—and, in the Ross case, led to the creation of a national investigative

---

[57] For extensive (and often colorful) discussions of such cases, see Metzger, pp. 139–93; Matthew W. Finkin and Robert C. Post, *For the Common Good: Principles of American Academic Freedom* (New Haven, CT: Yale University Press, 2009), pp. 26–45; and Veysey, among others. Veysey provides perhaps the most nuanced accounts (pp. 381–417).

committee of economists. But there was little if any concrete action until the AAUP's oft-quoted *1915 Declaration of Principles on Academic Freedom and Academic Tenure* and the constitution of its Committee A to address such issues. From the standpoint of our interest in the evolution of faculty roles in governance, the obvious question is: what explains the long hiatus between, for instance, the Ross case and the AAUP actions?

One explanation offered by Walter Metzger, who made a careful study of this question, is the nature of the scholarly workplace: highly individualistic. Even more important, according to Metzger, were institutional and disciplinary barriers that cut across the professorial community. There was also, in his words, "a deep aversion among academic men to entering into an organization whose purposes smacked of trade unionism," and this was combined with a "fear of administrative reprisal." In those days, the university was not a place where professors felt free to criticize their superiors.[58] In the Ross case, Veysey points out that a large majority of the Stanford faculty identified with the position of the administration. Their argument was "Why tear down a promising foundation over one incident?"[59]

58. See Metzger, pp. 468–80.
59. Veysey, p. 415. As this situation illustrates, faculty were protective of presidents and their institutions. More generally, Veysey tells us that the typical administrative response to these debates was to praise the ideal of academic freedom but also to stress the need for faculty to behave "responsibly" (p. 409). Administrators acted as devoted servants of institutions that it was their duty to protect. "During the decade after 1900, practically no American university president spoke of academic freedom without introducing . . . qualificatory overtones into his remarks" (p. 417). Veysey concludes: "It is important neither to exaggerate nor unduly to minimize the impact of the early struggle for academic freedom upon the American university as a whole. The problem became a running symptom of internal stress; it emphasized a cleavage between some faculty members and a larger group who sided, easily or reluctantly, consciously or covertly, with the administration and with the fundamental limitations upon deviance which the administration symbolized. In the end a mood of loyalty toward the institution widely prevailed" (p. 418).

This began to change. In the decade prior to 1915, a variety of forces worked to break down the barriers to collective action and a forceful assertion of faculty prerogatives, including, as Metzger puts it, the "spirit and ideology of Progressivism." Leading faculty members were also annoyed that the presidents of the research universities that formed the AAU in 1900 should have deigned to call themselves "*the* Association of American Universities" (our emphasis). A deeper current, we believe (to return to one of our recurring themes), was the growing market power of academics, and especially the most prominent ones, in the years marked by the emergence of the research university. It is no coincidence that the initiative for forming the AAUP was taken by a "few movers and shakers, by a few professors who, academically, had 'arrived.'" The formation of the AAUP was led by eighteen professors from Johns Hopkins, and by professors of the stature of John Dewey, one of the Progressive Era's most prominent public intellectuals. It is clear that the AAUP, as first envisioned, was to represent "the aristocrats of academic labor."[60]

The first task of those advocating academic freedom was to alter the idea that faculty were employees, serving at the sufferance of their employers. The 1915 *Declaration* asserted clearly that faculty "are the appointees, but not in any proper sense the employees," of universities; the example of judges was cited. The argument was that these appointees were responsible to a wider public, not just to their own trustees, for the fulfillment of the social function of the university.[61] Thus faculty leaders

60. Metzger, p. 203.

61. See Finkin and Post, pp. 33 and 40 ff. The *Declaration*, which is reproduced in full in the appendix to the Finkin-Post book, "sought . . . to change institutional practices by altering the perception of faculty status" (p. 115). As various authorities noted, faculty demanded dignity and respect. Veysey (p. 389) provides a long excerpt from a faculty member's statement in 1907 describing the plight of the faculty member as being "under" the administration.

appealed to professors as professionals, not as employees or as members of a union. The organizing committee specifically referred to the American Bar Association and the American Medical Association as models for a national association of faculty that viewed their role as "custodians of the interests of higher education."[62]

At its inception, the AAUP had two main goals: "The first was to place some limitation on the trustees' prerogative to fire teachers. Quite tentatively, the Association suggested that aberrant opinion should never be grounds for dismissal." It went on to propose that teachers should be entitled, before dismissal, to have charges against them in writing considered in a fair trial. The second objective was "to provide security and dignity in the academic job through definite rules of tenure."[63]

Both of these objectives were achieved, with lasting effects on both American higher education in general and, more specifically, on the effective role of faculty in one of the most critical aspects of governance: managing academic personnel matters related to freedom of utterance and assessments of professional competence. But this long-term success did not come instantly or without considerable struggle, as we will see when we discuss (in the next section) the challenges posed to the most basic concepts of academic freedom by what Geiger refers to as the "patriotic fervor" associated with the entry of the United States into "the European War."[64]

62. Metzger, pp. 478–80, and Philo A. Hutcheson, *A Professional Professoriate: Unionization, Bureaucratization, and the AAUP* (Nashville, TN: Vanderbilt University Press, 2000), p. 2.

63. Metzger, pp. 480–81. See John Dewey, "Address of the President: Delivered at the Annual Meeting of the Association, December 31, 1915," in *Bulletin of the American Association of University Professors* 1, no. 1 (December 1915): 7–13.

64. Geiger (2015), p. 423.

World War I and the Interwar Years

The Demand for "100 Percent Americanism"

It is an odd coincidence, and a reminder of the strange twists and turns of history, that only about two years after the AAUP's pathbreaking *Declaration of Principles,* the vicissitudes of World War I led to what Geiger calls a "repudiation" of these very principles. Context is important. Geiger argues:

> In terms of indoctrination through crude propaganda and suppression of civil liberties, World War I surpassed all other American wars. . . . Super patriots demanded national unity—100 percent Americanism—which targeted immigrants from eastern and southern Europe, radicals . . . , and German–Americans. . . . Campuses endured successive patriotic rallies. . . . A lack of enthusiasm could provoke charges of disloyalty, as happened at the University of Wisconsin. At Illinois, faculty were investigated for not buying Liberty bonds. . . . New wartime grounds for dismissal were approved. Universities were deemed justified in firing professors without due process. . . . Numerous dismissals occurred, often of war skeptics who were also disliked for holding radical views or for personal eccentricities. . . . The distinguished Columbia psychologist, James McKeen Cattell, long a thorn in the side of trustees and President Butler, was dismissed ostensibly for writing a critical letter to members of Congress. This action prompted the resignation of renowned historian Charles Beard, but such principled protest against war hysteria—and those who exploited it—was costly and rare.[65]

---

[65] Ibid., p. 424. Chapter 10 of Geiger's book, "Mass Education, 1915–1940," contains an extensive discussion of the World War I years. Geiger is scathing in his criticism of faculty members (whom he describes, on p. 425, as having "readily set aside the ethics of their profession"). He is surely right in the principles he espouses, but we are inclined to be at least somewhat more forgiving and less judgmental. The World War I years are a good reminder that there are times, fortunately not many, when "great waves" wash over many otherwise sensible people—it is hard to avoid thinking of some of the events at the time of the U.S. war in Vietnam as illustrations of this dictum.

Lest we underestimate the difficulty of asserting faculty prerogatives to speak out at this time in our history, it is well to remember that no less a person than Nicholas Murray Butler, president of Columbia University and a trustee of the Carnegie Endowment for International Peace, formally withdrew the privilege of academic freedom at his university during the war. In embracing America's wartime aims, Butler simultaneously placated Columbia's conservative trustees who had lingering doubts about his "alleged pacifism" and replaced his pro-German sympathies with a fervent patriotism that asserted the president's authority to dismiss any faculty member (or student) who criticized US policy.[66] At Princeton, President Hibben had a memorable encounter with an undergraduate, Henry Strater '19, who was a pacifist. When Hibben learned that Strater had invited the leading antiwar personage of his time, William Jennings Bryan, to speak at Princeton, he called Strater into his office and told him that he could not allow Bryan to speak on campus because he had already committed Princeton to a war policy.[67]

From the perspective of a basic commitment to freedom of expression ("utterance"), the "100 percent Americanism" con-

66. Michael Rosenthal, *Nicholas Miraculous: The Amazing Career of the Redoubtable Dr. Nicholas Murray Butler* (New York: Farrar, Straus and Giroux, 2006), pp. 225–26.

67. See William G. Bowen, *Lessons Learned: Reflections of a University President* (Princeton, NJ: Princeton University Press, 2011), p. 36. For other examples of a similar kind, see Jonathan Cole, *The Great American University: Its Rise to Preeminence, Its Indispensable National Role, Why It Must Be Protected* (New York: PublicAffairs, 2010), pp. 45–49. These actions by university leaders reveal a deeper truth about American higher education. It is only in more recent years that there has been a general understanding that the university should be the home of the critic, not the critic itself. For an excellent historical account of how long it took for the "new ideal" of openness and independence to prevail (as opposed to the "old ideal" of indoctrination and hewing to the party line), see the article "Princeton's Roots: An Amalgam of Models," by the distinguished historian Lawrence Stone in the *Princeton Alumni Weekly*, September 12, 1977, and Bowen's discussion of this entire subject in *Lessons Learned*, pp. 35–41, as well as the sources cited there.

cept was (and is) an abomination. Fortunately, the attempt to force near-total conformity of thinking during World War I proved to be an aberration. In the fullness of time, good sense prevailed. There was no escaping the practical need for freedom of expression and inquiry if research and teaching were to meet societal needs. However, between the end of World War I and the widely endorsed 1940 *Statement of Principles*, there were miles to go, much work to be done in gaining agreement on core principles between the AAUP and major college and university associations, and many dismissals that provoked controversy.

No one should expect (ever!) that institutions of higher education in America will move in lockstep, and it is hardly surprising that a wide variety of approaches to structuring active faculty involvement in academic personnel matters was evident in the interwar years. It took decades for the "new norms" that the AAUP espoused to take hold nationally. Both of our "old" case-study institutions, Princeton and the University of California, were apparently somewhat ahead of their time in having moved, as early as the 1920s, to governance systems that depended on regular, and influential, faculty recommendations concerning academic personnel decisions.

In the country at large, dismissals of faculty occurred and provoked claims of abuses of presidential power. The AAUP, however, was able to play only a limited role in attempting to adjudicate such disputes.[68] In Metzger's considered opinion, the AAUP (and its 1915 *Declaration of Principles*) "excited expectations among professors that it was unable and unwilling to fulfill." Due to limited resources and capacity, it "could not have served the academic world as policeman, judge, and jury."

68. See Carol S. Gruber, *Mars and Minerva: World War I and the Uses of the Higher Learning* (Baton Rouge: Louisiana State University Press, 1975). Columbia University President Nicholas Murray Butler's dismissive treatment of prominent free speech advocates like historian Charles A. Beard represented the weakness of the AAUP in its earliest years. See Rosenthal, pp. 230, 236–37.

It often tried to mediate, and Metzger concludes: "The AAUP investigations . . . served a limited purpose—to warn and to illustrate, rather than to avenge and redress."[69] This "limited purpose" was useful, however, and the AAUP's sometimes halting efforts to investigate unquestionably contributed to the evolving case law that in time protected faculty from being disciplined for unpopular utterance. It should also be noted that, after reviewing the records of many cases, Metzger concluded that "comparatively few . . . involved a clear violation of the right to free expression." Many involved presidential bungling, personal issues, and so on. It was also inevitable that, during the Great Depression, a number involved "the decision to cut down the staff in an effort to economize."[70] There were also some truly idiosyncratic situations.[71] Individual disputes notwithstanding, the 1940 *Statement*

69. Metzger, pp. 216–18. In tracing the origins of the "mixed" public–private system of education that emerged in this country, Clark Kerr similarly noted that "the primary governance model was Calvinist and particularly via Scotland. This has resulted in the existence of strong lay boards and of influential presidents that the public and state authorities can hold accountable." See Clark Kerr, "The American Mixture of Higher Education in Perspective: Four Dimensions," *Higher Education* 19, no. 1 (1990): 14.

70. Metzger, p. 218.

71. To cite one bizarre situation that occurred, as it were, "late in the game": In the winter of 1940, Bertrand Russell was invited to serve as a visiting professor by City College in New York. He had written *Marriage and Morals,* and various moralists objected to his views and sought to terminate his appointment. Albert Barnes, the strong-minded and highly opinionated head of the Barnes Foundation in Philadelphia, intervened and offered Russell an appointment at his foundation, which Russell accepted. But, not surprisingly, Barnes, who did not himself understand or accept the idea of academic freedom, then tried to control what Russell said at the Barnes Foundation (and also to keep Russell's wife from attending his lectures). Russell's appointment at the Barnes was terminated in December 1942. There was then this interesting (and encouraging) sequel. Over many years, Barnes initiated conversations with several educational institutions (including the University of Pennsylvania) to broaden the influence of his ideas. He offered to fund chairs on the condition that he name the incumbent, and so on. None of this came to anything, and Barnes could not understand why universities could not agree to his conditions. See Neil L. Rudenstine, *House of Barnes: The Man, the Collection, the Controversy* (Philadelphia: American Philosophical Society, 2012), p. 133.

of Principles was adopted by both the AAUP and by over two hundred educational organizations and institutions.[72]

Core Propositions about Academic Freedom

To cut to the proximate end of this hugely important topic, the historical evolution of principles of academic freedom suggests that, struggles and setbacks notwithstanding, there are four main conclusions germane to our study:

academic freedom

1. The basic argument for "academic freedom" was never that it was some kind of inalienable right. Rather, the basic argument for academic freedom was a highly practical, pragmatic one. In the words of legal scholars Matthew Finkin and Robert Post, the argument was "that the teacher's 'independence of thought and utterance' is *required* by the basic purpose of the university."[73] Without such independence, universities would be severely hampered in their ability to advance knowledge and educate properly new generations of students—a proposition being tested today by efforts to develop high-quality research universities in countries such as China, where there are limits on freedom of expression. "The basic claim is that researchers cannot

---

72. See AAUP, "Endorsers of the 1940 Statement," www.aaup.org/endorsers -1940-statement, accessed April 11, 2014.

73. Finkin and Post, p. xx, our emphasis. The Finkin–Post book is an excellent account by two leading legal scholars of the main contours of academic freedom, especially as revealed through the case law developed over the years by Committee A, the Committee on Academic Freedom and Tenure, of the AAUP. The authors explain that academic freedom is "conventionally understood as having four distinct dimensions: freedom of research and publication, freedom in the classroom, freedom of intramural speech, and freedom of extramural speech" (p. 7). They then discuss in detail the meanings (and limitations) of academic freedom in each of these contexts. Professor Finkin and Dean Post are past members of the AAUP's Committee A. Finkin, who chaired the committee, has also served as the AAUP's general counsel.

written?

1) *freedom of research*
2) *freedom in the classroom*
3) *freedom of intramural speech*
4) *freedom of extramural speech*

develop new knowledge unless they are free to inquire and to speculate."[74]

2. It has also been understood right along that "rights" are joined to professional "responsibilities." Finkin and Post are very clear on this point: "A second conceptual premise [in the development of the case for academic freedom] was that faculty are professional experts in the production of knowledge—they alone can judge the competence of other faculty as scholars. Lay governing boards are competent to judge concerning charges of habitual neglect of assigned duties, on the part of individual teachers, and concerning charges of grave moral delinquency. But in matters of opinion, and of the utterance of opinion, such boards cannot intervene." This is a claim for professional self-regulation. In short: "The traditional ideal of academic freedom [involves] twin commitments to freedom of research and to compliance with professional norms."[75]

3. With the passage of time, these closely linked propositions have become widely accepted. Notwithstanding challenges (some serious, as in McCarthyism and the "Red Scare" of the 1950s) and occasional efforts to set or expand limits, American higher education has successfully accepted the principles laid out in the 1940 Statement of Principles. Unlike many other consequential and complicated issues involving faculty roles, which we will explore in

74. Finkin and Post, p. 54.

75. Ibid., pp. 40 and 42. It is worth emphasizing here that, as with constitutionally guaranteed rights, there are no absolute academic rights or freedoms. Thus the freedom of research is not absolute because it may be regulated by the government (as in the case of institutional review boards). Institutions may also limit research due to concerns over conflicts of interest. Similarly, freedom in the classroom is not absolute. There is an obligation to grade fairly. A faculty member does not have the right to call on only men, or non-minorities. Nor do faculty members have complete freedom over how to teach. For example, a professor teaching human sexuality cannot provide live demonstrations in the classroom, as a Northwestern faculty member learned a few years ago.

chapter 4, questions of control over academic personnel matters related to utterance—as contrasted, for example, with control over staffing costs and teaching methods—are now more settled but not quite "off the table," as some recent examples suggest.[76] Today, no American college or university claiming academic respectability would seek to violate the norms articulated so clearly by Finkin and Post in their detailed elucidation of the meaning of the *1940 Statement*.[77]

76. Over the past few years, issues of academic freedom have surfaced most often around faculty members whose writings and speech support opposition to Israeli policy in the West Bank and the Gaza Strip. In the summer of 2014, the University of Illinois at Urbana–Champaign withdrew a recommendation for a faculty appointment with tenure, contingent on approval by the Board of Trustees, of a scholar in American Indian Studies. Although the university did not specify the reasons for its decision, and later admitted "some procedural missteps" in dealing with the candidate, there was widespread speculation that the faculty member's harsh comments in social media may have influenced the decision. See Scott Jaschik, "Out of a Job," *Inside Higher Ed*, August 6, 2014, available at www.insidehighered.com/news/2014/08/06/u-illinois-apparently-revokes-job-offer-controversial-scholar, and Peter Schmidt, "What's Next in the Steven Salaita Dispute?" *Chronicle of Higher Education*, September 12, 2014, available at www://chronicle.com/article/What-s-Next-in-the-Steven/148773. Our view is that this episode was handled very badly by the University of Illinois. At the minimum, there should have been a peer review of the reasons for not appointing the candidate. Moreover, it is not enough, in our view, for the "powers that be" to abrogate an appointment because the candidate has behaved in an "uncivil" manner. Professional norms should dominate all such discussions. There is a key distinction to be drawn between unpopular utterance, which may include a perceived lack of civility, and actions that call into question the capacities of a prospective faculty member to adhere to widely accepted professional norms in his or her teaching and research. See Peter Schmidt, "Pleas for Civility Meet Cynicism," *Chronicle of Higher Education*, September 16, 2014, available at www://chronicle.com/article/Pleas-for-Civility-Meet/148715. For a broader analysis of academic freedom issues in a digital environment, see Robert M. O'Neil, *Academic Freedom in the Wired World: Political Extremism, Corporate Power, and the University* (Cambridge, MA: Harvard University Press, 2008).

77. For a recent historical analysis of the evolution of academic freedom, especially from 1940 to the present, see Timothy Reese Cain, *Establishing Academic Freedom: Politics, Principles, and the Development of Core Values* (New York: Palgrave Macmillan, 2012).

4. Academic freedom is properly identified in the public mind as an individual liberty for faculty, but this protection depends on colleges' and universities' autonomy from external control, as illustrated by the examples of state interference in intellectual life that occurred during the McCarthy era and by earlier experiences in California with loyalty oaths. Although we view this kind of institutional or corporate autonomy as qualitatively different from the core notions of academic freedom afforded faculty, recent efforts at political interference in Virginia and Texas remind us that a reasonable degree of independence and autonomy is indispensable in protecting against abridgements of faculty freedoms by the state.[78]

A hint of things to come: As we will argue in some detail later, the more consequential danger to emerge over time is that faculty may overreach and seek to apply the basic principles of academic freedom to ancillary areas—a possibility with broad ramifications that we consider in chapter 5.

Putting aside the long-running debate over principles governing faculty utterance, and the development of the key role of the faculty in making professional judgments about academic competence, the decades between the two world wars posed many challenges for American higher education. These included exploring how to cope with the ever-expanding role of science in public life, as well as with the burgeoning number

78. We are grateful to Hanna Gray, president emeritus of the University of Chicago, for encouraging us to differentiate and link these two core notions. See David M. Rabban, "Academic Freedom, Individual or Institutional?" *Academe* 87, no. 6 (November–December 2001): 16–20, and Robert M. O'Neil, "University Governance and Academic Freedom," in William G. Tierney, ed., *Competing Conceptions of Academic Governance: Negotiating the Perfect Storm* (Baltimore: Johns Hopkins University Press, 2004), pp. 177–201. Drawing on Supreme Court cases since the *Bakke* decision (1978) and on recent federal circuit court opinions, Rabban and O'Neil acknowledge the potential for growing tension between these two core principles.

of high school graduates and the severe economic stress result-ing from the Great Depression. This period was complex, as we can see from Roger Geiger's detailed description of the dra-matic growth in enrollments, the origins of mass higher educa-tion, the effects of modern philanthropy, and the development of organized forms of scientific research.[79] This was also an important period from the standpoint of governance, in spite of (or as masked by) the decidedly slow aggregation of fac-ulty roles. The impacts on governance that occurred during this period were subtle and relatively quiet ones—certainly in comparison with the shocks to the system administered by the bookends: (a) the dramatic turn-of-the-century events that included the emergence of research universities and the prom-ulgation of basic concepts of academic freedom, and (b) the later events following the unprecedented explosion of spon-sored research in and after World War II, combined with the even more consequential explosion in student enrollments that accompanied the GI Bill and postwar demographic changes.

The Impact of the New Foundations

Historians of higher education writing about this period are consistent in the emphasis they give to the efforts by major new philanthropic foundations to shape the structure and function-ing of higher education—though, for understandable reasons, these authors do not share our special interest in the effects on faculty roles in governance.[80]

---

79. Geiger (2015), especially chapters 10 and 11.
80. Ibid., chapter 11, provides by far the most detail on the interwar years, including the roles of foundations, and we rely heavily on this carefully researched account. Another treatment, which is highly complementary, is The-lin, pp. 145–50. See also Ellen Condliffe Lagemann, *Private Power for the Public Good: A History of the Carnegie Foundation for the Advancement of Teach-ing* (Middletown, CT: Wesleyan University Press, 1988), and Condliffe Lage-mann and Jennifer de Forest, "What Might Andrew Carnegie Want to Tell Bill

In terms of their effects on higher education in this period, the two most important philanthropic initiatives, by far, were those established by Andrew Carnegie and John D. Rockefeller. These initiatives, which started roughly in 1900, took on a variety of corporate forms. In seeking to understand the objectives of these initiatives, it is important to remember that Carnegie and Rockefeller had amassed their fortunes by "imposing order and efficiency on the steel and petroleum industries, respectively." It is hardly surprising, then, that Rockefeller charged his General Education Board with promoting "a comprehensive system of higher education in the United States," and that the Carnegie Foundation was dedicated to "standardizing American education."[81]

Rockefeller's General Education Board first undertook to shore up the finances of American private colleges by a grant-making program that involved substantial matching components and that had two consequential effects on faculty: it increased their numbers and simultaneously led to much greater alumni involvement in all aspects of their affairs—thus further institutionalizing a broad form of lay control, as opposed to faculty control. The main instrument of Carnegie philanthropy in the early part of this period was the Carnegie Foundation for the Advancement of Teaching (CFAT), which established TIAA–CREF as the provider of portable pensions for academics at institutions that met CFAT standards. In a political climate increasingly sensitive to the need for raising standards and protecting professional prerogatives, CFAT trustees wished to encourage colleges and universities to standardize their admis-

---

Gates? Reflections on the Hundredth Anniversary of the Carnegie Foundation for the Advancement of Teaching," in Ray Bacchetti and Thomas Ehrlich, eds., *Reconnecting Education and Foundations: Turning Good Intentions into Educational Capital* (San Francisco: Jossey-Bass, 2007), pp. 49–67.

81. Geiger (2015), p. 480.

sions and enrollment policies and procedures, as well as their curriculums and course-credit requirements. One of the other stipulations, as David Nasaw notes, was the prohibition against the awarding of pensions to faculty at sectarian institutions. There was, therefore, as historian John Thelin notes, an element of both "coercion and coordination."[82]

A more controversial effort to make universities "business-like" was launched by President Henry Pritchett of the CFAT in 1909, when he commissioned Morris L. Cooke, a protégé of the scientific management guru Frederick Taylor, to study academic and industrial efficiency (the title of the report Cooke produced in 1910). Cooke sought to measure faculty efficiency in terms of student hours of instruction and, more generally, recommended removing faculty from all aspects of governance, which he thought should be "the exclusive prerogative of management." Geiger tells us that Cooke's study had little impact but exemplified "the deference to the new industrial order shared by CFAT board members, like Columbia president Nicholas Murray Butler."[83] Another historian of American higher education, John Thelin, notes:

> CFAT's advocacy of a corporate model for universities was reflected in the changing composition of academic boards and university presidencies. In 1880 the overwhelming majority of presidents and board members were drawn from the ranks of the clergy. By 1930, corporate executives, *corporate* lawyers,

82. Ibid., p. 481. See Thelin, p. 147, and David Nasaw, *Andrew Carnegie* (New York: Penguin, 2006), p. 671. The importance of the "portable" characteristic of these pension plans has been inadequately appreciated; it proved to be critically important in making faculty more mobile and thus enhancing their market power, as portable plans still do to this day. (It is mildly ironic that many other sectors of American society have, in recent years, adopted somewhat similar "vested" plans, which give employees much more freedom of movement and reduce the sense that one has to make a lifetime commitment to an employer.)

83. Geiger (2015), p. 483.

and bankers comprised over 73 percent of board positions at fifteen prominent private colleges and universities.[84]

More generally, this CFAT mindset did not, to say the least, encourage the more sophisticated concepts of appropriate roles for faculty that were to evolve later in the interwar years.

Around 1920, the foundations shifted their emphasis from seeking to change directly the way colleges and universities worked to seeking to improve American science nationally—an undertaking that was considerably more successful and that had consequential indirect effects on faculty roles. It is not part of our task to detail the efforts made to fund the National Research Council and other intermediate organizations, including the American Council of Learned Societies, the Social Science Research Council, and the National Bureau of Economic Research. Special attention was paid to medical research and education.[85] Large grants were also made to promote science in selected individual institutions, including Caltech. Geiger sums up: "By the end of the 1920s, there could no longer be any doubt that universities were the dominant institutions of American science."[86] One obvious consequence was a pronounced strengthening of the positions of leading scientists—whose wishes and needs had to be taken very, very seriously by presidents and trustees of universities that aspired to be centers of research and advanced training, as more and more did.

Faculty roles in the research universities during this period (especially during the Roaring Twenties) were mostly the

84. Thelin, p. 238, his emphasis.
85. The standard for all future scientific and educational scholarly surveys remains Abraham Flexner, *Medical Education in the United States and Canada,* Bulletin 4 (New York: Carnegie Foundation for the Advancement of Teaching, 1910).
86. Geiger (2015), p. 489, contains extensive documentation of these activities.

conventional ones: building departments, running research programs, training graduate students. One side effect of the expansion of undergraduate enrollments and graduate programs is that graduate students were now regularly enlisted as teachers. During the Great Depression, few faculty lost their jobs, even as they endured pay cuts (but cuts generally in line with declines in the cost of living). Universities coped with their financial problems in part by hiring larger numbers of assistants and instructors. There was, de facto, a "devolution" of authority at many of the larger research universities concerning the management of departmental affairs from the presidents and central officials to departmental "baronies," which were often conservative and not all that effective. Geiger concludes his long examination of experiences during the interwar years at many universities, including leading state universities, with these cautionary words: "Academic leaders recognized that the academic barons who had built departments and schools could become obstacles to further academic advancement."[87] This is a core organizational thesis that we will examine in its contemporary form in chapter 3, especially in the context of advances in technology, including new approaches to online learning. As we will see, Geiger's warning was prescient.

A Faculty Voice

But we should not get ahead of our story. Another development during the interwar years directly relevant to our interest in faculty roles in governance was the evolution of the desire of many for faculty to have a "voice" in the consideration of issues of all kinds affecting the colleges and universities that

87. Ibid., p. 538. See also a fascinating account of a "radical critique" of deans and department heads by John B. Johnston, an anatomy professor at the University of Minnesota in 1913 (pp. 500–501).

employed them. In considering the question of what kind of voice faculty should have, it is important not to let the discussion become overly complicated. There are really two basic issues: (1) how should colleges and universities structure the natural tendency of faculty to want to have a "say" in all kinds of matters that affect them and their institutions, sometimes in profound ways, and (2) can faculty who say "bad" things, from someone's perspective, either through formal channels or just "off the cuff," be penalized for their outspokenness?

As early as October 1917, almost immediately after the United States entered the "Great War" and barely two years after the AAUP's 1915 *Declaration of Principles,* members of Committee T of the AAUP began what became an elaborate consideration of questions such as these:

> What part should the faculty play in the determination of a university's fundamental educational policies; with regard, for example, to the establishment of new educational enterprises, such as new colleges, schools, and departments of instruction? What part should the faculty have in the selection of deans and president, in the selection and promotion of its own members, and in the making of the annual budget? Should there be explicit provision for representation of the faculty on the board of trustees, by way of members of the faculty? Or should the faculty be represented by way of faculty conference committees advisory to the board?[88]

At this juncture, our interest is not in whether faculty should serve on their own schools' boards of trustees (we think not, as a general rule, because of obvious problems of conflict of interest and because there are other ways for boards to gain access to faculty views) but in the larger question of

88. Committee T, "Report of Committee T on Place and Function of Faculties in University Government and Administration," *Bulletin of the American Association of University Professors* 6, no. 3 (March 1920): 18.

whether faculty should have some regularized voice in issues of all kinds affecting their institutions. Throughout the interwar years, the answer to this question was increasingly "yes," but almost always with the explicit understanding that the right to be heard did not translate into the right to prevail. Of course much depends on the specific issues under consideration. It was generally understood that faculty should have more influence and sometimes direct control over issues that are primarily academic, such as who should be authorized to teach, the criteria for awarding degrees, and so on. Other issues required what the AAUP committee leadership called "joint responsibility," with final authority residing in the board of trustees (and sometimes in the president). We note, however, that the recognition of legal realities did not signify full acceptance of such propositions or temper the AAUP conviction that boards of trustees should defer to the faculty in setting all consequential educational policies: "Except in financial matters, the trustees should not exercise directly the final power over educational policies and interests, which, at the present time, they legally possess in many cases."[89] We believe this is what the authors of the 1920 Committee T report may have meant by referring to the "spirit of joint responsibility and fuller cooperation."[90]

Our case studies of the University of California and Princeton are instructive. At the University of California in 1920, the Academic Senate "acquired from the regents formal recognition of its role in advising the president of the university." The Academic Senate was given the right "to lay its views before the board of regents through the president on any matter pertaining to the conduct and welfare of the university." As Angus Taylor observed in his history of the Academic Senate: "These historic principles still survive."[91] Not surprisingly, the actual

89. Ibid., p. 26.
90. Ibid., p. 24.
91. Taylor, pp. 1 and 4.

extent of consultation with the faculty has varied considerably over the years—depending in no small part on the preferences of the president. President Robert Sproul was not known for an inclination to consult, but he did appoint a Special Committee of the Academic Senate on Educational Policy, which later became a regular committee. During the Great Depression of the 1930s, the committee was asked to recommend how salary reductions were to be carried out—which it did, reducing the pay most of those who were highest paid.[92] It was, however, not until the time of Clark Kerr (1958–67) that extensive consultation became the norm at the University of California.

Presidents of Princeton have consulted the faculty informally on a wide range of issues since the university's earliest days. Of course, this was easier at Princeton than it would have been at many other institutions because of the small size of the university and the lack of professional schools (hence a single faculty). The informality of this process, which allowed an autocratic president such as Wilson to use it when and if he chose to do so, was altered under President Hibben in the early part of the twentieth century (as we noted earlier), when he "created a faculty-elected advisory committee to meet regularly with the trustees' curriculum committee."[93] This was the predecessor to the faculty Conference Committee of today, which was used for years by presidents of Princeton as a source of general advice, as well as both a vehicle for communication between the trustees and the faculty and an appeal body for aggrieved faculty.

A variety of mechanisms for encouraging faculty to "have a voice" were employed by leading state universities during the interwar years. For example, President George Vincent at the University of Minnesota is said to have "revitalized the faculty with careful appointments and given it a voice with a Univer-

92. Ibid., pp. 8–11.
93. Axtell, p. 77.

sity Senate." At the University of Michigan, President Alexander Grant Ruthven "displaced the ineffective senate (the total faculty) with a smaller University Council of elected faculty and administrators, [thereby] empowering the faculty."[94] Specific mechanisms for consultation must respect local traditions and circumstances. More important than the "forms" is the spirit in which expressions of opinion are sought and taken into account.

A critical aspect of the "right spirit" is a clear understanding that expression of unpopular opinion is just fine, and certainly no grounds for discipline. It took some time and effort for the AAUP to establish this now seemingly obvious point. In 1927, the AAUP concluded that a faculty member at the University of Louisville could not be dismissed because he was "disloyal" to the president. The Committee found that what the president of Louisville demanded was "not loyalty but subservience." In another case, the AAUP concluded that "dismissal for disagreement was 'a manifest infringement of academic freedom.'"[95] In short, "By 1933, the AAUP had come to view intramural expression as a full-fledged form of academic freedom. . . . Faculty might even have a 'professional responsibility' to express their considered views on 'educational matters.'"[96]

94. Geiger (2015), pp. 501–2.
95. Finkin and Post, p. 121. This was the Rollins case in 1933. See Finkin and Post for an extended discussion of these and other cases.
96. Finkin and Post, 123. We continue to hear from colleagues at a variety of institutions that administrators sometimes admonish faculty not to engage in obstreperous behavior and on occasion go so far as to argue that such speech should not be tolerated in the name of academic freedom. The lesson is that battles on this front, as on others, are never over—even as there is little evidence of any general crackdown on the right to disagree. Case in point: In the fall of 2014, the suspension (subsequently revoked) of a highly respected scholar by the University of Warwick, allegedly "for sighing, unfriendly body language and the use of irony," led to understandable concerns within the British academy about arbitrary punishment and faculty vulnerability. See Scott Jaschik, "British University Backs Down on Suspension for Sighing and Irony," *Inside Higher Ed*, October 27, 2014, available at https://www.insidehighered.com/news/2014/10/27/british-university-backs-down-on-suspension-sighing-and-irony.

Scale and Specialization

We turn now, in concluding this part of our study, to brief descriptions of two powerful currents that had long-lasting effects on the structure and organization of institutions of higher education—in spite of the fact that they are in some ways less visible than the interventions of the Carnegie and Rockefeller foundations—namely, the growing power nationally of science and the acquisition by many faculty of a voice in institutional affairs (especially in faculty personnel matters). We refer to (1) the "high school movement," which created the base needed for marked increases in total enrollments and in average institutional size, and (2) the pronounced increase in specialization within academia especially, but not only, in the sciences.

Accustomed as we are today to thinking of high school attendance as the norm in American life, it is important to recall that just over a hundred years ago, in 1910, "barely 9 percent of all American 18-year-olds graduated from secondary school and 19 percent of 15- to 18-year-olds were enrolled in a public or private high school." Just 30 years later, in 1940, "the median youth across the entire nation had a high school diploma and 73 percent of American youth were enrolled in high school."[97] This was the famous high school movement, and it had profound effects on American higher education for decades to come. For our purposes, it is especially significant to note that this burgeoning population of potential college students led not only to much higher total enrollments but also to large increases in the size of institutions, particularly those in the public sector. To illus-

97. See Claudia Goldin and Lawrence F. Katz, *The Race between Education and Technology* (Cambridge, MA: Harvard University Press, 2008), p. 195 and figure 6.1. Goldin and Katz provide a detailed and compelling account of the factors leading to this remarkable upsurge in schooling that includes a discussion of differences by region and gender.

trate: "Although the number of private and public institutions increased by 1.4 times from 1900 to 1933, the number of students increased almost fivefold."[98]

A concurrent development that has also had a lasting impact is the sharply increased specialization in academic disciplines that began in the late nineteenth century and then took off in the interwar years—as demonstrated, for example, not only by the growth in graduate and professional schools but also by the establishment of ever more narrowly defined "learned societies."[99] Universities greatly expanded their offerings, and faculty began to define themselves as occupying separate, specialized fields. The push for increased specialization is inexorable and derives, of course, from the continuing growth of knowledge.

Goldin and Katz were hardly the first to take note of these developments. In his 2002 introduction to a new edition of the widely cited Jencks and Riesman book of 1968, Jencks argues that the growth of professionalization and the leverage of distinguished scholars has transformed all institutions, not merely research universities, where one would find the greatest concentration of scholars, but other institutions as well, including church-related colleges whose character also began to change as a result of hiring faculty with "unconventional" views and ideas. "These changes transformed [some number of] small, sleepy, impoverished nineteenth-century colleges into larger, more affluent, and more cosmopolitan institutions."[100]

From early days, the professionalization of university professors brought conflict on many fronts. Jencks and Riesman

98. Goldin and Katz, p. 261. Data of the kind that they cite are extremely difficult to come by, and one of the many virtues of their study is that they explain in detail how they constructed the underlying data sets—no small achievement.

99. Goldin and Katz, pp. 262–66.

100. Jencks, p. x.

point to numerous late nineteenth- and early twentieth-century academic histories that report battles in which the basic question was whether the president and trustees or the faculty would determine the shape of the curriculum, the content of particular courses, or the use of particular books. The professors (for instance, Thorstein Veblen) lost most of the publicized battles, but they won the war. Today faculty control over these matters is rarely challenged, and conflict usually centers on other issues.[101]

From the perspective of our interest in faculty roles in governance, the general point to take away from this discussion is that the combination of scale and specialization made it impossible for trustees or presidents to exert the kind of hands-on control that had been possible in earlier days. To be sure, prior to World War II, as Christopher Jencks and David Riesman observed:

> Even senior scholars at leading universities did a good deal of scut work—teaching small groups of lower-level students, reading papers, grading exams, etc. Their labors were supplemented by aging but unscholarly instructors and assistant professors, who were not given tenure, status, or high salaries but were kept around precisely because there were lots of routine teaching jobs to be done and they were willing to do them.[102]

This pattern changed drastically after World War II, first at the leading research universities and then, by "contagious spread," at many other institutions. The growth in the authority of the department, and in some cases the departmental chair, is a fundamental fact of academic life that raises today quite profound questions about the "fit" between our inher-

101. Jencks and Riesman, p. 15.
102. Ibid., p. 40.

ited systems of governance and the present-day needs of society and the educational system created to meet them.[103] That is the subject of much of the rest of this study. We are reminded that sometimes today's "virtues" become tomorrow's "vices"— one of the sub-themes of the Goldin–Katz book.[104]

103. John Thelin argues: "Perhaps the major gain for faculty in terms of campus power [during the period from 1920 to 1945] was the emergence of the 'departmental chair' as a seigniorial role—an enduring source of local patronage and power, determined more by immediate campus politics than by national scholarly reputation" (p. 257).

104. Goldin and Katz, pp. 8 and 129–62. These "virtues" are also discussed in William G. Bowen, Martin A. Kurzweil, and Eugene M. Tobin, *Equity and Excellence in American Higher Education* (Charlottesville: University of Virginia Press, 2005), pp. 69–72. Of course, Goldin and Katz are talking about secondary education, and are asking if the forces (such as decentralization of much authority) that led to such a valuable expansion of students aiming for college in the interwar years continue to serve us well as we look ahead. An analogous question suggests itself when we consider, as we will in the next chapter, the evolution of higher education in this country since World War II.

3

Historical Overview, Part 2— World War II to the Present

THE UPHEAVAL OF waging total war transformed the United States, requiring an unprecedented national response from every corner of society. During World War II fifteen million men and several hundred thousand women joined the armed forces, and three-quarters of them served overseas. An additional fifteen million civilians changed their county of residence in the pursuit of jobs in wartime industries.[1] The incomprehensible stress and horror of World War II was a human tragedy, but in serving as the "great arsenal of democracy," the United States "banished the decade-long scourge of unemployment."[2] The unprecedented output of war materiel and the availability of generous wartime pay ended the Great Depression; it transformed at least temporarily economic prospects for women, especially married women who wanted to work outside traditional female occupations (like "Rosie the Riveter"); and, finally, it demonstrated for all to see the power of American science—which made great contributions to the war effort via the development of radar, the Manhattan Project, and in

[1.] David M. Kennedy, *Freedom from Fear: The American People in Depression and War, 1929–1945* (New York: Oxford University Press, 1999), p. 747.
[2.] Ibid., p. 644.

countless other ways.[3] Clark Kerr, in his memoirs, provides a succinct summary: "The battle of Waterloo may have been won on the playing fields of Eton, as the duke of Wellington said. World War II was won, to a major degree . . . in the laboratories of the [American] research universities."[4]

World War II and the Growth of Sponsored Research

There was phenomenal growth in federally funded research during and after World War II, and this infusion of support had profound consequences for higher education. From the standpoint of our interest in governance, there are two points to highlight, one generic and one organizational, both of which continue to matter.

First, the massive investment of government money in research, which in the United States (unlike the Soviet Union) mainly took the form of money provided in response to proposals from individual faculty members and research groups

---

3. Claudia Goldin, "The Role of World War II in the Rise of Women's Work," National Bureau of Economic Research Paper 3203 (December 1989), available at www.nber.org/papers/w3203; William H. Chafe, *The Paradox of Change: American Women in the Twentieth Century* (New York: Oxford University Press, 1991), pp. 121–74; Roger L. Geiger, *American Research Universities since World War II: Research and Relevant Knowledge* (New Brunswick, NJ: Transaction, 2004; originally published by Oxford University Press, 1993), pp. 3–29; and Jonathan R. Cole, *The Great American University* (New York: PublicAffairs, 2010), pp. 85–104.

4. Kerr, *The Gold and the Blue: A Personal Memoir of the University of California, 1949–1967,* vol. 2, *Political Turmoil* (Berkeley: University of California Press, 2003), p. 91. See also John R. Thelin, *A History of American Higher Education* (Baltimore: Johns Hopkins University Press, 2004), p. 258: "The major innovation for American higher education during World War II was that professors in a variety of fields demonstrated both expertise and a willingness to contribute that expertise to unprecedented wartime applications." The longer-term implications for a federal role in the support of research can be traced back, in no small measure, to the publication of Vannevar Bush, *Science, the Endless Frontier—A Report to the President* (Washington, DC: US Government Printing Office, July 1945).

at leading universities, had the generic effect of strengthening the position of science and scientists in major universities vis-à-vis other fields of study and other educational programs.[5] As Christopher Jencks and David Riesman note, the generous funding of scientific research via grants and contracts enhanced faculty status and in turn often allowed faculty to set their own working conditions. One result was a rapid decline in teaching loads for productive scholars, an increase in the ratio of graduate to undergraduate students, and the hiring of faculty members based on research accomplishments rather than teaching prowess.[6]

Second, there was a significant organizational innovation in the 1950s. To cite a specific institutional manifestation of a broader development: in 1958, the Princeton faculty voted to establish the University Research Board (URB).[7] The URB spent a great deal of time in its early years on the complicated issue of indirect cost recovery and on the even more contentious issue of classified research. The URB has always been chaired by a prominent faculty member; its first chairman was the distinguished scientist Professor Henry DeWolf Smyth. The growth of sponsored research and the establishment of two large-scale research programs (the Princeton–Penn Accelerator and the Princeton Plasma Physics Laboratory) led to the

---

5. The surprise launch of Sputnik by the Soviets in 1957 provided a further reason for spending ever more money on sponsored research. The US government established the Advanced Research and Projects Agency in 1958, and much subsequent funding flowed from this agency. Congress also passed the National Defense Education Act in 1958. See Homer Alfred Neal, Tobin Smith, and Jennifer McCormick, *Beyond Sputnik: U.S. Science Policy in the 21st Century* (Ann Arbor: University of Michigan Press, 2008).

6. Jencks and Riesman, *The Academic Revolution* (Garden City, NY: Doubleday, 1968; reprinted by Transaction, 2002), p. 15. The increased bargaining power of leading scientists had substantial spill-over effects because egalitarian impulses led other scientists and then social scientists and humanists to claim some of the gains scientists had achieved—for example, lower teaching loads.

7. See the Princeton case study.

recruitment by Princeton of a large number of highly qualified scientists who had minimal, if any, teaching responsibilities and who could not be incorporated readily within existing
departmental structures. Yet this important group needed, and
deserved, both status and an understood place in the institutional hierarchy. The URB was important in developing and
overseeing (with the Office of the Dean of the Faculty) specific and carefully defined policies governing this "professional
research staff."[8]

A potentially fruitful question to ponder is whether this
model could have value today in addressing the needs of the
growing corps of non-tenure-track faculty who are primarily
teachers, not researchers. Should more effort be devoted to creating one or more models of a "professional teaching staff"
that would be analogous to the model of the "professional
research staff" that evolved in the aftermath of the postwar
boom in sponsored research? As we will note later, such efforts
are already underway on a number of campuses, and we think
this organizational model will continue to evolve.

The "Red Scare" and the Loyalty Oath Controversies

In the late 1940s and 1950s, American higher education was
buffeted by Cold War fears of disloyalty and allegations of
espionage and subversion. The fears engendered by the "fall"
of China, the Soviet Union's unexpectedly early detonation of an atomic bomb, the Alger Hiss case, and the war in

---

8. Professional research staff structures were also established, for similar rea-
sons, at many other research universities. See Geiger (1993), pp. 198–229. One
of the authors of this study (Bowen) was asked by Princeton President Robert
Goheen to carry out a study of this area, which resulted in a 1962 report titled
"The Federal Government and Princeton University: A Report on the Effects of
Princeton's Involvements with the Federal Government on the Operations of the
University," located at the Seeley G. Mudd Manuscript Library, Princeton Uni-
versity, Princeton, NJ.

Korea contributed to a far-reaching, and at times irrational, preoccupation with security and loyalty—fears exploited by Senator Joseph McCarthy, as well as others. Several public universities and state legislatures responded to these unsettling events, and to fears that their campuses might be havens for disloyalty, by requiring all state employees to sign a disclaimer that they were not communists or members of any group that advocated the overthrow of the US government.

The quintessential case was at the University of California (see the case study). In March 1949, in an effort to prevent stronger action by the legislature's Committee on Un-American Activities, President Robert Sproul recommended that the regents add an explicit "anti-communist" proviso to the standard oath disavowing membership or belief in any organization that advocated the overthrow of the government. Although many faculty members had no substantive (political or ethical) objections to signing such a statement, they objected to the imposition on them of a special oath before one was required of all state employees. A number of states introduced similar loyalty oaths, but the California oath, as Clark Kerr emphasizes in his memoir, seemed qualitatively different because it was "imposed by the trustees of the university itself and . . . seemed to say that the administration and the regents considered faculty members to be a particularly suspect group."[9] A committee of the Academic Senate argued that loyalty oaths threatened academic freedom and tenure and reinforced stereotypes of the university as a haven for subversives. The regents rejected such arguments and issued an ultimatum, over Sproul's objections (he had reversed his position), insisting that all faculty sign the oath or be discharged. In August 1950, thirty-one faculty members were dismissed for refusing to sign: twenty-four at Berkeley, four at the University of California,

9. Kerr, vol. 2, p. 38.

Los Angeles (UCLA), two at Santa Barbara, and one at San Francisco. Other faculty members resigned in protest.

Twenty members of the Berkeley faculty took legal action through the District Court of Appeals to block the dismissals. The court decided unanimously that the firings were unconstitutional and that faculty could not be subjected to any narrower test of loyalty than the basic constitutional oath prescribed for all state employees. The Supreme Court of California upheld this decision. Although the ultimate outcome was the right one, it required a court order to break the impasse between the regents and the faculty and to protect the academic freedom of the faculty. This controversy eventually led some years later (in 1958) to the creation of a process whereby a faculty member with tenure who faced dismissal was entitled to a hearing before the properly constituted advisory committee of the Academic Senate.[10]

The consequences of this failure of governance were long-lasting. The loyalty oath crisis ripped apart the tenuous collegiality of shared governance at the University of California and left "a lingering enmity" that arguably contributed to the Berkeley Free Speech Movement of 1964.[11] This

10. Kerr, *The Gold and the Blue: A Personal Memoir of the University of California, 1949–1967*, vol. 1, *Academic Triumphs* (Berkeley: University of California Press, 2001), p. 33. See also Angus E. Taylor, *The Academic Senate of the University of California: Its Role in the Shared Governance and Operation of the University of California* (Berkeley: Institute of Governmental Studies Press, University of California, 1998), pp. 15–37; John Aubrey Douglass, *The California Idea and American Higher Education: 1850 to the 1960 Master Plan* (Stanford, CA: Stanford University Press, 2000), pp. 206–13; and Douglass, "Shared Governance at the University of California: An Historical Review," Center for Studies in Higher Education, Research and Occasional Paper Series 1 (March 1998), p. 6.

11. David P. Gardner, *The California Oath Controversy* (Berkeley: University of California Press, 1967), p. 249. In *The Gold and the Blue*, Clark Kerr recalls Roger Heyns, the chancellor at Berkeley (1965–71), saying that "every time he traced the origins of the problems he endured from the faculty in the second half of the 1960s, he was led back to the loyalty oath" (Kerr, vol. 2, p. 28).

controversy politicized the faculty and raised fundamental questions about academic freedom and the appropriate balance of power between the Board of Regents and the Academic Senate. According to a distinguished historian of the University of California (John Aubrey Douglass), the Academic Senate proved to be "a disjointed and poorly structured vehicle for presenting the collective opinion of the faculty."[12] A generational gap had emerged between the senate's veteran leaders and the newer, younger faculty hired since the end of World War II, who had no experience with the president or the board. As a result, senate negotiations with President Sproul and the regents in the 1950s often failed to represent the views of the faculty majority.[13] Faculty members grew disenchanted with the senate, and the formal and informal lines of communication between the regents, the president, and the faculty hardened. Sproul never recovered the trust of some of the regents, who were more evenly divided than the faculty on the issue of the oath, or the respect of the faculty, who resented the lack of consultation and the opprobrium of being singled out as a suspect group.[14]

This initially abrupt and then simmering controversy demonstrated that it can be a serious mistake to take for granted even concepts that one would think should be taken for granted. The debate over the loyalty oath demonstrated that the most fundamental principle of academic freedom (protection of the right to hold unpopular opinions), as articulated by the AAUP in 1915 and subsequently endorsed by nearly every organized group within higher education in 1940, was nonetheless at risk at times of great political upheaval. Once again, context (and nuance) are important. The regents of the University of California had been operating since October 1940 under a policy

12. Douglass (2000), p. 210.
13. Gardner, pp. 6–7.
14. Kerr, vol. 2, pp. 36–40.

of not hiring members of the Communist Party, and this policy had been accepted, de facto, by the Academic Senate. For some regents, the loyalty oath was "a test of their power to govern the university, just as for the faculty, it became a test of their power over academic affairs," particularly the responsibility to choose their own members.[15] As David Gardner observes, "The history of the conflict is a story of the failure of educated, competent, and allegedly rational human beings bound together in a good cause—the service of truth and knowledge—to resolve their differences without injuring the University as a whole."[16]

John Thelin reminds us of the widespread extent and the politically charged character of this debate over claims of loyalty versus claims of freedom of utterance:

> The investigations conducted by state legislatures and campus administrations showed that local politics were especially important in shaping academic freedom. Ellen Schrecker, in her exhaustive 1987 study, *No Ivory Tower*, documented a surprising phenomenon: numerous state university presidents took the initiative to subject their faculties to loyalty oaths and codes of conduct exceeding anything that vigilant congressional or state officials might have required. Many campus presidents proved to be more interested in defusing external scrutiny than in defending their professors' traditional rights of academic freedom.[17]

There is another lesson to be learned from this period. Although boards of trustees were not infrequently the source of challenges to free expression on campuses, trustees were also capable of being the staunchest defenders of core principles. A case in point is the widely publicized dispute at Princeton in 1956 over the invitation extended by a student group to Alger

15. Kerr, vol. 1, pp. 38–39.
16. Gardner, p. 245.
17. Thelin, p. 275, and Ellen W. Schrecker, *No Ivory Tower: McCarthyism and the Universities* (New York: Oxford University Press, 1986).

Hiss, a former State Department official, communist sympa-thizer, and "convicted perjurer," to speak on campus. Many alumni and conservative commentators of all kinds demanded that the university prevent Hiss, a former president of the Carnegie Endowment for International Peace, from speaking. The Princeton president deplored the invitation but also defended the right of students to hear speakers of their choice. Nonetheless, the uproar continued. Princeton was fortunate to have on its board at that time Harold R. Medina, the federal district court judge who had presided over the 1949 Smith Act trial of eleven leaders of the American Communist Party and who, in the words of one contemporary commentator, "stood pre-eminent as a foe of communist conspiracy." Medina was thus superbly positioned to lead the trustees in reaffirming the core principle that the university was open to speakers of all persuasions. The trustees decreed that the speech should be allowed to proceed—which it did, without serious incident. People calmed down; alumni giving held up. The main moral of the story is a simple one: trustees, such as Medina, are often more effective in defending campus rights in politically charged situations than are faculty and other "insiders." A secondary moral, and an encouraging one, is that if an institution does the right thing, for the right reasons, anger at initially unpopular decisions dissipates rather quickly.[18]

18. See William G. Bowen, *Lessons Learned: Reflections of a University President* (Princeton, NJ: Princeton University Press, 2011), pp. 47–48, and the notes therein for a full account of this set of events. Many other examples can be given of the value of lay boards in serving as intermediaries between the academic community and the broad society that academia serves. It is ironic, as our colleague Lawrence Bacow has observed, that roles seem now to have reversed. In the commencement season of 2014, pressures to discourage invited individuals (in this case, honorary degree recipients) have come from students and some faculty; it is now presidents, and occasionally trustees, who are struggling to maintain the openness of campuses to individuals who will challenge the views of some students. See Nathan Koppel, "Haverford Speaker Bowen Criticizes Students over Protests," *Wall Street Journal*, May 18, 2014.

At the very time of these rancorous disputes over loyalty oaths and freedom of expression, the entity that had been primarily responsible for articulating the concept of academic freedom for faculty—the AAUP—was itself in disarray. According to John Thelin, "One disappointing development between 1948 and 1953 was the collapse of the Association of American University Professors and its failure to provide faculty members and institutions with reliable representation throughout the assorted skirmishes and major battles."[19] As Walter Metzger notes, "The Association had paid dearly for its do-nothingism amid the commotions of the McCarthy period." The failure to issue a single report chronicling the violations of academic freedom at the Universities of California and Washington allowed other groups to "fix the boundaries between heresy and conspiracy, protected privacy and required candor, in a fashion that left academic freedom with a shrunken territory."[20] There was an internal cost as well. By remaining on the sidelines, the AAUP lost the confidence of existing members and of academics whose pleas for assistance went unheeded.[21] In another sense, however, the inability of the AAUP to be effective "across the board" is not at all surprising, and in fact could have been predicted by the changes/differences in faculty status by both field and institution. As faculty interests continued to vary by discipline, institutional type, seniority, and so on, it was probably inevitable that an organization such as the AAUP would not serve everyone. We see here one of the early fruits of the "fragmentation" of higher education that has been a major, ongoing, characteristic of the postwar period.[22]

19. Thelin, p. 276.
20. Metzger, "Ralph F. Fuchs and Ralph E. Himstead: A Note on the AAUP in the McCarthy Period," *Academe* 72, no. 6 (November–December 1986): 29.
21. Ibid., 30.
22. The problems of the AAUP today have been exacerbated by political disputes over what some see as extraneous matters—e.g., the proposed boycott by US colleges and universities of Israeli institutions. Interestingly, one of the

The Explosive Expansion of Higher Education, Leading to the "Golden Age" of the 1960s

An even more consequential development than McCarthyism was the unprecedented growth in enrollments that followed the end of World War II and lasted, with some interruptions, until the end of the 1960s. This growth in enrollments was fueled in the first instance by the GI Bill and then, later, by the arrival on campuses of the "baby boomers." These prolonged increases in the demand for higher education, along with the continuing growth of sponsored research, led to an unprecedented period of prosperity for institutions of higher education, as well as pressures of all kinds on colleges and universities to meet emerging societal needs.

According to William Zumeta et al., "By 1949–1950, 2.66 million students were enrolled, out of a population of 16.12 million 18- to 24-year-olds, an enrollment rate of 16.5 percent, and more than double the rate of 1929–1930. The success of the GI Bill launched the United States toward unprecedented rates of college enrollment and attainment." There was, however, a hiatus, and between 1950 and 1955 enrollment actually declined slightly. This pause in enrollment growth was not really consequential, however. "By the end of the 1950s, higher education leaders, having lived through the doldrums of smaller enrollments mid-decade, were well aware that a tidal wave was approaching, as the so-called baby-boom generation was nearing college age."[23]

---

co-authors of the leading book on academic freedom that we have cited repeatedly, Matthew Finkin, has been involved in this dispute and in fact resigned from the board of the AAUP's *Journal of Academic Freedom*. See Peter Schmidt, "AAUP Journal Is under Fire for Issue with 6 Essays Calling for Boycott of Israel," *Chronicle of Higher Education,* October 22, 2013, available at http://chronicle.com/article/AAUP-Journal-Is-Under-Fire-for/142525/.

23. William Zumeta, David W. Breneman, Patrick M. Callan, and Joni E. Finney, *Financing American Higher Education in the Era of Globalization* (Cambridge, MA: Harvard Education Press, 2012), pp. 61–63. This book is a useful summary of data for almost all of the postwar years.

Because the impending "tidal wave" (as it always seems to be called) of enrollments was rooted in well-known demographic data, it was hardly unanticipated; after all, the students who would descend on higher education in record numbers were already born. In this key respect, the impact of the tidal wave was in no sense a surprising external shock to the system, as Sputnik was. Even so, few people recognized, ahead of the fact, that enrollment growth would be as dramatic as it was, and that it would be driven by increases in participation rates as well as by the highly predictable increases in the sizes of the most relevant age cohorts. There were dramatic effects on the structure of the entire system of higher education: the number of community colleges nearly doubled over the decade of the 1960s. There was also staggering growth in graduate education as well as in government-sponsored research.[24]

California is once again the poster child. Clark Kerr introduced part 3 of the first volume of his memoirs, titled *Overarching Issues,* with this succinct account:

> Enormous as was the transformation for higher education in the United States at large, it was even greater for California. The impact on the state from the defense industry and defense-related university research was huge—twice the national average. In-migration to the state doubled the flow of students above the nationwide demographic tidal wave.[25]

Following an elaborate planning process, Kerr orchestrated not only the creation of new campuses at the University of California and an enrollment cap at campuses such as Berkeley and UCLA, but also the adoption of the famous *Master Plan for Higher Education in California* (1960). In essence, the Master Plan created a three-tiered system (the University of California,

24. Zumeta et al., pp. 63–67.
25. Kerr, vol. 1, p. 153.

the state colleges, and the community colleges), with specified admissions criteria for each, guaranteed transfer opportunities, and differentiated functions. The Master Plan is best understood as a pragmatically driven treaty that reduced the likelihood of warfare between the University of California and the state teachers colleges that would soon become the California State University system; it increased opportunity for students; and it saved taxpayer money by placing more of the educational burden on the less expensive (per capita) community colleges, and avoiding the creation of twenty or more additional research universities at high cost. It should be seen as an ambitious attempt to control costs—and, simultaneously, to enable the University of California to compete with the nation's most distinguished private as well as public universities.[26]

Through the Master Plan, Kerr sought to protect both the quality and the character of Berkeley especially (though of course he also cared about the University of California overall). He succeeded brilliantly in protecting, indeed enhancing, the quality of the faculty as measured, for instance, by institutional rankings.[27] But not even Kerr could protect the "character" of Berkeley, which was altered fundamentally by powerful external forces that drove the strengthening of graduate programs as well as research, diminished the appeal of undergraduate teaching, and altered fundamentally the roles played by senior faculty. Kerr's evocative discussion of the emergence of "two Berkeleys"

26. See the University of California case study and the references cited therein for a much more detailed explanation of the features of the Master Plan than we have space to provide here. There is today active debate over whether the Master Plan should be set aside altogether, as no longer serving the needs of the state, or modified in significant ways. See Saul Geiser with Richard C. Atkinson, "Beyond the Master Plan: The Case for Restructuring Baccalaureate Education in California," *California Journal of Politics and Policy* 4, no. 1 (January 2013): 67–123.

27. See Kerr, vol. 1, pp. 405–6. See also Roger Geiger, *Research and Relevant Knowledge: American Research Universities since World War II* (New York: Oxford University Press, 1993), pp. 79–80.

is emblematic of developments whose implications he understood much earlier, and much better, than almost anyone else.[28]

In commenting on his favorite campus in the context of the early 1960s, Kerr wrote: "Berkeley One was . . . a very attractive place for the best young faculty . . . in the nation, the ablest graduate students, the most talented undergraduates."[29] "Berkeley One" emerged from World War II as one of the University of California's two great research campuses—along with UCLA—but there were huge costs that accompanied the benefits of academic excellence. Pre-war Berkeley celebrated faculty who made their reputations in the classroom, pursued their research on weekends and during vacations, and devoted their careers to their students. After the war, attention shifted from legendary teachers to Nobel Prize winners and scholars with distinguished scholarly reputations, and Kerr observed poignantly that "a teaching university tends to unite teachers and undergraduate students, a research university to disunite them."[30] "Berkeley Two" had developed a different national reputation as "a fabled point of emanation for the counter culture and for radical political activities."[31] In general, and quite apart from the advent of the counter culture, Kerr observed, "Research replaced teaching; new and junior faculty and teaching assistants replaced senior faculty as student advisors. Celebration was in order but also consternation."[32]

28. See the University of California case study. Sheldon Rothblatt had the same sense we have of the importance of these developments. He titled his comprehensive review of the Kerr Memoirs "A Tale of Two Berkeleys" (*Minerva* 42 [2004]: 173–89). Key parts of the Kerr Memoirs are a reprise of Kerr's famous Godkin Lectures, given at Harvard in 1963. These lectures have been reprinted many times, with later commentaries by Kerr. The fifth edition is the most recent publication. See Kerr, *The Uses of the University*, 5th ed. (the Godkin Lectures on the Essentials of Free Government and the Duties of the Citizen) (Cambridge, MA: Harvard University Press, 2001).

29. Kerr (2003), vol. 2, p. 118.
30. Ibid., p. 14.
31. Ibid., p. 118.
32. Kerr (2001), vol. 1, p. 404.

80   Chapter 3

Operating at a radically different scale, the smallest of our case-study institutions, Macalester College, engaged in a major planning exercise of its own at the start of the 1960s that reflected both the exuberance of the times—evident in Minnesota as well as in California, albeit in less dramatic forms—and the generosity of DeWitt Wallace of *Reader's Digest* fame. In January 1961, the trustees created a Long-Range Planning Commission to study and make recommendations regarding the college's future purposes and goals, curriculum and instruction, faculty, student body, facilities, and administrative organization. The thirty-one-member commission, which was composed of fourteen trustees, six administrators, nine faculty members, and two "friends of the college," presented its report to the board in September 1961 at "the Stillwater Conference." Working through a series of committees, this "mixed" trustee–administrator–faculty group made sweeping recommendations for enrollment growth, changes in the curriculum, new facilities, and a major upgrading of the faculty that were approved by the trustees in just a year after the creation of the commission, in September 1961. Implementation followed quickly. Enrollment increased, a vigorous effort to recruit senior faculty succeeded, and the curriculum was modified. Macalester was transformed.[33]

Events during these years at our third case-study institution, the City University of New York (CUNY), were also emblematic of both the times and the impact of institution-specific factors—but the outcome was notably different. Many of the same reasons underlying the reorganization of the California system—including the evident need for more student places and the Cold War demand for research—led New York State to create CUNY as a PhD-granting umbrella for pre-existing city colleges in 1961. By 1970, CUNY had expanded to more

33. See the Macalester case study.

than double the original number of campuses, from seven to eighteen.[34] Unlike under California's Master Plan, however, the relationship among campuses and CUNY's expansion were heavily influenced by local pressures and did not feature strong central control or a clearly articulated overall plan. Near the end of the 1960s, there was a spirited debate over admissions standards, related to the perceived need (felt keenly in New York) to educate more students from under-represented minority groups at CUNY.[35] But that part of the CUNY story comes later, when we discuss more generally the effects of the Vietnam War, the Civil Rights Movement, and the widespread "student rebellions" that occurred in those years.

Overall, the most lasting effects of the 1960s "Golden Age" were both indirect and highly consequential for faculty roles in governance, though that was not so obvious at the time. The synergistic combination of continuing growth in sponsored research cum graduate education and rapidly increasing undergraduate enrollments meant that faculty bargaining power was very strong, especially in the sciences. Faculty hiring was highly competitive, with predictable results. Salaries increased; teaching loads were reduced sharply, especially at research universities; and administrators took pains to accommodate the interests of the most highly sought-after faculty members. At major research universities such as those within the University of California, departments grew markedly in size, and there was a pronounced increase in the use of teaching assistants.[36]

34. Sally Renfro and Allison Armour-Garb, "Open Admissions and Remedial Education at the City University of New York," a report prepared for the Mayor's Advisory Task Force on CUNY, 1999, pp. 14–15, table 2, www.nyc.gov/html/records/rwg/cuny/pdf/history.pdf, accessed December 20, 2013.

35. See the CUNY case study.

36. At Berkeley, Kerr tells us, "over half (61 percent) of the total teaching personnel in fall 1964 was teaching assistants and nontenured faculty . . . [and] one-fourth of the tenured faculty members were absent from their teaching duties on campus for at least half of the year from 1954 to 1964. The number of teaching assistants increased from about 500 to about 1,500 from 1953 to 1964"

Another significant development was the creation of "a new dimension to the eternal class struggles within a university . . . that between humanists and scientists," the academy's intramural version of C. P. Snow's celebrated *Two Cultures*. In his famous Godkin Lectures at Harvard in 1963, Kerr was both brave enough to call attention to this "divide" and clear in explaining its causes:

> The scientists, by and large, in the federal grant universities, get promoted faster, get more space, get more income through summer employment and consulting, have more secretaries and assistants, have greater access to travel funds and expense accounts, and accumulate a greater sense of status within and outside the academic community. Some humanists obviously resent all of this and consider it quite unfair, even though their own situation has improved, relative to what it used to be.[37]

These developments led to an increasing split of many major universities into semi-separate fiefdoms. The comparative neglect that humanists and social scientists felt with

---

(Kerr [2003], vol. 2, p. 113). As Jencks and Riesman reported earlier, "Today (1968), however, few well-known scholars teach more than six hours a week and in leading universities many bargain for less. Even fewer read undergraduate papers and examinations. At the same time, the American Association of University Professors and other faculty groups pushed through the 'up or out' rules on faculty promotion, so that the permanent assistant professor is now practically unknown at leading universities. The routine problems of mass higher education have therefore fallen by default to graduate students who assumed the role of shop stewards, mediating between the highly professionalized faculty who run the curriculum and the still amateur undergraduates who pursue it. Graduate teaching assistants handle quiz sections, read examinations, listen to complaints, and generally protect the faculty from overexposure to the ignorant" (Jencks and Riesman, p. 40). At that time (1968), Jencks and Riesman noted, most administrators were more concerned with keeping the faculty happy than with placating any other single group. This was probably especially true because of the shortage of good faculty that persisted at that time (Jencks and Riesman, p. 18).

37. Kerr (2001), pp. 45–46.

respect to their more generously funded colleagues in the sciences accentuated the growing sense of fragmentation. At work was not only the rise of the physical sciences to academic supremacy, but also the separation of advanced research from undergraduate teaching. Another factor leading to fragmentation then and now is the ever-growing specialization in essentially all fields of knowledge as disciplines continue to evolve and to proliferate. These powerful forces were felt first in the leading private and public research universities but then spread, as if by contagion, to mid-level universities and to liberal arts colleges. This "contagious spread" was a direct result of the strong market power of faculty in these years, and the inescapable tendency, in recruiting wars, for institutions at all levels of the academic pecking order to emulate practices at what were regarded as the most prestigious places. More generally, the euphoria of the Golden Age precipitated expectations that have proved to be long-lasting—and damaging in key respects.[38]

In his broad survey of the effects of the Golden Age, Thelin concludes:

At most colleges and universities, the biggest gains in income, power, prestige, and protections between 1945 and 1970 were those accumulated by the faculty. The prospect of a shortage of qualified college teachers, combined with the deference to expertise in some fields, gave a generation of professors unprecedented opportunities. The robust academic marketplace also had some spin-off in that faculty were sometimes able

[38] Hanna Holborn Gray, who served with distinction as acting president of Yale and then as president of the University of Chicago, in her Clark Kerr Lecture of 2009, noted that the decade of the 1960s set expectations that continue. In her words: "Decline in federal support and public favor is seen as a precipitous falling away from what once was and still ought to be the rightful norm in the world of higher education." Gray, *In Search of Utopia* (Berkeley: University of California Press, 2011), p. 65.

to negotiate gains in shared governance with presidents and boards, although this development remained highly uneven across the institutional landscape.[39]

As Thelin implies, the effects on faculty roles in governance exhibited divergent patterns. By no means did all faculty want to translate their increased market power into heavier involvement in decision-making (or into any involvement at all!), especially outside their own departments, and the status of key faculty allowed them simply to stand apart from all general manifestations of governance, if that is what they chose to do. But some faculty did want to be much more involved, and one result was far more extensive participation in decision-making of all kinds than had been the norm in earlier years. The Macalester case study illustrates how these "participatory" forces worked out at a good liberal arts college—and how faculty who wanted to be involved could become highly effective in contributing to responsible decision-making.

Desires for greater participation were not limited to faculty at "intimate" colleges such as Macalester. By the mid-1960s, having recovered from the nadir of the McCarthy years, many faculty members began to reassert their bargaining power with demands for greater involvement in college and university decision-making. In 1966 the AAUP issued the *Statement on Government in Colleges and Universities*, which it jointly published with the American Council of Education and the Association of Governing Boards. Although the statement reaffirmed

39. Thelin, p. 310. For evidence concerning changes in the "market power" of faculty, see the findings of Roy Radner and Charlotte V. Kuh that time-to-tenure dropped substantially in those years. They regard this as an instance of their general thesis that time-to-tenure (and, we presume, the probability of getting tenure) were responsive to the market. See Radner and Kuh, "Preserving a Lost Generation: Policies to Assure a Steady Flow of Young Scholars," *Carnegie Council on Policy Studies in Higher Education*, October 1978.

traditional faculty rights and responsibilities in the familiar areas of composition of the faculty, curriculum, admissions, student life, and academic freedom, it also emphasized "that all operations of the university bear upon one another."[40]

Throughout its hundred-year history, the AAUP has consistently acknowledged that governing boards and administrations have primary authority over matters affecting institutions' mission, planning, financial resources, and budgeting. By the late 1960s, however, the AAUP had begun to assert the faculty's consultative rights in all matters affecting college and university decision-making.[41] By expanding the definition of "educational policies," the AAUP adopted a "joint effort" model in which faculty would serve as co-managers, framing and implementing education policies and long-range plans affecting their institution's physical plant, budgeting, procedures affecting salary increases, and the appointment of the president and senior academic leaders.[42]

Reactions (and accommodations) to such arguments took many forms at different institutions. For present purposes, it is sufficient to note the clear evidence of the effects on governance of seismic shifts in the ebb and flow of faculty bargaining power (a recurring theme of this study). Faculty bargaining power declined sharply in the early 1970s, after its dramatic surge in the postwar years and the Golden Age of the 1960s, and an interesting question is whether its effects on faculty roles in governance were asymmetrical. Another key question is whether it is possible to identify pros and cons of highly participatory modes of faculty involvement in different settings.

40. Mary Burgan, "Why Governance? Why Now?" in William G. Tierney, ed., *Competing Conceptions of Academic Governance: Negotiating the Perfect Storm* (Baltimore: Johns Hopkins University Press, 2004), xii.

41. Neil W. Hamilton, "Faculty Involvement in System-wide Governance," in Tierney, p. 97.

42. George Keller, "A Growing Quaintness: Traditional Governance in the Markedly New Realm of U.S. Higher Education," in Tierney, p. 159.

However, before taking on either of these questions, we need to consider the intervening events of the late 1960s.[43]

Protests and Rebellions

In his introduction to Clark Kerr's memoirs, sociologist Neil J. Smelser, an astute observer of events at Berkeley and one of "Clark's boys," posed a question of great interest to contemporaries and historians: "Why was the university, born free as it were, destined to be the arena of so much political controversy?" The answer, Smelser suggested, has much to do with the university's special economic and cultural role in society and its susceptibility to internal and external forces that make it an object of periodic politicization and a symbol for rising expectations and dissatisfaction.[44]

43. The dramatic increases in the scale and complexity of university life that took place in the 1950s and 1960s also affected the distribution of authority within strictly administrative structures—and such re-distributions had their own effects on faculty roles. Again, the University of California experience is instructive (see the case study). Shortly after taking office in 1958, Kerr initiated steps to give more direct authority to the individual campuses. His experience as chancellor of Berkeley under Sproul had convinced him that the campuses needed greater control over their operations. He understood that a multi-campus, as distinguished from a flagship-based, system could not be tightly administered from a single, central presidential office (Kerr [2001], vol. 1, pp. 191–93 and 197–201). The number of presidential staff was reduced by 26 percent; chancellorships were established across the University of California system (with some budgetary authority); and the position of vice president–academic affairs, vacant since 1948, was filled to develop collaborative working relationships with campus administrators and the Academic Senate. These steps led to a much-needed reorganization of the senate. By 1963 the Northern and Southern sectional divisions, in which Berkeley and UCLA faculty exercised disproportionate influence, had become anachronisms. Kerr recommended a new federal system of nine Academic Senate divisions that redistributed authority across all campuses. Decentralization gave university faculty a more effective voice. See Douglass (1998), pp. 7–10.

44. Smelser, introduction to Kerr (2003), vol. 2, p. xvi. Smelser, along with colleagues at the University of California, Berkeley, Martin Trow, Sheldon Rothblatt, Earl "Bud" Cheit, and Fred Balderston, worked closely with Kerr throughout his presidency. See Smelser, *Dynamics of the Contemporary University: Growth, Accretion, and Conflict* (Berkeley: University of California Press, 2013), p. 2.

The protests and rebellions of the 1960s centered mainly on the war in Vietnam and the need to deal directly with the issues of race and poverty in America. In a memorable 1968 commencement speech, which he delivered during a particularly unsettling time at Columbia, Richard Hofstadter reminded his audience that student activism was an international phenomenon: "Not only in New York and Berkeley, but in Madrid and Paris, in Belgrade and Oxford, in Rome, Berlin, and London . . . students are disaffected, restive and rebellious."[45]

By far the best-known of the protests within the United States, prior to the tragic massacre at Kent State University (May 1970), was that of the Free Speech Movement led by Mario Savio at Berkeley (1964–65). In his Godkin Lectures in 1963, Kerr anticipated the student anger that was to erupt (though he surely underestimated its power, as anyone would have), and for the rest of his life he believed that the student unrest of the 1960s at Berkeley was a consequence of undergraduate neglect.[46] In any case, the history of this traumatic set of events is so well known, and has been described so often, including in our case study, that we need to spend no time recounting yet again what happened.[47] From the standpoint of our interest in faculty roles in governance, it suffices to note two points:

45. Hofstadter, "214th Commencement Address, Columbia University," *American Scholar* 37 (Autumn 1968): 583.

46. Kerr (2001), p. 49, and "The Frantic Race to Remain Contemporary," *Daedalus* 93, no. 3 (Fall 1964): 1051–70.

47. Kerr devotes the entirety of volume 2 of his memoirs to a detailed account of this period of "political turmoil." See Kerr (2003), vol. 2. Readers will also wish to consult Neil J. Smelser, "Berkeley in Crisis and Change," in David Riesman and Verne A. Stadtman, eds., *Academic Transformation: Seventeen Institutions under Pressure* (New York: McGraw-Hill and Carnegie Commission on Higher Education, 1973), pp. 51–69; Walter P. Metzger, "The Crisis of Academic Authority," *Daedalus* 99 (Summer 1970): 568–608; Todd Gitlin, *The Sixties: Years of Hope, Days of Rage* (New York: Bantam, 1987); David Burner, *Making Peace with the 60s* (Princeton, NJ: Princeton University Press, 1997); and Maurice Isserman and Michael Kazin, *America Divided: The Civil War of the 1960s* (New York: Oxford University Press, 2000).

- First, the "center" of the Berkeley faculty stayed on the sidelines for a long period of time; it was only with the election, by paper ballot, of an emergency executive committee on December 14, 1964, that the center of the faculty took hold. (This is, incidentally, a vivid example of the importance of something that may seem as trivial as an election procedure—if faculty members of the emergency committee had been chosen by voice vote or by a method that relied on plurality voting—rather than being required, through an iterative process, to receive a majority of votes for election—the outcome at Berkeley could well have been very different.) When it really counted, the center of the faculty coalesced as a responsible body. But it took a genuine crisis to energize as large and as diffuse a group as this one.

- Second, in a candid comment in his memoirs, Kerr acknowledged that he was slow in removing the overly rigid chancellor of the Berkeley campus, Edward Strong, because he was "fearful of faculty reaction."[48] Kerr had, after all, led the process of delegating authority to campus chancellors. This is an excellent illustration of the latent power of faculty over even presidents as well established as Kerr.

At CUNY, the last part of the decade of the 1960s was also a time of turbulence (see the case study). From 1965 to 1967, debates over admissions—and the related policies for tuition (which was still free at senior colleges) and state funding—divided the board and pitted the board chair against the university chancellor, Albert Bowker, whose roots were in California. In 1968, a Master Plan was adopted that included a proposal to transition by 1975 to a multi-tiered system of admissions similar to that employed in

48. Kerr (2003), vol. 2, p. 180.

California.[49] However, budget cuts were in the offing, and incremental plans were derailed by both financial uncertainties and increasing tensions on the campuses. A group of African American and Puerto Rican student activists took over part of the City College campus. The president of City College closed the campus for more than a month, refusing to negotiate with the students. When the college was reopened by court order, the students resisted and the police were called in. Protests spread to other campuses, and City College's president resigned.[50] Support for fully open admissions began to build. In July 1969, the Board of Higher Education voted to admit any New York City high school graduate who applied, beginning in 1970.[51] Less than a decade after its founding, CUNY had become a free and virtually open-access university.

Although it took more than a decade to play out, the experience of CUNY with open admissions could not be judged a success, certainly in hindsight. The perception of an educational system that was either "adrift" (the word used in the title of a 1999 report—CUNY: *An Institution Adrift*—of the Mayor's Advisory Task Force, which was chaired by Benno C. Schmidt, Jr.) or in decline, having lost much of its earlier reputation for excellence, led to major shifts in leadership, organization, and programmatic priorities that, in time, pitted the new chancellor of CUNY, Matthew Goldstein, against many of the faculty based on these campuses. From the standpoint of governance, this is the important part of the CUNY story, which we return to later in this narrative. The "turbulent sixties" served mainly to encourage faculty unionization and

49. Sheila C. Gordon, "The Transformation of the City University of New York, 1945–1970" (doctoral dissertation, Columbia University, New York, 1975), p. 223.
50. Gordon, pp. 215–17.
51. Ibid., p. 222.

to make clear to at least some observers that the highly decentralized structure of CUNY needed to be overhauled—as it was eventually, at the end of the 1970s.

Another important change that occurred in the 1960s at CUNY was the advent of collective bargaining over the terms and conditions of faculty employment. In the early 1960s, the Legislative Conference (LC) began to demand recognition as the collective bargaining agent for CUNY. In 1963, the United Federation of College Teachers (UFCT), a local of the American Federation of Teachers, also began to recruit within CUNY and challenged the LC's dominance. After 1967, when New York State passed the Taylor Law authorizing collective bargaining at public colleges, tenured faculty selected the LC as their bargaining agent, while non-tenured faculty selected the UFCT. Despite their rivalry, the two unions merged in 1972 to form the Professional Staff Congress.[52] We interpret this advent of collective bargaining as yet another reflection of the increased bargaining power of faculty members in the 1960s. It was, however, the political stresses and strains of the 1960s, not such seemingly mundane matters as struggles for power over terms of employment, that were all-consuming in these years. The impact of the era's incivility and disruption on faculty roles is difficult to calculate. Although many, if not all, faculty would have agreed "that in ultimate reality . . . they *are* the university," their collective involvement in students' moral and spiritual development had long since passed.[53] Protests directed against the Reserve Officers' Training Corps (ROTC), the Central Intelligence Agency, and

52. Irwin Yellowitz, "Academic Governance and Collective Bargaining in the City University of New York," *Academe* 73, no. 6 (1987): 8.

53. The quotation is from Richard Hofstadter's 1968 commencement speech at Columbia; see Wilson Smith and Thomas Bender, eds., *American Higher Education Transformed, 1940–2005* (Baltimore: Johns Hopkins University Press, 2008), p. 384. See also Jencks and Riesman's discussion of faculties' changing character, pp. 38–40.

military contractors like Dow Chemical, as well as activism aimed at creating a more multicultural curriculum and the hiring of more faculty of color, reflected the degree to which student activists held the university responsible for society's faults and expected immediate remedies.[54] As Richard Hofstadter advised the Columbia University class of 1968, the university serves society's interests best as "an intellectual and spiritual balance wheel," but "it is hardly surprising that we have some trouble in getting it fully accepted by society or in living up to it ourselves."[55]

Princeton, privileged institution that it was, showed that no college or university that enrolled students concerned about events in the world could be immune to the tensions of the Vietnam era (see the Princeton case study and the references therein). In May of 1968 there was a demonstration unprecedented in its size in which protestors criticized government policies related to Vietnam and, at the other end of some spectrum, campus issues such as parietal rules. The demonstrators also challenged Princeton's decision-making procedures in general, and President Robert Goheen responded immediately by constituting the Special Committee on the Structure of the University, chaired by Professor Stanley Kelley (known always as the Kelley Committee), which included a carefully chosen mix of faculty members, students, and administrators.

An Interim Report submitted in November 1968 addressed eight controversial issues, including "rights and rules" of conduct, research contracts, relations with outside organizations (the Institute for Defense Analysis), and conflicts of interest. None of these issues had a direct bearing on faculty roles. The campus community, and especially the students, were much

54. Smith and Bender, p. 345.
55. Ibid., p. 384.

more interested in challenging trustee oversight of university affairs; "Power to the People" was one slogan.[56] (The ensuing account tracks Princeton's experience in crafting governance responses to these events in considerable detail—in part because we know it so well. However, a far more important reason is that this history contains wide-ranging lessons of continuing import.)

As is so often the case, there were major failures in communication and a general lack of understanding of key distinctions, such as the one between de jure and de facto authority. Working closely together, the Kelley Committee, other administrators, and trustees crafted a *Statement of Policy on Delegation of Authority* that was adopted by the trustees in October 1969. It has remained, to this day, both a centerpiece of Princeton's system of governance (it is required reading for all new trustees) and a prototype for similar statements and policies adopted by other colleges and universities.[57] It "has passed the test of time." The *Statement on Delegation* distinguishes among matters where the trustees exercise only "general review" (e.g., faculty appointment processes, curricular decisions, and other academic matters), matters where trustees exercise "prior review" (when there is a claim on funds, including the setting of budgets), and matters where there is "authority directly

---

56. See James Axtell, *The Making of Princeton University: From Woodrow Wilson to the Present* (Princeton, NJ: Princeton University Press, 2006), pp. 348–58, for a description of the events at Princeton in the 1960s, the setting in which the Kelley Report was prepared, and its major conclusions. An even more authoritative account of all aspects of the work of the Kelley Committee is to be found in "The Governing of Princeton University: Final Report of the Special Committee on the Structure of the University," April 1970, including the appendix materials. This report, drafted by a distinguished political scientist, contains perhaps the best analytical discussion extant of the governance of institutions of higher education in all of its dimensions (at, to be sure, a private research university with the special characteristics of Princeton).

57. The *Statement on Delegation* is discussed in Bowen, pp. 9–10. Because of its importance, it is reprinted in full as an appendix to the Princeton case study and as an appendix to the Kelley Report.

exercised" by the trustees (investments, real estate transactions, and so on). When authority is delegated by the trustees to the faculty, it is always delegated through the president. This document proved highly reassuring to all parties except the most radical students.[58]

Another major accomplishment of the Kelley Committee was the formulation of a series of recommendations that led to the creation of a university-wide deliberative body, the Council of the Princeton University Community, or CPUC, which is charged with considering all kinds of questions of policy and with making recommendations to other entities with decision-making authority. The president chairs the CPUC, which continues to serve as a "place to go" when there is controversy or debate of almost any kind. The CPUC also spawned the creation of a series of important campus-wide committees that have served to organize consideration of matters as varied as "rights and rules" and, perhaps most important, a "Priorities Committee," chaired by the provost, that plays the critical role in formulating budgets, which are reviewed by the president and then presented to the trustees for action.[59] This rather elaborate committee structure has been found, not surprisingly, to have its pros and cons, which we will discuss in the next chapter, when we focus on mechanisms for channeling faculty viewpoints of various kinds.

There were, of course, moments of stress and strain in crafting the *Statement on Delegation*, in establishing the CPUC machinery, and in responding to later protests related to the US

58. To our knowledge, few other universities have adopted as explicit a statement of delegation as this one. It would be nice to know why this is so. Part of the answer, we suspect, is that achieving agreement on such principles on anything like an "across-the-board" basis is difficult and very time-consuming. Princeton's relatively simple structure, with no professional schools and a single faculty, certainly made it easier than in other university settings to craft an explicit statement of delegation.

59. See the Kelley Report for a detailed explanation of all of these committees.

incursion into Cambodia and other war-related events. Still, overall (and certainly by the standards of the time), the process was remarkably civilized and free of rancor.[60] This achievement, which is what it was, can be attributed in large part to the close working relationships and multiple friendships developed over the years between the faculty and the leaders of the administration, almost all of whom had come directly from the faculty. It is hard to exaggerate the importance of this subtle, obviously informal, "cultural" determinant of faculty influence in governance.[61]

From the standpoint of our focus on the evolution of faculty roles, this is the first of several important takeaways from Princeton's response to the turmoil of the late 1960s and early 1970s. But we should not overgeneralize. It is possible in a university as relatively small and cohesive as Princeton to develop a web of inter-connected loyalties, and thus to inculcate an attitude toward "academic community" that discourages skepticism if not downright hostility between faculty and administration; larger, more complicated, institutions lack this formidable luxury. And even in the Princeton case,

[60] Bowen remembers one vivid exception to this generalization. In the absence of President Goheen, Bowen (then the provost) was chairing a large and rather contentious faculty meeting in the 1970s. A faculty member known for his liberal sympathies expressed the view that the faculty at large should "follow the lead of the students," who were demonstrating loudly outside the meeting room. Another faculty member, the redoubtable Marion J. Levy Jr. (author of *Levy's Laws of the Disillusionment of the True Liberal*) responded in words to this effect: "*Sir* [his emphasis], you are seeking to lick a boot that has yet to be raised in your direction." That comment ended the discussion.

[61] David Dobkin, retiring dean of the faculty at Princeton, said in an interview (reported in the Princeton case study): "In general, there is and has been for many years, an exceptionally good working relationship between the administration and the faculty—with most academic administrators coming directly from the faculty ranks. There is very little 'we–they' thinking. This excellent relationship is built on trust, which has been developed over many years." Dobkin went on to refer to his lasting impression of a dinner he attended at the president's house for new members of the faculty. "There is a tone to this place that I learned at that dinner that has served me well ever since."

one has to wonder if it would have been possible to develop this comprehensive governance structure in the absence of a crisis environment such as existed in the late 1960s. It is far from obvious that, starting from scratch, it would be possible today to mobilize the energy and broad sense of institutional commitment needed to create this kind of governance machinery.

A second takeaway from this entire set of experiences is that personalities, and particularly the personality and leadership style of the president, make an enormous difference. At Princeton, President Robert Goheen's ability to walk forthrightly, and with no evident fear, into a potentially lethal stew of angry voices outside Nassau Hall in 1968 was due in no small measure to his character and background as an assistant professor of classics when he was elected president and, before that, as a World War II hero. Goheen demonstrated over and over again, in every phase of his life, impeccable integrity, a Calvinist-like set of values, and an abundance of common sense. His understated manner was perfect for communicating that the debate at Princeton was not at all about him; rather, it was about the very purposes of a great university that he felt privileged to serve. One thinks immediately of other examples of leaders ideally suited to their circumstances: for instance, Clark Kerr, the Quaker-inspired visionary and leader of an incredibly complicated set of individuals at Berkeley and the University of California; Matthew Goldstein, whose strength of personality and outgoing manner were just what CUNY needed at a decisive time in its history (see below); and Robert Gavin, the determined president of Macalester, who changed the character of that college through aggressive recruitment of faculty. Readers will think of other examples, and of course the contrast with the autocratic and "distant" style of Nicholas Murray Butler at Columbia (and the near-term consequences for Butler's university) is not to be missed.[62]

(3) The third and last major takeaway is the value of having strong, legitimized processes in place ahead of crises. This was not the case at Princeton in 1968—hence the need for the Kelley Committee—but it was true after the development by the committee of the *Statement on Delegation* and the creation of the CPUC, both of which antedated, fortunately, later disputes over how to respond to the Cambodia incursion and what to do about ROTC. There is no need to recount how the CPUC channeled angry debate over the later stages of the Vietnam War into generally constructive channels, but it is worth pausing for a moment to look at the handling of the highly contentious ROTC issues. Fundamental faculty prerogatives were respected, especially the right to decide what curricular offerings qualified for credit toward graduation and the right to decide which teachers should enjoy faculty status—both direct reflections of the *Statement on Delegation*. At the same time, even staunch anti-war activists had to accept, like it or not, the authority of the trustees over the "corporate" relationship between the university and the government's Department

---

62. The personalities and histories of key trustees are also obviously very important. At Princeton in the raucous 1960s and 1970s, the active involvement of both Nicholas deB. Katzenbach, former attorney general, and John Doar, former assistant attorney general (1960–67) and former chief counsel for the US House Committee on the Judiciary (1974), on the board of trustees was pivotal. It was hard for even the most strong-willed protestor not to be impressed by these two individuals, who, at great personal risk, had, as it were, "stood in the schoolhouse doors" at the Universities of Alabama and Mississippi when it was necessary to confront Governors George Wallace and Ross Barnett. Mention should also be made of at least one key administrator other than the president. At Princeton, the hero of the protest era was Neil Rudenstine, then dean of students, later provost at Princeton and then president of Harvard University. Dean Rudenstine had many of President Goheen's characteristics: he was incredibly smart, courageous, and unflappable, and was a highly effective, always restrained, defender of core values.

of Defense. As a result, the Army ROTC program remained at Princeton through this troubled time (though it did not at many other places), but under faculty-controlled rules governing course credit and faculty status. Being clear about where de facto authority rested for different aspects of the ROTC role at Princeton was critical in bringing about a resolution that was widely, if not universally, accepted. Ambiguity has its advantages, but also serious limitations.[63]

Retrenchment in the 1970s—and Subsequent Ups and Downs

Before considering the impact on higher education of rising fuel costs, slower economic growth, double-digit inflation, and unsteady student enrollments, we pause to acknowledge the experience of women faculty in the academy and their postwar pursuit of equity—which proved to be an excruciatingly slow process. Although the nation's women's colleges had employed women faculty from their earliest days and helped develop outstanding future scientists and academic leaders, broader educational opportunities for women scholars, especially at the nation's most prestigious research universities, awaited larger social, political, and cultural changes. During the long interim period, which began in the middle of the past century, women academics found a home in higher education's less prestigious sectors—in two-year colleges, normal schools, teachers col-

---

63. For a full discussion of the application of governance principles in the ROTC case, see Bowen, *Lessons Learned: Reflections of a University President* (Princeton, NJ: Princeton University Press, 2011), pp. 21–23. The same book also contains discussions of other war-related issues, including the (not very successful, at the time) handling of the disruption of a talk by Secretary of the Interior Walter Hickel (pp. 49–50). Hundreds of protests were directed at ROTC programs and buildings at colleges and universities across the United States. See Todd Gitlin, *Years of Hope, Days of Rage* (New York: Bantam Books, 1993 ed.), p. 409.

leges, small Catholic institutions, and, most notably, land-grant schools not yet transformed into major centers of research and scholarship. Just as the progress made by women scientists during World War II proved transitory, women faculty who had served as deans during the war years were moved in the postwar period to less prestigious positions. As historian Linda Eisenmann notes, "When faculty openings occurred [in the 1950s], few institutions hired the women who had gained considerable experience during the war years." Instead, as Margaret R. Rossiter observes, "a woman-dominated 'parafaculty' developed as 'faculty wives' seized long-term research associate and other non-tenure-track jobs—the only jobs open to them in a time when nepotism rules prohibited employment of both members of a married couple."[64]

During the expansion of higher education in the 1960s, a great many public colleges and universities tried to emulate the research-centric model. As Eisenmann and Rossiter note, once scholarly credentials supplanted good teaching and character building as preferred faculty traits, young men became more highly valued than experienced older women. Rossiter points to a survey conducted in the 1950s by the National Education Association, which demonstrated that the largest percentages of women faculty taught at teachers colleges (23.5 percent), while only 7.2 percent had positions at private research universities.[65]

In the 1960s and 1970s, the combined effects of Affirmative Action, Title IX, the coeducation of a number of previously

---

64. See Eisenmann, "Women, Higher Education, and Professionalization: Clarifying the View," *Harvard Educational Review* 66, no. 4 (Winter 1996): 858–73 (quotations on p. 868), available at http://hepg.org/her-home/issues/harvard-educational-review-volume-66-issue-4/herarticle/clarifying-the-view_252. See Rossiter, *Women Scientists in America: Before Affirmative Action, 1940–1972* (Baltimore: Johns Hopkins University Press, 1995), especially pp. 122–48.

65. Eisenmann, online version.

all-male institutions of prominence, and the feminist movement began to chip away at the deep-seated, pernicious ideology that had marginalized and undervalued women faculty members' teaching and scholarship as less serious and more transitional than those of men. Societal change and legislation enabled women to challenge discriminatory practices and to demand equal pay. By the 1970s, when women faculty in growing numbers entered public university systems, their presence disrupted the overwhelmingly white, male faculty world. Tensions rose, gender equity remained elusive, and women faculty encountered familiar problems of under-representation in prestigious disciplines and unequal pay in almost all disciplines—problems that were aggravated by a sluggish economy.[66]

The calming of the political waters as the war in Vietnam slowly came to an end was accompanied by serious financial pressures on all of higher education. The publication in 1971 of Earl Cheit's *The New Depression in Higher Education,* based on visits and interviews at forty-one colleges and universities, was a wake-up call for both the educational establishment and the country at large.[67] Sponsored research declined at the same time that educational costs rose rapidly. The oil shock of 1973 (the quadrupling of oil prices) helped to trigger a recession that occurred alongside steeply rising prices of goods and services of all kinds to produce a "stagflation" that lasted until Chairman of the Federal Reserve Paul Volcker tightened monetary policy in the early 1980s.

66. See Judith Glazer-Raymo, *Shattering the Myths: Women in Academe* (Baltimore: Johns Hopkins University Press, 1999); Linda Eisenmann, "A Time of Quiet Activism: Research, Practice, and Policy in American Women's Higher Education, 1945–1965," *History of Education Quarterly* 45, no. 1 (Spring 2005): 1–17; and Eisenmann, *Higher Education for Women in Postwar America, 1945–1965* (Baltimore: Johns Hopkins University Press, 2006).

67. See Zumeta et al., pp. 67 ff, for a lengthy discussion of the economics of higher education throughout the 1970s and beyond (including citations of Cheit's book and other studies).

In seeking to chart a reasonable path through truly troubled times, Princeton administrators consulted not only with faculty but also with students and staff (as a result of the establishment of the CPUC, described earlier). There were no overt changes in faculty roles, but the need to make hard choices, including the need to impose very large tuition increases, led to some fraying of nerves, especially on the part of elected student participants in the governing process.[68] Macalester College experienced far more serious financial challenges than Princeton during the first half of the 1970s. On top of the problems facing all of higher education at this time, Macalester was hard hit by the decision of DeWitt Wallace, the college's principal benefactor, to withdraw his financial support.[69] In April 1971, the faculty minutes recorded that "a special committee was created to deal with faculty reductions for 1972–73." This committee was composed of three faculty members and three administrators. Ultimately, twelve full-time (non-tenured) faculty

[68] Consulting with the faculty in such circumstances had long been the practice at many institutions. Recall the use of faculty advisors by President Robert Sproul at the University of California in addressing Depression-era problems in the 1930s. It was the broadening of consultative processes during the period of campus turmoil at Princeton that precipitated the inclusion of students and others in such processes at that school in the 1970s and thereafter. See Bowen's "The Economics of Princeton in the 1970s: Some Worrying Implications of Trying to Make Do with Less," *Report of the President* (February 1976), especially pp. 30–33, for a discussion of "the fraying of nerves" that occurred in the mid-1970s.

[69] The withdrawal of Wallace's support may have been connected to an unpleasant experience that Tricia Nixon, one of President Richard M. Nixon's daughters, had while visiting Macalester during the Vietnam era. According to the *Papers of the Nixon White House*, part 5, H. R. Haldeman, *Notes of White House Meetings, 1969–1973*, Nixon's chief of staff, Robert "Bob" Haldeman recorded this entry on the evening of October 15, 1970: "Called tonight all cranked up because Macalester College kids gave Tricia a bad time with obscene signs. Wants DeWitt Wallace, who funds the place, to put the screws on them." See H. R. Haldeman, *The Haldeman Diaries: Inside the Nixon White House* (New York: Berkley Books, 1995), p. 242. The telephone log entry can be found in Joan Hoff Wilson, ed., *Papers of the Nixon White House* (Bethesda, MD: University Publications of America, 1993), available at http://roosevelt.nl/topics/papers_nixon.pdf. (See the Macalester case study.)

members (approximately 10 percent of the full-time faculty) were "let go" and about the same number of administrative staff members left the college. As our case study attests, many at Macalester testified that the faculty helped develop important strategies to make it possible for the college to get through the "tough years" and emerge as a stronger institution.

Reflecting a broader perspective, Thelin emphasizes that in the post-Vietnam years, higher education faced circumstances that were quite different than they had been earlier:

> By 1972 the end of a fifteen-year hiring boom had left the academic profession with reduced mobility and little leverage in their power to influence institutional decisions. . . . At the same time that the national job market for academics was reaching saturation, the expanded number of Ph.D.-granting programs were tooled up to assure a constant flow of new Ph.D.'s into the academic market for years to come. . . . In the array of problems facing presidents and boards, faculty were not a primary object of concern. One reason was that presidents and provosts enjoyed a buyer's market. . . . And since few tenured professors had the option to consider good jobs elsewhere, the balance of governance power shifted away from the faculty back to the administration.[70]

70. Thelin, pp. 331–32. There were also important developments in the community college sector during these years. Due in no small part to the influence of the Carnegie Commission, the community colleges had been undergoing a transformation from an earlier emphasis on their serving as transfer-oriented pathways to four-year institutions to an emphasis on their serving as low-cost, vocationally oriented institutions. Compositional/demographic changes played an important role in the late 1970s and early 1980s in accelerating this transformation; there was a massive influx of non-traditional students to community colleges during the latter part of the 1970s. (See Steven Brint and Jerome Karabel's history of the community college movement, *The Diverted Dream: Community Colleges and the Promise of Educational Opportunity in America, 1900–1985* [New York: Oxford University Press, 1991], pp. 103–28.) The surge in community college enrollments has been accompanied by campaigns for faculty unionization, many of which have succeeded, but it has not produced important debates over traditional faculty governance issues.

Even so, and in spite of financial pressures and changes in the academic labor market, there was a continuing spread of the faculty staffing policies/practices now prevalent at leading research universities to other institutions. As Thelin puts it:

> The expectation that professors should publish and should obtain external research funding worked its way increasingly into both the customary and formal codes for tenure and promotion at the state regional comprehensive universities and at many liberal arts colleges—institutions that had little if any involvement in doctoral programs. This expectation had some plausibility because these institutions increasingly hired new professors who had studied for the Ph.D. at major research universities and understood what research was about.[71]

However, continuing financial pressures, combined with the spread of new teaching technologies such as online learning, raise real questions about the long-term viability of this model—a proposition that we will explore more fully in chapters 4 and 5.

Also relevant in this context is a national decision made in the 1960s: the decision, in 1967, to outlaw mandatory retirement as a result of the passage of the Age Discrimination in Employment Act; there was then a grace period that delayed the effects of the end of mandatory retirement until the end of 1993.[72] Colleges and universities to this day continue to seek

---

71. Thelin, p. 356.

72. See National Research Council, *Ending Mandatory Retirement for Tenured Faculty: The Consequences for Higher Education* (Washington, DC: National Academies Press, 1991). In 1986 the "House and Senate reached agreement on legislation amending the Age Discrimination in Employment Act (ADEA) of 1967 to prohibit mandatory retirement on the basis of age for all workers except for tenured faculty in higher education, police officers, fire fighters, and a few executives and high-level policy makers. The exemption for tenured faculty, which terminates at the end of 1993, permits mandatory retirement of any employee who is serving under a contract of unlimited tenure at an institution of higher education and who has attained 70 years of age" (ADEA, 1986, Section 12(d)).

ways to cope with the rising salary and benefits costs imposed by the presence of larger numbers of well-paid senior faculty, as well as with diminished opportunities to rejuvenate and redeploy faculty ranks by replacing older faculty with newly minted PhDs. The impact of demographic trends related to the spurt in hiring in the 1960s deserves more attention than we can give it here. One still developing mode of adaptation to staffing issues has been the "rise of the adjunct (non-tenure-track faculty member)" as colleges and universities have made changes in staffing policies intended both to curb increases in the costs of traditional tenure-track faculty and to gain more flexibility in allocating teaching slots.[73] The implications of this shift in the staffing mix for faculty roles in governance, as well as for doctoral education, are still being sorted out, and one intriguing approach to this complicated set of issues (the creation of a "professional teaching staff") is discussed in chapter 4.

Both the 1980s and the 1990s began with economic contractions, followed by the dot.com boom in the stock market in the late 1990s, and these economic ups and downs, which continued into the next century, made for hazardous planning and decision-making.[74] In addition, these overarching swings in economic activity were sometimes exacerbated by

73. See Thelin, p. 332. In 2002 David Kirp noted that in the California state university system half of all appointments in the 1990s were off the tenure track, and more than half of all courses were taught by "disposables" (Kirp, "Higher Ed Inc.: Avoiding the Perils of Outsourcing," *Chronicle of Higher Education*, March 15, 2002, pp. 13–14). See John G. Cross and Edie M. Goldenberg, *Off-Track Profs: Nontenured Teachers in Higher Education* (Cambridge, MA: MIT Press, 2009). See also Ben Cosman, "Universities Are Cutting Tenured Faculty While They Load Up on 'Non-Academic' Administrators," www.thewire.com, February 7, 2014, www.thewire.com/politics/2014/02/universities-are-cutting-tenured-faculty-while-they-load-non-academic-administrators/357858/, accessed February 10, 2014.

74. See Zumeta et al., especially chapter 4, for a detailed description of economic events in these decades.

institution-specific developments, as in the case of Macalester College. Idiosyncratic events related to this college's large holding of *Reader's Digest* stock had major reverberations. During Michael McPherson's term as president, 1996–2003, the college had to cope with a decline of about 25–30 percent in the value of its endowment because of a drastic decline in the value of the *Reader's Digest* stock. The value of this single holding, which constituted the majority of Macalester's endowment, fell by half over three years.[75]

As McPherson explained, "The challenge facing the College was to restrain spending in the near term to reflect the substantial decline in income from the (now reduced) endowment, while not cutting spending so severely as to undermine in a lasting way the investments in improving the College that were underway. To accomplish these twin goals, the Trustees needed to spend a larger annual percentage of the (now diminished) endowment than was the norm, and the faculty and staff needed to accept more restraint in salary gains and funds for innovation than was habitual." This strategy succeeded, a result that McPherson attributes to several factors: "First, the College's wealth was a recent phenomenon. Unlike institutions whose faculties had become accustomed to abundant resources, the Macalester faculty's 'sense of entitlement' was much more limited. Second, the administration created a Long-Range Planning and Budget Committee and its strong faculty and staff representatives, who were widely respected by the College's leadership, recognized that pressing for short-term spending might imply consuming the 'seed corn.' Third, the Board recognized that its responsibilities were broader than maximizing the value of the endowment and appreciated that one role of endowment is to provide a resource to be drawn

---

75. This lack of diversification was not Macalester's fault. Rather it was the result of unwise limitations imposed from outside (see the case study).

on when times demanded it."[76] At one point, McPherson notes, "the faculty were demanding more severe cuts in program and salaries while Trustees urged an increase in spending from the endowment"—a combination McPherson rightly regards as "remarkable."[77]

Looking back on those years and reflecting on our interest in faculty roles, McPherson made the important observation that it is easier to work with faculty to economize when they have not had time to become used to affluence:

> The lesson I want to draw . . . is this: it was so much easier to manage through this strenuous situation at Macalester than it . . . would have been at Williams [where McPherson had been dean of faculty] or a similarly long established place. At Mac, major wealth was quite a new experience, and there were still faculty around who had experienced the earlier rollercoaster years of the late 60s and early 70s. The faculty at Macalester . . . were far more willing to make sacrifices like pay freezes, postponement or cancellation of planned physical improvements, faculty expansion plans, etc. Indeed, I actually had to struggle with a faculty committee on priorities that wanted to make cuts that I thought would do lasting damage.[78]

Some years later, the Macalester faculty became, in our view, less responsible. During 2012–13, in the wake of fall-

76. The ability to effect institutional change depends on a shared vision, the absence of intractable interests, and the capacity to recruit and energize campus leaders. In spite of vast differences in scale and mission, the same sense of urgency and clarity of vision that contributed to organizational change at Macalester in the late 1990s is evident today at a large public institution, Arizona State University, where President Michael Crow has made change and innovation the foundation of what he calls "the new American University." See Kevin M. Guthrie, Christine Mulhern, and Martin A. Kurzweil, "In Pursuit of Excellence and Inclusion: Managing Change at Arizona State University," Ithaka S+R, January 2015.

77. Michael S. McPherson to the authors, November 27, 2013, personal correspondence.

78. Ibid.

ing enrollments in Russian and a small number of majors, the Educational Policy and Governance committee (known as EPAG) recommended discontinuing the Russian Studies major. However, to take effect, such a proposal had to make its way through the full faculty. The *Faculty Handbook* provides that such a recommendation will not prevail if two-thirds of the faculty oppose it.[79] That is exactly what happened. Apart from the wisdom of giving the faculty, as a body, veto power over what is really a resource allocation matter, there are broader questions about the effects of such a policy on faculty participation in governance. We are told that today at Macalester one of the major concerns among faculty is the difficulty of convincing their colleagues to stand for election to major committees (see the case study). This situation appears, in part, to reflect the increasing specialization and professionalization of faculty that has taken place across essentially all sectors of higher education. But there may also be another lesson to be learned from this episode. At liberal arts colleges like Macalester (and at many universities, too, we suspect), faculty may well become

[79]. The *Macalester Faculty Handbook* states that EPAG's responsibility includes "consideration and recommendation to the general faculty of changes in the organization of academic departments including their creation, significant modification, or elimination." A subsequent section of the handbook outlines the procedure for "Discontinuance of a Department, Major and/or Minor." The procedure includes the following statement: "EPAG shall make a written report and recommendation to the faculty regarding the proposed discontinuance.... If EPAG recommends discontinuing a department, it shall provide its full report to the faculty a minimum of ten days before the next faculty meeting, at which its recommendation may be discussed. A voting member of the faculty at that meeting may present a motion to reject EPAG's recommendation, and such a motion may be discussed, but a vote on the motion shall be postponed until the next regular meeting of the faculty. In order to be adopted, such a motion to overturn EPAG's recommendation shall require the support of at least two-thirds of the members of EPAG voting, a quorum being present. The recommendation of EPAG shall become effective in the absence or failure of such a motion." See *Macalester College Faculty Handbook,* section 4: "Curricular Policies and Procedures," III C.5, p. 13, available at www.macalester.edu/provost/facultyhandbook/04curricularpolicies/curricular-policies.pdf.

increasingly wary of investing substantial amounts of time in standing committees when their recommendations can be rejected by the faculty at large.[80]

Operating at the opposite end of the size spectrum, CUNY was changed more profoundly by the economics of the 1970s than any of our other three case-study institutions. In 1976, New York City was on the brink of bankruptcy, and it announced quite suddenly that funding for CUNY would be cut by a third. This unexpected and significant decrease in funding forced the entire university to close for two weeks in June. Over the next several years, CUNY had to lay off thousands of faculty and staff. In 1979, the city and New York State reached an agreement under which the state would assume financial responsibility for the senior colleges and continue to share responsibility for the community colleges. The agreement also required all institutions to begin charging tuition. The 1979 CUNY Financing and Governance Act, which implemented these changes in financing, also reorganized the Board of Higher Education into the Board of Trustees. Instead

---

80. Exemplifying this dilemma is a recent change in the faculty by-laws that makes it possible for nominations for major faculty committees to be based on $x + 1$ nominations (e.g., if a committee needs three new members, the election can be based on four nominees for that committee), whereas for more than forty years it was required that there be $2x$ nominees (e.g., six nominees for three openings). There is speculation that the hesitance to serve on major committees is based on at least two issues: (1) a perception that service to the college is not valued significantly in decisions related to promotion, tenure, and salary improvement, and (2) a perception that when dealing with some recent issues (such as the proposed discontinuation of the concentration in Russian Studies), the faculty as a whole did not support the recommendation of a committee that had worked very hard to bring that recommendation to the faculty. One current faculty member felt that faculty involvement in the budgeting process has been getting weaker. Another colleague commented that the faculty have a lot of power, but now there seems to be a lot of distrust across academic divisions and between the faculty and the administration. Smaller departments worry about the future of their departments, and the allocation of resources is increasingly seen as a zero-sum game. If a faculty position is to be added to Department X, it will probably be taken from Department Y. (See the Macalester case study.)

of twenty-one members appointed by the mayor, the Board of Trustees would have fifteen appointed members, with ten appointed by the governor and five appointed by the mayor. By 1999, the board membership had largely turned over to reform-oriented appointees of Mayor Rudolph Giuliani and Governor George Pataki. In the summer of 1999, the board recruited Matthew Goldstein—who had left Baruch, one of the CUNY senior colleges, to become president of Adelphi University a year earlier—as university chancellor, and tasked him with implementing the recommendations in *CUNY: An Institution Adrift*. As a condition of his appointment, Goldstein insisted that the campus presidents report to him rather than to the board.

In time, these major changes in organization and leadership led to a very different alignment between the locus of decision-making power and system-wide issues of control over graduation requirements and transfer policies—as we will see when we discuss CUNY's controversial Pathways Initiative. There have been major consequences for the faculty role in governance, and it seems clear (certainly in settings like this one) that such realignments of decision-making authority can occur only in the wake of far broader changes in an entire governing structure. This is another lesson with definite implications for the long-term evolution of faculty roles.

The Real Estate "Bubble" Breaks—and Fiscal/Political Realities Take Hold (or Do They?)

The 1990s and early 2000s were rollercoaster years for higher education. The recession at the start of the 1990s led to the first absolute decline in state appropriations for higher education since records have been kept.[81] Appropriations then recovered,

81. Zumeta et al., p. 82.

as they have traditionally following recessions, but less rapidly than in the past—in part because a great many states were experiencing structural deficits.[82] For institutions with fundraising capacities, the dreary economic outlook of the early 1990s was offset in large part by a soaring stock market later in the decade, fueled by rapid increases in the prices of shares of technology companies. But the dot.com bubble then burst and, following the 2000–2001 recession, the Dow Jones average hit a five-year low in October 2002. There was another sharp drop in state appropriations. State systems experienced real adversity, with state appropriations per full-time-equivalent student hitting their lowest level in a quarter of a century.[83] As the skies cleared, the stock market rebounded once again, and many well-endowed institutions with aggressive investment management policies benefited greatly—at least for a time. Another day of reckoning came when the real estate bubble burst in 2008–09. Among large endowments, the mean drop in market value was almost 21 percent.[84]

State appropriations did not regain anything like all of their lost ground, and, as is well known, public universities responded by raising tuition aggressively—thereby putting a larger share of responsibility for covering educational costs on

82. For a detailed account of these years, see Zumeta et al., chapters 1 and 4, and also the endnotes in William G. Bowen, *Higher Education in the Digital Age* (Princeton, NJ: Princeton University Press, 2013).

83. See reports released by the state Higher Education Executive Officers; see also Bowen (2013), part 1, n. 44.

84. Andrew Golden, president of the Princeton University Investment Company, to Bowen, April 25, 2014, personal communication. Princeton's own endowment declined 23.5 percent in FY 2009, but this result must be seen in the context of an average annual return of 9.7 percent over the previous ten years. As Golden observes, "Better to have made a ton of money and then lost some, than to have never made it at all." The Princeton trustees concluded that their borrowing capacity (with interest rates very low), and their long-term investment results, made it wise to borrow some money to meet some part of their current commitments rather than sell assets at depressed prices. Princeton, in company with other universities, also made major budget cuts.

students and their families. The wisdom of this privatization of public higher education is controversial, and a story in its own right—but it is not our story. There have been innumerable expressions of concern about "affordability," some justified and some not. The wealthiest institutions have used generous financial aid policies to offset increases in "sticker price," which has forced less fortunate colleges and universities to increase their discount rates to unsustainable levels. Moreover, private returns to investments in education, certainly for the ablest students at the most selective institutions, have remained high. These situations, however, are a truly tiny slice of the pie, and we should not allow them to distract us from broader concerns. At the national level, serious questions about fairness, and the ability of American higher education to continue to be an "engine of opportunity" rather than a "bastion of privilege," have been joined to concerns about the failure of our system of higher education to meet the overall needs of the country for human capital formation at a time when international competitiveness depends more than ever before on knowledge and brain power.

Many of us doubt that there is likely to be a return to what some think of as "the halcyon days of yore," and there have been numerous suggestions that we have encountered a "new normal" for higher education.[85] The economic and political environment does seem to have changed fundamentally. How widely this is understood—or, if understood, accepted—is an open question. Writing for the 1995 edition of his Godkin Lectures, Clark Kerr made this observation about the inclinations of those facing constrained resources at that time: "The first reaction on campus was to try to ignore (or deny) what was happening—a reaction still prevalent among many faculty members. A second has been for administrators to take

85. See, for example, Zumeta et al., p. 98.

band-aid actions."[86] This lament has a familiar ring to it, and we will comment at greater length in chapter 5 on the dangerous tendency simply to "wait for the sun to shine again." We anticipate that discussion here by citing Kerr once again, who went on to suggest (in his 1995 essay) that "a third [reaction] is still evolving, and it potentially involves both administrators and faculty."[87] Kerr was prophetic as always. His use of the modifier "potentially" applies in 2014 as surely as it did twenty years earlier, in 1995.

The chief relevance of these debates for our focus on evolving faculty roles lies primarily, though not exclusively, in the pressures generated for new approaches to the management of institutions of higher education. There is no denying the fact that institutions in general have been under great pressure to be more efficient in their business practices.[88] They have also been challenged to search for fundamentally different ways of delivering instruction cost-effectively and to identify, if they can, new sources of revenue.

The Impact of Experiments with Online Learning

Searches for "magic bullets" are inevitable in such circumstances, and advances in information technology have inspired legislators, regents, and commentators of all kinds to urge institutions of higher education to re-engineer themselves. Much of this activity has been naïve, if not destructive, and it is hard to forget the abortive effort of the Board of Visitors of the University of Virginia to fire their newly elected president, Teresa

86. Kerr, *The Uses of the University*, 4th ed. (the Godkin Lectures on the Essentials of Free Government and the Duties of the Citizen) (Cambridge, MA: Harvard University Press, 1995), p. 165.

87. Ibid.

88. See Bain-Berkeley 2010 report, "Achieving Operational Excellence at University of California, Berkeley," available at http://oe.berkeley.edu/sites/default/files/diagnostic%20report%20bain%20uc%20oberkely.pdf.

Sullivan, at least in part because of her alleged slowness in employing digital technologies to attack such problems.[89] But it would be a serious mistake to underestimate the potential power of the new technologies to alter modes of instruction—even as we discount the superficially appealing "disruption" ideology, which sometimes suggests that a whole new world, without many classrooms, is to appear suddenly (we do not believe that).[90]

We see all around us examples of efforts to harness online learning technologies of many kinds, all in an effort to impart knowledge. Sometimes such efforts have been the product of concerns with the "new normal" in higher education finance, but sometimes they have resulted simply from faculty having embraced exciting opportunities to teach in new ways. In fact, the existence of so many "flavors" of online learning, intended to serve many different purposes, makes it difficult to sharpen conversations. We will resist doggedly the temptation to provide any kind of survey of this amorphous field of activity, because that would shift attention from our focus on evolving faculty roles.[91]

[89.] See Andrew Rice, "Anatomy of a Campus Coup," *New York Times*, September 11, 2012, available at www.nytimes.com/2012/09/16/magazine/teresa-sullivan-uva-ouster.html?pagewanted=1&_r=0.

[90.] See Clayton M. Christensen and Henry J. Eyring, *The Innovative University: Changing the DNA of Higher Education from the Inside Out* (San Francisco: Jossey-Bass, 2011). As Peter Drucker mused in his book *The New Realities,* back in 1989, "Will tomorrow's university be a 'knowledge centre' which transmits information rather than a place that students actually attend?" For a critique of the "gospel of disruptive innovation," see Jill Lepore, "The Disruption Machine," *New Yorker,* June 23, 2014, available at www.newyorker.com/reporting/2014/06/23/140623fa_fact_lepore?currentPage=all.

[91.] In *Higher Education in the Digital Age,* Bowen provides a general introduction to this set of activities and to their potential economic significance. That book also contains an appendix in which Kelly Lack provides a useful description of the contours of the field and notes distinguishing characteristics of different approaches to online learning (pp. 72–77). See also two British publications: K. Stepanyan, A. Littlejohn, and A. Margaryan, "Sustainable e-Learning: Toward a Coherent Body of Knowledge," *Educational Technology and Society*

In the main, and with rare exceptions, consideration of the applicability of these technologies has served to highlight issues pertaining to faculty roles, not to resolve them. The widely publicized introduction of MOOCs (massive open online courses) has affected faculty first by giving those with the talent, inclination, and institutional support the opportunity to experiment with methods of teaching that reach hundreds of thousands of students. The two best-known of these platforms, Coursera and edX, are still evolving, and one of their impacts on faculty roles is that they are forcing educational institutions, and their faculties, to confront profound questions about the ownership of intellectual property rights, and especially of content that is produced through collective activity involving a number of people with varied skills (and certainly with technological support that is often substantial).[92] Questions of control over the distribution of such content across institutional lines, and about its sustainability, are enormously important and are the subject of a companion project being undertaken by ITHAKA.[93] Right now, there are few well-established protocols.

A second impact is on faculty and staff who are wondering whether it is possible to adapt MOOCs to serve the needs of *institutions* as well as *individuals*. The right relationship between MOOC providers and local "adapters" is

---

16, no. 2 (2013): 91–202, and *The Maturing of the MOOC: Literature Review of Massive Open Online Courses and Other Forms of Online Distance Learning*, Department for Business Innovation & Skills, BIS Research Paper 130, London, September 2013. As the subtitle suggests, this latter publication contains an extensive literature review.

92. See www.coursera.org/ and www.edx.org/.

93. ITHAKA is a not-for-profit organization that helps the academic community use digital technologies to preserve the scholarly record and to advance research and teaching in sustainable ways. ITHAKA provides three innovative services that benefit the academic community: JSTOR (http://about.jstor.org/10things), Portico (http://www.portico.org), and Ithaka S+R (http://www.sr.ithaka.org/clientservices).

very much open for discussion. As of the moment, it is fair to say that there is no evidence that MOOCs can address the pressures facing higher education to deliver instructional content leading to degrees in more cost-effective ways than previously. San Jose State University has been one pioneer in testing online course offerings by Udacity, and studies of outcomes, which were bedeviled by methodological problems of all kinds, raised serious questions as to whether at-risk students, in particular, could be expected to benefit from this approach.[94]

The advent of MOOCs has had a third impact. In some settings, it has raised the question of where the locus of authority rests for institutions and their faculty members to decide whether to participate in such collective enterprises at all. At Amherst, the president decided to defer to the wishes of the full faculty in deciding whether to accept an invitation from edX to participate in its program; after months of discussion, the faculty voted "no" rather overwhelmingly, preferring to "chart their own course."[95] Our colleague Lawrence Bacow observed, "It is hard to imagine any other organization in which a subgroup could unilaterally claim the right [or be given the right] to limit the capacity of the head of the organization to enter into contracts on behalf of the organization."[96] The much more common approach has been to allow individual faculty

94. See Carl Straumsheim, "After Weeks of Delays, San Jose State U. Releases Research Report on Online Courses," *Inside Higher Ed,* September 12, 2013.

95. See Ry Rivard, "Despite Courtship Amherst Decides to Shy Away from Star MOOC Provider," *Inside Higher Ed,* April 19, 2013; see also Steve Kolowich, "Why Some Colleges Are Saying No to MOOC Deals, at Least for Now," *Chronicle of Higher Education,* April 29, 2013.

96. Bacow to Bowen, November 18, 2013, personal e-mail correspondence. Faculty at Middlebury have recently urged the college to terminate its relationship with a for-profit company, K12, but in this instance the president is resisting this course of action and the board retains final decision-making authority. See Steve Kolowich, "Middlebury Faculty Seeks to Cut Ties with Online-Education Company," *Chronicle of Higher Education,* May 21, 2014.

members to decide for themselves whether or not to enter into these relationships.[97]

In examining faculty roles in making judgments of this kind, it is worth noting that there are faculty roles on both the "receiving" and "sending" ends of pedagogical links. The Department of Philosophy at San Jose State reacted angrily to a suggestion from "on high" that the department consider using the popular "Justice" course developed by Professor Michael Sandel at Harvard to supplement normal course offerings. The faculty at San Jose State were concerned that their role would be diminished to that of "glorified TAs (teaching assistants)." The provost responded that it was entirely up to the department to decide whether or not to use the Sandel course. On the "sending" end of the link, Sandel responded by saying that he is only trying to make material available to the public and that he certainly did not want his lectures "to be used to undermine faculty colleagues at other institutions."[98] Some faculty creators of content at other universities have also been leery of being seen as "undermining" colleagues at "receiving" institutions. These debates raise fundamental—and as yet unresolved—questions of institutional roles, as well as faculty roles, in deciding how, if at all, instructional content should be

97. A decision by the Duke faculty not to join the "2U" consortium may seem analogous, but there is a crucial difference. In the Duke case, the proposal was not to join a MOOC, but rather to participate with other institutions in creating a pool of for-credit courses for undergraduates. The vote in the faculty was actually against granting Duke credit to Duke students who would have taken online courses from the pool. The authority of faculty over the granting of credit is long-standing and different in character from decisions to prohibit faculty from providing offerings for MOOCs. Duke remains a member of Coursera. This particular case, which was also said to reflect some faculty "frustration" with the Duke administration, reminds us that votes on questions of this kind often reflect a variety of considerations and should not be interpreted in too single-minded a way. See Ry Rivard, "Duke Faculty Reject Plan for It to Join Online Consortium," *Inside Higher Ed,* April 30, 2013.

98. Quoted in Ry Rivard, "San Jose State University Faculty Pushes Back Against EdX," *Inside Higher Ed,* May 3, 2013.

shared across institutions in a digital age. Who should have the authority to make such decisions?

There is another, quite different, motivation that has driven some institutional efforts to do more with online learning—namely, the desire to increase enrollments without commensurate increases in costs, thereby both serving more students and increasing revenue. The University of Massachusetts is one (among many) institutions that have followed this path.[99] UMassOnline, the online learning consortium that provides marketing and technological support for the university's vast array of online offerings, reports impressive gains in enrollment and revenue.[100] The New America Foundation has published a report, *The Next Generation University*, which describes in considerable detail the apparent successes of six other public universities (Arizona State University, Georgia State University, the State University of New York–Buffalo, the University of California–Riverside, the University of Central Florida, and the University of Texas at Arlington) that they believe have demonstrated a capacity to increase enrollments and become more efficient—often by using online technologies.[101] Much more rigorous research is needed to confirm some of the claims in this report, but the report is, at the minimum, encouraging in

99. It is worth recalling that the 2012 Ithaka S+R study "Barriers to Adoption of Online Learning Systems in U.S. Higher Education" (led by Lawrence S. Bacow, with William G. Bowen, Kevin Guthrie, Kelly A. Lack, and Matthew P. Long) found that revenue generation was a major motivator for introducing online courses.

100. See "UMassOnline Reports a 12% Increase in Enrollments and a 16% Increase in Revenue Generated by Online Courses Offered through University of Massachusetts Campuses in FY11," *Business Wire*, July 6, 2011. See also "UMass Online Education Program Generates More Than $78 Million in Revenue," educationnews.org, September 24, 2013, available at www .educationnews.org/online-schools/umass-generates-over-78-million-in-revenue -from-online-programs/.

101. Jeff Selingo, Kevin Carey, Hilary Pennington, Rachel Fishman, and Iris Palmer, *The Next Generation University* (Washington, DC: New America Foundation, May 2013).

suggesting that institutions "on the way up" can and do innovate. Changing approaches may be easier for these institutions than for institutions that are, for one reason or another, more "fixed in place." One lesson to be drawn from these six case studies is that it may be appreciably easier to gain efficiencies when enrollments are growing rapidly than when the student base is static. Providing online learning at scale enables innovative institutions to expand enrollment, especially among underserved students, and to increase revenue relatively quickly.[102]

The contrast between such experiences, particularly the experience of the University of Massachusetts and the experience of the now-defunct effort at the University of Illinois to develop Global Campus as a for-profit entity, is instructive. Global Campus was established in 2007 to further the university's land-grant mission by expanding educational opportunities for non-traditional students. Conceived as a separate accredited entity that would enroll students in degree and certificate programs in such fields as business administration, nursing, and recreation, sport, and tourism, Global Campus was intended to combine the business model of a for-profit with the academic integrity and quality of a flagship public university. In retrospect, it seems clear that Global Campus suffered from both an overblown sense of what was possible from a business standpoint in an increasingly competitive field and, even more, from a failure to recognize that faculty criticism of course quality would prove devastating—certainly in the setting of a "brand" as well established as that of the University of Illinois. This is a clear example—and there are many others (including the efforts of the president's office at the University of California to launch an online program, which we discuss below)—of the need for strong faculty support of initiatives

102. The January 2015 Ithaka S+R report on Arizona State University documents many of these propositions in a specific setting. See Guthrie, Mulhern, and Kurzweil.

that threaten academic reputation. Faculty do not like to have anyone challenge, directly or subtly, their authority over content intended to lead to the granting of degrees.[103]

Several of the lessons identified in this brief description of how various institutions have addressed the potential of online learning in the "new normal" are illustrated nicely by the experiences of CUNY, which had made very limited use of online learning prior to the founding of the School of Professional Studies (SPS) as a subsidiary of the Graduate School and University Center in 2003 (see the case study for both more detail and references). Efforts to explore online initiatives in earlier years had revealed that at least one of the leaders of the University Faculty Senate, the faculty governance body for university-wide academic matters, was opposed to online instruction as a matter of principle, viewing it as a pathway to "automating faculty out of existence." A more general problem was that online instruction and online degrees were simply not priorities for most faculty leaders. SPS had the advantage of having been founded with a mix of adjuncts and faculty from other CUNY campuses. Thus SPS was able to cherry-pick among interested faculty, choosing those who were highly motivated to do something new; and SPS did not have to cope with faculty being forced to change their ways. Also highly relevant is the fact that consortial work is given greater leeway under the release time rules of the collective bargaining agreement, and faculty could be (and were) compensated for making extra efforts to develop new pedagogies. All were *very* considerable advantages!

Having initially offered extension programs that were not all that threatening to other units of CUNY, SPS soon expanded its portfolio to encompass a broad range of certificate and

103. See Steven Kolowich, "What Doomed Global Campus?" *Inside Higher Ed,* September 3, 2009.

degree programs, most entirely online. This is, as our case study makes clear, an example of the approach the Goldstein administration used to create several new, streamlined, and demand-sensitive initiatives that might have been held up if they had been pursued through more traditional means. It is also an example of what can be accomplished by starting anew in developing online pedagogies—provided, as was the case here, that the new structure has strong support from the central administration, which in turn has the strong backing of a board with real authority.

We complete this discussion of faculty roles in the online technology environment by commenting on the widely noted effort by Mark Yudof and colleagues in the president's office at the University of California to respond to calls (including calls from the governor) to see if greater use of technology could not ease somewhat the seemingly inexorable pressures on the finances of the entire University of California system. Also relevant was the widespread appreciation of the fact that potential students of all ages were by now accustomed to using technology every day in ways that would have been unthinkable even a decade ago.

This complex and troubled story, which we discuss below in some detail because it is so instructive (and which is told in even more detail, complete with a timeline and references, by Derek Wu in the appendix to our University of California case study), serves as a sharp reminder of the fragility of shared governance. By essentially everyone's account, this initiative was not successful. It is worth thinking hard about why Berkeley, in particular, did well in dealing with the reorganization of the biological sciences in the 1970s and the creation of a new school of information studies shortly thereafter—and why the later university-wide online learning effort has been much less successful. One obvious explanation is the lack of faculty leadership at the start of the online initiative, along with the subsequent difficulty in obtaining faculty buy-in, but that is not all that there is to the story.

The initiative was introduced to the public prominently via an op-ed in the *Los Angeles Times* in July 2009, written by Christopher Edley Jr., dean of Boalt Hall, the Berkeley School of Law, an active member of the University of California Commission on the Future, who was serving as co-chair of the Education and Curriculum working group and as a senior advisor to President Yudof. Edley introduced the idea of a "virtual" eleventh UC campus devoted solely to awarding online degrees to UC-eligible students. Such a plan, in his eyes, would offer education more cheaply (improving student access and diminishing institutional cost burdens) while maintaining quality. At the outset, Edley was very confident in the potential to raise the resources necessary for an upfront investment in this "virtual campus" (the program for which came to be called the University of California Online Education Initiative, or UCOE) and believed that faculty members were cautiously supportive of such an endeavor.

Several months later, in October 2009, Daniel Greenstein, vice provost for academic programs and planning and co-leader with Edley of UCOE, met with the Academic Senate's University Committee on Education Policy (UCEP) to provide an overview of both the broader initiative and a related—yet distinct—pilot project that would implement online courses at a more modest level to see if there were "opportunities that UC [was] not taking full advantage of."[104] In fact, the idea behind the pilot project originated from the senate divisions on one or more campuses (which included the University of California, Berkeley). Although there was discussion about possible faculty concerns and how this pilot would be evaluated, the committee

104. See University of California Academic Senate, University Committee on Education Policy, Meeting Minutes, Monday, October 5, 2009, available at http://senate.universityofcalifornia.edu/committees/ucep/ucep.10.5.09.minutes.pdf.

stated that there did not appear to be any senate policies that would impede its progress and recommended that Greenstein and his partners develop a preliminary proposal and determine the direction of the pilot.

For the next several months, Greenstein and Edley worked on the planning stages of the pilot project, which called for offering twenty-five high-demand, lower-level gateway courses online, for which professors would compete for development grants awarded through a process run by the Academic Senate. However, the approval process for these system-wide courses would have to cross multiple hurdles, starting with recommendation and review from each campus's Committee on Courses, before seeking approval by each campus division of the Academic Senate and, subsequently, by the system-wide UCEP. Although Edley acknowledged that the approval process might make it difficult to move the project forward, there was hope that the Faculty Senate would quickly endorse the initiative, and that classes would be taught as soon as 2011. In fact, Edley and Greenstein had proceeded to distribute funding for the online courses (hoping to immediately facilitate their development), even before the Academic Senate passed judgment on whether or not to approve them. Although Edley's "eagerness to reshape the university [was] seen by many faculty members as either naïve or dangerous," he remained ambitiously adamant that the University of California should be at the forefront of an inevitable movement to deliver quality online education for credit—and ultimately for degrees.[105]

In May 2010, Greenstein received a letter from the system-wide Academic Council (the administrative arm of the Academic Senate), which unanimously endorsed—based on UCEP's

105. Josh Keller and Marc Parry, "U. of California Considers Online Classes, or Even Degrees," *Chronicle of Higher Education,* May 9, 2010, http://chronicle.com/article/In-Crisis-U-of-California/65445/, accessed November 1, 2014.

recommendation—proceeding with the online learning pilot project, *contingent on the procurement of external funds*. A few days later, the Berkeley Faculty Association, an advocacy group, released a report raising serious concerns about Edley's plan for a "cyber campus," which included "profoundly degraded undergraduate education, eroded faculty governance and control over curriculum, research delinked from teaching . . . and squadrons of [graduate student instructors] at the frontline of online contact . . . in courses whose sole purpose is revenue generation."

Expressions of faculty concerns failed to forestall progress on the project. Immediately following a presentation by Greenstein and Edley in July 2010, the University of California regents responded enthusiastically to Edley's belief in the potential of online instruction to enhance the University of California's ability to serve its mission and voted to endorse the pilot program. Over the next few months, Edley and Greenstein worked on selecting the courses that would be offered as part of the initiative, and on securing private grants for the pilot project—a fundraising effort that achieved only minimal results ($750,000 rather than $7 million).[106] At the same time, it was announced that the project had taken out an interest-free $7 million loan from the University of California Office of the President, to be paid back over the next seven years, primarily through revenue to be generated by tuition payments from non–University of California students. Many faculty members responded critically to the announcement of the loan. They felt that Edley reneged on his original commitment to pursue external funding and instead tapped directly into their "monetary share" at a time when the University of

106. It was only in March of 2012, nine months after the regents approved the endeavor, that the pilot project obtained its first extramural grant—one of $750,000 from Next Generation Learning Challenges, an initiative managed by EDUCAUSE with funding from the Gates and Hewlett Foundations.

California was struggling to deal with a recent $500 million cut in state support.

In a May 2011 letter to President Yudof, Daniel Simmons (chair of the University of California Academic Senate)—who had previously supported the pilot program and the need to experiment with online education even during times of financial crises—expressed concern about the opportunity costs of the $7 million loan and the ambiguity surrounding the pilot program's objectives (e.g., expanding access versus raising revenue). He noted that the senate had not yet received any course proposals for approval (even though it had previously been told that courses would be offered beginning in the fall), and that many unanswered questions remained about program evaluation and the focus on lower-division requirements. As a result, Simmons wrote that the Academic Council—reversing its position from a year prior—advised that no additional online pilot courses be developed until things were evaluated in a more rigorous fashion.

Nonetheless, the pilot moved forward despite these concerns from the faculty. In July 2011, Simmons wrote another letter—this time to University of California Provost Lawrence Pitts—endorsing UCEP's recommendation from a month earlier that the council appoint an independent "blue-ribbon panel" of experts (from both inside and outside UC) to report periodically to the senate on the progress and results of the pilot. A few months later—in September 2011—Greenstein announced preliminary plans to repay the loan, which included selling five thousand places (out of seven thousand) in the online classes to non-UC students, such as military personnel and international students.

In June 2012, Keith Williams (former chair of UCEP and now UCOE faculty advisor) announced that he would be taking over as interim director of UCOE (working with approximately ten staff members), following Greenstein's impending departure. In the same announcement, he wrote that UC Online anticipated rolling out an additional nineteen courses over the next nine months (which, together with the six released in spring 2012, would total twenty-five) and would begin marketing efforts to enroll non-UC students in July. However, Williams acknowledged that cross-campus enrollment would likely not happen before 2014. In July of that year, Williams stated that UC Berkeley was beginning to look into offering more courses through Coursera in a way that would complement University of California Online.

A total of seven hundred students took University of California online courses in the spring and summer semesters of 2012, but because they were already enrolled in the University of California system, no additional revenue was generated. At the same time, UCOE spent $4.6 million developing and marketing its project in the 2011–12 school year. In November 2012, the "blue-ribbon panel" released the first iteration of its evaluation, painting quite a critical picture of the initiative. The panel was dissatisfied with the program's unclear goals and narrow-mindedness, and it was also concerned about UCOE's inability to provide timely progress reports of suitable scholarly quality (all while continuing to tap loan funds). It recommended that the program be delayed until a fuller evaluation of results could be performed for all online courses offered. In a February 2013 revision, the panel reiterated the original points in its November report while acknowledging that some progress had been made, particularly with respect to generally positive attitudinal results from students and faculty involved with UCOE.

As of spring 2013, University of California Online offered fourteen courses (with twenty-one additional UCOE-supported courses in development), having enrolled—up to that point—seventeen hundred UC students (who took UC Online courses primarily as offerings from their home campuses) and only eleven non-UC students. These non-degree students paid between $1,400 and $2,100 in tuition for each class, depending on the number of credits offered and the length of each course. As a result, by the end of the 2012–13 academic year, UC Online had generated no more than $23,100 in tuition revenue from non-UC students in an effort to repay the loan. UC Online is now looking at other ways to bring in much-needed revenue to pay back the loan, including offering its course development services (perhaps through licensing) to other outside programs interested in developing online courses, and actively targeting both community college students hoping to transfer to a University of California institution and California residents who meet University of California eligibility criteria.

Edley, who no longer leads the effort, acknowledges that the dream of a "virtual" University of California campus is all but over. Once problems began arising with the pilot, various parties came to view the pilot project as an end in itself. Today, the University of California has largely shifted gears from UCOE's top-down strategy to a campus-by-campus innovation system that cultivates the creativity of individual faculty members in devising approaches that incorporate online and blended learning. In the meantime, individual campuses and the UC system have made concerted efforts to broaden and diversify their online learning efforts. Individual experiments too numerous to list abound, but we should note that the University of California, Berkeley, joined the edX consortium and there is now a system-wide Innovative Learning Teaching Initiative that seeks to create both a pilot cross-campus enrollment webpage and a formal approval process for cross-campus course credit that will enable students university-wide to enroll in courses at other campuses.[107]

107. Carl Straumsheim, "A Changing Economy Changes Online Education Priorities at the U. of California," *Inside Higher Ed*, August 13, 2014, available at www.insidehighered.com/news/2014/08/13/changing-economy-changes-online-education-priorities-u-california.

What are we to conclude from this blow-by-blow account of an initiative that now belongs to history? There are, perhaps, four main lessons. First, institutions as well as individuals have personalities, which have to be respected. An aggressive, top-down approach had little chance to succeed in the University of California context, where faculty prerogatives are deeply embedded and prized. Whether a similar approach could have succeeded in a different setting is problematic, but less clear. Second, this tale illustrates some of the special complications posed by online initiatives that cut across institutional as well as departmental boundaries; we will discuss later whether course approval processes that worked well in a simpler day are viable in a digital age. Third, it is evident in retrospect that projects of this kind, especially when undertaken at a time of general financial stringency, must have a coherent business plan and acknowledge, up front, potential conflicts between educational and financial objectives. Fourth, everyone should recognize the strong aversion, especially on the part of faculty (but sometimes on the part of administrators, too) to any discussion of cost savings in the case of educational programs. On the website of the Berkeley Resource Center for Online Education, there was at one time a list of goals and "anti-goals," and one anti-goal was to lower costs. We return to all of these points in chapter 5, where we make some suggestions concerning faculty roles going forward. Some changes in established assumptions seem definitely in order.

The Pathways Initiative at CUNY

Online activities, important and newsworthy as they are, do not constitute anything like all responses to the changed economic circumstances confronting all of higher education, and particularly the public sector. We conclude this part of our study by discussing in detail the Pathways Initiative at CUNY, which is an interesting, very different, and highly instructive example of how an enterprising institution ought to change—and did change—faculty roles (see the case study for more detail and references). Among other lessons, this provocative history demonstrates the potential value of strong leadership from on high—the unfortunate counter-example of President Yudof's efforts to introduce big changes at the University of California notwithstanding.[108]

Although CUNY's Board of Trustees has legal authority over academic policy, from 1961 until the mid-2000s each CUNY campus was given broad leeway to define its academic requirements, including which credits earned at other campuses would count on the "home" campus. The faculty on each campus had little incentive to accept credits from other campuses because doing so meant that there was less demand for courses (and instructors) and a smaller budget; faculty also had an understandable, if self-serving, belief that students were best served by taking *their* courses, as opposed to analogs at other campuses. The same factors led faculty on some campuses to raise the number of general education credits required for a degree to one of the highest levels in the nation. As a result, CUNY students who transferred between campuses—an increasingly common occurrence—were often required to earn many more than 120 credits during their academic career in order to graduate: the average CUNY baccalaureate graduate earned 130 credits to obtain a 120-credit degree. Of course, many students who might have earned a degree if they had been able to transfer their credits never earned one at all. We should pause right here to note this dramatic fail-

108. The CUNY and University of California case studies illustrate well that leadership from on high can either succeed or fail, depending on circumstances—including both the skills of the respective leadership teams and specific institutional settings. As the CUNY case study explains, the system leadership had the great advantage of a state law that gave it the authority (as courts later confirmed) to initiate curricular changes. In California, on the other hand, the Academic Senate had a long and well-established history of control over many curricular matters.

ure of "the system" to align decision-making with key variables affecting both educational outcomes and costs. Incentives and responsibilities simply have to be aligned properly—as we will emphasize in chapter 5.

The Pathways Initiative, passed by the board in June 2011, required the chancellor to establish a task force to develop common transfer and general education policies for the university—which he did, in spite of a general lack of cooperation from the University Faculty Senate (UFS) and campus faculty councils (see the case study). In December 2011, following extensive consultation, the task force generated recommendations for a common general education framework and a process for transferring credits across campuses, which the chancellor accepted. Campuses were then tasked with matching their courses to the new framework. The new system took effect in the fall semester of 2013.

The Pathways Initiative was very popular among many students but very unpopular among a vocal group of faculty. After declining to nominate members of the task force, the UFS, along with the faculty union, filed suit to block the initiative. The plaintiffs alleged that the board resolution breached an earlier settlement, which, they argued, confirmed that the faculty had authority over matters of curriculum—effectively, that the board could act only on curriculum matters first approved by the faculty. The AAUP also wrote a letter protesting the Pathways Initiative as an infringement on faculty governance. In February 2014, the trial court in the UFS/union suit to block the Pathways Initiative ruled for CUNY. The court reaffirmed that the Board of Trustees was the sole body authorized by state law to "govern" and "administer" the university, including its academic policies, and that neither its by-laws nor the settlement agreement in the earlier case granted a veto over curricular matters to the faculty. The trial court's decision may not be the final word on the matter—the UFS and the union have appealed the ruling, and there are indications that CUNY's new administration is backing away from some of the Pathways Initiative's policies. But for now, at least, it stands as a powerful vindication of the administration's and board's authority to lead on academic matters, even over faculty opposition.

This initiative is an excellent example—the best one we have found—of the need for a "central authority" with the power to make what are clearly system-wide decisions. The effects of the Pathways Initiative are being closely monitored; there is every reason to expect that it will lead to both higher completion rates and faster time-to-degree. The opposition from campus-based faculty is hardly surprising, not only because of concerns for their "authority" over such matters but also because of concerns about effects on enrollments, budgets, and the number of staffing positions on individual campuses. Here we see a clear example of the conflict between understandable "local" concerns and "the greater good"—viewed from the perspectives of individual students and their families and the societal need for improved educational outcomes. CUNY's leadership saw that it had an opportunity and, one might say, a responsibility, to help students complete their degrees within the system in a timely way. The court decision rejected categorically the argument that only the faculty can initiate proposals of this kind. If the court had agreed that the faculty had a "sole right-to-initiate," this would have given the faculty a de facto right to veto any new initiatives that they didn't like by simply refusing to "initiate" anything. This, then, is an instance in which an institution was able to respond positively to the need for more cost-effective outcomes—something desirable under any circumstances but nearly essential in the "new normal" facing higher education.

4

Faculty Roles Today and Tomorrow—
Topical Issues

OUR HISTORICAL OVERVIEW demonstrates convincingly that, both in the decades leading up to World War II and in the postwar years, neither faculty roles nor governance practices in general should ever be thought of as immutable. Over the centuries they have responded to the changing needs of the society that higher education exists to serve, and also to the changing character of the higher education enterprise itself as institutions have evolved. This unending, highly iterative process warns us against thinking that we are in a settled place today. Indeed, significant changes in governance practices seem both more imminent, and more necessary, than they have been at any point in recent memory. This does not, however, make it easy to predict the course of events.

In this chapter we discuss the current status of faculty roles in some key areas of governance, noting where they do (and do not) seem to be working well. Then, in the next chapter, we offer our own thoughts about some potentially overarching challenges that we believe deserve serious attention—even as long-lasting "fixes" are elusive.

We begin with an important if obvious proposition: many (most) individual decisions about research and teaching are

???   *Huh?*

made informally outside formal governance structures. This informal "system" has worked exceedingly well, and the vast majority of such decisions are considered "the most accepted, the least contested, and . . . the most legitimate."[1] So why change what many consider a soundly functioning system? As Clark Kerr observed some twenty years ago, changes in formal governance structures have often made little difference: "All that effort, all that passion, all that turmoil was mostly for naught, but it was also mostly inevitable given the conditions of the times."[2] True enough. But in our judgment, the "conditions of the times" are different today—and call for modifications in established approaches to some, but by no means all, governing policies and practices.

The most fundamental questions are these: Does higher education today, operating in a rapidly evolving digital world marked by both high expectations concerning educational outcomes and tough budgetary constraints, need new approaches if not some new governing machinery? And, if so, what might such modifications look like? Needless to say, in presenting our own views on this fundamental pair of questions, in this chapter and the next, we do not intend to compromise the reader's prerogative of mining the historical data and the case studies presented here to produce a different set of propositions (which, fortunately, is impossible in any case!). We would like to think we are engaging in a conversation with the reader, not preaching to a world that is hardly waiting, breathlessly, for instruction from us or from anyone else.

In the interest of economy, we will pass over without comment some areas of decision-making that seem both less important than others and largely non-controversial. Examples

1. See Clark Kerr, *The Uses of the University,* 5th ed. (the Godkin Lectures on the Essentials of Free Government and the Duties of the Citizen) (Cambridge, MA: Harvard University Press, 2001), p. 135.
2. See Kerr, p. 137.

are faculty authority to determine who qualifies for course credit and for degrees, and the faculty role in student discipline.[3] Here is the short list of topics we will consider:

1. the selection and tenure of the president;
2. the faculty appointment process, including oversight of dismissals;
3. the role of faculty in giving advice on matters of all kinds;
4. the role of faculty in budgetary and staffing questions that include the conditions of employment for non-tenure-track (NTT) faculty;
5. faculty responsibility for maintaining academic standards in admissions, curricular content, and grading; and
6. authority to determine teaching methods, which includes, in a digital age, decisions about the creation and ownership of online platforms and content, as well as control over both the distribution of access to such resources and their sustainability.

The Selection and Tenure of the President

Lay boards of trustees/regents are an enduring, as well as unique, characteristic of American higher education, and it is almost universally accepted today that such boards have the final authority to hire and dismiss a president. But it is also widely understood now, as it was not always, that boards are well advised to consult the faculty when a president is to be named.[4] It should be equally clear that boards should

3. We note, however, that growing public concern regarding the protection of students from sexual harassment and assault has raised questions about the need to overhaul college and university policies and the role of faculty members in adjudicating an unfamiliar and highly contentious set of issues.

4. In 2014 there appeared a tendency, not really evident before, for legislatures and others in public university settings to seek to impose "big names" on institutions. Faculty are still involved in search processes, but big names

not remove a president precipitously, without at least some faculty involvement in the decision-making process. This is, however, not always understood, and when boards try to remove a president without warning or consultation, major governance issues can ensue—as the Board of Visitors of the University of Virginia learned when they tried to dismiss their president, Teresa Sullivan, by a peremptory strike. An ensuing (and predictable) faculty revolt resulted in Sullivan's reinstatement.[5] This bizarre set of events led to a loss of respect for the board and, paradoxically, to the creation of a situation in which the president may feel unnecessarily beholden to the faculty for her survival. The convoluted dispute at the University of Texas at Austin, over the continued tenure in office of William C. Powers as president, illustrates both the politicized nature of decisions concerning the leadership of many public university systems and the power of faculty, along with

can drive other aspirants from the field and make faculty involvement in the selection process more pro forma than it should be. Some recent examples include the appointment of South Carolina's former lieutenant governor, Glenn McConnell, as president of the College of Charleston and the hiring of former Ohio State University football coach Jim Tressel as president of Youngstown State University. In what may become a precursor of future faculties' displeasure with "narrowed" presidential searches, the Florida State University Faculty Senate voted "no confidence" in a search firm that appeared (initially) to limit consideration to State Senator John Thrasher, a former member of the Florida State Board of Trustees who had served as chairman of the incumbent governor's re-election campaign. Of course, even if a president is chosen in this way (as Thrasher was), he or she will still have to function going forward—and at least a modicum of faculty and student support is likely to be essential for survival. See Ry Rivard, "Florida State U. Faculty Open New Front in Battle over Presidential Searches," *Inside Higher Ed,* June 6, 2014, available at www.insidehighered.com/news/2014/06/06/florida-state-u-faculty-open-new-front-battle-over-presidential-searches, and Peter Schmidt, "Florida State U. Picks Politician as President Despite Widespread Protest," *Chronicle of Higher Education,* September 24, 2014, available at http://chronicle.com/article/Florida-State-U-Board-Picks/148975.

5. See Sara Hebel, Jack Stripling, and Robin Wilson, "U. of Virginia Board Votes to Reinstate Sullivan," *Chronicle of Higher Education,* June 26, 2012, available at http://chronicle.com/article/U-of-Virginia-Board-Votes-to/132603/.

other groups, to push back against efforts to dismiss a popular president.[6]

Largely as a result of weak academic labor markets, considerable power has gravitated over past decades, really since the "Golden Age" of the 1960s, from faculties to presidents—or at least to presidents interested in exercising strong leadership. When academic labor markets are weak, administrators are much less prone to give faculty members all kinds of perks, including quasi-decision-making authority, than they are when faculty are in high demand and it is difficult to recruit and retain the ablest individuals. Even so, presidents remain dependent in almost all instances on faculty support. As our experienced colleague Lawrence Bacow likes to say, "No president ever truly wins a 'no confidence' vote." Once doubts in the president's leadership surface, his or her authority diminishes. The latent power of the faculty over even very strong presidents has long been recognized by astute leaders, as we are reminded by Clark Kerr's acknowledgment of this fact of academic life at the University of California in the 1960s (see the case study). In the case of lesser, less-secure leaders, the opposition of even a few key faculty can be paralyzing.[7] More generally, we have been told of situations in which fear of antagonizing the faculty, especially on the part of administrators who may hope

6. See Katherine Mangan, "Texas Showdown Is Averted, with the President to Stay on for a Year," *Chronicle of Higher Education*, July 10, 2014. After asking for his resignation early in the new academic year, the chancellor of the Texas system backed down and agreed that President Powers can serve through the 2014–15 academic year.

7. In conducting a study of communication patterns and levels of influence exerted by different individuals and groups on fifteen campuses, Ithaka S+R found instances of presidents who either felt completely paralyzed by strong academic leaders who opposed their efforts to make change or worked at the margins of institutional change instead of attempting to deal with faculty resistance. A long-standing culture of faculty governance in each instance kept the institutions from experimenting with online education or with any kind of new business models.

to be considered for other leadership positions, has led to weak responses to faculty demands for more teaching credit or reduced teaching loads.

As a general rule, this check-and-balance machinery, which is what it is, seems to us the right way to handle a matter of such supreme importance as the selection/tenure of the president. Unlike some other aspects of governance, this is not one in need of extensive fixing. But its continued effectiveness does depend on the exercise of a modicum of good judgment by faculties, presidents, and boards. Also required, now especially, are courage and the will to act on the part of presidents—in short, a willingness to take some risks. Looking back in later years on the 1960s, from his vantage point as chairman of the Carnegie Commission on Higher Education, and later as a prescient elder statesman, Kerr did not pull any punches:

> I would argue for giving leadership a better chance to exert itself. Most successful new policies in higher education have come from the top. We need to reverse the denigration of leadership. . . . It was denigrated by students in the late 1960s and early 1970s. . . . Presidents were used like Kleenex. The institutions survived, but their leaders did not. Yet in a time of troubles, as then loomed and now looms again, leaders are more needed but are harder to get to serve and to keep. To the list of presidential attributes I gave in the original [1963 Godkin] lectures, I would now add the ability to withstand the frustrations from all of the checks and balances, and the criticism from all of the more active and vocal participants; that is, the possession of nerves like sewer pipes.[8]

Effective leadership comes in many forms and is often accompanied by enthusiastic testimonials and simultaneous charges of

8. See Kerr, p. 137.

arrogance. At Arizona State University, President Michael Crow's insistence that a flagship university should enroll and graduate an increasing number of students who match the state's diversity, and also enhance quality (in teaching and research) while reducing costs through the use of technology, has made his claims for "The New American University" a flashpoint of innovation and resistance. Thirteen years into the Crow presidency, the "shared sense of urgency and enthusiasm for change" reflect the institutionalization of a compelling vision, persistence in spite of spirited resistance, and the implementation of substantial transformation. In retrospect, it is clear that Arizona State's success reflects the importance of the "fit" between presidential style and institutional circumstances, a willingness to encourage the departure of obstructive senior leaders, and the recruitment of deans and faculty who are eager to embrace and implement new directions.[9]

To reiterate, faculty have a definite role to play, along with other actors, in judging presidential capacities—both when presidents are being chosen and then after they have been in office for a time. Care does need to be taken, however, in parsing out exactly what lessons one should take from faculty assessments of the current needs of their institutions. One poorly understood risk of heavy faculty involvement in the process of searching for a president is that relying too heavily on current faculty to help define what a new president needs to do can mislead a board as to the needs of the institution. Current faculty may not see the need for a rather drastic upgrading of faculty quality or academic rigor that can be evident to outsiders. A "blind spot" of this kind can contribute to the selection of a president not well equipped to lead a needed revitalization

9. Kevin M. Guthrie, Christine Mulhern, and Martin A. Kurzweil, "In Pursuit of Excellence and Inclusion: Managing Change at Arizona State University," Ithaka S+R, January 2015.

of the faculty or unwilling to recommend the reallocation of instructional resources.[10]

Consistent with our interest in specifying faculty roles with some precision, we hasten to add that assigning an appropriate role to the faculty in assessing the president's effectiveness does not imply that a faculty representative should be given a seat on the board of trustees/regents. In fact, as we have said before, we believe that assigning a board seat to an elected faculty representative is neither necessary nor wise—it creates conflicts of interest and can put a faculty representative in an awkward position.[11] A general rule of the road is that board members should not represent constituencies. Trustees should bring to the board table a wide range of perspectives—related, for example, to age, race/ethnicity, where individuals live, and vocation—but each member should then seek to do what seems best for the institution overall, not to serve a narrower set of interests.[12]

10. Boards have an important role to play in, as David Riesman often said, "protecting the future from the present." Both faculty and administrators may have a tendency to place too much emphasis on meeting immediate needs (or satisfying instant desires). Boards can be a valuable balancing element—provided, of course, that they do not claim to know too much or to have an expertise that they lack. There is a principle of comparative advantage that needs to be respected, in this context and in others. Boards have a certain kind of expertise, and should have a long-term perspective; faculty have an obvious comparative advantage in academic areas; and presidents/deans have a comparative advantage in putting all the pieces together, developing coherent long-run plans, and linking resource requirements to institutional priorities.

11. Suppose that the faculty representative has a different view on a subject than the faculty at large has expressed. What is the faculty representative to do—express a contrary position or simply repress his or her own thoughts? See the Kelley Report, "The Governing of Princeton University: Final Report of the Special Committee on the Structure of the University," April 1970, including the appendix materials, for a cogent discussion of this often misunderstood issue. A far better approach is to gain faculty perspectives by consulting faculty on the home campus in some other way and/or including on the board one or more respected faculty members from other institutions.

12. Judith Shapiro, former president of Barnard, points out that having faculty serve as *non-voting* members of boards can be useful in, among other things,

138 Chapter 4

The Faculty Appointment Process—
Criteria and Decision-Making Authority

This is a second area in which major progress has been made in codifying a set of principles and practices that protect the ability of educational institutions to engage in the unfettered pursuit of ideas that is necessary for both excellent research and high-quality teaching. Faculty have an essential role to play in selecting new colleagues, evaluating the professional competence of peers on an ongoing basis, and providing proper procedures for ensuring that individuals are not dismissed for wrong reasons. Specific organizational mechanisms for discharging this key set of responsibilities will vary by institution (and both our historical overview and the case studies illustrate some effective processes and procedures).

Whatever the mechanism(s) chosen, no reputable college or university today would fail to respect the freedom of faculty members to speak their minds, verbally and in print, *so long as they adhere to professional norms.* The italics in the previous sentence emphasize that this core freedom of utterance does not mean that faculty can say or do absolutely anything that comes to mind. Not at all. Matthew W. Finkin and Robert C. Post explain cogently that freedom of thought and expression in the academy is part of a social compact that derives from societal needs and is tied inextricably to responsibility to adhere to professional standards. The unqualified use of the word *rights* can be highly misleading.[13]

As our historical overview reminds us, these core principles/ protections have by no means always been in place in this

---

promoting friendly relations between boards and faculties. Even so, we suspect that on some issues of both confidentiality and willingness to speak frankly, a proper separation of roles remains appropriate.

13. See Finkin and Post, *For the Common Good: Principles of American Academic Freedom* (New Haven, CT: Yale University Press, 2009).

country, and they certainly are not accepted worldwide today. The AAUP and numerous college and university associations deserve great credit for having accomplished so much in clarifying and enforcing the absolutely central faculty role in ensuring that this selection/review process works as it should. Occasional outrages occur, and backsliding is, as we have noted, always possible. This is yet another instance in which eternal vigilance is in order. Also, there are ongoing issues to debate (e.g., the murky line between the right to be outrageous and impermissible hate speech).[14] There is still more progress to be made, and four specific questions deserve to be addressed:

1. First, is there a role for the president/provost/dean in working with faculty, indeed in leading them, to upgrade faculty quality when this is needed? Our answer is emphatically "yes." History is replete with examples of how much strong leadership from "on high" can accomplish; all four of our case studies illustrate this fundamental point.[15] The most successful colleges and universities pride themselves on enjoying a strong partnership between administrators and faculty in rejecting candidates for promotion who are not

14. Today, most "free speech" controversies seem to involve the right of students to speak out, often collectively, on sensitive issues such as legalization of marijuana, as well as on highly charged political questions such as Israeli–Palestinian disputes. See Jennifer Medina, "Advocacy Group Sues 4 Universities in Challenge to Policies It Says Curb Free Speech," *New York Times,* online edition, July 1, 2014, www.nytimes.com/2014/07/02/us/advocacy-group-sues-4-universities-in-challenge-to-policies-it-says-curb-free-speech.html?_r=0, accessed July 1, 2014.

15. See also the results achieved by Frederick Terman at Stanford, some grumbling notwithstanding. As dean of the School of Engineering and later as university provost, Terman promoted the expansion of the STEM fields (science, technology, engineering, and mathematics) and created the intellectual and financial conditions that helped transform Stanford into a world-class university. See C. Stewart Gillmor, *Fred Terman at Stanford: Building a Discipline, a University, and Silicon Valley* (Stanford, CA: Stanford University Press, 2004).

up to high standards, in tying advancements in rank and salary to stellar performance, and in insisting that searches for new faculty aim high enough. To achieve good results, we think there is much to be said for appointing, not electing, departmental chairs—albeit after close consultation with departmental faculty. Elected departmental chairs can end up protecting mediocrity in situations in which stronger leadership is required at the departmental level. We would also argue against the notion that the chairmanship should rotate automatically to the next person in line. Good leadership is hard to find and should supplant a misguided commitment to evenhandedness or seniority.

2. Second, are our colleges and universities doing a good enough job of post-tenure review? The answer is surely "sometimes yes, and sometimes no." The University of California has been a leader in insisting that all faculty need and, for that matter, *deserve,* periodic peer-to-peer reviews of their strengths and weaknesses. The end of mandatory retirement in the 1990s, the aging of faculties, and the use of phased retirement incentives to encourage institutional renewal make this responsibility much more important than it was in days gone by. It is far easier for faculty to accept the desirability of such post-tenure reviews if they are assured, as they should be, that they have to be the active evaluators, and that they are protected against foolish abuses of the information obtained through such processes in subsequent decisions concerning salaries, perks, and even dismissals.

3. Third, are we doing an adequate job of handling the increasing numbers of NTT teachers, whether they are called faculty or not? The answer once again varies widely, especially vis-à-vis different types of contingent faculty, and some real progress is being made right now on this front; but we suspect that there is more to be done in thinking through

Faculty Roles Today and Tomorrow 141

sensible policies and in regularizing procedures. Important efforts are underway at a number of institutions to improve and regularize procedures in this area, and we discuss (later in this chapter) the case for establishing a "professional teaching staff."

4. Fourth, does the increasing use of online technologies, which often cuts across departmental lines, and the growing value of inspired uses of technology, suggest that criteria for appointments and advancements should be reviewed to see if adequate attention is being paid to creative contributions to pedagogy? We suspect that the answer to this question is "yes."

The Role of the Faculty in Giving Advice of All Kinds

There are ample historical precedents, going back at least to the early 1900s, of formal provision for consultation with faculty on essentially all subjects. (See, for instance, the example provided by our case study of the University of California, where this role of the faculty was recognized explicitly in the 1920s.) But history also makes clear that for a long time much depended on presidential attitudes—on the extent to which presidents in fact relied on such channels. We have seen, for example, the difference between the uses made of faculty advice by Presidents Sproul and Kerr at the University of California. Sproul's autocratic tendencies led him to make use of faculty counsel only when it was absolutely necessary (for example, in the Great Depression of the 1930s). Kerr's Quaker background and experience as a mediator led him, in sharp contrast, to consult and consult and consult.

The highly imprecise specifications of faculty roles in shaping university policies (from the earliest times) led to efforts by the AAUP's Committee T, starting in 1917, to claim legitimacy for significant faculty roles in many areas of decision-making, extending well beyond the faculty appointment and advancement process.[16] The 1940 *Statement of Principles on Academic Freedom and Tenure,* adopted by the Association of American Colleges along with the AAUP, "effectively institutionalized tenure as a safeguard for academic freedom at most American colleges and universities," but it did not do more than this, and it left open the many questions about broader faculty roles that are still being debated.[17] The powerful market position of faculty in the heady years of the strong post–World War II demand for faculty, coupled with the pressures exerted by the student rebellions of the late 1960s, led to more regularized procedures at many institutions. (Note, for example, the creation of new consultative machinery at two of our case-study institutions, Macalester College and Princeton.)

In these years, there was a definite push by faculty at many institutions, and certainly by the AAUP as an organization, to gain a prominent place for faculty "at the table" when issues of all kinds affecting them and "their" institutions are being discussed and, in some cases, negotiated through collective bargaining. As already noted, in 1966 three associations—the AAUP, the Association of Governing Boards (AGB), and the American Council of Education (ACE)—jointly drafted the *Statement on Government of Colleges and Universities,* which recognized, albeit in very general terms, the desirability of affording faculty

16. For a detailed historical account of AAUP activities in this area, and of responses to these efforts, see Larry G. Gerber, "Professionalization as the Basis for Academic Freedom and Faculty Governance," *Journal of Academic Freedom* 1 (2010), online journal of the AAUP, www.aaup.org/sites/default/files/files/JAF/2010%20JAF/Gerber.pdf, accessed July 10, 2014. This article is valuable in providing insights into the thinking behind AAUP efforts over many decades, but it needs to be understood as written by a proponent of extensive faculty participation in governance at all levels. In addition, Gerber's recent book, *The Rise and Decline of Faculty Governance: Professionalization and the Modern American University* (Baltimore: Johns Hopkins University Press, 2014), provides a valuable historical overview of the long sweep of faculty governance. We respect his scholarship but disagree with his interpretive framework.

17. Gerber (2010), p. 15.

a major voice in governance. In many areas of governance (including, for example, strategic planning), the 1966 *Statement on Government* calls for "joint effort" among faculty, administrators, and trustees. But the lack of specificity in the agreed-upon language led the AAUP to develop its own clarifying policy documents in, for example, its 1972 statement, *The Role of the Faculty in Budgetary and Salary Matters*.[18]

Although administrators and trustees at many colleges and universities have welcomed faculty participation in many areas of decision-making (and thus have given faculty the "voice at the table" that they had long sought), there has been no widespread institutionalization of faculty authority outside the basic areas of faculty appointments/advancements and responsibility for maintaining academic standards. The extensive opportunity for faculty to "have a say" in matters of all kinds is illustrated vividly by the list of no fewer than thirty-three standing faculty committees at Berkeley, which cover topics of every kind, including admissions, student life, educational policy, computing, the operations of the library, faculty awards, and university–emeriti relations.[19] Patterns naturally vary across institutions, and there are also innumerable ad hoc committees. The impact of faculty advice varies, as it should, with the relevance of faculty expertise to the matter at hand—and also with myriad idiosyncratic factors affecting individual campuses.[20]

18. Ibid., p. 19. See also *The Role of the Faculty in Budgetary and Salary Matters*, Reports and Publications, Washington, DC, AAUP, www.aaup.org/report/role-faculty-budgetary-and-salary-matters, accessed July 8, 2014.

19. See "About the Committees," Academic Senate, Berkeley, Regents of the University of California, 2014, http://academic-senate.berkeley.edu/senate-committees, accessed November 1, 2014.

20. In the investment area, Stanford recently decided to divest holdings in coal companies after active faculty participation in reviewing the issues at stake. See "Stanford to Divest from Coal Companies," *Stanford News*, May 6, 2014, available at http://news.stanford.edu/news/2014/may/divest-coal-trustees-050714 .html. See also David Oxtoby, "Divestiture Is Nothing but a Distraction," *Chronicle of Higher Education*, September 18, 2014, http://chronicle.com/article/Divestiture-Is-Nothing-but-a/148789?cid=megamenu, accessed September 18,

The key point is that in almost every area, faculty have an opportunity, collectively as well as individually, to weigh in—whether they choose to use it or not. It can be argued that in some situations, faculty collectively have not just an opportunity to be heard, but an *obligation* to defend core principles. As this text is being drafted (in early July 2014), there is a real question as to why faculty collectively have not been more front and center in addressing the issues of openness and civility raised by the plethora of apparently controversial commencement speakers who have chosen not to speak in the face of protests by students and others (including some faculty). Here is an instance in which a firm voice, expressed by the faculty collectively, would have served institutional purposes very well indeed. Odd as it may seem to those concerned about too much faculty power, both sizable parts of the academic community and the public at large seem to be more troubled by the lack of clear expressions of faculty sentiments on core principles (and by a general tendency for the broad "middle" of campus communities to be overly passive in response to protests) than by concerns about faculty overreaching.[21]

2014. Trustees by no means always follow the recommendations of campus-based groups in deciding such issues, including how to vote on proxies. See President Goheen's comment on the importance of maintaining final trustee authority over such matters in his Annual Report for 1970: Robert F. Goheen, *Princeton University: The President's Report,* 1970. More generally, it is instructive to note that even the AAUP-inspired 1966 *Statement on Government* recognizes that in "'exceptional circumstances and for reasons communicated to the faculty,' a president (or, by analogy, a provost, dean, or department head) might reverse a faculty judgment if an entrenched majority of faculty have become implacable defenders of an unproductive status quo" (Gerber [2010], p. 18).

21. One of us (Bowen) spoke on this subject at the Haverford commencement in May 2014, and his views, criticizing both the tone/approach of student protestors and the failure of an invited recipient of an honorary degree to come to commencement and deal directly with the protestors, have been widely disseminated. See, for example, Susan Snyder, "Haverford College Commencement Speaker Lambastes Students," *Inquirer,* May 18, 2014. At one college involved in disputes of this kind (Smith), large numbers of faculty did, in the aftermath of the decision by Christine Lagarde not to accept an honorary degree offered by Smith, express strong support for the president's position regretting this decision.

The subject of intercollegiate athletics is sui generis, too complicated to go into in any detail here, but noteworthy, we believe, as an example of the immense challenges facing even well-governed institutions. There is almost always a faculty committee on athletics. Faculties have felt free to comment on compromises with academic standards, and they have had a real effect in some egregious situations (such as the need to address the blatant disregard for meeting minimal requirements that occurred at the University of North Carolina [UNC]–Chapel Hill).[22] The UNC experience is, however, an outlier. In general, faculty have been unsuccessful in their efforts to reign in abuses in intercollegiate sports—in spite of the clear disconnect between highly questionable practices and academic values. This is not, of course, a "faculty" failure as much as it is a reflection of the power of entrenched interests in what are money-driven enterprises, coupled with an understandable reluctance of most university leaders, including trustees/regents, to expend valuable capital fighting with ferocious, single-minded adversaries ("wrestlers are different . . . wrestlers are fighters") when they have so many other important battles to wage.[23]

22. Mention should also be made of Professor William C. Dowling's determined, but ultimately unsuccessful, effort to right the balance between the emphases on intercollegiate athletics and academics at Rutgers (following in the footsteps of no less distinguished an academic than Milton Friedman). See William C. Dowling, *Confessions of a Spoil Sport: My Life and Hard Times Fighting Sports Corruption at an Old Eastern University* (University Park: Penn State University Press, 2007). Nationally, the work of the Drake Group, which "aims to defend academic integrity in higher education from the corrosive aspects of commercialized college sports," is perhaps the best-known faculty effort to have an effect on athletics policies—but we do not have the impression that they have had much impact. See http://thedrakegroup.org.

23. The quotation comes from a comment made to President Harold Shapiro at Princeton by Trustee Donald Rumsfeld when Princeton attempted (ultimately unsuccessfully) to cut back its support of intercollegiate wrestling. See James L. Shulman and William G. Bowen, *The Game of Life* (Princeton, NJ: Princeton University Press, 2002), pp. xxix–xxx of paperback edition.

Putting to one side the near-universal use of standing committees to consider recurring questions ranging from admissions to athletics, many institutions have learned that it can be helpful to have an established structure in place that gives individuals a "place to go" to express displeasure on matters of any kind or simply to ask for clarification. Faculty senates, councils, and campus-wide bodies of various kinds exist to meet this need. Easy as it is for busy deans and faculty to be impatient with such machinery, it is wise to remember the old bromide "An ounce of prevention is worth a pound of cure." Picking up the pieces after an unnecessarily rancorous, confused, and divisive battle can be far more time-consuming than patiently attending calmer meetings intended to find common ground when there is still time to do so, or at least to be sure that the reasons for taking a particular position are clear. "Giving reasons," a wise student of governance once explained, "is the ultimate test of accountability."

Defining faculty roles in this area is far from straightforward, however. There is abundant evidence that ambiguity concerning the optimal degree of faculty involvement—in, for example, decisions as wide-ranging as the establishment of affiliated institutional relationships and real estate development— can lead to controversy. Recent examples include the debate at Yale over the creation of the Yale–NUS (National University of Singapore) College, the objection raised by faculty at New York University to the university's plan for the redevelopment of space in downtown Manhattan, and faculty complaints at the University of Michigan about the proliferation of "image-building" in non-academic areas and the use of bonuses and salary supplements to reward high-performing administrators.

One source of frustration for all involved in such debates is the difficulty in knowing when enough consultation is enough. There are also often charges by faculty and students that administrators have just been going through the motions in "seeming to listen"; such complaints are frequently followed by the countervailing assertion by administrators that faculty and students fail to understand the distinction between listening and agreeing. We see no formulaic way of resolving such differences in perspective. Yet again, there is no substitute for the exercise of common sense.

History does teach us, however, that certain general rules apply. In times of genuine crisis (Berkeley in the mid-1960s), there is no substitute for some accepted means of ascertaining the *legitimacy* of collective expressions of faculty views. Having in place machinery for formal consultation ahead of time can be a meaningful advantage. In this regard, established secret-ballot methods of electing faculty representatives are of great importance—they can ensure that it is not just the most vocal who are heard. Even so, it is notoriously difficult to obtain anything approaching a common view from a heterogeneous set of faculty members (note the lack of a strong consensus view by the University of California Senate at the time that Proposition 209 was facing a vote).[24] Finally, experience teaches us that, in advance of real "shootouts," it is very useful for the community at large to have a reasonably clear understanding of where, at the end of the day, the locus of authority rests for decisions of various kinds; there should not be too much ambiguity.[25]

24. Proposition 209, the so-called California Civil Rights Initiative, was a state-wide proposition approved by the voters in November 1996. It amended the state constitution to prohibit public institutions from discriminating on the basis of race, sex, or ethnicity in the areas of public employment, contracting, and education. Proposition 209 effectively banned the proactive use of race in college and university admissions.

25. Materials supporting these propositions are presented in chapter 3 (and in some of our case studies). See especially the discussion of the handling of the ROTC matter at Princeton at the time of the Vietnam War. It is very important that presidents avoid the creation of what Lawrence Bacow has called "blocking coalitions." As Bacow points out: "When presidents really fail, it is not because

Still, there is no escaping the inherent tension between, on the one hand, expending the energy needed to manage processes intended to ensure that faculty (and others) have a regularized voice at the table and, on the other hand, avoiding consultative machinery that simply wastes time or that forces people with serious work to do to listen to too much uninteresting talk. Adlai Stevenson once put it this way: "The sound of tireless voices is the price we pay for the right to hear the music of our own opinions." Stevenson then added this wise observation: "There is also, it seems to me, a moment at which democracy must prove its capacity to act. Every man has a right to be heard; but no man has the right to strangle democracy [or decision-making in an academic setting] with a single set of vocal chords."[26]

Robert Goheen, like Clark Kerr, was prescient, and in the immediate aftermath of the successful use at Princeton of the newly established CPUC to diffuse campus conflicts related to the Vietnam War, expressed this "longer range concern [that] has no easy solution":

> Active participation in the affairs of the Council and its committees puts inordinate demands upon the time of the senior University officers, faculty members, students, staff and alumni involved. . . . The price of such service to the University can be high. . . . How long such participation can be sustained . . . is uncertain. . . . Of course, should the University be entering calmer, easier seas, and should that respite last, the demands placed upon the Council and its members will lessen. . . . In such periods, the CPUC perhaps might serve the community

---

they fail on a single issue. Rather, they have clumsily stepped on enough toes over time that blocking coalitions become far easier to form" (Bacow to Bowen, June 26, 2014, personal e-mail correspondence).

26. Stevenson, speech given in New York City, August 28, 1952, in Walter Johnson, ed., *The Papers of Adlai E. Stevenson*, vol. 4 (Boston: Little Brown, 1974), p. 63.

best by meeting only occasionally. . . . But in times when the winds of change blow hard . . . the Council will always be confronting fresh tasks, and election to it will be no sinecure.[27]

Goheen was surely right when he went on to suggest that a simple way of minimizing unnecessary frustration over "too many meetings" is for the convener to be quick to cancel any that seem unnecessary or unlikely to be productive. No one (or almost no one!) has ever complained about not having to go to a predictably boring meeting. Since the early 1970s, much thought has been given at many places (including Princeton) to ways of preventing excessive demands on faculty time in the service of consultation.[28]

More generally, the challenging economic circumstances of the 1970s and subsequent decades led to various calls for a more "efficient," business-like approach to college and university governance. Especially noteworthy was the 1996 publication by the AGB of a report titled *Reviewing the Academic Presidency: Stronger Leadership for Tougher Times*. Some have interpreted this report as a direct attack on collegial decision-making and a call for a more corporate model of management in which a college's or university's chief executive officer "must resist academia's insatiable appetite for the kind of excessive consultation that can bring an institution to a standstill."[29]

We have no way of assessing whether there has in fact been a general shift in attitudes toward consultation in response to the concerns expressed in the AGB report. There is, however, absolutely no doubt about the increasing focus of everyone on decisions (and hence on the locus of decision-making authority) pertaining to overall levels of faculty staffing, the composition of

27. See Goheen, p. 18.
28. Evan Radcliffe, "Faculty Adopts Thompson Time-Saving Proposals," *Daily Princetonian* 99, no. 109, November 4, 1975.
29. Gerber (2010), p. 22.

the teaching staff, and the circumstances of the rapidly increasing number of NTT faculty—the topics to which we turn now.

The Role of Faculty in Staffing Decisions—and the Rise of Non-Tenure-Track Faculty (the New Majority)

The AAUP was right in deciding that the financial retrenchments of the 1970s meant that the most pressing governance issue of that decade, and of succeeding ones, would be the role of faculty in influencing, nay controlling, staffing decisions. In budgetary matters, some institutions—especially those in privileged positions and not facing the need to make drastic shifts in the mix of teaching staff—have enjoyed marked success in utilizing mechanisms such as the Priorities Committee at Princeton to include faculty prominently in discussions, and in de facto decision-making, about how to allocate resources. But it is essential to recognize that administrators have been actively involved in such processes and normally have been "at the head of the table." Trustees have, of course, retained final authority over budgetary decisions.

A critical reason that faculty have not been given more final authority over budgetary matters is that they are clearly interested parties when difficult choices have to be made regarding conflicting claims on scarce resources—between, for example, claims for more faculty support, financial aid for graduate and undergraduate students, library acquisitions, and investments in technology and infrastructure. Increasingly, prospective students and their families have also been seen as interested parties when trade-offs have had to be made between increasing tuition and cutting budgets. Faculty expertise is essential in arriving at wise decisions—on academic matters certainly—but it would be hard to defend giving faculty anything approaching final authority over matters in which their self-interest is so clearly involved.

This proposition holds across the board, at all times and in all places, but it is even more consequential in settings in which major changes in the mix of teaching personnel are taking place—as is the case at many institutions today. A quick review of "big picture" facts is in order.[30]

- In 1969, tenured and tenure-track faculty accounted for over three-quarters of all faculty (78.3 percent); in 2009, tenured and tenure-track faculty accounted for just over one-third of all faculty (33.5 percent). As many people have noted, the ratio simply flipped.
- Among NTT faculty, both full-time and part-time staff have increased, but part-timers have increased faster (by over 400 percent between 1970 and 2003).
- The ratio of tenure-track to NTT faculty varies by sector, and increases in the relative number and scale of NTT faculty at community colleges (where NTT faculty are especially numerous) have affected the overall numbers; but NTT faculty increased markedly relative to tenure-track faculty across the board and are now a majority in all sectors, in-

30. Reliable data on staffing patterns are notoriously difficult to obtain. Definitions vary widely, and self-reporting is far from reliable (not so much because institutions "cheat" or deliberately mislead as because of the lack of clarity in defining categories and applying the definitions that exist). Scholars who have focused on these questions, as our colleagues Michael McPherson and Charles Kurose at the Spencer Foundation are doing now, are very cautious about putting great weight on the seeming precision of data from the Integrated Postsecondary Education Data System (IPEDS). See also the commentary by John C. Cross and Edie Goldenberg on these questions in *Off-Track Profs: Nontenured Teachers in Higher Education* (Cambridge, MA: MIT Press, 2009), where they demonstrate that colleges and universities do not systematically track these data and that much that is shared with the Department of Education is largely guesswork that creates a "fictitious precision" (p. 23). The data summarized in the text are from Adrianna Kezar and Daniel Maxey, "The Changing Faculty and Student Success: National Trends for Faculty Composition over Time," Rossier Pullias Center for Higher Education, University of Southern California, Los Angeles, 2012, especially p. 5. The reader is warned again not to put too much weight on speciously precise figures; but the general pattern is unmistakable.

cluding research universities and comprehensives. Although much less of a factor at liberal arts colleges, NTT faculty have long been an important part of the teaching faculty, especially (but not only) at small independent colleges in metropolitan areas and among proximate institutions operating within consortia.

This shift in the mix of the teaching staff is truly *revolutionary* (the right word here, as it often is not) and shows no signs of abating. It is hard to predict how far this shift will go. In a forthcoming publication, Gary Saul Morson and Morton O. Schapiro at Northwestern suggest that by 2040 "only around 10% of positions will be held by tenured and tenure-track professors."[31] We are not at all sure the decline in the relative number of tenure positions will go this far, but it could. (This unmistakable shift in the mix of teaching staff should not be confused with often misleading allegations that faculty generally are being replaced by administrators and other non-teachers—a different issue, and a far more complicated and less clear-cut proposition.[32])

The forces driving the shift in the mix of teaching staff are readily identifiable. First, there has been the need felt by many

31. See Morson and Schapiro, eds., *The Fabulous Future? America and the World in 2040* (Evanston, IL: Northwestern University Press, forthcoming).

32. For a statement of the claim that there has been a decided shift toward the employment of administrators rather than faculty members, see Michael J. Cripps, "Essay Calls for New Model Job of Faculty Member Administrator," *Inside Higher Ed,* May 12, 2014. The data reported in this essay are, however, subject to quite different interpretations, and our colleague, Michael McPherson (writing to Bowen on May 12, 2014, in a personal e-mail) points out that in fact the trend over the past thirty-five years has been toward a decline in the number of non-professional staff and an increase in the "other professional" categories. The growing number of other professionals includes many people working in support functions, including as computer specialists. This is exactly the same kind of trend that has been evident throughout the economy as people in higher-skilled service jobs have displaced clerks. It also represents a shift away from faculty carrying out various functions such as counseling and academic advising. McPherson points out that the category of "executive/administrative/managerial" as a share of all staff has changed relatively little.

institutions to curb increases in staffing costs and thus to hire fewer tenured faculty when vacancies exist; tenure-track faculty are generally paid more, enjoy costlier benefits, and teach less than other staff.[33] (Inspection of available data suggests that, overwhelmingly, NTT faculty have been hired when there have been new positions to fill; the aggregate number of tenure-track faculty has not gone down and has even increased modestly.[34]) Second, the end of mandatory retirement has undoubtedly contributed to the reluctance of many institutions to take on what amount to fixed costs for an indeterminate period; by adding NTT faculty, institutions have gained flexibility and greater control over future staffing patterns. Third, increases in research support in research-intensive universities have often led to the hiring of more NTT faculty as tenure-track faculty have bought their way out of teaching commitments to devote more time to research.

There is, in addition, a supply side to this equation: the increasing glut of individuals seeking teaching positions (because of the increase in doctoral recipients, combined with the drop-off in demand for traditionally trained candidates) has made it far easier than it would have been in earlier days

33. Lawrence S. Bacow points out that the appeal of lower-cost teaching resources today has a strong historical precedent in the "cheap labor" argument for using tutors in early American colleges. See chapter 2.

34. See US Department of Education, Institute of Education Sciences, National Center for Education Statistics, http://nces.ed.gov/. We are indebted to Charles Kurose at the Spencer Foundation for having reviewed carefully the available data. According to his analysis, these data are about Title IV institutions that existed in IPEDS in both 2002 and 2011. According to these data, over this time period the number of tenured or untenured but tenure-track faculty actually did increase by 4.6 percent, or about 20,000 positions. But both of these figures are much smaller than the figures for non-tenure-track (NTT) faculty—over this time period the number of NTT faculty grew by 31.8 percent, or about 223,000 positions. This suggests that the percentage of all faculty who have tenure or are on the tenure track has been declining not because the number of positions has been declining, but because the number of NTT faculty positions has been growing so much faster.

to make the staffing substitutions that have occurred. There is also another factor that has not had great quantitative effects as yet, but could have a considerable impact going forward. We refer to the "unbundling" of aspects of teaching as a result of MOOCs and other online technologies—which can imply less need than before for tenured and tenure-track faculty to take responsibility for all aspects of a course.[35]

The broad effects on faculty roles in governance of this dramatic shift in the mix of teaching staff are still being sorted out. It is clear, in any event, that the power of tenure-track faculty has been diminished simply as a result of the decline in their relative numbers. Markets are unrelenting, and the decline in the demand for tenure-track faculty relative to other teaching staff that started in the early 1970s has taken its toll—albeit perhaps more in its effects on faculty mix than in its effects on the roles and expectations of the remaining tenure-track faculty. However, on some campuses the pressures on administrators to yield to any new requests by current or prospective tenure-track faculty for a "stronger voice" have surely abated as the demand for tenure-track faculty has declined markedly in the decades since the "Golden Age" of the 1960s.

The status of NTT faculty is very much in flux. Adjunct faculty (generally defined as part-timers, paid per course) have, not surprisingly, unionized in some places. We expect this process to continue across all sectors of higher education,

<hr/>

35. For discussions regarding "unbundling," see William G. Bowen, "Academia Online: Musings (Some Unconventional)," Stafford Little Lecture, Princeton University, October 14, 2013, pp. 3–5, and William G. Bowen, *Higher Education in the Digital Age* (Princeton, NJ: Princeton University Press, 2013), p. 66. According to a recent ACE report (funded by the Gates Foundation), unbundling is occurring in "myriad ways," and the uses of technology, rather than accelerating the decline of the "complete scholar," can help integrate teaching and research in ways that strengthen student learning. See Colleen Flaherty, "ACE Studies on Faculty Roles and Business Models," *Inside Higher Ed*, July 17, 2014, available at https://www.insidehighered.com/quicktakes/2014/07/17/ace-studies-faculty-roles-and-business-models.

especially as the American Federation of Teachers (AFT) and the Service Employees International Union (SEIU) accelerate their already aggressive efforts.[36] All is not smooth sailing for the unionization movement, however. At the April 2014 annual conference of the National Center for the Study of Collective Bargaining in Higher Education and the Professions, there was frank acknowledgment by union leaders of some opposition from tenure-track professors who do not want to see their numbers diminished or their role in governance diluted; also, some contingent faculty seem to want to "pass" as tenured faculty and thus resist being labeled as anything except "professors."[37]

This already muddled situation is muddled all the more by the heterogeneity of the large and rather amorphous NTT group. Sarah Turner, professor of economics and chair of her department at the University of Virginia, thinks it is helpful to separate out a group she calls "master teachers," who are full-time, receive benefits and, unlike transients, teach on a continuing basis. These master teachers have much heavier teaching loads than tenure-track faculty, but are not expected to produce publishable research. Many of them could do other things, but often prefer "life in the classroom." If carefully chosen, these individuals can be highly effective, especially in teaching basic courses, and, Turner points out, they are far less expensive than other staffing options—including

36. See, for example, the success of the SEIU in unionizing adjunct faculty at Northeastern, Lesley University, and Tufts in the Boston area (*Chronicle of Higher Education*, May 16, 2014). The SEIU has also had notable success in Washington, DC.

37. Peter Schmidt, "Union Efforts on Behalf of Adjuncts Meet Resistance within Faculties' Ranks," *Chronicle of Higher Education*, April 9, 2014. Michael McPherson tells us (in his April 12, 2014, e-mail) that he is reminded of the literature on businesses run as cooperatives, like the kibbutzim in Israel. When such businesses expand, they should, on egalitarian principles, add more partners. But that would mean a dilution of existing worker–owners' property value, so there is a tendency to hire workers instead (e.g., Thai laborers in Israel).

bottom line educational priorities demonstrate!!

not only tenure-track faculty but also graduate TAs—when proper account is taken of required tuition payments as well as stipends.[38]

Perhaps the most rigorous study of the teaching effectiveness of full-time NTT faculty who are routinely reappointed (and are akin to Turner's "master teachers") has been carried out at Northwestern University by Professor David Figlio and his colleagues.[39] This study focuses on a wide gamut of courses taken during a student's first term at Northwestern and examines differences between tenure-track faculty and "contingent" faculty in their effects on lasting student learning (measured by subsequent course elections and performance). The study finds "consistent evidence that students learn relatively more from contingent faculty in their first-term courses" (abstract). The results are especially pronounced for Northwestern's mid-level and less academically qualified students. Of course it is

measure ?? X?
?

38. Turner to Bowen, July 8, 2014, personal phone conversation. Other sub-categories include the occasional visiting professor who is well qualified by any standard to teach a particular course (e.g., the Federal Reserve Bank person who teaches money and banking). There is also the larger group of ad hoc, temporary, part-time teachers who are paid by the course. Decisions to hire these part-timers are often impromptu and incremental, driven by particular needs of the moment, such as the need to replace someone who goes on leave, but it can then be highly tempting to keep such (usually) conscientious and (often) overqualified people in place. These categories do not have a great deal in common, except for the existence of serious concerns about equity and fairness; almost all institutions are wrestling with the question of how to manage/govern them. Even at an elite liberal arts institution such as Williams College, we are told (by Michael McPherson, who was a dean at Williams) that there are NTT teachers in fields such as K–12 teaching who don't fit readily into any established staffing structure (McPherson to Bowen, January 29, 2014, personal e-mail). At Columbia, faculty and students have protested the university's decision not to renew the contracts of two noted NTT professors in sociomedical sciences because the faculty missed obligations to raise 80 percent of their salaries through outside grants (www.insidehighered.com/news/2014/03/10/columbia-criticized-not-renewing-long-term-professors-over-their-failure-pay, accessed September 19, 2014).

39. David N. Figlio, Morton O. Schapiro, and Kevin B. Soter, "Are Tenure Track Professors Better Teachers?" NBER Working Paper 19406, September 2013, www.nber.org/papers/w19406, revised August 28, 2014, accessed November 2, 2014.

important to recognize that these results apply only to the effectiveness of contingent faculty in beginning courses and not to the effectiveness of various sets of faculty in stimulating and overseeing independent work. Still, the study warns against cavalier assumptions that NTT faculty are poor substitutes for tenure-track faculty in teaching introductory material. Quite the contrary.

There are other examples of efforts to engage full-time NTT faculty in regularized teaching responsibilities. Rutgers University, New Jersey's flagship public university, offers one model. Full-time NTT professors at Rutgers are part of an AAUP–AFT bargaining unit that achieved important goals in their 2014 contract. Career titles have been established for teaching positions, explicitly non-renewable positions have been abolished, five-year appointments will be the norm, and advance notice of non-reappointment is required. These NTT professors comprise 29 percent of full-time faculty, and number more than eight hundred. There are, however, another thirteen hundred part-time adjuncts at Rutgers who are in a separate AAUP–AFT bargaining unit and are not affected by this contract.[40]

The University Senate Faculty Affairs Committee at the University of Maryland has recommended a plan that would create regularized promotional opportunities for NTT faculty. The committee's recommendations would eliminate "faculty research assistant," and "research associate" positions, with faculty now holding such titles to transfer to new positions on clearly defined professional ladders. The committee is also charging the Office of Faculty Affairs with developing stan-

40. See Rutgers AAUP–AFT, "Full-Time Faculty Non-Tenure Track," New Brunswick, NJ, 2014, www.rutgersaaup.org/members/full-time-faculty-non-tenure-track, accessed November 2, 2014. See also "Rutgers Full-Time Adjuncts Win Long-Term Contracts," *Inside Higher Ed,* February 4, 2014, www.insidehighered.com/quicktakes/2014/02/04/rutgers-full-time-adjuncts-win-long-term-contracts, accessed February 4, 2014.

dards and methods of evaluation, which are to be an integral part of the review and promotion process.[41]

At the University of Michigan, there is an elaborate set of provisions governing the status of approximately fifteen hundred lecturers. Arrangements for matters of all kinds, including appointments, salaries, benefits, duties, and management rights are spelled out in a 183-page collective bargaining agreement between the Regents of the University of Michigan and the "Lecturers' Employee Organization" (LEO).[42] Included in this bargaining unit are all NTT instructional staff; excluded are all tenure-track faculty, clerical staff, and supervisors. There are nine titles for NTT staff, an explicit explanation of which classes of lecturers enjoy a "presumption of renewal," detailed salary information, and many, many other provisions. This is the most elaborate set of arrangements for NTT staff of which we are aware, and it deserves careful study by other institutions contemplating the development of structures of this kind. Needless to say, such structures can be either the result of collective bargaining agreements, as this one is, or the result of actions initiated by the institution on its own.

A more extreme approach to the emergence of "new-style" faculty is found at the online college of Southern New Hampshire University (SNHU), which is avowedly designing a "new template" for its faculty. The college has relied on a stable of twenty-seven hundred adjunct instructors to staff its online courses in a year-long pilot, and it was prepared to hire forty-five full-time faculty by the end of the summer of 2014. These faculty will not conform to the classic model. They will

41. Jon Banister, "Non-Tenure-Track Faculty Framework Moves Forward," www.diamondbackonline.com, February 25, 2014, www.diamondbackonline .com/news/campus/article_e1d63b0e-9ddf-11e3-8dc7-001a4bcf6878.html, accessed November 2, 2014.

42. See www.hr.umich.edu/leo/agreement.pdf. We are indebted to Professor Joel Slemrod at the University of Michigan for guiding us to relevant documents.

work remotely, not on a campus. They will not be encouraged to publish, and if they "perish" it will be, according to an SNHU faculty member, because they fail to provide frequent, helpful feedback to students. None of these faculty will be on a tenure track (all will hold annual appointments), but the chief academic officer says that the assumption is that faculty will be with the college for a long time unless "something goes particularly wrong."

It does not sound as if these faculty will have a significant role in any aspect of governance, and they cannot be expected to exercise a significant check on administrative authority. SNHU says it believes that all faculty should have the freedom "to express themselves on controversial issues without fear of retaliation." It is unclear, however, what machinery, if any, is in place to protect faculty expressions of controversial views in this setting—just as it is unclear how, in practice, accrediters will monitor the need for some set of continuing faculty to demonstrate the required commitment to ensure that students meet their in-class and out-of-class responsibilities. It could well be that, as one faculty member put it, "we are the canaries in the coal mine of higher education."[43]

The value of canaries notwithstanding (and it is real), we are skeptical that the SNHU online college model has applicability to the need for modified faculty governance structures at institutions that have a campus and that use a blend of online and face-to-face instruction. And, of course, it remains to be seen how effective the new template at SNHU's online college proves to be in its own, very special, setting. We believe that the incipient developments at institutions such as the University of Maryland and the University of Michigan

43. This commentary and all of the quotations in this paragraph are from Steve Kolowich, "Southern New Hampshire U. Designs a New Template for Faculty Jobs," *Chronicle of Higher Education*, May 8, 2014, http://chronicle.com/article/Southern-New-Hampshire-U/146443, accessed May 9, 2014.

need to dispense, for the most part, with NTT faculty!
non academically speaking!

are more relevant to defining roles for teaching staff at colleges and universities in general.

There is, in our view, an important opportunity at this particular stage in the evolution of faculty roles for new thinking about structures. The benefits of new thinking could be substantial. We hearken back to the development of professional research staff structures in the aftermath of the post–World War II explosion of sponsored research in science and engineering (see the Princeton case study, as one example among many). What was clear then was that research universities needed to rely on significant numbers of highly qualified individuals who could not be accommodated within the regular faculty ranks without totally unbalancing the disciplinary mix of the faculty, and without upsetting well-established principles that tenured faculty would teach as well as do research. The creation of a "professional research staff" structure was a way of meeting the felt needs of critically important research personnel for both status and an understood place in the scheme of things (with specified terms of appointment, procedures for advancement, protections against unfair treatment, and so on).

In light of the forces driving the huge increase in NTT faculty—forces that are highly unlikely to go away—universities would be well advised to acknowledge (as some already are) that full-time NTT faculty have been filling essential teaching roles for many years, and to move expeditiously to consider creating analogous "professional teaching staff" structures. Tenure-track faculty should cooperate with such efforts and not simply bemoan reductions in their relative numbers. There is surely a place in academia, and it should be a respected place, for talented individuals who do not aspire to publish the truly distinguished work of scholarship that would make them top candidates for a tenured position at a university that prides itself on producing outstanding

PhDs, or at a college committed to inculcating scholarly skills among undergraduates.[44]

We should create conditions that will honor the master teachers, who deserve to find a regularized, respected, decently paid way of toiling in their chosen teaching vineyards. The shifting demands of the academic marketplace writ large tend increasingly to favor the master teacher, and colleges and universities alike should create structures that will provide the right incentives for full-time NTT academics who prove their worth in the classroom. The need (and the opportunity) to capitalize on this set of circumstances varies greatly across the higher education landscape—these challenges are less urgent for the wealthiest privates than for the harder-pressed institutions in both the private and public sectors. But the desirability of gaining legitimacy for the concept of a fairly compensated professional teaching staff should resonate broadly and restore a needed measure of mutual respect and equity within the academy.[45]

It is not for us to suggest the details of how such a concept could best be given flesh and blood (which will, in any event, need to vary widely across institutional types, as incipient efforts demonstrate). But we can suggest a few principles that should be considered in most settings; implications for

---

44. We link the PhD-producing universities and those institutions, including elite liberal arts colleges, that focus great effort on training undergraduates to do original research because we believe that faculty at both kinds of institutions need to be active on the research front if they are to be effective in guiding others seeking to learn how to do research.

45. The importance of this subject is underscored by the reaction of some adjuncts and NTT faculty to the report of the Modern Language Association (MLA) on doctoral education in modern languages and literature. The report was criticized on the ground that it did not address the egregious working conditions of many adjuncts and NTT faculty today. See Vimal Patel, "MLA's Effort to Reshape Ph.D. Misses Mark, Some Say," *Chronicle of Higher Education*, June 4, 2014, http://chronicle.com/article/MLA-s-Effort-to-Reshape/146913/.

faculty governance are embedded within these propositions. We believe that it is desirable to do the following:

- Have a well-formulated set of titles along with, of course, compensation and benefits that are commensurate with contributions. Titles should capture what members of the teaching staff are expected to do and should convey respect—for example, "lecturer" and "senior lecturer."
- Be clear about terms of appointments and opportunities for reappointment. Three-year appointments, after some probationary period, seem appropriate in most settings, and such appointments should be renewable; there should be an opportunity to qualify for "continuing status" in lieu of being able to compete for tenure. Many institutions have adopted similar approaches, for example, in defining relationships with librarians, physical education staff, and coaches. We do not think the conferring of tenure is necessary or desirable for professional teaching staff, given institutional needs to preserve staffing flexibility.[46]
- Have a well-defined evaluation process to be used in making decisions about advancements, promotions, and non-reappointments for professional teaching staff. Institutions should be clear where authority rests for making appointments, reappointments, and salary decisions—presumably with the departmental chair, at least in the first instance.
- Provide basic organizational protections (such as appeal processes) for the core elements of academic freedom—

46. The financial pressures that we expect to continue to beset many colleges and universities make it unwise to demand that all non-reappointments be justified on the grounds of "financial exigency" (a standard cited frequently when reductions in tenure-track faculty are being considered). The need for some degree of flexibility in making staffing decisions is, as we have noted, one factor that has driven the shift in the mix of teaching staff.

rights of "utterance" and protections against reprisals and unprofessional assessments of qualifications for promotion, advancement, and retention. NTT faculty must have the freedom to think, to teach, and to write as they see fit. The core values of academic freedom should not be tied too tightly or narrowly to tenure-track or tenured faculty.

- Encourage suitably qualified members of the professional teaching staff (defined, perhaps, by their having been given lecturer or senior lecturer titles) to participate generally in the life of their institution; treat them as members of the faculty, and make them eligible to serve on appropriate faculty committees (for example, admissions, course of study, and examinations and standing). A good example of the integration of NTT faculty into the mainstream of faculty governance is provided by the decision of the University of Southern California's Academic Senate to choose—for the first time—a NTT faculty member as its president.[47]

- Include members of the professional teaching staff in the same administrative "chain of command" as tenure-track faculty, responsible not only to a departmental chair but ultimately to an appropriate dean or associate dean (as is generally the case with professional research staff).

More generally, it would be helpful if the established higher-level organs of college and university governance (such as the ACE, the AAU, the Association of Public and Land-grant Universities, the National Association of Independent Colleges and Universities, the American Association of Community Colleges, and the AGB) welcomed and, we would hope, endorsed the development of organizational structures of this kind.

47. Andy Thomason, "Non–Tenure Track Professor Will Lead Southern Cal's Academic Senate," *Chronicle of Higher Education,* May 29, 2014, available at http://chronicle.com/blogs/ticker/non-tenure-track-professor-will-lead-southern-cal-s-academic-senate/78825.

Faculty Responsibility for Maintaining Academic Standards in Admissions, Curricular Content, and Student Performance

Since at least the latter half of the nineteenth century, a principal faculty role has been to be "Horatio at the Gate," protecting academic standards against all who would sully them. This responsibility should not change. It is exercised via several steps. First, at many private colleges and universities (and at some publics as well), faculty normally serve on admissions committees that are meant to protect standards at the point of entry to membership in the academic community. Today only a relatively small number of colleges and universities are selective (and admission to these institutions receives a grossly disproportionate amount of attention in the press); be that as it may, faculty at these institutions need to be involved, along with administrators, in balancing what are bound to be competing claims on a limited number of places. Public universities are subject to state laws and regulations that may restrict, for instance, the capacity of institutions to take race into account in making even holistic judgments about the allocation of places in an entering class. Nonetheless, faculty should not hesitate to "lean in" when the wisdom of such restrictions is being debated.[48] In what are, de facto, open admissions situations, faculty should have a strong role in deciding what constitutes the threshold for admission, but it is also proper for there to be system-wide policies governing matters such as which institutions should be responsible for developmental work.[49] At the

[48] Our case study of the University of California reports concern among some faculty and administrators that the university-wide Faculty Senate did not "push back" vigorously enough when this issue arose—in spite of the strong and unusual provision in California law that gives faculty control over admissions. As we noted in the case study, it may be difficult to marshal needed faculty support in divisive and politically charged situations such as this one.

[49] See the CUNY case study for an important example of the latter point.

graduate and professional levels, authority for admissions decisions almost always rests primarily, if not solely, at the level of the department or institute, and this is proper.

The second stage is the development and oversight of curricular content. Since at least the interwar years, faculty in American universities have been entrusted with the responsibility, operating within budgetary constraints, for ensuring that curricular content is coherent and qualitatively sound. This is especially true when individual courses are being evaluated, and the University of California is an excellent example of an institution that has long insisted that approval of all such courses is entirely a faculty prerogative, not one shared with administrators (see the case study). As a matter of general principle, no one, we hope, would question the authority of faculty members to determine the intellectual content of courses for which they are responsible. External pressures in high-stakes, intercollegiate athletics can lead, as we have said, to the raising of eyebrows about the academic quality of courses or the widespread practice of steering athletes to "majors in eligibility."[50] But it is wrong, as we said earlier, to blame the individual teacher in such a situation—surely it is the "system" that deserves, at the minimum, searching scrutiny.

Even in the straightforward case of faculty teaching standard courses in mainline departments, there are two caveats (qualifiers) to the altogether proper delegation to the individual faculty member of responsibility for setting the content to be

50. See these online stories: Brad Wolverton, "Need 3 Quick Credits to Play Ball? Call Western Oklahoma," *Chronicle of Higher Education*, September 12, 2014, http://chronicle.com/article/Need-3-Quick-Credits-to-Play/135690/; "College Athletes' Studies Guided toward 'Major in Eligibility,'" *USA Today*, November 18, 2008, http://usatoday30.usatoday.com/sports/college/2008-11-18-majors-cover_N.htm; Brad Wolverton, "The Education of Dasmine Cathey," *Chronicle of Higher Education*, June 2, 2012, http://chronicle.com/article/TheEducation-of-Dasmine/132065; and Amy Julia Harris and Ryan Mac, "Stanford Athletes Had Access to List of 'Easy' Courses," *Stanford Daily*, March 9, 2011, www.stanforddaily.com/2011/03/09/1046687/, all accessed June 1, 2014.

covered by his or her students. First, faculty teaching sections of a large course must conform to decisions regarding material to be covered by the colleague(s) in charge of the course. Second, some courses that function as prerequisites must include material that is necessary for students to grasp before they can move on to higher-level courses in the same area. Departmental authority must be acknowledged in both of these situations.

When entire courses of study are being considered, the ground shifts somewhat. Here it is necessary to have broader administrative/trustee approval of the resource commitments that are generally involved (again, see the University of California case study). Such approval is not sufficient, however. Faculty approval is also a requirement for moving ahead—certainly if a new program is part of the established academic structure. Even if a new curricular venture is a "spin-off," it is dangerous to proceed without faculty support. The demise of the Global Campus initiative at the University of Illinois (see the earlier discussion in chapter 3) is an excellent example of the ever-present need to be sure that faculty are satisfied that some new curricular innovation is not going to threaten the academic reputation of *their* institution (their "brand" in the vernacular). In short, it is extremely risky, even if it is "legal," to impose a new curricular initiative if faculty harbor serious doubts about its academic value.

There is, however, an important asymmetry in faculty roles vis-à-vis the broad contours of the curriculum. As we have just said, faculty approval should be required, as is almost always the case today, when new programs of study are proposed or when major modifications are made in existing programs. But we do not think that faculty approval should be required when decisions are made to close programs or, for that matter, entire courses of study. "Negative" decisions of the latter kind should be the province of administrative decision-makers and trustees, who are ultimately responsible for priority-setting, as well as what are almost always difficult decisions about resource allocation and fundraising. To be sure, academic expertise is a critically important element in a sound decision-making process, and there is everything to be said for extensive faculty involvement in making such decisions, and in advising administrators in proposing alternative professional responsibilities for faculty about to be displaced; also, of course, contractual obligations to faculty involved in such programs must be respected. But none of this means that faculty should be given a veto over decisions to discontinue programs.[51]

3. The third stage in maintaining academic standards is oversight of the process of assessing the performance of individual students. There is almost always a faculty committee on "examinations and standing" that discharges this responsibility. In the main, there is every reason to think that this machinery works well. When there appear to be serious slippages of standards—as, for example, in the case of the UNC–Chapel Hill athletes noted earlier—it is almost always the result of inadequate or inappropriate exercise of authority delegated to someone (in this case, it would appear that the main culprit was the former chair of the Department of African, African American, and Diaspora Studies), but broader issues of culture, expectations, and complicity are also involved. In such situations, remedial action has to be taken, as it has been at UNC.[52]

Aberrations aside, we conclude that faculty continue to be given, and to exercise, responsibility for maintaining academic

51. Our case studies illustrate that there have been occasions when faculty have exercised such a veto—see the discussion of the failure of the Macalester faculty to approve the recommendation of a faculty committee that the Russian Studies program be ended (noting that here it was an explicit faculty committee recommendation that was rejected).

52. See Paul M. Barrett, "UNC Academic Fraud Scandal Sparks Racial Recriminations," *Businessweek*, February 4, 2014, www.businessweek.com/articles/2014-02-04/unc-academic-fraud-scandal-sparks-racial-recriminations, accessed November 2, 2014. See also Jack Stripling, "Widespread Nature of Chapel Hill's Academic Fraud is Laid Bare," *Chronicle of Higher Education*, October 23, 2014, http://chronicle.com/article/Widespread-Nature-of-Chapel/149603, accessed November 2, 2014.

standards. This is not only the practice today, it is also an absolutely central principle going forward. Faculty alone have the expertise to make the necessary qualitative judgments.

In a simpler age, we might have been able to end this part of our story right here. But we live in a digital age, and advancing technology is insistent in raising new questions—and is no respecter of conventions that historically have worked quite well. In this regard, the last of our sections in this chapter has to do with the locus of authority for determining the uses made of new technologies—both on the "home campus" and beyond.

Control over New Teaching Methods—Online Learning

We now enter truly treacherous territory, without a clear North Star to guide us. Our focus continues to be on faculty roles—and, in this instance, on how online technologies affect the locus of authority for teaching methods in the digital age. First, however, we have to take a sidestep and describe the context within which these questions present themselves. Let us recapitulate, ever so briefly, key points referenced in our discussion in chapter 3 of recent experimentation with online learning.

Early hype notwithstanding, online technologies, including MOOCs, have not transformed the academic landscape. College settings are still easily recognizable by those who grew up in a pre-digital age. (Some believe that they are much too recognizable!) At the same time, new online technologies have not proven to be a fad. They are constantly improving and are, without doubt, here to stay.[53] As we saw in our earlier

[53] For a much fuller exposition of Bowen's views on the status and impact of online technologies, see *Higher Education in the Digital Age* (Princeton, NJ: Princeton University Press, paperback edition, 2014), and "Technology: Its Potential Impact on the National Need to Improve Educational Outcomes and Control Costs," paper presented at DeLange Conference IX, Addressing the Challenges of a Changing Landscape: Teaching in the Research University of Tomorrow, Rice University, October 13, 2014, available at www.sr.ithaka.org/blog-individual/technology-educational-outcomes-cost.

discussion, there have been both promising efforts and real disappointments, and both have important lessons to teach us.

Here is a brief catalog of successes:

- MOOCs (such as those launched by Coursera and edX) have had an undeniable and highly positive impact on access to knowledge by aspiring students of all ages around the world.[54] There is also growing anecdotal evidence that faculty participation in the use and development of MOOCs encourages broader faculty interest in hybrid or blended learning, and a re-examination of traditional methods of teaching.

- "Adaptive learning" approaches to the study of subjects such as beginning statistics, with sophisticated feedback loops, have been demonstrated to be effective with students of all backgrounds.[55]

- A recent Ithaka S+R study involving campuses within the University System of Maryland demonstrates that participating faculty enjoyed using more active learning practices and the opportunity to teach their courses in different ways. Faculty members were also pleased with their students' engagement and learning outcomes.[56]

54. See Carl Straumsheim, "For Stanford U. MOOC Instructors, Trial and Error Breeds Success," *Inside Higher Ed,* February, 18, 2014, available at www.insidehighered.com/news/2014/02/18/stanford-u-mooc-instructors-trial-and-error-breeds-success. See also Christina C. Davidson, "MOOCs and the Promise of Internationalization," *Chronicle of Higher Education,* January 29, 2014, available at http://chronicle.com/blogs/future/2014/01/29/moocs-and-the-promise-of-internationalization/.

55. See William G. Bowen, Matthew M. Chingos, Kelly A. Lack, and Thomas I. Nygren, "Interactive Learning Online at Public Universities: Evidence from Randomized Trials," Ithaka S+R, May 22, 2012. Regrettably, the pioneer in this area, Carnegie Mellon University, seems to have given up its "first-mover" advantage in this potentially very important field—adaptive learning is an expensive approach if pursued rigorously.

56. See Rebecca Griffiths, Matthew Chingos, Christine Mulhern, and Richard Spies, "Interactive Online Learning on Campus: Testing MOOCs and

- Automated grading programs have been successful in reducing the tedium of grading in some courses.[57]
- The University of Massachusetts and other institutions have succeeded in using online technologies to expand dramatically their distance-learning capabilities.[58]
- A number of other public universities (including Arizona State University, Georgia State University, and the State University of New York–Buffalo) have increased both enrollments and revenues by judicious deployment of online technologies.[59]
- The College of Online and Continuing Education at SNHU is serving the needs of approximately 37,000 students, mostly working adults, and may represent a model for other non-profit universities that wish to build large-scale programs. The pilot program is also exploring whether the use of full-time NTT instructors improves student performance and retention in writing-intensive courses.[60]
- Countless numbers of individual colleges and universities have used simple online technologies to post content and assist instruction in many other ways.

Other Platforms in Hybrid Formats in the University System of Maryland," Ithaka S+R, July 10, 2014, available at http://sr.ithaka.org/research-publications/Interactive-Online-Learning-on-Campus.

57. See John Markoff, "Essay-Grading Software Offers Professors a Break," *New York Times*, April 4, 2013, available at www.nytimes.com/2013/04/05/science/new-test-for-computers-grading-essays-at-college-level.html?pagewanted=all&_r=0.

58. See "UMassOnline Reports a 12% Increase in Enrollments and a 16% Increase in Revenue Generated by Online Courses Offered through University of Massachusetts Campuses in FY11," *BusinessWire*, July 6, 2011, available at http://www.businesswire.com/news/home/20110706005892/en/UMassOnline-Reports-12-Increase-Enrollments-16-Increase#.VFp7imeiE_Q.

59. See Jeff Selingo, Kevin Carey, Hilary Pennington, Rachel Fishman, and Iris Palmer, *The Next Generation University* (Washington, DC: New America Foundation, May 2013).

60. Steve Kolowich, "Southern New Hampshire U. Designs a New Template for Faculty Jobs," *Chronicle of Higher Education*, May 8, 2004, available at http://chronicle.com/article/Southern-New-Hampshire-U/146443.

It cannot be said, however, that there has been much progress to date in (a) adapting the best-known MOOCs to meet the urgent needs of large campuses seeking improved ways to achieve good learning outcomes at sustainable costs, or (b) developing customizable platforms that individual institutions could use in cost-effective ways.[61] This lack of success represents a void in efforts to meet critically important national needs—to improve educational attainment overall and to address equity/social mobility issues. Odd as it may seem to emphasize governance issues in a technological age, we believe that they are of critical importance. In some of the most important sectors of higher education, a substantial modification in administrative/governance mechanisms, including faculty roles, is one of several "levers" that must be employed if we are to increase the odds of addressing successfully the formidable set of intertwined challenges in this area.[62]

61. Ithaka S+R worked with the University System of Maryland and with Coursera, Carnegie Mellon University, and Pearson to test out a number of efforts to adapt these technologies in Maryland settings. Some mildly encouraging results have been reported, consistent with the findings of Ithaka S+R's earlier study, "Interactive Learning Online at Public Universities: Evidence from Randomized Trials"—but no big breakthroughs. See Griffiths et al. For a discussion of the barriers that have to be overcome, see Lawrence S. Bacow, William G. Bowen, Kevin M. Guthrie, Kelly A. Lack, and Matthew P. Long, "Barriers to Adoption of Online Learning Systems in U.S. Higher Education," Ithaka S+R, May 2012, available at www.sr.ithaka.org/research-publications/barriers-adoption-online-learning-systems-us-higher-education.

62. See Bacow et al. A recent report by Ithaka S+R of an online pilot project hosted by the University System of Maryland, "Interactive Online Learning on Campus: Testing MOOCs and Other Platforms in Hybrid Formats in the University System of Maryland," Ithaka S+R, July 10, 2014, identified a number of issues that require closer faculty and administrative negotiation than currently exists at most institutions. First, the report reaffirms a fundamental point identified in the "Barriers" study—that participating faculty are enthusiastic about the learning outcomes and pedagogical benefits of online learning and that widespread faculty adoption of MOOCs and hybrid courses depends on the faculty's ability to customize their courses. Customization is key. Second, public university systems are well positioned to accelerate potentially transformative change—not by top-down directives, but by joining with faculty and departments in strategic initiatives that create incentives that are clearly aligned with system-wide plans

To be absolutely blunt, it is time for individual faculty to give up, cheerfully and not grudgingly, any claim to sole authority over teaching methods of all kinds.[63] In exchange, faculty should be given an important seat at a bigger table—a table at which collaborative decision-making is needed on four aspects of online learning: (1) decisions concerning investments to be made locally either in designing online platforms that enable faculty to customize their courses or in doing the customization;[64] (2) decisions concerning the uses at "home" of online technologies designed locally or externally; (3) decisions concerning the sharing of online technologies across institutions; and (4) decisions concerning the adoption of a "portfolio" approach to curricular development that involves a blend of courses, some mainly online, some "hybrid," and some face-to-face.[65]

The need for a highly collaborative approach is rooted directly in, first, recognition of both the importance of scale in contemplating potentially large investments in this area and

and objectives. The need for high-level, coordinated strategic planning in this area is obvious, and it is equally obvious that most governance structures today do not support this approach.

63. In fact, there have always been limitations on faculty control of methods—for example, faculty cannot simply assume that any number of TAs is available to teach sections of courses, and access to space and facilities can also affect how course material is presented.

64. An obvious question is what "return" can be expected and whether the resources required justify the proposed outlay. Returns on such investments can of course take many forms—improving teaching on the home campus; extending the reach of faculty on the home campus to other campuses within the same system or even more broadly; conceivably generating increases in enrollment and in revenues, as some institutions have done; demonstrating to skeptics (including, perhaps, regents and legislators) that the institution is "in the game" and not hopelessly behind others in entering the digital age; and, finally, simply satisfying the felt need of interested faculty to be active experimenters in this area—perhaps collaborating with colleagues in other institutions.

65. For an explanation of what we mean by a "portfolio" approach to curricular construction, see Bowen, *Higher Education in the Digital Age*, paperback edition (2014), p. 68.

the broad ramifications of such investments. Second, there are
obvious "collective" aspects to many modes of online teaching, which can require the involvement of multiple members
of the teaching staff, graduate students, master teachers, librarians, and instructional technology support personnel. Third,
there is a clear need for institutional policies regarding both
ownership/control of the content of online courses and long-
run institutional responsibility for the sustainability of such
offerings.

This is an area in flux, and there is a pressing need for new
protocols that institutions can consider. It can be tempting for
institutions to change as little as possible and, for example,
simply to assert that whatever "rights" faculty currently enjoy
in owning intellectual property that they were largely responsible for creating (albeit almost always with some contribution
of university resources) should apply here as well.

We are skeptical, however, that such a "business-as-usual"
approach is wise—in part, but only in part, because needed
institutional contributions of resources can be substantial, as
can, in some situations, monetary pay-offs to the licensing of
content. There are, in addition, very important broader issues
to be considered. A narrow vesting of "ownership" of digital
content and control over its distribution may not serve larger
institutional (or societal) purposes. There are, for example,
important questions concerning responsibility for the sustainability of technologically enhanced digital course materials to
be addressed. Will a newly developed online course be available in the future, even if the person most responsible for its
creation moves to another location or dies? And who will be
responsible for upgrading the content and presentation of material over time? The history of the JSTOR database of scholarly
journals is replete with lessons applicable to online learning,
and one of the most important has to do with sustainability.
JSTOR would never have become the success that it is today

(having just signed up its nine thousandth participating institution worldwide) had it not been able to persuade librarians and university administrators that it was sustainable—with the resources and the commitment to maintain and upgrade itself. Librarians, and those responsible for library construction, had to be confident that JSTOR would "be there" in the long run.[66]

In an increasingly digital environment, the major decisions regarding curricular structure require a modernized conception of shared governance (see the last section of chapter 5 for an elaboration of this point). Decisions of all kinds concerning online technologies must rely heavily on faculty expertise, but they must also reflect institution-wide decisions concerning facilities, scheduling, "pricing" (tuition and financial aid), and obligations to meet the needs of various sub-sets of potential students—including, especially, low- and moderate-income students, and students from otherwise disadvantaged backgrounds.

Tempting as it is to offer our own highly provisional answers to this list of far-reaching questions, that is a task for another day.[67] Our purpose right now is simply to emphasize that the technological advances underpinning online learning argue against compartmentalized decision-making and lead inexorably to the need for collaborative approaches. In short, these technological advances compel us to argue for a form of "shared governance" that blends multiple perspectives and takes full advantage of faculty expertise—but that leaves final authority for most of these complex matters with administrators and trustees. In our view, faculty should retain primary

66. See Roger C. Schonfeld, *JSTOR: A History* (Princeton, NJ: Princeton University Press, 2003).

67. Bowen's views on a number of these substantive issues may be found in *Higher Education in the Digital Age* (2013); "Academia Online: Musings (Some Unconventional)," Stafford Little Lecture, Princeton University, October 14, 2013; and "The Potential for Online Learning: Promises and Pitfalls," *EDUCAUSE Review* 48, no. 5 (September–October 2013). See also Bowen's 2014 DeLange Conference paper.

control over the content of course materials (consistent with institutional missions, available resources, and historical practice), but not over teaching methods per se.

The proverbial bottom line is that decisions of many kinds concerning technologically enhanced course offerings cannot be left solely to faculty members. Easy assumptions about faculty roles in this area, many with deep historical roots, have to change—which is certainly not to say that faculty perspectives and insights can be ignored. Not at all. Faculty expertise is indispensable, as is faculty enthusiasm for innovative approaches. Ways have to be found to incorporate faculty perspectives within a broader decision-making framework. Here again, institutional mechanisms will surely differ markedly, and historical practices assuredly need to be taken into account— but in the context of a very different environment.

All that said, faculty should understand, as many will, that their interests will be best served in the long run by working cooperatively with others to craft new rules of the road. It is wrong to assume that faculty in general will simply be naysayers. When approached in the right way, treated as valued participants in a shared enterprise, and provided with appropriate tools and incentives, faculty should be (must be!) highly constructive participants in shaping a new order. Their understanding and support are essential.[68] We are reminded of an old adage from industrial relations: in working with other parties, one gets (not always, but by and large) the relationships one deserves; treat others with respect, and they are likely to treat you that way, too.

68. Readers may want to refer back to the case-study discussion of the aborted effort of the University of California to introduce online learning from the president's office.

5

Overarching Challenges

WE NOW STEP BACK from considering how to view faculty roles in specific contexts—such as making faculty appointments and deploying new teaching methods—and comment on four overarching challenges. We will adopt a decidedly normative tone because we think that, right or wrong as our propositions may be, adopting an assertive posture is the best way to encourage debate and fresh thinking.

Confronting Trade-offs and the Need for Upfront Consideration of Costs

First on our short list is the need for faculty and administrators alike to do what for many of them is a difficult thing: avoid treating educational quality, important as it obviously is, as the only crucial variable in making major decisions. As in every walk of life, trade-offs are unavoidable. A regrettable and long-lasting legacy of the "Golden Age" of the 1960s is a tendency on the part of some to believe that it is sufficient to focus solely on educational outcomes, and on how to improve them, and that the availability of resources will somehow take care of itself. As we have seen repeatedly, it is all too easy simply to

Here's the nut of the matter

ignore costs. The most vivid example of this tendency gleaned
from our case studies is the listing on a University of California, Berkeley, website of efforts to seek cost savings as an "anti-
goal."[1] Apparently this listing has now been taken down from
the website in question, but the mindset it represents has a lingering presence—and by no means at Berkeley alone. In the
1995 edition of his Godkin Lectures, Clark Kerr offered this
provocative observation: "The call for effectiveness in the use
of resources will be perceived by many inside the university
world as the best current definition of evil."[2]

1. We asked C. Judson King, provost and senior vice president–academic
affairs, emeritus, University of California, and director, Center for Studies in
Higher Education, University of California, Berkeley, about this, and he reports
that he was unable to bring up the cited website. King then adds: "Perhaps the web
site has been redone since you consulted it. Hence my answer will reflect what I
think may be at play. The BRCOE [Berkeley Resource Center for Online Educa-
tion] and MOOCLab are designed to stimulate and help faculty get going in devising on-line approaches to higher education. In that sense citing opportunities and
available assistance would be designed to get the faculty doing things, while citing
cost savings would not incentivize and stimulate the faculty much if at all. In that
the goal is to get the faculty moving with regard to on-line methodology, the web
site may have been created to stress the things attractive to faculty and eliminate
or minimize any implication that on-line methodology is going to displace faculty. With regard to the thinking that 'online learning technologies are not going
to reduce costs,' I don't think that feeling is universal at Berkeley. The statement
probably reflects a feeling that online components will be an add-on, without significant reduction in current costs; i.e., the faculty will continue to 'teach' as much
or nearly as much. It is true that enhanced delivery and pedagogy through the use
of on-line elements can be attractive to many faculty members, and there is probably substantial feeling that the best role of on-line education, as it now stands,
is to enrich courses rather than to supplant the need for the instructor. I think
there is general appreciation that the use of on-line methodology can and should
change the nature of classes, i.e., by adding components beyond the classical lecture. Finally, the typical cost structure of on-line education (of the quality in which
most faculty believe) is a substantial cost out front for development of the on-line
component, followed by little or very small cost per usage hereafter. In that sense,
someone looking at the cost of on-line instruction in the short run will see it as an
added cost, and it takes an appreciation of the longer term to see the savings." King
to Bowen, February 2, 2014, personal e-mail.

2. See Kerr, The Uses of the University, 4th ed. (the Godkin Lectures on the
Essentials of Free Government and the Duties of the Citizen) (Cambridge, MA:
Harvard University Press, 1995), p. 181.

[Handwritten marginalia:]
? Clark Kerr — Bowen's idol
Here's an idea — reduce admin & perceived cut their outrageous salaries
When cuts have to be made, start with the admin — Cuts in faculty + educational programs are a matter of last resort!!

We have encountered, over and over, a decided aversion to talking about costs, as if this were, indeed, sacrilegious. Another adage comes to mind: "The best is the enemy of the good." Let us consider a sharp-edged example. If teaching method "A" yields results that are not "the best," not quite as good as those obtained in another way—say, the new results are 90 percent as good as those yielded by teaching method "B"—but if A costs two-thirds as much as B, that ratio has to be taken into account in deciding which teaching method to adopt. Resources saved in one corner of the educational enterprise can be used in another, or can be used to reduce the costs of attending college. It is responsible, not sacrilegious, to seek to use limited resources in the most productive way.[3]

As we have argued in our historical overview of the post–World War II years, the decade of the 1960s was an anomaly. Hanna Holborn Gray, in an underappreciated and trenchant set of lectures, has called attention to the aftereffects of the 1960s. She points out that the decade set expectations that continue. In her words, "Decline in federal support and public favor is seen as a precipitous falling away from what once was and still ought to be the rightful norm in the world of higher education." Gray goes on to observe that "the critical fact [is] that available resources could not continue to keep pace with the expansion of knowledge and its technologies

---

3. A colleague has suggested that the problem is even more serious than our "hard-edged" example suggests. He notes that there is resistance to taking account of cost savings even when it can be demonstrated (as an Ithaka S+R study did in an examination of the use of the Carnegie Mellon statistics course) that using an adaptive learning approach "does no harm" in that learning outcomes are unaffected. An eminent doctor said that exactly the same thought process exists in health care. He said that he is something of an enigma to some of his colleagues because he cares about costs of treatments as well as their results. It isn't, he said, that he is against spending money on health care. It is just that he wants to spend the available resources as wisely as possible. One of our colleagues has suggested that it is only in education and health care that such a mindset would be regarded as odd or in need of justification.

and capital requirements or with the accelerating growth in the university's functions and programs." It is, she concludes, "naturally tempting to take the option of muddling through. . . . But that will scarcely offer long-term health. . . . Questions raised by current economic circumstances serve to expose and force us to confront longer-existing issues and deeper fault lines that have been building over the past decades."[4] It will not do to be caught up in nostalgia for a Golden Age of the 1960s that cannot be considered in any way typical and is certainly not a norm for today. We are reminded of the words Cervantes has Don Quixote uttering on his deathbed: "One should never look for the birds of this year in the nests of yesteryear."[5]

We are not suggesting that cost considerations are generally absent from decision-making. Hardly. There is too much evidence of the pain of retrenchment to believe that. Nor is it fair to use experiences at a leading flagship public university like the University of California, Berkeley—never mind a privileged private university such as Stanford or an elite private college such as Williams—to make points that are meant to apply to institutions that are much harder pressed.[6] (We will say more shortly about the increasing fragmentation and stratification

4. See Gray, *Searching for Utopia: Universities and Their Histories* (Berkeley: University of California Press, 2011), pp. 68–69. An exception to the tendency to downplay cost issues in the 1960s is Clark Kerr's reference, in his 1963 Godkin Lectures, to "problems related to costs, identified particularly by Beardsley Ruml—faculty–student ratios, fuller utilization of the calendar, excessive numbers of courses, mechanization of instruction . . . ." See Kerr, *The Uses of the University,* 5th ed. (Cambridge, MA: Harvard University Press, 2001), p. 79.

5. Miguel de Cervantes Saavedra, *Don Quixote of La Mancha,* ed. and trans. by Walter Starkie (New York: Signet, 1974), p. 1048.

6. Trade-offs are particularly painful for under-resourced public institutions. In the fall of 2014, the California State University system's twenty-three campuses enrolled almost ten thousand more students than in the previous year, but another ten thousand applicants, including qualified transfers from the state's community colleges, were denied admission when state appropriations fell short of supporting the hiring of additional faculty. See Carla Rivera, "Cal State Lowers Enrollment Growth, Other Expenditures for Fall," *Los Angeles Times,* July 22, 2014, available at www.latimes.com/local/lanow/la-me-ln-calstate-trustees-20140722-story.html.

of higher education, with growing divisions between "haves" and "have-nots.") The serious generic problem is that too often cost considerations drive decisions at hard-pressed institutions *only when there is no other way to go*—when "muddling through" has hit a wall.[7]

There is also a polar tendency, at least as dangerous, that is seen most often in calls by legislators, regents, and trustees, for institutions to move aggressively (with or without adequate faculty consultation) to introduce cost-saving technologies. Unfortunately, far too many calls to action are made in the absence of any real concern for quality, or any appreciation that it is less well-prepared and disadvantaged students who are most likely to be harmed by such an approach. Our plea is a *modest* one for occupying what Isaiah Berlin once called the "ungrateful middle ground," and dealing directly, upfront, and unapologetically with trade-offs when that can be done thoughtfully and ahead of some make-or-break crisis.[8]

It is also the case that at many institutions, both private and public, the issue is not how to teach more efficiently, at lower cost, but how to make do with insufficient resources. One commentator on a draft of this manuscript pointed out that the problem at a great many resource-starved institutions is not that they fail to be concerned about costs, but that they are just too poor—too "bare bones."

7. Based on research and interviews at public institutions, Deanna Marcum and colleagues at Ithaka S+R report that even where state appropriations have been cut significantly, administrators and faculty are reluctant to engage cost questions in any significant way. Marcum et al. to the authors, June 7, 2014, personal correspondence.

8. Isaiah Berlin is famous for, among other things, his discussion of the moral dilemmas faced by nineteenth-century Russian writers as many of them sought to balance a yearning for absolutes with the complex visions that they simply could not push from their minds. Berlin writes with special empathy about Alexander Herzen and others, "who see, and cannot help seeing, many sides of a case. . . . The middle ground," Berlin writes, "is a notoriously exposed, dangerous, and ungrateful position." Berlin, *Russian Thinkers* (New York: Penguin, 1994), p. 297.

Aligning Roles and Responsibilities

In addition to the need for all parties to consider trade-offs in a direct and timely way, sound decision-making requires that higher education address deep-seated organizational issues and, in particular, improve alignments between roles and responsibilities. For faculty, the basic unit of organization is the department (sometimes the center or institute). Departments are, generally speaking, well suited to make judgments about the professional qualifications of peers and to monitor standards of academic achievement by students. However, as Clark Kerr explained cogently in the 1995 edition of his Godkin Lectures, and as we noted in chapter 1:

> The professoriate is not well organized to consider issues of efficient use of resources. Many decisions with heavy cost consequences, including faculty teaching loads and size of classes, are made at levels far removed from direct contact with the necessity to secure resources. Departments usually operate on the basis of consensus, and it is difficult to get a consensus to cut costs. And among departments, the rule is senatorial courtesy—not to interfere with the conduct of others, however inadequate it may be.[9]

True as this statement was when Kerr made it over twenty years ago, the first part (about the disconnect between the locus of some kinds of decision-making and the locus of responsibility for garnering resources) is even truer in today's digital age, marked as it is by the need for decisions regarding the development and deployment of technologically enhanced teaching methods that often cross departmental boundaries. There is no denying the need to invent effective decision-making mech-

9. Kerr (2001), p. 180.

anisms that are collaborative, if they do not exist already, to address such issues. As we have argued repeatedly, faculty are an absolutely essential source of both expertise and enthusiasm in a process that, more and more, will transcend departmental lines. Still, it is an open question whether, as Kerr asked in the mid-1990s, faculty "can work effectively on a large scale, whether [they] can agree on more than preservation of the status quo."[10] It may well be, and we suspect strongly that this is the case, that much stronger high-level leadership is going to be required than past practice would intimate—but strong leadership that recognizes the need to engage faculty as genuine participants, rather than as co-combatants, in the decision-making process.

To continue our ongoing dialogue with the Clark Kerr of decades ago in the context of our own time, we believe an observation he made in the mid-1990s warrants reconsideration:

> When change comes it is rarely at the instigation of this group of [faculty] partners as a collective body. The group is more likely to accept or reject or comment, than to devise and propose. The group serves a purpose as a balance wheel—resisting some things that should be resisted, insisting on more thorough discussion of some things that should be more thoroughly discussed, delaying some developments where delay gives time to adjust more gracefully to the inevitable. All this yields a greater sense of order and stability.[11]

We do not think that the most urgent need today is for "a greater sense of order and stability." It is rather for organizational machinery that can facilitate an all-encompassing set of strategic decisions that allocate human and capital resources effectively and provide a compelling set of incentives for faculty

10. Ibid., pp. 32–33.
11. Ibid., p. 75.

to pursue system-wide goals.[12] Such machinery cannot be simply consensus-driven; real leadership from those in positions to garner resources is essential. Perhaps a visual image will help. Traditionally, much of academia has been organized vertically, with the department as the key, largely self-contained, unit. Going forward, we suspect that a much more horizontal structure is going to be required, because decisions of many kinds are going to transcend departmental structures. We have in mind decisions about the deployment of technology, about new approaches to teaching at least some kinds of content, and about the reallocation of teaching resources. "Horizontal thinking" will require both effective leadership from senior officers and a much less compartmentalized and, perhaps, a more "networked" way of approaching issues; an essential element is the willingness of key faculty to think broadly about institutional needs, without expecting to control outcomes. Skeptics are not wrong to warn that ever-stronger disciplinary ties impede the willingness of many of the ablest faculty to play such institutionally oriented roles. But they are wrong if they suggest that this contest for loyalty and institutional commitment should simply be given up as an artifact of a bygone era.

Some faculty (and others) will also no doubt object to this formulation as favoring a "corporate" as opposed to an "academic" or guild orientation. This semantic and often symbolic distinction may, however, obfuscate rather than clarify organizational choices. The extent of autocratic decision-making

12. We are impressed by the results of the ongoing university-wide reorganization at Arizona State University that focuses on investing resources in online education and empowering the faculty to increase quality, scale, efficiency, and productivity simultaneously. An important takeaway from the Ithaka S+R study of Arizona State is that entrepreneurial activity often starts with professional programs and schools (nursing, mass communication, and education) when administrators and faculty have clear external incentives to improve student credentials and pass rates on state-wide qualifying examinations. See Kevin M. Guthrie, Christine Mulhern, and Martin A. Kurzweil, "In Pursuit of Excellence and Inclusion: Managing Change at Arizona State University," Ithaka S+R, January 2015.

in the best-run companies of today is frequently exaggerated. In fact, in corporate America as well as in the academy, support for leadership from "below" has been essential for some time.[13] There are, to be sure, differences in cultures and contexts, but we should not confuse ourselves by overstating them. A proper alignment between roles and responsibilities is essential in every setting. We recognize that there is often a difference between corporate America and academia in the ability to move quickly—and this difference has to be narrowed, but surely not in the direction of even more cumbersome and compartmentalized decision-making in the academy. In today's digital world, it is hard to exaggerate the importance of having educational institutions (and their offspring) benefit from the ability to make decisions promptly, and then to change course if need be. Nimbleness is a real virtue, and it is one reason that some entities have decided to move out from under a university umbrella and to operate either as independent not-for-profits or as for-profits.[14] At the same time, although we admire the

13. For a dramatic example of the power of this proposition (albeit in an extreme situation), see the account in the *Washington Post* of the resignation of James Robinson as chairman/CEO of American Express—an outcome driven in no small part by dissatisfaction with Robinson's leadership on the part of many staff members. See Brett D. Fromson, "American Express Chairman Steps Down amid Pressure from Directors," *Washington Post,* January 31, 1993. We are told by a knowledgeable colleague that these same points about corporate America apply to the military as well.

14. The decision of Highwire Press to leave Stanford is an excellent example of decisions of this kind. See Carl Straumsheim, "The 19-Year-Old Startup," *Inside Higher Ed,* June 4, 2014. Bowen's favorite example of this point is from the history of JSTOR (which was, and is now, an independent not-for-profit entity). In the earliest days, when decisions were being made about which ten economics journals should be included in the pilot, Bowen was asked how long he thought it would take for agreement to be reached on this question—six months of committee meetings, a year? Bowen's answer was "Twenty-four hours!" He then made a dozen calls to economists in different fields and assembled a provisional list of the first ten journals—an easy task because there was so much agreement. Bowen then said to those who were taken aback by the quick (if ad hoc) decision as to which journals were to be included: "If we got it wrong, we'll fix it. What's important is not which journal is number ten or number eleven, but to get started."

speed with which for-profit online providers adjust to market changes, the sometime absence of consultation with faculty represents a dangerous exclusion of an indispensable voice.[15] We believe that there are ample opportunities within a shared governance model to accommodate consultation without sacrificing timely decision-making.

Issues of alignment in academia reach well beyond the individual campus. The CUNY case study is an excellent illustration of the progress that can be made when a proper alignment of roles and responsibilities is achieved. So long as individual campuses at CUNY had near-complete control over their own degree requirements and over how they would treat efforts to transfer credits from another campus to their own, inefficiency and wasted motion (judged from a system-wide perspective) were inevitable. Completion rates and time-to-degree suffered. It is hardly surprising that students—as well as the leadership of the system, which properly felt responsible for system-wide outcomes, including completion rates and time-to-degree—were frustrated. Once the central "system" exerted leadership, and established some norms via the Pathways Initiative, the incentive structure changed—with the expectation that improvements in completion rates and time-to-degree would follow.

Because what was at issue was mainly efficient "flow through the system," it was essential to align decision-making authority with the overall responsibility for outcomes. There was an evident need for some common conventions as to how students could garner and transfer credits. The lack of central direction and coordination was paralyzing. The attempt to realign the system required enormous effort and dedication from administrators who were more committed to what

15. We wish to express our appreciation to Henry S. Bienen, president emeritus of Northwestern University, for sharpening our understanding of these differences.

they viewed as good policy than to enhancing their own popularity. Faculty on many CUNY campuses to this day resent what they see as the wrongful intrusion of the system into "their" domain (see the case study). Even after a state trial court reaffirmed the authority of the central system to initiate this kind of curricular reform and rejected what was, in effect, a claim by faculty on individual campuses to veto power over such changes, opponents of the policy continue to challenge it. In this sense, the Pathways Initiative reveals another key lesson: it is not enough to initiate a systemic efficiency; at least an equal amount of effort is required to protect it against retrenchment.

The limited capacity of inherited organizational structures to meet today's needs is, if anything, even more evident at the regional/national level when we consider how to provide the necessary incentives and resources for the development of technologically enhanced platforms that can be customized on a wide variety of campuses.[16] As we have noted already, praiseworthy efforts by Coursera and edX, among others, to develop platforms that can serve a variety of users have not solved this problem (at least thus far). This apparent disconnect, for which none of the principal actors is to blame, illustrates vividly the lack of alignment between national needs and the organizational capacity/commitment to address them. Entities such as Coursera and edX have, understandably, their own priorities. Putting these entities to one side, it is tempting to think that collaborations of institutions with similar objectives would meet

16. For discussions of this problem, see William G. Bowen, *Higher Education in the Digital Age* (Princeton, NJ: Princeton University Press, 2014), and Lawrence S. Bacow with William G. Bowen, Kevin M. Guthrie, Kelly A. Lack, and Matthew P. Long, "Barriers to Adoption of Online Learning Systems in U.S. Higher Education," Ithaka S+R, May 2012. See also Rebecca Griffiths, Matthew Chingos, Christine Mulhern, and Richard Spies, "Interactive Online Learning on Campus Testing MOOCs and Other Platforms in Hybrid Formats in the University System of Maryland," Ithaka S+R, July 10, 2014.

this national need. However, much experience teaches us that collaboration as a mode of decision-making within academia is fraught with problems, especially when the prospective collaborators are also competitors. Trying to reach common agreements, when hard choices have to be made, can be extremely time consuming (frustrating in the extreme) and can lead to lowest-common-denominator decisions. Collaborators have an easier time simply exchanging information and ideas than making tough decisions.[17]

Required, we suspect, is a new initiative that would respect the need for prompt and efficient decision-making and that would be focused laser-like on the needs of the large number of mid-level public institutions in this country that would benefit greatly from the creation of a new, broad-based platform that many of them could customize. It is far from obvious, however, how this objective can be addressed in the context of this country's historical emphasis on institutional independence. We see an analogy with the discussion by Claudia Goldin and Lawrence F. Katz of the historical development of pre-college schooling.[18] Goldin and Katz recognize that, in their terminology, some of the "virtues" of the past (features of our system that promoted the vast expansion of the base of college-ready students) may be the "vices" of the future. In particular, the existence of a great many small and fiscally independent school

17. In September 2014, eleven public universities (with significant socioeconomic diversity in their student populations) announced the creation of the "University Innovation Alliance" with the goals of strengthening multi-institutional collaboration, improving completion rates, and reducing costs. The alliance, which consists of two flagship public universities, five land-grant institutions, and four relatively young publics, will use adaptive learning, pre-college outreach, and extensive data sharing to achieve its objectives. See Paul Fain, "Sharing Intel on Completion," *Inside Higher Ed,* September 17, 2014, www.insidehighered.com/news/2014/09/17/university-innovation-alliance-kicks-big-completion-goals, accessed September 20, 2014.

18. Goldin and Katz, *The Race between Education and Technology* (Cambridge, MA: Harvard University Press, 2008), especially pp. 129–32.

districts was valuable at one point in our history but today may be a source of growing inequalities and inefficiencies. Stronger central direction is political anathema to many, but it could prove necessary to strengthen educational capacities at both pre-college and college levels.[19] Informal "coalitions of the willing," which are possible, are very hard to create, and even harder to sustain.

Coping with an Ever-Changing Academic Landscape

In thinking about faculty roles going forward, there is no denying the need to recognize basic characteristics of the ever-changing educational landscape within which faculty operate. It will not do to wish for a return to a Golden Age (that fewer and fewer academics personally remember) or even to the conditions before the Great Recession. Nor, as Hanna Gray has reminded us, should we believe that exhortation alone will suffice to change funding trends and underlying political realities. Leaders of educational institutions and faculty alike need to cope thoughtfully with a reconfigured academia. Two words, especially, encapsulate deep-seated changes to which everyone must adapt: *fragmentation* and *stratification*.

By *fragmentation* we mean simply that it is harder and harder to assume that faculty in general share a great many common characteristics, including aspirations, priorities, and views as to where authority should rest. The inexorable increase

19. In the case of higher education, our intuition is that the best hope for making real progress lies in creating, somehow, a viable partnership among (a) one or more funders willing to make the substantial investment required, (b) an educational "system" (beyond a single campus) eager to serve as a test bed and capable of making prompt and binding decisions, and (c) institutions with real technical capacity and a willingness, as well as the ability, to design the basics of a platform that others could customize. Brokering such a tri-partite partnership would require the leadership of either a well-staffed funder or some respected third party. Faculty involvement at all levels would be essential, but faculty could not expect to have a final voice or veto in decision-making.

in specialization, as fields of knowledge splinter and then splinter again, is a basic driver of this phenomenon—which Clark Kerr identified earlier than most people when he commented on "the two Berkeleys." The increasing reliance on NTT faculty has been another source of fragmentation. This fragmentation phenomenon is most evident in large institutions, but it exists within even liberal arts colleges (see the Macalester case study).

The continuing proliferation of "centers" and "institutes" has some real intellectual advantages but also contributes to fragmentation as well as to non-trivial increases in administrative costs (because each unit of this kind needs a leader and some supporting staff). As Neil Rudenstine points out:

> Centers often have a great deal more autonomy than departments (and lots less committee work, etc. because they rarely make their own appointments, etc.). So they add to the sense of fragmentation, even though they also extend research and teaching "horizontally." They also impede, because of their comparative autonomy, the process of administrative efforts to unify the faculty at an institution in order to make efficiencies.[20]

One implication of increased fragmentation for faculty roles in governance is that it is ever more difficult to assume that there is "a faculty view" on issues of many kinds. It is equally important to distinguish among faculty as individuals, as members of a department, and as citizens of an institution. Differences—and tensions—within faculty ranks and between departments have always existed and have to be regarded as normal. Decision-making processes need to recognize this diversity of circumstances within "the faculty," and not just between scientists and everyone else. A related implication is that it is only in a very limited number of settings that meet-

20. Rudenstine to Bowen, August 2014, personal e-mail correspondence.

ings of the faculty as a whole can be expected to be productive. A residential liberal arts college is generally thought to be the prototypical example of such a setting, but questions are being raised (by, for instance, Brian Rosenberg, president of Macalester) as to the reality of this assumption.[21] Even in such settings, the ideal of "coming together" is exceedingly hard to attain when the stakes are high, tempers flare, and time is short.

President Rosenberg has concluded that we should "rely more heavily for important decisions on representative rather than direct democracy." Here is his argument:

> All-faculty meetings are simply the wrong place to make decisions that have a serious strategic or financial impact on an institution. There is neither the time nor the base of information nor, at most colleges, the appropriate atmosphere necessary for careful and informed deliberation. Better outcomes are likely to come from elected faculty committees whose members have the time and willingness to study complex issues. These committees should be more fully empowered to make decisions and not just to offer recommendations to the full faculty.[22]

One point is very clear to us. In thinking about "representative governance" models, careful attention needs to be paid to how members of a faculty senate (or some such body) are chosen. Both nomination and voting processes need to be designed to ensure, as best one can, that able individuals are chosen from various parts of the body politic. There is also an uncomfortable "fact of life" to be taken into account: namely, the oft-stated observation that it has become more and more difficult to persuade the "right" faculty to serve on key committees.

21. See Brian Rosenberg, "Shared or Divided Governance?" *Inside Higher Ed,* July 29, 2014, available at www.insidehighered.com/views/2014/07/29/essay-new-approach-shared-governance-higher-education.

22. Ibid.

as well as in faculty senates—or to lead internal efforts to address sensitive questions.[23]

We see no magic solution to this problem, which is compounded by the pressures many faculty feel to make their way up whatever promotion ladder exists in a more and more stressful academic labor market. High-level encouragement for faculty involvement can definitely help, albeit to a limited extent. Faculty at large need to respect and thank colleagues who are willing to take on onerous institution-specific tasks rather than insult them with sometimes rude criticisms of their work. (We know of one case in which an able faculty member took on the thankless task of studying a highly sensitive question concerning equity issues in compensation only to be bedeviled by criticisms, some ill informed; this faculty member has resolved never again to take on such a task.)

Another form of fragmentation involves the professionalization of administration, as evidenced by the proliferation of graduate programs in the field, as well as "how-to" seminars for aspiring or newly chosen deans and presidents. Today it is less common than in days gone by for administrators to come up through local faculty ranks. An increasing number of administrators are appointed from outside the institution to handle specific and often highly specialized tasks.[24] This source of a sharper division between faculty and administrators contributes to the difficulty of achieving something approaching a common view of an institutional mission and,

23. President Gray has the impression "that the vigor of faculty participation or interest in general university affairs has atrophied somewhat as faculty live increasingly within their departments. . . ." She also notes more emphasis on "independent entrepreneurship." See Gray, p. 85.

24. According to the ACE's 2012 study of the college presidency, 34 percent of current presidents served as provosts or chief academic officers. See Bryan J. Cook, "The American College President Study: Key Findings and Takeaways," ACE, Washington, DC (Spring Supplement, 2012), available at www.acenet.edu/the -presidency/columns-and-features/Pages/The-American-College-President-Study .aspx.

more than that, a sense that "we are all in this together." (We should not, however, exaggerate the lasting nature of faculty appreciation for the fact that administrators were once faculty—all too soon, faculty-turned-administrators are seen as individuals who have "crossed over.") Faculty–administration fragmentation, to whatever degree it exists, obviously makes it more difficult to achieve the kind of truly collaborative shared governance that we favor (see later discussion).

The effects of fragmentation on academia are both complicated and compounded by *stratification*, by which we mean the increasingly evident tendency for a fragmented system of higher education to be divided into tiers, with pronounced differences between sets of institutions with respect to financial resources (and then with respect to faculty salaries, teaching loads, and perks). There are also increasing differences in selectivity, in class sizes and curricular options for students, in socioeconomic diversity, and in status.[25] These dimensions, and others, are of course correlated. For our purposes, focusing on inflation-adjusted differences in "educa-

---

25. It is worth noting that, at the same time that greater differences have appeared across tiers of higher education, there has been a tendency for institutions within certain tiers to look more alike. President Gray argues convincingly that intensifying competition has had "the perverse effect of making institutions in some respects to be more rather than less similar to one another. . . . Universities have moved in a more homogeneous direction, and in their turn colleges have in some respects become more like universities in their culture and aspirations." Her conclusion is that "we would do well to return to basics." But in doing so, we "need to avoid the temptations of easy nostalgia and begin from where we are. . . . It seems clear that universities need to confront some painful realities and become more deliberatively selective in what they choose to do. . . . Universities are overstretched. . . . The competition among them has led to greater homogeneity rather than a constructive diversity of institutional profiles and distinctive individual excellence. . . . Greater differentiation among institutions might encourage each to focus on its own particular mix of academic priorities and responsibilities." Gray favors what she calls "the stripped down university" (Gray, pp. 85 ff). There is, we agree, much to be said for more focus and more willingness to live with limited resources, and to celebrate rather than bemoan differences among institutions.

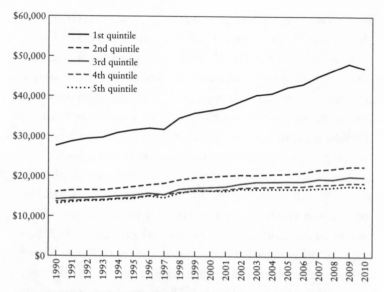

FIGURE 3 Education and related expenditures per full-time-equivalent student for private four-year institutions, 1990–2010 (quintiles)
Source: National Center for Education Statistics, Delta Cost Project Database.

tion and related" (E&R) expenditures per full-time-equivalent (FTE) student seems to be the best way to capture the key trends. Thanks to the excellent work of Charles Kurose at the Spencer Foundation, we present, as figures 3 and 4, two graphs that summarize differences in E&R expenditures per FTE student between 1990 and 2010 by selectivity tier within the private sector and by flagship/non-flagship status within the public sector.[26]

These data are striking. Within the private sector, they demonstrate, first, that spending per student is light years greater within the top quintile of private institutions than within the bottom four quintiles. In 2010, the top-quintile private

---

26. For explanations of terms and methodology, consult Charles Kurose at the Spencer Foundation.

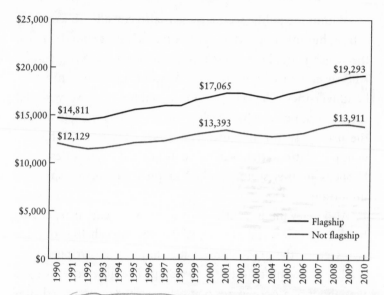

FIGURE 4 Education and related expenditures per full-time equivalent student for public four-year institutions, flagship and all other, 1990–2010
Source: National Center for Education Statistics, Delta Cost Project Database.

institutions spent over $45,000 per student (and the top decile spent over $60,000!), as compared with roughly $20,000 per student in the four other quintiles. Second, this huge gap within the private sector has been growing steadily. Kurose has also demonstrated (data not shown) that these stark differences in resources spent have *not* come primarily from differences in net tuition payments; on the contrary, the gap in resources spent per student from sources other than tuition (often called the "average subsidy") is even greater and has grown even faster than the gap in total E&R spending per student. The power of large endowments, and of highly sophisticated fundraising machinery, is evident. It is easy to see why students fortunate enough to attend the top-tier private institutions feel (or should feel!) very privileged—as should the faculty/administration at these institutions.

Within the public sector, there is also considerable stratification, but much less than within the private sector. In 2010, the flagship public universities spent just over $19,000 per FTE, as compared with roughly $14,000 spent by other public universities. This gap within the publics has also widened since 1990, but not by nearly as much as has the gap within the private sector. Because such a large fraction of the student population attends public colleges and universities, what happens in this sector, looked at on its own, is especially important.

Also relevant is evidence of a growing gap in spending between privates and publics. Within the top echelons of these two sectors, the private universities have far outstripped their public counterparts in E&R spending. The difference in 1990 was about $12,000; in 2010, it was nearly $30,000.[27] Private-public stratification is important because the leading privates and the leading publics compete aggressively with each other—especially for faculty and for research funding. Such competition is healthy for all concerned, and it is worrying that the publics may be losing the capacity to compete effectively.

Both the extent of stratification and its rate of increase have major implications for public policy questions of all kinds, including prospects for students' social mobility and whether it is healthy from a societal perspective for there to be such great, and growing, differences between the "have" and "have-not" institutions. (We think not.) These are, however, questions for another day. Our interest continues to be in faculty roles in governance. From this perspective, the extent of stratification reinforces a point we have made earlier: it is less and less realistic to expect faculty to speak with one voice. There are such wide differences in circumstances

27. These comparisons are far from precise, in part because the figures are all averages and fail to take account, among other things, of scale effects. Still, they are rough indicators of real differences.

that faculty in different selectivity tiers have quite different points of view on many issues, including those having to do with potentially revolutionary applications of technology to teaching methods.

These data on E&R expenditures have another, in some ways more powerful, implication for faculty roles and responsibilities. They demonstrate yet again that costs have been rising steadily within all tiers in both the private and the public sectors. It is highly unlikely (as Kurose notes in a personal memorandum to us) that these rates of increase, which have been fueled almost entirely by net tuition increases in all tiers excepting the top tier of private institutions, are sustainable. We conclude, along with many others, that active efforts have to be made to reduce costs while sustaining (if possible, improving) educational outcomes. Such efforts are most needed, it seems clear, in both public institutions in general (perhaps excluding, at least temporarily, the best-positioned flagship universities) and the "regional" private institutions below the top selectivity tier. And there are reasons to believe that costs also matter—and perhaps ought to matter more than they sometimes seem to—even within the elite private institutions.[28]

It is revealing that a summer 2014 survey found that "many campus chief financial officers lack confidence in the sustainability of their colleges' business model over the next decade—but they also seem loath to take cost-saving measures that

---

[28] Here are three reasons that costs should matter at these more affluent private institutions: (1) they set an example for others, and growing expenditures at these institutions put pressure on institutions just below them in the hierarchy; (2) even with heavy subsidization, some deserving students from less privileged backgrounds may be discouraged from applying or risk being passed over in the admission/aid process—at all but the very wealthiest institutions with exceptionally generous financial aid programs; and (3) higher education is losing the battle of public opinion, which in time could affect research support and, conceivably, lead at some future time to taxes on endowment, and so on. We are indebted to Lawrence Bacow, Kevin Guthrie, and Michael McPherson for emphasizing these points in discussions with us.

could ignite campus controversy."[29] The survey found that fewer than a quarter of business officers "strongly agree they are confident in the sustainability of their business model for the next five years, and only 13 percent strongly agree they are confident in their model over the next 10 years." Yet, "when it comes to specific ways to balance their budgets, CFOs are wary of several ideas that could agitate key campus groups. Do they have any plans to have senior faculty teach more undergraduates, revise tenure policies, promote early retirement for administrators and staff, outsource more academic programs or cut funding for intercollegiate athletics? A quarter or fewer of the CFOs said they planned to try each of those tactics." Here again, we find evidence of not just an aversion to confronting cost pressures directly, but a fear of antagonizing key constituents, especially faculty. It is hard to see how a "head-in-the-sand" approach can lead to good decisions.[30]

29. See Scott Jaschik and Doug Lederman, eds., "The 2014 Inside Higher Ed Survey of College & University Business Officers," conducted by Gallup. Nor are private institutions immune from these worries. According to the survey, "Forty-five percent of private college CFOs (and 50 percent of those at private baccalaureate colleges) agreed that their tuition discount rate is unsustainable" (http://publicsearch.kctcs.edu/publication/lists/todaysnews/allitems.aspx?Paged=TRUE&p_Created=20140721%2013%3A18%3A56&p_ID=3452&PageFirstRow=511&&View={9F63CB88-CC0E-4F27-A7C7-025B09C4BC14}). Mention should also be made of a recent report by Moody's Investors Service, in which Moody's expressed a continuation of its negative outlook for the whole higher education sector in part because it found that colleges are "living with increased operations, maintenance, and debt service costs even as a new cycle of capital investment builds" and even as tuition revenue remains stagnant. See "Negative Outlook for US Higher Education Continues Even as Green Shoots of Stability Emerge," Moody's Investors Service, July 11, 2014. See also "Amid 'Negative Outlook' for Higher Ed, Moody's Finds Optimism," *Inside Higher Ed*, July 15, 2014.

30. We are far from alone in expressing these sentiments. Taylor Reveley, president of William & Mary, puts it this way: "We desperately need to get tenured faculty to accept that just as great change has come to the professional lives of physicians, lawyers, and corporate executives, [it is] now coming to those of us in higher education, like it or not, and we can either get in gear and try to shape change in productive ways, or we can wait to be blown like a leaf in a gale" (Reveley to Bowen, August 6, 2014, personal e-mail correspondence).

198   Chapter 5

In addition to the obvious need to confront reality, two specific, straightforward implications for faculty roles stand out. First, the unrelenting cost pressures that are so evident at all but the most fortunate institutions increase the stakes involved in finding effective uses of technology to control rates of increase in instructional costs—and these pressures should also increase the willingness of faculty to consider some of our earlier suggestions as to how they might look at their roles in decision-making. Second, these same cost pressures increase the inclination of institutions to use NTT faculty, which in turn means that it is all the more important to address the legitimate professional needs of this group—perhaps by, as we have argued, increased efforts to create professional teaching staff structures. Tenure-track faculty, as well as NTT faculty, should support such initiatives.

There is another, highly sensitive and highly controversial, question that we believe deserves more careful consideration than it has received. This question concerns the supply side of the academic labor market and the desirability of asking, as Robert Berdahl (then president of the AAU) did bravely but without great success in 2009: how many research-intensive universities, and how many PhD programs, does the country really need? The decreasing demand for newly minted, research-oriented PhDs is driven in part by the cost indicators we have just presented—combined, of course, with cutbacks in state support, increasing resistance to tuition increases, and the possibility of using technology in more effective ways. It is hardly surprising that, in these circumstances, leaders of hard-pressed institutions seek ways to avoid paying the costs of supporting research activities of faculty by giving them teaching loads that allow them to pursue traditional modes of scholarship alongside their teaching; hence, the rise of the NTT faculty and the need to recognize and support a professional teaching staff.

Established faculty and their professional associations are understandably reluctant to enter this fray, but we believe their long-run interest will be advanced by thoughtful reconsideration of how many scarce resources should be invested by hard-pressed universities in traditional doctoral training.[31] We hasten to add that this is not to deny the value to the country of continuing to support vigorously the "right" number (whatever that is) of strong PhD programs; and it is certainly not to speak against emphasizing the synergy of research and teaching when the two really go together. But it is to argue, once again, for upfront consideration of trade-offs and for avoiding sentimentality—even if that means being labeled an elitist.[32]

a little walking back here

Princeton et al can carry on as usual!

31. A related question is whether this is the right time (as it could be) to ask again if the structure of current graduate programs is well suited to the need for more teaching professionals going forward. This question concerns not just the length—overly long—of current programs but also whether, in their totality, they put too much emphasis on traditional forms of scholarship and research. The traditional emphasis on originality and rigor seems just right for individuals heading for tenure-track positions, but it may not be right for aspiring "master teachers." In May 2014 the Modern Language Association (MLA) Taskforce on Doctoral Study in Modern Literature recommended a major redesign of doctoral programs that would shorten the timeline, emphasize new pedagogies, and encourage new scholarship beyond the traditional national literature–history paradigm. See Coleen Flaherty, "5-Year Plan," *Inside Higher Ed*, May 28, 2014, available at www.insidehighered.com/news/2014/05/28/mla-report-calls-phd-program-reform-including-cutting-time-degree. We note, however, that the MLA report rejects reducing the size of doctoral programs as representing a threat to graduate student diversity. And the report does not address the question we have raised concerning the very structure of programs that should be designed to meet the needs of prospective master teachers. It may be unrealistic to expect professional associations such as the MLA to tackle such sensitive issues—but if they will not address these questions, who will? — _not Bowen, I hope, n folks like Bowen!_

32. In a widely discussed report by the New America Foundation, Kevin Carey takes the AAU to task for putting too much emphasis on research spending as a membership criterion and urges the organization to broaden its membership considerably. The AAU responded immediately by arguing that it puts more weight on student education than Carey recognizes. See Paul Basken, "AAU Is Accused of Glorifying a Limited View of Higher Education," *Chronicle of Higher Education*, June 3, 2014. Although we are sympathetic to some of the concerns Carey expresses about higher education overall, we do not agree with his sharp,

Current training of Ph.Ds is designed in large measure to produce master teachers, teachers with active scholarly interests

yes. keep up with it

Clarifying Notions of "Academic Freedom"

"Academic freedom" is an iconic concept that has lasting value. But it can be abused. Under the rubric of academic freedom, faculty can be tempted to claim too much authority in a broad array of areas—thereby risking support for the core values that the concept should continue to represent.

At the end of chapter 2, we cited the work of legal scholars Matthew W. Finkin and Robert C. Post, who have emphasized that academic freedom is primarily about "the teacher's 'independence of thought and utterance,'" and that this independence is not some inalienable right handed down from on high but rather is "required by the basic purpose of the university."[33] Without such independence, universities would be severely hampered in their ability to advance knowledge and educate properly new generations of students. There is an important corollary: "Independence" of thought is linked to professional "responsibilities," which include the obligation to adhere to professional norms and to discipline those who fail to do so. This is a claim for professional self-regulation. In short: "The traditional ideal of academic freedom [involves] twin commitments to freedom of research and to compliance with professional norms."[34]

These core propositions can be threatened in many ways—both directly and indirectly. In the summer of 2014, lawmakers in South Carolina proposed cutting the budgets of the College

---

even strident, criticism of the AAU as an organization that "harm[s] the cause of higher learning in America." Indeed, we think that it is important that some modest number of leading research-intensive universities meet together to consider issues such as the one we have just discussed (the scale of doctoral education). It would also be helpful, as the higher education landscape continues to evolve, for broader-based organizations such as the ACE to play an even larger role than at present in national debates about priorities.

33. Finkin and Post, *For the Common Good: Principles of American Academic Freedom* (New Haven, CT: Yale University Press, 2009), p. xx.

34. Finkin and Post, pp. 40 and 42.

of Charleston and the University of South Carolina Upstate "as punishment for recommending that incoming students read books with gay characters and themes."[35] Threats come from both ends of this ideological spectrum. In Virginia, a gay rights advocacy group asked UVa to disclose a faculty member's e-mail correspondence and other personal records because they claim that the professor's work is being used to support anti-gay and pro-life legislation. The university has resisted this request. There is an understandable concern that such requests, if honored, could have a chilling effect and be intimidating— even as they do not challenge directly the faculty status of individuals.[36] A well-intentioned effort of a very different kind at the University of Oregon, intended to apply academic freedom policies to students and staff as well as faculty, raises other issues.[37] We have no quarrel with the basic objective here, which is to protect rights of expression for members of the larger academic community. But we do have a concern that lumping students and staff with faculty is risky in that it dilutes the basis for defending the freedoms of faculty to express views of every kind. Students and staff differ from faculty in that they are not so clearly "required" (in the phraseology of Finkin and Post) to exercise such freedom in order to advance knowledge, and they do not have the same concurrent obligation to protect professional norms.

In a similar vein, it is hardly surprising that faculty groups have sought to extend the well-established core principles of

35. See Eric Kelderman, "S.C.'s Public Colleges Find Themselves Caught in Election-Year Grandstanding," *Chronicle of Higher Education*, May 5, 2014.

36. Colleen Flaherty, "Gay Rights Group's FOIA Request for Professor's Research Pits Privacy vs. Academic Freedom," *Inside Higher Ed*, May 29, 2014. It is also worth recalling our earlier discussion of the controversy at the University of Illinois over whether the anti-Israeli views of a prospective faculty member led the chancellor to decide not to forward a recommendation for the individual's appointment to the regents.

37. See Peter Schmidt, "U. of Oregon's New Academic-Freedom Policy Protects Students and Staff," *Chronicle of Higher Education*, May 29, 2014.

academic freedom, covering independence of thought and expression, to support claims for faculty authority in other realms of university life. The general counsel of CUNY, Frederick P. Schaffer, has provided a succinct account of the AAUP's efforts to extend the principles of academic freedom:

> The AAUP's vision of academic freedom has been encumbered by the addition of numerous policies, procedures, rules and prohibitions as an old ship accumulates barnacles. The AAUP, of course, deserves great credit for having put academic freedom on the map and having investigated and reported on a number of important cases involving significant violations of its principles. However, there is hardly any aspect of university life on which the AAUP has not expressed an opinion and which, according to the AAUP, is not an aspect of academic freedom. These include such diverse matters as detailed procedures relating to the renewal or nonrenewal of appointments, dismissal and suspension, including the permissible grounds for such action, standards for notices of non-reappointment, the use of collegiality as a criterion for faculty evaluation, post-tenure review, the status of part-time faculty, non-tenure track appointments and the status of such faculty, the use of arbitration in cases of dismissal, operating guidelines for layoffs in cases of financial exigency and so on.[38]

In previous sections we have given our views on the proper locus of authority in many of these specific areas, and there is no need to repeat that commentary here. Some of the topics Schaffer lists belong within the scope of the core principles of academic freedom (a good example is the need for NTT faculty to have full freedom of expression), but many do not. We reiterate our sense that trends in academia today—in particular

38. Schaffer, "A Guide to Academic Freedom," *CUNY Bulletin*, January 2, 2012, available at www1.cuny.edu/mu/vc_la/2012/01/02/a-guide-to-academic-freedom/.

the combination of unrelenting financial pressures and accelerating technological change—argue against compartmentalized decision-making. Vigorous efforts to seek too powerful a place for faculty in major decision-making roles are entirely understandable but could end up being counter-productive. Again, Schaffer puts the central point very well:

> To link to academic freedom every policy and procedure that a professional association or labor organization might want for its members is to drain the concept of all meaning and to lend credence to the unfortunate view of some that academic freedom is no more than special pleading on behalf of a privileged elite. Because there are, and will continue to be, real and serious threats to academic freedom, it is important to all who care about universities to be clear about its meaning, to exercise restraint in its invocation and to support true claims with vigor.[39]

Ours is an increasingly polarized and politicized era in which it seems harder and harder for legislators to find common ground and easier and easier for individuals in positions of power to insist on adherence to their conception of ideological purity. Such attitudes breed assaults on original and, at times, unorthodox thinking that have to be repelled. We have argued in this book that many aspects of the role of faculty in governance need to be refined and even rethought. But respect for the core principles of academic freedom—genuine independence of thought and expression—does not belong on this list. It is, if anything, more important than ever before that legitimate claims to academic freedom be both applauded and upheld. There should be absolutely "no give" in insisting on the centrality of the faculty role in this aspect of governance.

39. Ibid., our emphasis.

204   Chapter 5

The sometime tendency to link the focused concept of academic freedom (as we, in company with Finkin and Post, would define it) to the much broader concept of "shared governance" reinforces the need—present in any case—to re-examine how shared governance should be thought about. The first thorough-going attempt to link these two concepts of which we are aware is the adoption in 1966 by the AAUP of its *Statement on Government of Colleges and Universities (Statement on Government)*, which it had jointly formulated with the ACE and the AGB.[40] Then, in 1998, the AGB issued its own *Statement on Institutional Governance*, which was widely read as pushing back on active faculty involvement in addressing issues of many kinds.[41]

At one point in our research we were inclined to drop references to shared governance altogether and to argue for avoiding all use of the phrase. We were troubled by the vagueness of the concept, the lack of even rough agreement as to what it meant, and inclinations to use the phrase in sloganeering efforts of various kinds. We are now persuaded that the term is here to stay and in fact can have useful connotations. It cannot, however, be expected to settle most issues of consequence having to do with the precise definition of faculty roles—it remains too amorphous, and subject to too many interpretations, to serve that purpose. Moreover, as we have argued throughout

40. We were surprised by how recent the emphasis on shared governance seems to be, and we asked Susanne Pichler (librarian of the Andrew W. Mellon Foundation) to search for uses of the phrase *shared governance* in relation to higher education. She reports that JSTOR indicates zero instances between 1600 and 1970, and a first occurrence in 1975, with 23 others between 1971 and 1980, 98 between 1981 and 1990, 214 between 1991 and 2000, and 369 between 2001 and 2010.

41. For a good account of these developments, see Frederick P. Schaffer, "A Guide to Academic Freedom," *CUNY Bulletin*, January 2, 2012, available at http://www1.cuny.edu/mu/vc_la/2012/01/02/a-guide-to-academic-freedom/.

this study, market conditions and local circumstances have affected faculty roles since the days of the colonial colleges and will continue to do so; the variety of such forces means that there will always be institution-specific answers as to how the role of the faculty should be defined.

We understand why the AGB thought it necessary in 1998 to argue against some of the sweeping claims for shared governance in the 1966 *Statement on Government* adopted by the AAUP. Too much consultation and an inability to respond nimbly in addressing issues of new kinds had, by the late 1990s, taken a toll. More generally, the impact of continuing developments in digital technologies cannot be underestimated. Currents that are both deep and strong are washing over all of us, as Kevin Guthrie, writing in his role as president of ITHAKA, has explained cogently:

> In the last decade billions of people around the world have become connected. They are connected to each other and to products, content and services by way of a network that is enabling new forms of communication, collaboration and commerce. If a product or experience can be converted readily to a digital form—for example a page of content, or piece of music, or a videotape of a lecture—it can be transmitted across the globe instantly via the network at extremely low marginal costs. This compression of time and space related to digital communication is creating new industries and threatening existing ones. It has unleashed forces that are having transformative impact. In just a few years companies like Google, Facebook and Amazon grew to generate billions of dollars of revenue by providing services that had never previously existed. These and other companies are also stealing attention and customers from long-lived industries like newspaper publishing and music.
>
> What is the impact of these forces on colleges and universities? That is a matter of great debate, with many people willing to argue the extremes, either that higher education institutions

are doomed, or that the importance of face-to-face interaction protects them from threat. While the ultimate impact on individual institutions or the sector at large cannot be known, it is not credible to argue that higher education will be unaffected, since the very essence of the enterprise—the creation and diffusion of knowledge—can in substantial measure be digitized and transmitted over the network. The sector therefore cannot insulate itself completely from these forces and will have to face down the challenges and embrace the opportunities that come along with them.[42]

The key point is that lines between content, technology, and pedagogy have blurred. This is a major reason that vertical modes of decision-making in the academy, focused on departmental authority, have to give way to more horizontal ways of organizing discussion of new approaches to teaching and learning. Pendulums swing, and we are persuaded that carefully considered arrangements for an even broader sharing of perspectives, cutting across departmental lines, have become more, not less, essential. But this is not to suggest a sharing of final decision-making authority, which, in our view, needs to be located unambiguously in the hands of senior administrators with campus, university, and sector-wide perspectives—who can be, and should be, held accountable for their decisions.

There is, in any case, an ever more insistent need to find fresh ways of testing out both new teaching methods and new ways of organizing and scheduling academic work in many (not all) settings. Right now, such efforts are often hamstrung by (a) inertia, present always but driven ever more powerfully today by interdependencies among the curriculum, the calendar, physical facilities, and scheduling—a lethal combination that can make change seem so overwhelmingly complex that

42. Guthrie to Bowen, August 16, 2014, private e-mail correspondence.

it is not worth even considering new approaches; (b) mindsets that resist thinking hard about costs and trade-offs until too late; and (c) the perception of many potential contributors of new teaching methods that faculty resistance is *the* daunting obstacle. The result, too often, is an inanimate coalition of the unwilling that seems mired in place.

We need new ways, maybe even radically new ways, of engaging faculty and administrators in discussions of options, and how to seize them, that will, as we have said, often be "horizontal" rather than "vertical"—that is, that will often cut across departmental lines and at times across campus and even institutional boundaries. Exactly how this is to be accomplished will have to be worked out at the level of individual institutions, or perhaps at the level of institutional systems. But three things are clear to us:

1. Faculty cannot be given a veto over the introduction of new approaches to teaching content, and we do not think that, with proper incentives in place, many faculty would expect such veto power. It is all too easy, and self-defeating, simply to assume faculty resistance when that need not be the attitude or reality at all.

2. Faculty expertise and faculty enthusiasm are indispensable to finding cost-effective ways of delivering excellent educational content. Absent significant faculty involvement in designing, customizing, and implementing new approaches, frustration and, yes, failure are inevitable.

3. College and university presidents must engage (or re-engage) in academic matters.[43] We do not propose that leaders

[43] As Derek Bok notes, "Presidents who are not perceived to be participating actively in the promotion of education and research are less likely to acquire the moral authority and respect of the faculty that academic leaders need in order to guide an institution composed of independent professors." In a recent (2010) survey on how college and university presidents spend their time,

immerse themselves in the minutiae of course development, for that would be foolish and unproductive. But we encourage presidents to exert academic leadership by appointing deans, provosts, and department chairs with distinguished credentials, high academic standards, and a commitment to academic rigor. Presidents should draw faculty attention to the importance of academic research on the development of cognitive skills. They should establish priorities for key academic initiatives, actively recruit faculty to lead such endeavors, use their influence to insist on rigorous external reviews of all academic programs, and never accept inferior quality or lack of commitment to institutional priorities.[44]

We hasten to observe that the arguments in favor of adopting new ways of thinking about teaching methods and curricular development are far stronger at some institutions than at others. We can hear colleagues saying, "Wait a minute, all is

academic matters ranked last among six responsibilities. See Bok, *Higher Education in America* (Princeton, NJ: Princeton University Press, 2013), p. 399, and his essay "The Questionable Priorities of University Presidents," *Change: The Magazine of Higher Learning*, 46, no. 1 (2014): 53–57. By comparison, a 2001 AAUP survey found that faculty authority was concentrated in traditional academic areas, such as curriculum, degree requirements, tenure, appointments, and degree offerings, and that faculty members played a much smaller role in decisions regarding the size of disciplines, budgets, salary compensation, and the planning of construction projects. See Gabriel E. Kaplan, "How Academic Ships Actually Navigate," in Ronald G. Ehrenberg, ed., *Governing Academia* (Ithaca, NY: Cornell University Press, 2004), p. 177. These are classic examples of "divided governance," a concept that we attribute to Macalester College President Brian Rosenberg.

44. Presidential leadership in the academic arena comes in many forms, often from the leaders of institutions whose missions focus on improving educational attainment. For an insightful explication of the nuanced differences in the assessment of "competence" in using knowledge versus the "mastery" of a body of knowledge, and what one external degree-granting institution (Excelsior College) is doing to demonstrate its students' preparation, see John F. Ebersole, "Let's Differentiate between Competency and Mastery," *Inside Higher Ed*, July 25, 2014, available at www.insidehighered.com/views/2014/07/25/lets-differentiate-between-competency-and-mastery-higher-ed-essay.

fine here at College/University X; we don't need to consider radical changes in how we operate." That may well be true at X, at least for now, but the number of institutions that fall in the "X" category are small and may well diminish over time. Also, we would hope that even the best-established, wealthiest, most selective institutions would want to cooperate, in whatever ways are appropriate, in helping higher education in general meet the pressing needs we identified in the introduction to this book.

So, what should *shared governance* mean, looking ahead? We agree that it should include the parsing out of some tasks with, for example, faculty responsible for decisions about selection, advancement, and termination of peers, and trustees responsible for investing institutional resources. There are, of course, innumerable decisions to be made in the vast territory between these two "bookends," and in this study we have tried to indicate how we believe roles of faculty should be thought about in particular areas and particular circumstances. We do not believe, however, that efforts to refine the shared governance concept should focus primarily on seeking to identify with ever greater precision which issues "belong" to the faculty and which issues "belong" to administrators and trustees. More compartmentalized governance is not going to be effective in addressing the complex issues facing higher education today. Shared governance should not mean, in the words of Brian Rosenberg, "divided governance."[45]

Simplistic as it may sound, we believe that shared governance should be viewed, not so much in terms of "who owns

45. See Rosenberg (2014). Another trusted colleague has pointed to the tension that exists when faculty see their roles as protecting and defending the *faculty's* prerogatives rather than the social, cultural, and economic benefits that faculty are entrusted with creating. Jo Ellen Parker to the authors, July 19, 2014, private correspondence.

what," but as embracing a commitment to a genuine sharing of perspectives—to the avoidance of constituency-based thinking (to the extent that this can be achieved in a world of real human beings!). What is most needed on the part of all parties, including both faculty and administrators, is not just a willingness to reject "we" versus "they" thinking, but an eagerness to embrace good ideas generated by others. Such mutual openness to good ideas from all sources should be accompanied by recognition that nimble decision-making is required. Nimbleness implies a need for a well-understood locus of authority, with administrators expected to listen carefully to those with ideas and expertise to contribute, but then to have the confidence and courage to decide.[46]

Those responsible for deciding should be expected to give reasons for their decisions and should be held accountable for outcomes.[47] They should also take pains to explain that in seeking to avoid compartmentalized decision-making, they are not attempting a "land grab" by administrators or trustees. As Neil J. Smelser wisely observes:

> Given *both* the value and indispensability of shared governance *and* its deterioration, the only proper course is for administration and faculty to confront one another openly and frankly about their values and frustrations, about what is working and not working in shared governance, and initiate joint efforts to

46. The willingness of a college or university president or provost to take risks, rather than just "keep the boat afloat," requires acceptance of the fact that this may be the last full-time administrative position the person will hold. See the CUNY case study of the Pathways Initiative. Ithaka S+R's study of organizational change at Arizona State University suggests that adherence to a stable set of widely accepted principles encourages engagement and cooperation between senior administrators and faculty. See Guthrie, Mulhern, and Kurzweil.

47. A wise trustee, deeply conservative on almost all issues, said that he opposed formulaic approaches to decision-making and favored giving considerable latitude to presidents and other officers to make decisions—because, in his words, "If you get too many things wrong, I can fire you!"

yeah, let's form a committee meeting! That'll do it!

diagnose problems, identify points of vulnerability, and attempt to overhaul and streamline archaic structures.[48]

Important as the right words of explanation are, they must be accompanied by the right actions, which in this case means a demonstrated willingness by administrators to follow wise counsel provided by colleagues who are not primarily administrators. Faculty need to be given evidence that they are indeed genuine partners in a shared undertaking.

cheap posturing
cheap + meaningless because insincere!

Whatever the mode of decision-making, mistakes will of course be made. We are persuaded, however, that good will and a modicum of good luck will allow institutions to fix most errors. A key is to establish trust—an elusive but critically important determinant of success or failure. Brian Rosenberg puts this point very well: "I think organizations with a culture of suspicion make decisions to avoid the worst, while those with a culture of trust make decisions to aspire to the best."[49] Trust, in turn depends on a well-defined and broadly understood sense of institutional mission. Faculty and administrators alike generally believe strongly in the value of what they are doing—otherwise many would have chosen different life paths. In thinking about roles, it is much better to err in the direction of assuming the best about faculty and administrative colleagues than assuming bad behavior that may, in fact, be brought about only by the assumption that it is likely. This has been our collective experience and we think it will serve our successors equally well.

blather

this passes for wisdom in some quarters apparently!

48. Smelser, *Dynamics of the Contemporary University: Growth, Accretion, and Conflict* (Berkeley: University of California Press, 2013), p. 66.
49. Rosenberg (2014). In personal correspondence with the authors (July 2, 2014), President Rosenberg goes on to suggest that in believing so strongly in the importance of trust, he may be regarded as "either hopelessly naïve or a dinosaur." Some degree of naïveté may in fact be useful in pressing for changes in culture, but there is nothing to be said for going back to the age of the dinosaur.

But a lot may be said in favor of asking what worked so successfully for so many years

Case Studies

Introduction to the Case Studies

FROM THE EARLIEST DEVELOPMENT of this project, colleagues reinforced our belief in the importance of creating case studies that would chronicle the evolution of governance practices—and especially the authority granted to faculty at four-year colleges and universities across different sectors of American higher education. The advantage of a case study approach is of course the ability to look almost microscopically at institution-specific documents (faculty handbooks, faculty meeting minutes, institutional archives, oral histories, and published histories) and to identify precipitating events and points in time when faculty authority, responsibilities, and obligations changed, and then to ask why. Some specific questions that we have tried to address in these case studies include: What was the event and what triggered it? What were the issues? Who were the parties involved, and what were their respective interests? Who has the authority to make decisions? How was the issue resolved? What were the long-term implications in terms of faculty and administrative responsibilities and perceived prerogatives? Was a formal report or policy created as an outcome?

Although we and our collaborators consulted formal institutional documents, we understood that, in many cases, the written record would be of limited value. The study of governance may leave an extensive paper trail but it is not always a fruitful or revealing one. We were looking for evidence that is often hidden, sometimes intentionally buried in dry, antiseptic minutes and in institutional statements that are frequently devoid of context and that have been scrubbed clean for protection of people and places. Nonetheless, the opportunity to work closely with colleagues with vast institutional knowledge has compensated for the silence or sparseness of institutional records. There is simply no substitute for the knowledge of individuals who know an institution well and have ready access to local files and records that can be used to check recollections.

Readers will want to know why we chose these four institutions, if they are "representative," and why we believe their experiences bear directly on issues facing a far more variegated, heterogeneous, and diverse collection of colleges and universities. Our original intention was to commission ten case studies, but it proved exceptionally difficult to construct a credible account of faculty governance roles based on available public sources because so many important developments were not part of the historical record. Because we felt a strong need to "anchor" impressions and commentaries in written historical records, this represented a severe constraint on how broadly we could reach in developing case studies. Fundamentally, we came to the conclusion that the notion of a "representative sample" was an illusion and that our most important contribution would be to start a conversation with our readers based on a close analysis of a small number of colleges and universities whose experiences have had an outsize influence nationally and/or are broadly representative of specific sectors within American higher education. We turned to institutions that we knew through personal and professional relationships and whose examples provide texture and help make broader points. We also immersed ourselves in the rich scholarship on the history of higher education and have drawn general conclusions from our examples only when there is other evidence on which to base such conclusions. We have tried to be transparent about both the evidence and the perspectives that shape our judgments, but ultimately readers will need to draw their own conclusions.

Our four case studies encompass a variety of institutions and governance processes: public and private; graduate and undergraduate; research-centered and teaching-focused; unionized and non-unionized; faculty-senate and single-faculty forms of participation; a multi-campus flagship public university; an elite private research university (with no professional schools); a stand-alone liberal arts college; and the largest urban university system of two- and four-year colleges in the United States. A comparative analysis of our two oldest institutions, Princeton University and the University of California, reveals remarkable parallels in the delegation of authority to faculty in the early twentieth century, reflecting the leadership of strong presidents. There are obviously vast (and instructive) differences between those years and the post–World War II period as matters of scale, wealth, and mission have become increasingly important. It would be foolish to contrive a comparison of Macalester College, a liberal arts college with 2,000 students and approximately 170 faculty, and the City University of New York (CUNY) system of twenty-four community and senior colleges and graduate schools, with 270,000 students, 7,000-plus full-time faculty, and 11,000 adjunct faculty. But we can say that in both situations, the roles of faculty are best understood in the context of institution-specific governance policies and practices that continue to evolve and that have dramatically influenced their directions. CUNY is not only the largest and most important urban university system in the country, but we believe it is also a rare example of an important institution that has experienced a truly transformative change in governance structure.

Our four case studies reaffirm our conviction that governance, far from being a dry, mundane process detached from the "real" work of teaching, learning, and the creation of knowledge, is an indispensable element whose smooth functioning requires constant attention—and even re-invention.

The University of California

William G. Bowen and Eugene M. Tobin

> The two greatest gifts to the University of California have been the institutional autonomy given to its Board of Regents in the Constitution of 1878 and the unprecedented grant of authority the board assigned to the Academic Senate in 1920.
>
> Clark Kerr, September 1997[1]

Prologue

"The governance of the University of California," writes historian Roger L. Geiger, "depended upon the balanced working of four sets of actors: the regents, the president, the chancellors, and the Academic Senate."[2] We would add a fifth actor, the state's legislative and executive branches, which take an understandable interest in the expenditure of taxpayer funds, and, on occasion, have expressed a more questionable interest in the political opinions of university faculty and administrators.

We are especially interested in the faculty role in governance, but that role must be understood in the context of broader policies and practices, including the authority exercised or delegated by the regents, the president, and other key administrators and the political, sectarian, and partisan influences that buffet state institutions. More specifically, our focus on the faculty role carries the risk that we will understate (undervalue) the importance of presidential leadership.

1. Clark Kerr, "Foreword," in Angus E. Taylor, *The Academic Senate: Its Role in the Shared Governance and Operation of the University of California* (Berkeley: Institute of Governmental Studies Press, University of California, Berkeley, 1998), p. xi.

2. Geiger, "Making the University of California," review of Clark Kerr, *The Gold and the Blue: A Personal Memoir of the University of California, 1949–1967*, vol. 1, *Academic Triumphs* (Berkeley: University of California Press, 2001), in *Science* 296 (April 5, 2002): 52.

On the broad subject of change in higher education, here is a comment by Clark Kerr, former chancellor of the Berkeley campus (1952–58) and university president (1958–67):

> Heraclitus said that "nothing endures but change." About the university it might be said, instead, that everything else changes, but the university mostly endures. [Kerr then paraphrases another version of his reference to the approximately sixty-six institutions that existed in the Western world in 1530 and have endured to this day and finally concludes:] Looked at from within, universities have changed enormously in the emphasis in their several functions and in their guiding spirits, but looked at from without and comparatively, they are among the least changed of all institutions.[3]

We would modify Kerr's observation by noting that change certainly does occur within both individual institutions and higher education as a whole, but that it tends to be gradual and evolutionary and almost always reflects societal needs and circumstances. Given this perspective, we have chosen to organize our case study of governance within the University of California by first presenting a broad historical perspective that covers the period up to Clark Kerr's dismissal in 1967. Then, in the second part of this study, we use a topical structure to discuss the more recent (current) role of the faculty in governing the university. We pay some special attention to the Berkeley campus, but our interest is system-wide.

A Brief Interpretive History of Faculty Governance, 1868–1967

At the Beginning

In 1868, when the California Legislature enacted legislation creating a state university, governing authority was vested in a Board of Regents that "for all practical purposes . . . was involved in virtually all mat-

---

3. Kerr, *The Uses of the University,* 5th ed. (the Godkin Lectures on the Essentials of Free Government and the Duties of the Citizen) (Cambridge, MA: Harvard University Press, 2001), p. 289.

ters of university management with one exception."[4] The exception to complete board and presidential authority was the authority granted to a newly created Academic Senate composed of all the faculties and instructors, and presided over by the president, which was "created for the purpose of conducting the general administration of the University."[5] In reality, during these early years the faculty had very little influence over educational policy. The regents made all decisions affecting admissions and the curriculum and determined the relationship of the senate to the board and president.[6] The establishment of a Board of Regents with nearly plenipotentiary powers, at the same time as the role and responsibilities of the Academic Senate were slowly evolving, guaranteed that "there would be long and continuing debate over the proper domain of faculty."[7]

One of the earliest formative influences on the management and governance of the University of California resulted from a new state constitution (1878) that established the university as a "public trust." Although not quite the "fourth branch of state government" that the university's champions have claimed, the legislation enabled the regents to operate with relative independence but with a watchful eye on developments in Sacramento.[8] Benjamin Ide Wheeler's decision to accept the university presidency in 1899, in spite of its serious financial problems (declining state appropriations) and a series of short-lived

4. John Aubrey Douglass, *The California Idea and American Higher Education: 1850 to the 1960 Master Plan* (Stanford, CA: Stanford University Press, 2000), p. 42.

5. "An Act to Create and Organize the University of California," passed March 23, 1868, *California Statutes of 1867–68,* p. 248. Unlike modern academic senates that denote a subset of a college or university faculty who represent the faculty at large, the Academic Senate created by the Organic Act (1868) included all full-time faculty.

6. John Aubrey Douglass, "Shared Governance at the University of California: An Historical Review," Center for Studies in Higher Education, University of California, Berkeley, Research and Occasional Paper Series 1 (March 1998), p. 2.

7. Douglass (2000), p. 1.

8. Ibid., pp. 65 and 69. As many subsequent events (including the firing of Clark Kerr) revealed, no state university can really be immune from political currents in the state; and of course the state political situation affects the university in many ways, and in all days—through the appropriations process and regulatory processes, as well as state-wide referendums, and so on.

presidential predecessors, depended not only on his willingness to raise substantial public and private funds, but also on the regents' readiness to give him an unusually free hand in all areas of university governance. The regents agreed to stop micromanaging and gave the new president complete authority over faculty appointments, dismissals, compensation, and educational policy. Under Wheeler's nearly autocratic control, which allowed for neither consultation nor negotiation, the faculty reorganized the curriculum, introduced twenty new academic departments, established articulation agreements with the state's normal schools and emerging two-year colleges, raised admission standards, and adopted the first system of peer review for faculty appointments and promotion.[9] Although many faculty objected to Wheeler's autocratic methods, they respected his academic judgment and admired his success in garnering resources that materially strengthened the university and attracted scholars with national reputations.[10] The faculty recognized, however, that their influence on the academic program depended entirely on the president's relationship with the regents, and Wheeler demonstrated no interest in codifying the faculty's role.

The most significant changes in faculty governance occurred at the end of Wheeler's second decade in office. An increasingly disgruntled faculty used the president's pro-German sympathies, which had become a political embarrassment during the First World War, to precipitate a crisis of confidence that led to his forced retirement in July 1919. During Wheeler's last year in office, the Board of Regents created a Council of Deans to exercise presidential responsibilities, but this misguided experiment occurred at a time of institutional instability and proved to be a disaster. Emboldened by the regents' action (and by the lack of presidential leadership), the Academic Senate asked for board approval to play an advisory role in the selection of the next president and for formal powers to choose

9. Douglass (1998), pp. 3–5.

10. See Roger L. Geiger, *The History of American Higher Education: Learning and Culture from the Founding to World War II*, chapter 8, "The Creation of American Universities" (Princeton, NJ: Princeton University Press, 2015), and an earlier work by Verne A. Stadtman, *The University of California, 1868–1968* (New York: McGraw-Hill, 1970), pp. 179–201.

their own leaders and make decisions regarding educational policy. In June 1920, the regents approved a series of Standing Orders that codified the senate's authority, subject to the board's approval, over the conditions of admission, degree requirements, and educational policy. These new arrangements gave the senate an advisory role to the president on faculty personnel policy, budget issues, the appointment and dismissal of deans, and the right to choose its own committees and to determine its own rules and organization.[11] This evolution of faculty authority, known as the "Berkeley Revolution of 1919–1920," represents a "watershed moment" in the history of shared governance.[12]

11. Readers interested in the history of faculty governance at the University of California should consult Angus E. Taylor, *The Academic Senate of the University of California: Its Role in the Shared Governance and Operation of the University of California* (Berkeley: Institute of Governmental Studies Press, University of California, Berkeley, 1998). As part of the Standing Orders adopted by the Board of Regents in 1920, Taylor notes that membership in the Academic Senate was defined as consisting of "the president, deans, directors recorder, librarian and all professors and instructors giving instruction . . . but instructors of less than two years' service" were not entitled to vote (p. 3). At its inception, the senate was authorized to choose its own chairman, but beginning in 1933, President Robert Sproul served as chair ex officio of the entire senate, and the Northern and Southern Sections each had a faculty member as vice chair (p. 12). Individual faculty began serving as chair of the Academic Senate in the early 1960s. Today Academic Council chairs are chosen by the Academic Council, the university-wide governing body of the Academic Senate. As a result of the 1919 "Berkeley Revolution," the senate was authorized to choose its own committees. As Taylor notes, this was "the basis for the senate's early establishment of a Committee on Committees . . . [which] is, arguably, the cornerstone of the senate's power to act independently of the administration" (p. 3n3). But in the senate's formative years, the president exercised some influence through the dean of faculties, who chaired the Committee on Committees. Today members of the Committee on Committees on each university campus are elected by the senate members on that campus, and the Committee on Committees determines its own chair. This is important. Note the contrast with Princeton, where the president and senior deans play a substantial role in determining faculty membership on committees.

12. Taylor, pp. 2–5, and Douglass (1998), p. 5. As we will see, the parallel with Princeton University is striking. At Princeton, President Woodrow Wilson, like Wheeler, focused on improving the faculty, but, again like Wheeler, Wilson kept control and used faculty supporters when and as he chose. After Wilson, there was a devolution of authority to the faculty. In both settings, presidential success

The Wheeler–Sproul–Academic Senate Model

In his unusually perceptive personal memoir, Clark Kerr characterized the changes made under Wheeler and his successors, particularly the shift of academic responsibility from the regents to the president and Academic Senate, as "a clear victory for the 'academic' university."[13] The "Wheeler–Sproul–Academic Senate model," as Kerr calls the organization of University of California governance during this period, continued until 1950. During this momentous half-century, which encompassed the Great Depression, World War II, and the postwar Red Scare, President Robert Sproul (1930–58) consolidated administrative authority and used his large presidential staff for decision-making but had "little organized administrative machinery for consultation."[14]

Prior to assuming the presidency in 1930, Sproul, a member of the class of 1913, held four university appointments simultaneously: controller, land agent, secretary of the regents, and vice president in charge of business and financial affairs.[15] Although faculty might have been expected to object to the new president's lack of academic credentials, Sproul was widely respected for the tenacity and the eloquence with which he defended the academic program. Sproul brought to the presidency an unrivalled knowledge and understanding of university operations and finances, along with an exceptional talent for lobbying the legislature, defending the university's budget, and strengthening academic quality. During a time of economic constraints, he convinced the people of California that their university brought value to the state. Sproul supported the development of a

---

in strengthening the faculty created an environment in which faculty naturally expected a larger role in governance and were capable of exercising more authority. Also, following strong presidencies, there was, in the case of the University of California, a "vacuum" at the top, and, in the case of Princeton, a successor president who was happy to delegate power to the faculty. See our parallel case study of the faculty role in governance at Princeton.

13. Kerr (2001), vol. 1, p. 144.

14. Ibid., p. 19.

15. In his memoir (2001) Kerr notes (vol. 1, p. 17) that in terms of daily operations, Sproul was actually the "operational president" from 1920 to 1958, having effectively aggregated every significant budgetary and administrative responsibility in his multiple positions.

multi-campus flagship university, particularly the growth of the former "southern branch" (which had been renamed the University of
California, Los Angeles [UCLA]), as well as campuses at Davis, Riverside, Santa Barbara, and La Jolla, but he was reluctant to delegate significant administrative responsibility, even as the university grew from
twenty thousand students in 1930 to approximately fifty thousand
by 1950. Sproul's penchant for micromanagement, which had always
been both a notable strength and a potential weakness, did not survive the loyalty oath controversy that fractured university governance
during the years from 1949 to 1952.

The Loyalty Oath Controversy

The controversy was fueled by Cold War fears of disloyalty and allegations of espionage and subversion by government workers, union
members, and academics. The "fall" of China, the Soviet Union's
unexpectedly early detonation of an atomic bomb, the Alger Hiss
case, and the war in Korea contributed to a far-reaching, at times irrational, preoccupation with security and loyalty. In March 1949, in
an effort to prevent stronger action by the legislature's Committee
on Un-American Activities, known as the Tenney Committee, President Sproul recommended that the regents add a proviso to the standard oath disavowing membership in or belief in any organization
that advocated the overthrow of the government. Although many
faculty members had no political or ethical objections to signing
such a statement, they objected to the imposition of a special oath
before one was required of all state employees. A number of states
had introduced loyalty oaths to cover all state employees, but the
California oath, as Clark Kerr emphasizes in his memoir, seemed
qualitatively different because it was "imposed by the trustees of the
university itself and . . . seemed to say that the administration and
the regents considered faculty members to be a particularly suspect
group."[16] A committee of the Academic Senate argued that loyalty

16. Clark Kerr, *The Gold and the Blue: A Personal Memoir of the University
of California, 1949–1967*, vol. 2, *Political Turmoil* (Berkeley: University of California Press, 2003), p. 38.

oaths threatened academic freedom and tenure and reinforced stereotypes of the university as a haven for subversives. The regents rejected such arguments and issued an ultimatum, over Sproul's objections (he had reversed his position), insisting that all faculty sign the oath or be discharged. In August 1950, thirty-one faculty members were dismissed for refusing to sign: twenty-four at Berkeley, four at UCLA, two at Santa Barbara, and one at San Francisco. Other faculty members resigned in protest.

Twenty members of the Berkeley faculty took legal action through the District Court of Appeals to block the dismissals. The court decided unanimously that the firings were unconstitutional and that faculty could not be subjected to any narrower test of loyalty than that in the basic constitutional oath prescribed for all state employees. The Supreme Court of California upheld this decision. Thus it took a court order to break the impasse between the regents and the faculty and to protect the academic freedom of the faculty. This controversy led to the creation of a process whereby a faculty member with tenure who faced dismissal was entitled to a hearing before the properly constituted advisory committee of the Academic Senate.[17]

The loyalty oath crisis ripped apart the tenuous collegiality of shared governance and left a "lingering enmity" that arguably contributed to the Berkeley Free Speech Movement of 1964.[18] The controversy politicized the faculty and raised fundamental questions about academic freedom and the appropriate balance of power between the Board of Regents and the Academic Senate. The senate proved to be "a disjointed and poorly structured vehicle for presenting the collective opinion of the faculty."[19] A generational gap had emerged between the senate's veteran leaders and newer, younger faculty hired since the end of World War II, who had no experience

17. Kerr (2001), vol. 1, p. 33. See also Taylor, pp. 15–37; Douglass (2000), pp. 206–13; and Douglass (1998), p. 6.

18. David Gardner, *The California Oath Controversy* (Berkeley: University of California Press, 1967), p. 249. Clark Kerr recalls Roger Heyns, the chancellor at Berkeley (1965–71), saying that "every time he traced the origins of the problems he endured from the faculty in the second half of the 1960s, he was led back to the loyalty oath." Kerr (2003), vol. 2, p. 28.

19. Douglass (2000), p. 210.

with the president or the board. As a result, senate negotiations with President Sproul and the regents often failed to represent the views of the faculty majority.[20] Faculty members grew disenchanted with the senate, and the formal and informal lines of communication among the regents, president, and faculty hardened. Sproul never recovered the trust of some of the regents, who were more evenly divided than the faculty on the issue of the oath, or the respect of the faculty, who resented the lack of consultation and the opprobrium of being singled out as a suspect group.[21] In 1952, over Sproul's opposition, the board created the position of chancellor at Berkeley, appointing Clark Kerr, a distinguished labor economist, negotiator, and Berkeley faculty member. Raymond Allen, the former president of the University of Washington, who had guided that university through its own loyalty oath crisis, was appointed chancellor at UCLA.[22]

The controversy revealed how much the growth of the university had outpaced administrative and governance processes.[23] The Academic Senate had been divided since 1933 into northern and southern sections with corresponding advisory committees responsible for informing the president on faculty views and attitudes. The committees lacked meaningful access to general faculty opinion and were dominated by faculty from Berkeley and UCLA, whose greater numerical representation effectively disenfranchised the other campuses. When the two sections disagreed or failed to act in a timely fashion, as was the case during the loyalty oath crisis, academic governance suffered.

20. Gardner, pp. 6–7.
21. Kerr (2003), vol. 2, pp. 36–40.
22. Douglass (2000), p. 211.
23. President Sproul and his large administrative staff "abhorred decentralization," whereas most campuses, abetted by local regental support, demanded greater autonomy and more responsibility, including the appointment of chancellors as chief operating officers. In 1952, when Clark Kerr was appointed chancellor of the Berkeley campus, he had no assignments and had to ask for secretarial assistance. President Sproul's administrative secretary reluctantly gave Kerr three "ancient folders" that included complaints about fleas, ticks, and lice; a petition to ban dogs on campus; and a demand to prevent dogs from using a water fountain in front of a campus library. See Kerr (2001), vol. 1, pp. 40–43.

now Ludwig's fountain!?
(?)

"The great mystery of the University of California, and particularly of its Berkeley campus," Kerr notes in his memoir, "is how it could achieve so many academic triumphs while being subject to so much political turmoil and how these two aspects of its histories were inter-related."[24] A brief analysis of the *Master Plan for Higher Education in California, 1960–1975,* and the conditions that contributed to the Free Speech Movement of 1964, suggests a few explanations. As the 1960s progressed, public research universities like the University of California faced three significant challenges: (1) the launch of Sputnik and the Cold War put new emphasis on scientific research, especially defense-related research and development; (2) the pressure on public institutions to create spaces for the "tidal wave" of new students raised profound questions regarding the transition from an elite to a mass-based system of higher education; and (3) an unprecedented period of economic prosperity generated new resources that created boundless expectations and market pressures on research institutions.[25] The *Master Plan* and the politicization of campus life that led to the Free Speech Movement raised governance questions that are best understood within institutional and societal contexts rather than as abstract "things" that occurred independent of circumstances.

During the 1950s, when California's population was increasing at a substantial rate and discharged veterans were settling in the state in record numbers, the University of California had to make a series of decisions regarding student growth, including the possibility of setting limits on prospective enrollments. In 1954, the combined Committee on Educational Policy (CEP) of the Northern and Southern Sections of the Academic Senate attempted to respond to President Sproul's request for advice on how to address anticipated enrollment pressures. The CEP considered various options, but no conclusion was reached. In October 1957, the regents agreed to proceed with the planning for two new campuses, and they appointed Clark Kerr to succeed Sproul as university president in July 1958.[26] During the Kerr

24. Kerr (2003), vol. 2, xxviii.
25. Kerr (2001), vol. 1, pp. 153–71.
26. Taylor, pp. 39 and 47.

years (1958–67), enrollments at the university doubled, three new campuses were built, missions were refocused, competition increased, and expansion accelerated administrative decentralization.

In retrospect, the *Master Plan* "looks like a grand design to achieve great purposes"—universal access to higher education, scientific and technological advancement, and skill development to meet the rapidly changing labor market needs of the people of California. Contemporaries, like Kerr, however, viewed their work as a "desperate attempt" to prepare for an unprecedented increase in new students, while avoiding a civil war among competing public education rivals, and simultaneously fending off legislatively imposed policies that were viewed as the worst possible outcome. "The Master Plan was 'a treaty ... a process ... and a vision,' but it was also a product of stark necessity, of political calculations, and of pragmatic transactions."[27]

The *Master Plan* reduced the likelihood of warfare between the University of California and the state teachers colleges, which would soon become the California State University (CSU) system. "It increased opportunity for students; saved money by placing more of the burden on the less expensive (per capita) community colleges and by avoiding the creation of twenty or more unneeded research universities at high cost; and fully served the labor market, particularly through the CSU with its polytechnic programs."[28] Community colleges were to be open to all qualified students, and transfer opportunities were guaranteed, with many upper-division places at Berkeley (and other University of California campuses) reserved for transfer students. The plan also included very specific admissions policies for each sector. In later years, as California struggled to balance its commitments to universal access, degree completion, and world-class educational excellence, many comments were made about the gap between the *Master Plan*'s promise and its limited accomplishments. In retrospect, it is important to recognize that the *Master Plan* was an ambitious attempt to control costs and to enable the University of California to compete with the nation's most distinguished private as well as public universities.

27. Kerr (2001), vol. 1, pp. 172–73.
28. Ibid., p. 188.

The Two Berkeleys

"There were coming to be two Berkeleys," Kerr observed of his favorite campus in the context of the early 1960s. "Berkeley One was . . . a very attractive place for the best young faculty . . . in the nation, the ablest graduate students, the most talented undergraduates." Berkeley Two had developed a different national reputation as "a fabled point of emanation for the counter culture and for radical political activities."[29] Berkeley One emerged from World War II as one of the University of California's two great research campuses—along with UCLA—but there were huge costs that accompanied the benefits of academic excellence. Pre-war Berkeley celebrated faculty who made their reputations in the classroom, pursued their research on weekends and during vacations, and devoted their careers to their students. After the war, attention shifted from legendary teachers to Nobel Prize winners and scholars with distinguished reputations. As Kerr observed, "A teaching university tends to unite teachers and undergraduate students, a research university to disunite them."[30] Berkeley's academic triumphs directly contributed to its political turmoil. "Research replaced teaching: new and junior faculty and teaching assistants replaced senior faculty as student advisors. Celebration was in order but also consternation."[31]

Berkeley's enrollment increased from approximately 18,000 students in 1952 (with approximately 13,500 undergraduates) to 27,500 (with approximately 18,000 undergraduates) a decade later.[32] Under Kerr's direction, and with regental support, subsequently approved by the legislature under the *Master Plan*, a cap was set at 27,500 students, approximately a third of whom would be graduate students, whose training occupied more and more of the faculty's time. Departments grew in size, faculty devoted themselves to highly specialized research areas, and teaching loads were reduced by half, first in the

29. Kerr (2003), vol. 2, p. 115.
30. Ibid., p. 14.
31. Kerr (2001), vol. 1, p. 404.
32. See Verne A. Stadtman, *The Centennial Record of the University of California* (1967) at http://content.cdlib.org/view?docId=hb4v19n9zb&chunk.id=div00459&brand=calisphere&doc.view=entire_text, accessed March 15, 2014.

sciences and then across the board. The better-endowed private universities had low student-to-faculty ratios and abundant resources. The University of California could compete for government and corporate research support only by matching their peers' lower faculty teaching loads; this led to the neglect of undergraduate education. Kerr warned about the teaching–research trade-offs in the Godkin Lectures at Harvard (1963), and for the rest of his life he believed that the student unrest of the 1960s was a consequence of undergraduate neglect.[33] The "flight from teaching" had been underway since the 1950s, when Berkeley consciously moved from a teaching- to a research-centered environment and the university turned to junior faculty and teaching assistants (TAs) to pick up the slack. As a result of this shift, the number of TAs increased from about 500 in 1953 to approximately 1,500 by 1964. By the mid-1960s, TAs were responsible for half of all instructional hours with first- and second-year students; these trends represent a very early point in the emergence of contingent and non-tenure-track (NTT) faculty as a growing percentage of the teaching faculty.[34]

As Berkeley faculty burnished their national and international reputations, many withdrew from meaningful contact with undergraduates. In the words of sociologist Max Heirich, "The earlier function of senior faculty members as informal links between administrators, junior faculty, and students was largely vacated."[35] The older, more conservative faculty who had acted as mediating agents in undergraduate life were replaced by teaching assistants and younger faculty with more progressive views and varying degrees of resentment toward the university. Many TAs in the humanities worked six or

33. The Godkin Lectures were published as Kerr, *The Uses of the University*, 5th ed. (2001). See Sheldon Rothblatt's essay review, "A Tale of Two Berkeleys," *Minerva* 42 (2004): 185.

34. Kerr (2003), vol. 2, p. 113, and (2001), vol. 1, p. 404.

35. Max Heirich, *The Spiral of Conflict: Berkeley 1964* (New York: Columbia University Press, 1968), p. 58, quoted in Kerr (2003) vol. 2, p. 113. C. Judson King does not believe that the shift from teaching to research was as stark as Kerr concluded, or "at the very least not universal across the campus. The teaching commitments in engineering, physical sciences, and professional schools have not been reduced this much, if at all." King to Bowen, March 15, 2014, personal correspondence.

avg. time to degree in English has always been close to 10 years at least since the 60s to the present

Ph.D

eight years and left without PhD degrees. Faculty dissatisfaction and the potential for political dissent were also evident in the comparative neglect that humanists and social scientists felt in comparison with the celebrity status enjoyed by their more generously funded colleagues in the sciences.[36] Enrollments in humanities and social science departments at Berkeley had tripled between (1953) and (1963), and students with more liberal political opinions arrived on campus eager to engage in the political debates stimulated by the Civil Rights, feminist, and anti–Vietnam War movements.[37] These "outside intrusions," as Kerr calls them, "had obvious impacts on academic life: on disturbances in the classrooms, on debates in the Academic Senate, on budgets from Sacramento, on the tenure of administrators."[38] No governance structure could have prevented the political turmoil that stemmed from these major transformations, but the effects could have been moderated, especially in student life.

Turn on, drop out / We're talking here about a set of this national phenomena at this time, though perhaps

Decentralization, Shared Governance, and Student Life

Student life represented an area of governance in which Kerr, as Berkeley chancellor and later as University of California president, hoped to make a substantial contribution, but he first had to deal with the legacy of an unusually restrictive set of rules and procedures. In order to protect the university from the Depression era's tumultuous political cross-currents, the regents had issued Rule 17, a part of the so-called

36. In recent years, American higher education has experienced a similar degree of fragmentation in the faculty ranks, particularly with respect to a substantial differentiation in compensation and perquisites. Sarah Turner has pointed to these differences as a causal factor in the growing difficulty in getting faculty to "pull together," except perhaps at times of extreme crisis (e.g., the clumsy attempt by the Board of Visitors to fire Teresa Sullivan as president of the University of Virginia, with no consultation or discussion).

37. Kerr (2003), vol. 2, p. 111. In his introduction to the second volume of Kerr's memoirs, Berkeley sociologist of education Neil Smelser argues that Kerr was "one of the architects of his own revolution," in the sense that changes he introduced in making ROTC voluntary, establishing open forums for political discussion, allowing Communist Party members to speak on campus, and prohibiting discrimination in campus fraternities and sororities, created a more liberal campus environment. See Kerr (2003), vol. 2, p. xix.

38. Kerr (2003), vol. 2, p. 14.

Sproul Directives (1938), which included a prohibition on the use of university facilities for student political activities. In practice, at Berkeley this meant that speakers and public demonstrations had to gather "off campus" in Stiles Hall (the university YMCA) or on the streets of the city of Berkeley just outside Sather Gate. In Kerr's mind, it was incongruous that these policies still existed in the late 1950s at a major research university located in one of the nation's most liberal cities. "Here was a dragon I decided I had to confront."[39] In the fall of 1959, with the regents' approval, and following consultation with the Academic Senate, Council of Chancellors, and deans of students, the Sproul Directives were liberally amended and reissued. In particular, Kerr removed restrictions on the uses of university facilities and encouraged all campuses to create convenient "Hyde Park" areas for speakers of all persuasions.[40] Of course, as Kerr later observed, "This large body of existing rules . . . could be made to look both new and oppressive."[41] This is precisely what happened, in part because Kerr had delegated to campus chancellors and deans of students the responsibility to consult with students, something that was done haphazardly or not at all.

Shortly after taking office in 1958, Kerr initiated steps to give more direct authority to the individual campuses. His experience as chancellor of Berkeley under Sproul had convinced him that the campuses needed greater control over their operations. He understood that a multi-campus, as distinguished from a flagship-based, system "could not be tightly administered from a single, central presidential office."[42] The number of presidential staff was reduced by 26 percent; chancellorships were established across the University of California

39. Kerr (2001), vol. 1, p. 95.
40. See ibid., pp. 93–96 and 109, and Kerr (2003), vol. 2, pp. 122–29. As Kerr notes in volume 2 of his memoirs, "When the university decided to use the area from Sather Gate to Bancroft Way for the new student union complex, I realized that somehow the Sather Gate tradition had to be preserved. . . . So I proposed that space of approximately 26 feet by 40 feet at Bancroft and Telegraph be turned back to the City of Berkeley as a 'freedom of expression' area to replace the former area in front of Sather Gate" (Kerr [2003], vol. 2, p. 130).
41. Kerr (2003), vol. 2, p. 154.
42. Rothblatt, 179–80, and Roger L. Geiger, "Making the University of California," Science 296 (April 5, 2002): 52.

system (with some budgetary authority); and the position of vice president–academic affairs, vacant since 1948, was filled to develop collaborative working relationships with campus administrators and the Academic Senate. These steps led to a much-needed reorganization of the senate.[43] By 1963 the Northern and Southern sectional divisions, in which Berkeley and UCLA faculty exercised disproportionate influence, had become an anachronism. Kerr recommended a new federal system of nine Academic Senate divisions that redistributed authority across all campuses. Decentralization gave university faculty a more effective voice,[44] but Kerr's single-minded focus on decentralization led to serious misjudgments. By delegating all student affairs responsibilities to the campuses, Kerr treated the rules governing students' political activities as part of the decentralization process. This was a serious mistake because no one in the administration anticipated the adverse impact that liberalizing the Sproul Directives would have on campus. The administration and regents were focused on Sacramento. "We were fearful," Kerr admitted, "that the legislature might take away some of our institutional autonomy or reduce our financial support if we began allowing our property to be used for direct political actions."[45] This clear illustration of the latent power of the state led the university to defend a position that was "no longer legally defensible."[46]

By the early 1960s, direct action and civil disobedience had become prominent elements in civil rights sit-ins, effectively blurring the lines between speech and action. The university tried to maintain a murky distinction between "free speech," defined as the spoken and written word, and "advocacy," which the Board of Regents defined as actions related to speech, such as fundraising and political recruit-

---

43. Douglass (1998), p. 8. In March 1961, the Sixteenth All-University Faculty Conference was held on the Davis campus on the general topic "The University in a Period of Growth." A new university-wide Academic Assembly was created, with membership consisting of the University of California president, chairs of each senate division, leaders of the Committee on Educational Policy and the Committee on Budget and Interdivisional Relations, and delegates to the assembly selected on a proportional basis from the divisions. See Taylor, p. 55.

44. Kerr (2001), vol. 1, p. 199.

45. Kerr (2003), vol. 2, pp. 142–43.

46. Ibid., p. 143.

ment. Kerr and the regents believed that the Sather Gate and Hyde Park tradition would allow the university to keep political advocacy off campus, thereby reducing the prospect of politicizing academic life. The university could claim that it recognized free speech at the same time as it refused to allow campus property to be used to mount political attacks against the state or society at large. Kerr understood that the university had entered "a maze with no easy way out."[47]

In September 1964, when Berkeley Chancellor Edward Strong (1961–65) directed Dean of Students Kathleen Towle to revoke the cherished Sather Gate tradition, Kerr (by his own admission) compounded the misstep by not rescinding the order immediately. Kerr was also slow to recognize the need to dismiss Chancellor Strong. His decision to wait says much about the latent influence of different actors in the governance process. As the principal author and advocate of decentralization, Kerr did not want to violate the spirit of his own policy. He also believed that some Berkeley faculty members were in a rebellious mood and was "fearful of faculty reaction."[48] In time, the actions of student activists in the Free Speech Movement, which culminated in the occupation of Sproul Hall in early December 1964, created an environment in which a variety of faculty voices, representing ad hoc and standing committees, seized control of the situation from Chancellor Strong and gradually coalesced around a centrist solution to end the crisis.[49]

47. Ibid., pp. 138–39 and 142.
48. Ibid., pp. 180–81. This is an excellent example of the latent power of the faculty over even as accomplished and powerful a leader as Clark Kerr.
49. At the December 18, 1964, meeting of the Board of Regents, Kerr made two sets of propositions that were approved by the regents. The first offered a general expression of appreciation to the Academic Council of the university-wide Academic Senate for its constructive proposals and analysis of recent developments, a reaffirmation of faith that the university's faculty and students would find the "means to combine freedom with responsibility under today's new circumstances," and a reaffirmation of the regents' commitment to the First and Fourteenth Amendments. The most important set of proposals urged the regents to direct the administration "to preserve law and order on the campuses and to take the necessary steps to insure orderly pursuit of its educational functions." Kerr's propositions also reconfirmed "that ultimate authority for student discipline within the University is constitutionally vested in the Regents, and is a matter not subject to negotiation." Implementation of policy would continue to be

The Firing of Clark Kerr

Following the election of Governor Ronald Reagan, and in the context of the times, the Board of Regents fired Clark Kerr as president on January 20, 1967, by a vote of 14–8. Kerr refused suggestions that he resign. He wanted to demonstrate that the initiative for his separation came from the regents and the governor, not from him. The chancellors and the faculty overwhelmingly expressed strong support for Kerr and opposed both any suggestion that he resign and his firing—to no avail.[50]

The Faculty Role in More Recent Years

In General

We are now going to take a topical approach as we consider the faculty role at the University of California in more recent years. In taking this approach, we are well advised to heed the admonition of C. Judson King, director of the Center for Studies in Higher Education at the University of California, Berkeley, and a long-time participant in and observer of the university's history, who has identified three distinct levels of articulation around the faculty role in governance: (1) formally delegated responsibilities where faculty have clear dominion over a decision-making area, such as approval of courses and degree contents, definitions of conditions of admission, and the right of the senate to organize its own work as it sees fit; (2) issues where faculty provide advice that is almost always followed, including recommendations regarding academic personnel and departmental and program reviews; and (3) issues where faculty are consulted and listened to, but where

delegated by the regents to the president and chancellors, "who will seek advice of appropriate faculty committees in individual cases." Kerr's recommendations also proposed a review of all university policies, "with the intent of providing maximum freedom on campus consistent with individual and group responsibility." See Kerr (2001), vol. 1, pp. 233–34.

50. There is a long account of these events, and of the subsequent establishment by the Berkeley faculty of the Clark Kerr Award (with Kerr as the first recipient), in the oral history by Ewald T. Grether, dean of the School of Business at Berkeley (included in Taylor, pp. 73–82). See also Taylor, pp. 69–71.

there is no expectation that faculty will make the decision, so that decisions that go a different way are not controversial.[51] It is important to note, as one scholar observes, that "the root of the contemporary notion of shared governance [at the University of California] . . . emerged not only from the formal delegation of authority to the [Academic] Senate, but also from informal modes of involving faculty in the management of the nation's largest land-grant university."[52]

A general observation: Berkeley is very "faculty-centered," and administrators expect to "work with the faculty; they don't try to force them to do anything."[53] Also, as we have seen in the historical overview, the University of California has benefited from a very high degree of congruity between its faculty structures, beginning with the Academic Senate, and a deeply held commitment to the "spirit of shared governance" that unites faculty and administrators in a common commitment to academic excellence. Shared governance is not a panacea; in fact, as the later discussion of online learning illustrates, it can make it harder to get things done. But it definitely provides a forum for alternate views and for building faculty support.

Choosing "the Faculty" Whose Voices Are to Be Heard

As a rule, the faculty express themselves, and act, through committees and representatives. Thus, in discussing the various faculty roles, a recurring—and very important—question is what process is followed in choosing the faculty whose voices are to be heard. As we have seen, prior to the "Berkeley Revolution" of 1919–20, President Wheeler appointed the faculty committees whose advice he sought with respect to the appointment and advancement of professors.

51. King to Bowen, January 5, 2014, personal correspondence.
52. Douglass (1998), p. 1.
53. Tyler Stovall, dean, Undergraduate Division, College of Letters and Science, University of California, Berkeley. Armando Fox, professor in residence, Electrical Engineering and Computer Science (and the creator of the apparently highly successful automated grader system), repeated this same sentiment: "Berkeley has a special tradition of faculty governance. . . . You cannot tell a Berkeley faculty member what to do." (Stovall and Fox, interviews by Kevin Guthrie, September 2013.) Other interviews that Guthrie conducted in September 2013 captured this same theme.

The Standing Orders adopted in 1920 defined the membership of the Academic Senate (AS) very inclusively: the president, deans, other administrators, and "all professors and instructors." The AS was authorized to "choose its own chairman and committees in such manner as it may determine," and Taylor notes that this was "the basis for the senate's early establishment of a Committee on Committees."[54] Today, members of the Committee on Committees on each campus are elected by the senate members on that campus, and the Committee on Committees determines its own chair. Also, although the top officers of the administration are indeed members of the AS (many of them by virtue of their faculty appointments), they are not actual participants in senate activities. Academic Council chairs are chosen by the Academic Council, the university-wide governing body of the AS.[55]

Throughout the materials describing events at the University of California over the years, there are mentions of faculty voting on matters of many kinds, including appointments to key committees, by secret, mail-in ballot. A good example is the handling of the Free Speech Movement crisis in 1964. In the second volume of his memoirs, Kerr tells us that in December 1964, the faculty at Berkeley finally took charge of managing the crisis. They created an emergency executive committee to represent faculty across all divisions. The faculty members of the emergency executive committee were elected by secret (mail-in) ballot.[56]

---

54. Taylor, p. 7. In the early years, the president had some influence through the dean of faculties, who chaired the Committee on Committees. In the words of President Barrows in 1922, "This arrangement would seem to assure a proper consideration of the President's desires in the composition of committees" (minutes of the meeting of the Board of Regents of the University of California, December 12, 1922, quoted in Taylor, p. 7n6). This is no longer the case.

55. C. Judson King to Bowen, February 3, 2014, personal e-mail.

56. Kerr (2003), vol. 2, p. 226. This involved a rather cumbersome process of rounds of voting that, however cumbersome, worked. The process was more complicated than the "single transferrable vote" (and "alternative vote") machinery that Professor Stanley Kelley put in place at Princeton in the late 1960s—which is explained in an appendix to the Kelley Report ("The Governing of Princeton University: Final Report of the Special Committee on the Structure of the University," Princeton University, April 1970). Kelley, a political scientist, borrowed this highly effective electoral process from the Irish government.

Selecting Chancellors

The president selects the chancellors, as was the case in the recent selection of Nicholas B. Dirks at Berkeley by President Mark G. Yudof, but there is active faculty involvement in the selection process. According to a press release from the Office of the President (December 12, 2012), the selection was made after a six-month search process. There was an advisory committee of University of California faculty, students, staff, regents, alumni, and foundation representatives that was involved in screening candidates and conducting interviews. Regents then approved the appointment and the terms (salary, etc.) of the chancellor.

Selecting Departmental Chairs

As is evident in the following discussion of the process of appointing and advancing faculty, chairs of departments are tremendously important. Chairs are chosen by administrative officers after consultation with the faculty; they are not elected by their faculty colleagues. The dean of the school in question consults the faculty of the department individually and then reports the general sense and spread of faculty views to the provost when asking for approval of his or her selection. Chairs typically serve three to five years. Some serve longer, with continual consultation by the dean with the faculty if they are to serve longer. This responsibility is not spread around. Only about 10–30 percent of faculty members become chairs eventually, depending on the size of the department.[57]

The Faculty Review Process for Appointments and Advancements

The real test of governance is not only how well colleges and universities respond to crises but how effective and flexible they are in addressing the myriad daily demands of institutional life—of which the judicious handling of faculty personnel matters is of first importance.

57. C. Judson King to Bowen, March 15, 2014, memo.

In his foreword to Angus Taylor's history of how the AS handled eleven crises, Kerr writes: "These crises constitute what might be called the 'public life' of the Academic Senate since the end of World War I. The Academic Senate has also had a 'private life' comprised of the work of its . . . many committees. . . . In its public life, the senate has made significant contributions to solving major problems before the university. In its private life, the senate has made equally great contributions in shaping effective ongoing policies and in making critically important individual judgments, particularly on faculty appointments and promotions." Kerr adds: "I think the academic success of the university is based more on the contributions of the AS than on any other factor. The AS holds the most important share in this system of *shared governance* particularly in the review of all academic appointments and promotions."[58]

The faculty's key role in the appointment, promotion, and advancement process has continued to the present day. C. Judson King has observed that this process "is singular, and many of us feel that it is the single most important reason for the success of the university." Faculty are reviewed repeatedly and thoroughly by a faculty-led process throughout their careers, and their advancement and salary are tied to these reviews. In this sense, the University of California has had post-tenure review since the 1930s. There is a similar, intense review at the time of approval of the initial appointment. To be sure, faculty committees only recommend actions to the campus chancellor, but these recommendations are approved "99.44%" of the time.[59]

58. Taylor, pp. xi–xiii (quote on p. xiii, our emphasis). In the concluding section of his history, Taylor concurs with Kerr's judgment about the preeminent importance of the faculty role in the faculty personnel process (p. 112).

59. King to Bowen, January 5, 2014, personal e-mail. The process is described in great detail in a paper by Ellen Switkes, "University of California Peer Review System and Post-tenure Evaluations," *Innovative Higher Education* 24, no. 1 (1999): 39–48. This elaborate peer review process involves ad hoc committees and the solicitation of outside letters for appointments to tenure and for major faculty promotions; the faculty committee's role is advisory, however, and each faculty file is forwarded "to the Chancellor's office for a decision" (Switkes, p. 45). Daniel F. Melia, associate professor of rhetoric and Celtic studies at the University of California, Berkeley, told Kevin Guthrie (in a September 2013 interview) that recommendations are approved "nearly all the time, except for some token refusals to make clear that the power remains there if absolutely necessary."

everybad idea!!!

In many colleges and universities, final action on at least tenured faculty appointments is reserved to the trustees/regents. This is not the case at the University of California. Authority in all faculty personnel matters has been delegated to the faculty (and the chancellors) by the regents and the president. Real authority rests with the Senate Committee on Academic Personnel at each individual campus.[60] These committees are chosen by the campus Committees on Committees, and the chair of each committee is one of the members in his or her final year of service on the committee.[61]

should be solely in the hands of the faculty!

This could well be the most thoroughly faculty-driven review process in the country, and Kerr has referred to his "unstated reservations about removing the regents entirely from the process of approving appointments and promotions to tenure—the most important series of actions a university ever takes." Kerr continues, "To this day, I regret that I did not ask for more detailed consideration of this basic change in university policy, but I did not: an annual presidential post-review of the quality of actions at the campus level and, perhaps, monthly reports would have kept the regents informed about the chancellors' actions and the quality of the faculty being developed. Actually, in practice, the campuses made better decisions than I had feared. But the change isolated the regents from this essential aspect of university life."[62]

wisely so *very* *rightly so!*

60. To the best of our knowledge, the last real test of faculty control of the appointment process was the Angela Davis Case in 1969, when the regents attempted to dismiss Davis from the UCLA faculty because she was a member of the Communist Party. This action was blocked by a summary judgment of the court that enjoined the university from taking an action to terminate based solely on membership in the Communist Party. The Academic Council of the Academic Senate then passed a resolution specifying that lawful political affiliation, including membership in the Communist Party, cannot be the basis for disqualification for membership in the university faculty. See Taylor, pp. 98–100, for a full account of this historically important controversy.

angela davis

61. The members of the Committees on Committees are elected by the members of each campus Faculty Senate division. Faculty members volunteer themselves for these assignments, gather three or four endorsements from around the campus, and then appear on the ballot. According to C. Judson King (writing to Bowen on February 3, 2014, in personal correspondence), "Voter judgments tend to be made on how well known and respected the person and/or his/her endorsers are."

62. Kerr (2001), vol. 1, p. 211.

There is another special feature of the California system, as C. Judson King has explained (in the same personal correspondence cited above):

> This process is exercised for appointments and advancements at new campuses from the start, with the role of the Senate Committee on Academic Personnel being taken by a Committee on Academic Personnel for the new campus composed of faculty members from the existing campuses. We just went through that, successfully I think, over the past 13 years to form the initial faculty for the new Merced campus. As best I know, this review and advancement process is unique.

However, not everyone believes that this university-wide approach is wise, and some have questioned whether it makes sense to have the same processes and standards on very different campuses.[63]

Oversight of Curriculum and Academic Program

The regents' Standing Order 105.2 explicitly delegates to the AS oversight of academic decisions involving admissions, degree status, and the curriculum. As C. Judson King observes, the oversight of academic decisions, such as control of the curriculum, rests clearly with the division senates, working with the departments. So any new course at Berkeley must be proposed by the department to the division senate. The decision as to whether it is approved rests with the senate, not with the administration. In general, these decisions also stay at the division/campus level. Only very large decisions that have substantial budget impact have to go to the system-wide senate.[64]

63. Michael S. McPherson, president of the Spencer Foundation, commented as follows (writing to Bowen on January 6, 2014, in personal correspondence): "Some administrators responsible for the development of the new University of California campus at Merced questioned the wisdom of imposing exactly the same processes and standards regarding faculty rules, including recruiting and tenure, at both Berkeley and a start-up campus aimed at disadvantaged students. They thought it was kind of crazy."

64. Paraphrase based on an interview with C. Judson King conducted by Kevin Guthrie in September 2013.

The important distinction between faculty authority over individual courses (exercised through the AS) and authority over organizational units such as schools, colleges, and departments—where the administration has authority, with approval by the regents when needed—is well represented by the replacement at Berkeley of the School of Library and Information Studies with the School of Information Management and Systems (now the School of Information). This organizational transformation was accomplished through close collaboration between the AS and the administration.

Even more massive departmental reorganizations were required in two colleges to replace numerous existing departments in the biological sciences with a smaller number of larger, better-focused units. It was evident in the 1970s that effective organization of research and teaching at the forefront of the life sciences now related much more to scale (molecular, cell, etc.) than to the classical divisions by classes of species. One factor explaining Berkeley's success in accomplishing a vast reorganization of these fields was that the chancellor at the time, Michael Heyman, enlisted excellent academic leadership from the biological sciences in key posts. A special internal Biological Sciences Review Committee of faculty (appointed by the administration) recommended the creation of a Chancellor's Advisory Committee on Biology (CACB), composed of eminent Berkeley biology faculty. This recommendation was adopted, and the committee reported directly to the chancellor and vice chancellor and took on many important roles, including recommending fields in which new hires should be made, suggesting search committees, and developing an overall space plan, which in turn led to major fundraising successes. The new space became a major lure to move things along—an excellent incentive.

From a governance perspective, it is important to note how relations with the AS were handled. The principals chose not to pose issues for the AS and await responses—which might have led to impasses and inaction. Rather, the CACB took intellectual leadership, informed the AS and its committees of plans as they evolved, and in effect put the burden on the AS to take the initiative if it wanted to question something or stop something. Hence, the involvement of the AS was substantially less than it might have been otherwise. The success of the effort to reorganize within the College of Letters and Science then made it easier to accomplish a reorganization within the College of Natural Resources (which was the home of many other biologists and botanists). Success breeds success.

To sum up: at Berkeley, the reorganization of the biological sciences and information sciences demonstrated a high degree of collaboration between faculty structures (operating through the AS) and the university administration. It appears that formal lines of authority were respected, but ways were also found to get the relevant parties working together, whatever the structures. The "spirit of shared governance" so evident in these experiences may well be more important than specific mechanisms used to address particular problems.

The infamous (and much earlier) Eldridge Cleaver case, in the late 1960s, provides a very different example of the faculty role in overseeing courses, and it illustrates a key distinction between oversight of course content and responsibility for deciding who will teach a course.[65] From September 1968 through the summer of 1969, there was a long-drawn-out struggle involving the regents, the Berkeley faculty, and University of California President Charles J. Hitch over whether an "experimental course" titled Dehumanization and Regeneration in the American Social Order could be offered with Eldridge Cleaver (of Black Panther fame) as principal lecturer. The public was outraged. Roger Heyns, chancellor of Berkeley, was urged to intervene but declined to do so because he said that the AS, not the administration, had the power to authorize and supervise courses of instruction. The controversy continued.

When the matter was discussed at a meeting of the Academic Council, President Hitch shifted the argument away from Cleaver per se and drew a sharp distinction between (1) having an outside speaker brought in once or twice as an invited guest to present a point of view and (2) appointing a qualified outsider as a temporary visiting faculty member to make a substantial contribution to a course. The Academic Council subsequently endorsed the princi-

65. For a detailed history of this controversy, see Taylor, pp. 83–87.

ple that any person who has substantial responsibility in a course of instruction must have the appropriate instructional title and that normal controls over the appointment process must apply. Cleaver did not pass this test. After much debate, the chancellors and the Academic Council adopted the position that the action taken concerning this course (not to allow it to be offered for credit, as originally proposed) was justified on the ground that "the assignment of responsibility to teach is an administrative responsibility, separate and distinct from the senate's control over the plan and subject matter of a course." Hitch said that approval of the resolution in question involved no violation of academic freedom (it did not refer to Cleaver, as various other draft resolutions had, but focused on policy). Hitch kept emphasizing that they were dealing with an issue of personnel policy, not an issue of academic freedom. (This is an absolutely key distinction that is relevant to our broader interest in online learning.)

Although faculty are understood to have clear dominion over the curriculum and courses, there is less agreement over the effectiveness of the faculty in providing campus-wide coordination of what it means to have an undergraduate degree. This oversight role is left to the division senate, which has delegated considerable responsibility to departments, and some faculty whom we interviewed questioned how much real oversight is exercised. Others, however, pointed to the existence of clear university-wide requirements, campus-wide requirements, and requirements for students within the College of Letters and Science at Berkeley. Each of the four other undergraduate colleges has its own set of requirements. All of these have been approved by the campus division of the AS, in line with the delegation of degree requirements by the regents directly to the senate. The AS on each campus has a Committee on Courses of Instruction, to which all courses are submitted by departments for approval before they can be taught for the first time. There is, nonetheless (as we think all would agree), a challenge to provide, in fact as well as in the abstract, close attention on a faculty-wide basis to overall educational philosophy at a time of more and more faculty specialization and inevitable tensions between interests of individual faculty in research and their concern for the educational program writ large. This is, of course, a challenge for all research universities, and for many colleges as well. It is not an issue of where de jure authority rests.[66]

The Faculty Role in the University of California Online Education (UCOE) Initiative

The University of California's recent—difficult—experience with online learning, which is discussed in detail in the appendix to this case study, serves as a sharp reminder of the fragility of shared governance. It is worth thinking hard about why Berkeley did well in dealing with the reorganization of the biological sciences and the creation of a new School of Information, and why the university-wide online learning effort has so far been much less successful. One obvious explanation is the lack of faculty leadership, and the lack of faculty buy-in, in the online case.

A heavy-handed, top-down approach had little chance to succeed, especially in the University of California context, where faculty prerogatives are deeply embedded and prized. There is no doubt that the online experience illustrates well the centrality of faculty authority in curricular matters at the University of California. This experience also illustrates some of the special complications posed by online initiatives, particularly when, as in this instance, the initial impetus came from the president's office without much, if any, direct faculty involvement. Other factors contributing to the difficulties with the online project include the lack of a business plan, the fact of scarce resources, and the conflict (if not stated) between educational objectives and financial objectives.

It is well worth noting the strong aversion, especially on the part of faculty (but sometimes on that of administrators, too), to any discussion of cost savings, certainly in the case of educational programs.

66. C. Judson King made this comment (writing to Bowen on March 15, 2014, in a personal e-mail): "The issues of undergraduate education, as a whole and including general education and distribution requirements, have been considered sporadically by a university-wide committee (the Pister Report), by the College of Letters and Science at Berkeley (and similar colleges on other campuses), the Center for Studies in Higher Education at Berkeley (Smelser–Schudson committee of the early 2000s), and the Academic Senate (with regard to the Berkeley campus-wide requirement on American Cultures)."

Berkeley has made a major effort to save on *administrative* costs, via a project known as Operational Excellence. In the academic area, our interviews with faculty and some academic administrators indicate that the focus invariably seems to be on educational outcomes, not on educational outcomes at a specified cost. One senses little if any inclination to think in terms of trade-offs. On the website of the Berkeley Resource Center for Online Education (BRCOE), there was at one time a list of goals and "anti-goals," and one anti-goal was to lower costs.[67]

We have to ask if there is not even more to the story. Are there specific aspects of efforts to move ahead in the online area that posed (and continue to pose) unusually difficult governance challenges? We suspect that there are. In a companion project, we will try to spell out such challenges and suggest governance arrangements (including possible protocols for handling intellectual property [IP] issues) that could make it easier to succeed in the online area.

67. We asked C. Judson King about this, and he reports that he was unable to bring up the aforementioned website. King then adds (writing to Bowen on February 2, 2014, in a personal e-mail): "Perhaps the web site has been redone since you consulted it. Hence my answer will reflect what I think may be at play. The BRCOE and MOOCLab are designed to stimulate and help faculty get going in devising on-line approaches to higher education. In that sense citing opportunities and available assistance would be designed to get the faculty doing things, while citing cost savings would not incentivize and stimulate the faculty much if at all. In that the goal is to get the faculty moving with regard to on-line methodology, the web site may have been created to stress the things attractive to faculty and eliminate or minimize any implication that on-line methodology is going to displace faculty. With regard to the thinking that 'online learning technologies are not going to reduce costs,' I don't think that feeling is universal at Berkeley. The statement probably reflects a feeling that on-line components will be an add-on, without significant reduction in current costs; i.e., the faculty will continue to 'teach' as much or nearly as much. It is true that enhanced delivery and pedagogy through the use of online elements can be attractive to many faculty members, and there is probably substantial feeling that the best role of on-line education, as it now stands, is to enrich courses rather than to supplant the need for the instructor. I think there is general appreciation that the use of on-line methodology can and should change the nature of classes, i.e., by adding components beyond the classical lecture. Finally, the typical cost structure of on-line education (of the quality in which most faculty believe) is a substantial cost out front for development of the on-line component, followed by little or very small cost per usage hereafter. In that sense, someone looking at the cost of on-line instruction in the short run will see it as an added cost, and it takes an appreciation of the longer term to see the savings."

Faculty Responsibility for Student Life
and Student Discipline

As our historical overview reminds us, in the mid-1960s there was tremendous turmoil at Berkeley (as well as at many other institutions), and there were major debates concerning the role of the faculty in student life, and especially in student discipline. Kerr concluded his detailed explication of student unrest in the fall of 1964 by comparing the university's response to student civil disobedience with later events at the University of Chicago, Columbia, and Harvard:

> The Berkeley faculty alone said, no academic discipline. It alone never completely condemned coercive disobedience. But it also did not have the two to five years of experience the others had. The Heyman report [issued by the Committee on Student Conduct of the Berkeley Academic Senate]—as endorsed by the department chairs in December 1964 and the Academic Senate in connection with the disturbances of December 1966—had created the model of faculty assurance and student anticipation that there would be no academic discipline for student political behavior. Why? I do not understand why.[68]

As previously noted, at the December 18, 1964, meeting of the Board of Regents, Kerr urged the regents to direct the administration "to preserve law and order on the campuses" and to take "the necessary steps to insure orderly pursuit of its educational functions." Kerr's recommendations to the regents also reconfirmed "that ultimate authority for student discipline within the University is constitutionally vested in the Regents, and is a matter not subject to negotiation." Implementation of policy would continue to be delegated by the regents to the president and chancellors, "who will seek advice of appropriate faculty committees in individual cases."[69]

In more recent years, the matter of the faculty role in student discipline has not been questioned or debated, and today the Berkeley campus has regulations and procedures, involving both administra-

68. Kerr (2003), vol. 2, p. 226.
69. Ibid., p. 234.

tive officers and a faculty committee, that are similar to what is found at many other colleges and universities.[70]

The Faculty Role in Advising and Consultation in General

In 1920, the AS "acquired from the regents formal recognition of its role in advising the president of the university." The AS was given the right "to lay its views before the board of regents through the president on any matter pertaining to the conduct and welfare of the university." As Angus Taylor observed: "These historic principles still survive."[71]

Today, the chair and vice chair of the Academic Council have seats at the meeting table of the regents, can engage fully in discussions and present senate views—but have no vote. C. Judson King observes:

> In practice, the administration brings virtually all major matters pertaining to the administration of the University to the Senate for its advice. Although it is not explicitly stated, the Academic Senate has the primary role in the review of tenure track faculty members for promotion and advancement, with the advice of the pertinent Senate committees in that regard nearly always followed by the administration [see the earlier discussion of this topic]. Advice in other areas is taken seriously but is nowhere nearly as controlling as it is in the area of promotion and advancement of faculty.[72]

Historically, the use of the AS for broad consultation has varied greatly. President Sproul was not known for emphasizing consultation, but he did appoint a Special Committee of the Academic Senate on Educational Policy, which later became a regular committee. During the Great Depression of the 1930s, the committee was asked to recommend how salary reductions were to be carried out—which

70. C. Judson King, e-mail of February 2, 2014. Today's procedures are given at http://sa.berkeley.edu/conduct/overview and http://safetycounts.berkeley.edu/content/disciplinary-action.

71. Taylor, pp. 1 and 4.

72. King, "Change at the University of California: The Roles of Governance," report to ITHAKA, New York, January 2014, p. 4.

it did, reducing most the pay of those who were highest paid.[73] Following World War II, a major issue was how to respond to anticipated needs for major increases in enrollment. In the spring of 1954, "the combined Committee on Educational Policy of the Northern and Southern Sections [of the AS] tried to respond to a request from President Sproul for advice." The committee considered various options, but no conclusion was reached.[74]

It was not really until the time of Clark Kerr that extensive consultation became the norm. In his memoirs, Kerr emphasizes the critical importance of consultation and the amount of time he devoted to meeting with the Academic Assembly, Academic Council, and university-wide senate committees. He writes: "The purpose of all this consultation was to share information, elicit suggestions, agree upon decisions, and get acquainted. There were face-to-face negotiations and a certain amount of conciliation to achieve consensus or at least consent."[75] Kerr's collaborative and mediating instincts were deeply rooted in his personal and professional life, which clearly influenced his presidential style. As an undergraduate at Swarthmore College (class of 1932), he joined the Quaker meeting, spent summers working as a "peace caravaner" with the American Friends Service Committee, and came to believe that "there is that of good in every person." Later in life, Kerr had a distinguished career in industrial relations and was a skilled labor mediator.[76]

It is striking, and not surprising, that during the Kerr years, which represented an unprecedented period of change and expansion, the Berkeley faculty focused on "macro" questions, especially on how to cope with pressures for greatly increased enrollment. More recently, the faculty has focused much of its attention on the academic issues discussed earlier, including the reorganization of the biological sci-

73. Taylor, pp. 8–11.
74. Ibid., p. 39.
75. Kerr (2001), vol. 1, p. 201.
76. Kerr (2001), vol. 1, pp. 13–14. This is an excellent example of the importance of a person's upbringing and personal inclinations in shaping how he or she handles an activity such as consultation. One has to ask whether Kerr's sense of collegiality and professional courtesy still exist in meaningful ways at most large public universities—or at private institutions of almost any size, for that matter.

ences, the creation of the School of Information, and the online learning initiative. Of course, much attention has been given to funding cuts imposed by the state legislature.

One of the most difficult and contentious issues of general policy to arise centered on affirmative action/race/admissions. This set of issues has been present in one form or another almost everywhere, prompting major court cases and extensive debates over admission policies, but they surfaced in a particularly virulent form in California in the mid-1990s. The debate in California was triggered by the regents' resolution (in 1995) eliminating racial and other preferences in admissions, hiring, and contracting. The president of the university, all the chancellors, and all vice presidents opposed the resolutions in a public statement. Nonetheless, Kerr noted that the question of how to respond proved divisive within the faculty: "Berkeley, the campus most devoted to 'diversity,' was more affected than any other campus because it had the most pressure on admissions. . . . The Regents had not sought the Academic Senate's advice and Berkeley protested. The other campuses did not support the Berkeley protest in an effective way."[77]

It is unclear why the Academic Council did not itself ask to review the resolution on admission, because "the conditions of admission" fall squarely under the senate's purview. According to C. Judson King, it remains something of a mystery as to why the senate did not assert itself more strongly here and push back, as it did during the Kerr years. Part of the explanation may be time pressures, because things were moving so fast. Also, there could well have been divisions within the senate on this issue, and King's guess is that the senate was probably divided, with a substantial minority that were not for affirmative action and/or thought that affirmative action had gone too far. That minority may have been sufficient to freeze the senate into inaction.[78] This entire episode reminds us again that whatever formal delegations of authority may exist, it is difficult, if not impossible, for a public university to prevent a determined set of political actors from setting broad policies when an issue becomes as politically charged as affirmative action.

77. Kerr (2001), vol. 1, p. 356.
78. King to Bowen, March 15, 2014, memo.

In any case, the senate and the university-wide administration decided to work together (rather than have the senate work on its own) in deciding precisely how to adjust policies in light of the regents' resolutions and the passage of Proposition 209, which banned all affirmative action in government employment and public education. Pursuant to a resolution adopted by the regents, the university moved to create an "Outreach Task Force" that was designed to find ways to increase the eligibility and attendance of disadvantaged students in a race-neutral context. Four regents were included on the task force. Two persons were named by the Academic Council to serve on the large (thirty-six-member) task force, which was co-chaired by the provost (C. Judson King at the time) and a prominent person from the private sector. The task force held public meetings.

Various staff studies were made available to the Board on Admissions and Relations with the Schools (BOARS), the committee of the AS charged with studying and recommending the conditions of eligibility and admissions. The president met with BOARS, and many complicated approaches were discussed and adopted. The president at the time, Richard Atkinson (1995–2003), was a distinguished psychologist whose specialty was standardized testing, and presidential leadership was important in gaining approval by the senate of proposals that placed more emphasis on achievement than aptitude as a reliable predictor of students' future success. In short, the president and other key administrators were effective in working with the senate to develop specific modes of adaptation to the regents' Resolution SP-1 and Proposition 209.[79]

Looking Ahead

Clark Kerr was very clear, and ahead of his time, in noting the growing specialization of faculty roles, the growing "professionalism," and the growing emphasis on research and consultation—sometimes at the expense of undergraduate teaching. It remains to be seen how

79. See C. Judson King, "Change and Governance at the University of California: Comparative Case Studies," Research and Occasional Papers Series CSHE.11.14, Center for Studies in Higher Education, University of California, Berkeley (2014), pp. 10–14.

these developments will affect notions of "shared governance," and, more specifically, the willingness of key faculty to invest substantial time and energy in serving on key committees (with the probable exception of committees on appointment and advancement).

In recent years, another concern has emerged that will require careful and thoughtful attention. Faculty serving on campus- and university-wide committees of the AS are all from "traditional" faculty ranks. If the percentage of lecturers and contingent faculty continues to grow, traditional faculty will represent a decreasing percentage of the overall community of teachers and educators. This is a nationwide trend, which is already being reflected in pressures for unionization of teaching staff and also in broader debates over how the composition of the teaching cadre should be determined and how much authority should be given to subsets of teaching staff, and not just to traditional tenure-track faculty members. As one of our colleagues is fond of saying, "Stay tuned."

APPENDIX: THE UNIVERSITY OF CALIFORNIA ONLINE EDUCATION INITIATIVE

Derek Wu
March 4, 2014

In an op-ed in the *Los Angeles Times* in July 2009, Christopher Edley Jr.—dean of the University of California, Berkeley, School of Law—introduced the idea of a "virtual" eleventh University of California campus devoted solely to awarding online degrees to University of California–eligible students.[80] Such a plan, in his eyes, would offer education more cheaply (improving student access and diminishing institutional cost burdens) while maintaining quality. At the time, in

Derek Wu is a research analyst at Ithaka S+R, where his work focuses on examining the effects of changing higher education costs on student enrollment and outcome patterns and on assessing the implications of online learning in higher education with regard to costs, productivity, and changing governance structures.

80. http://articles.latimes.com/2009/jul/01/opinion/oe-edley1.

addition to his role as a dean, Edley was an active member of the University of California Commission on the Future (serving as co-chair of the Education and Curriculum working group) and a senior advisor to University of California President Mark Yudof. At the outset, Edley was very confident in the potential to raise the resources necessary for an upfront investment in this virtual campus and believed that faculty members were cautiously supportive of such an endeavor.[81]

Several months later, in October 2009, Daniel Greenstein—vice provost for academic programs and planning and co-leader with Edley of the UCOE—met with the AS's University Committee on Education Policy (UCEP) to provide an overview of both the broader initiative and a related—yet distinct—pilot project that would implement online courses at a more modest level to see if there were "opportunities that UC [was] not taking full advantage of."[82] In fact, the idea behind the pilot project originated from the division senates on one or more campuses (which included the University of California, Berkeley).[83] Although there was discussion about possible faculty concerns and how this pilot would be evaluated, the committee stated that there did not appear to be any senate policies that would impede its progress and recommended that Greenstein and his partners subsequently develop a pre-proposal and determine the direction of the pilot.[84]

For the next several months, Greenstein and Edley worked on the planning stages of the pilot project, which called for offering online twenty-five high-demand, lower-level gateway courses, for which professors would compete for development grants awarded through a process run by the AS.[85] However, the approval process for these system-wide courses would have to cross multiple hurdles, starting with recommendation and review from each campus's Com-

81. http://chronicle.com/article/Online-Campus-Could-Solve-Many/47432.

82. http://senate.universityofcalifornia.edu/committees/ucep/ucep.10.5.09.minutes.pdf.

83. C. Judson King to Kevin Guthrie, February 5, 2014, personal e-mail.

84. It bears mentioning that the chair of this committee—Keith Williams—would later become a faculty advisor to the University of California Office of the President and ultimately interim director following Greenstein's departure.

85. http://chronicle.com/article/In-Crisis-U-of-California/65445/.

mittee on Courses before seeking approval by each campus division of the AS and, subsequently, by the system-wide UCEP. Although Edley acknowledged that the somewhat complex nature of the AS's approval process might make it difficult to move the project forward, there was hope that the Faculty Senate would quickly endorse the initiative and that classes would be taught as soon as 2011.[86] In fact, Edley and Greenstein had proceeded to distribute funding for the online courses—hoping to immediately facilitate their development—even before the AS passed judgment on whether to approve them. Although "[Edley's] eagerness to reshape the university [was] seen by many faculty members as either naïve or dangerous," he remained ambitiously adamant that the University of California should be at the forefront of an inevitable movement to deliver quality online education for credit—and ultimately for degrees.[87] Whether what was being worked on was a pilot project or the first step in a much larger effort to develop a new permanent program in online education seems to have been a source of misunderstanding and tension among the program's leadership and others at the university, especially faculty. Testing something of this magnitude would require significant resources and changes in approach.

In May 2010, Greenstein received a letter from the system-wide Academic Council (the administrative arm of the AS), which unanimously endorsed—based on UCEP's recommendation—proceeding with the online learning pilot project, contingent on the procurement of external funds.[88] A few days later, the Berkeley Faculty Association released a report raising serious concerns about Edley's plan for a "cyber campus," which included "profoundly degraded undergraduate education, eroded faculty governance and control over curriculum, research delinked from teaching . . . and squadrons of [graduate student instructors] at the frontline of online contact . . .

---

86. http://cshe.berkeley.edu/virtual-universities-ucs-eleventh-campus. In an e-mail conversation with Bowen in April 2010, Dan Greenstein was optimistic that faculty approval could be obtained for every course because faculty members themselves would be the ones developing them.

87. See source in footnote 85.

88. http://senate.universityofcalifornia.edu/reports/HP_LP_Greenstein_reonline pilot.pdf.

in courses whose sole purpose is revenue generation."[89] In particular, many faculty members were reminded of a similar project at the University of Illinois (the Global Campus initiative) that had imploded after two years.[90]

Nevertheless, these concerns proved not enough to forestall progress on the pilot project. Immediately following a presentation by Greenstein and Edley in July 2010, the University of California regents responded enthusiastically to Edley's belief in the potential of online instruction to enhance the University of California's ability to serve its mission (even though Edley emphasized that online degrees were not currently on the table) and voted to endorse the pilot program.[91] Edley's working group initially anticipated finishing the pilot and interpreting the data in the next year or two, a plan that the Berkeley Division of the AS deemed "impossibly optimistic."[92]

Over the next few months, Edley and Greenstein worked on selecting the courses that would be offered as part of the initiative and securing private grants for the pilot project. In February 2011, a peer review committee selected twenty-nine University of California faculty members who would receive funds to develop the pilot project's first batch of courses (with seventy professors having applied to participate). These courses would be offered for the first time in January 2012. Two months later (and nine months after the regents approved the endeavor), the pilot project obtained its first extramural grant—one of $750,000 from Next Generation Learning Challenges, an initiative managed by EDUCAUSE with funding from the Gates and Hewlett Foundations.[93] At the same time, it was announced that the project had taken out an interest-free $7 million loan from the Uni-

89. www.scribd.com/doc/31893477/BFA-Report-on-UCOF-OnLine-Ed. It is important to note that many faculty members have always viewed the pilot project and "online campus" endeavor as interlinked, such that any progress on the pilot initiative would necessarily translate to moving closer to a fully online degree program.

90. www.sfgate.com/opinion/editorials/article/Mortarboards-without-the-bricks-3181746.php.

91. www.sfgate.com/education/article/UC-regents-endorse-test-of-online-instruction-3181427.php.

92. www.insidehighered.com/news/2010/08/03/california.

93. www.universityofcalifornia.edu/news/article/25296.

\$ 1 million at a year perhaps!

versity of California Office of the President, to be paid back over the next seven years, primarily through revenue generated by tuition from non–University of California students.[94]

Many faculty members responded critically to the announcement of the loan. They felt that Edley had reneged on his original commitment to pursue external funding and instead tapped directly into their "monetary share" at a time when the University of California was struggling to deal with a recent \$500 million cut in state support.[95] In a May 2011 letter to President Yudof, Daniel Simmons (chair of the AS)—who had previously supported the pilot program and agreed that there was a need to experiment with online education even during times of financial crises—expressed concern about the opportunity costs of the \$7 million loan (i.e., cutting funding to other successful programs) and the ambiguity surrounding the pilot program's objectives (e.g., expanding access versus raising revenue).[96] Other issues raised in the letter included the fact that the AS had not yet received any course proposals for approval (even though it had previously been told that courses would be offered beginning in the fall) and that there remained many unanswered questions about program evaluation, the focus on lower-division requirements, and so on. As a result, Simmons wrote that the Academic Council—reversing its position from a year prior—advised that no additional online pilot courses be developed until things were evaluated in a more rigorous fashion.

Nonetheless, the pilot moved forward despite these concerns from the faculty.[97] Two months later, in July 2011, Academic Council Chair Simmons wrote another letter—this time to Provost Lawrence Pitts—endorsing UCEP's recommendation from a month earlier that the council appoint an independent "blue-ribbon panel" of experts (from

94. http://dailybruin.com/2011/05/05/uc_plan_for_online_classes_lacks_funding_uc_takes_out_a_6-9_million_loan/.

95. http://chronicle.com/blogs/wiredcampus/reversing-course-u-of-california-to-borrow-millions-for-online-classes/30853.

96. http://senate.universityofcalifornia.edu/reports/DS_MGYreonlinepilot_May2011_FINAL.pdf.

97. http://senate.universityofcalifornia.edu/news/source/onlinepilot.may2011.html.

both inside and outside the University of California) to report periodically to the AS on the progress and results of the pilot.[98] A few months later—in September 2011—Greenstein announced preliminary plans to repay the loan, which included selling five thousand places (out of seven thousand) in the online classes to non–University of California students, such as military personnel and international students.[99] This announcement did little to mollify the University Council–Academic Federation of Teachers (the union that represents the University of California's non-tenured lecturers), which feared that a push toward online education could threaten the status of its members' jobs.[100] Such a possibility led Union President Bob Samuels to contentiously say that language in the recently ratified online pilot contract gave the union the power to stop or delay the project if lecturers' jobs were indeed affected.[101] However, this minor controversy did not amount to much.

By early 2012, the pilot project had introduced its first course—Preparatory Calculus—at the University of California–Merced.[102] A total of six courses ended up being offered in the spring semester of 2012, all of which were offered only to University of California students enrolled at the instructors' home campuses.[103] Before University of California Online could offer any online course beyond its campus of origin, it needed to define—in consultation with the AS—an administrative and policy structure to facilitate student registration and enrollment. Cognizant of the need to bring in large numbers of non–University of California students in a timely fashion (to generate revenue), the leaders of the pilot project were hope-

98. http://senate.universityofcalifornia.edu/reports/DS_LPreUCOEevaluation plan.pdf. By the time UCEP made this recommendation, its former chair—Keith Williams—had stepped down.

99. www.sfgate.com/education/article/UC-investing-millions-in-new-cyber -studies-program-2309838.php.

100. www.huffingtonpost.com/2011/10/23/uc-online-instruction-pilot_n_ 1027170.html.

101. http://californiawatch.org/dailyreport/uc-online-instruction-pilot-sparks -excitement-controversy-13185.

102. www.dailycal.org/2012/02/20/uc-inaugurates-pilot-program-for-online -classes/.

103. www.ucop.edu/uconline/_files/KWilliams_UCOnline_update.pdf.

ful that the AS would quickly approve policies allowing University of California Online courses to award University of California credit to non-matriculated students while simultaneously moving forward with soliciting letters of intent for the development of a second wave of courses (against the advice of the Academic Council to slow down).[104] In fact, in a February 2012 update to the Academic Council, Greenstein and Keith Williams (former chair of UCEP and now UCOE faculty advisor) anticipated enrolling 3,700 non–University of California students over the first year and 5,000 non–University of California students in the second.[105]

Two months later, in another update to the Academic Council, Greenstein and Williams reiterated the importance of timing as well as patience with regard to the evaluation process while also saying that UCOE had made an effort to anchor courses (along with the revenues derived from offering them to non–University of California students) in their respective departments.[106]

In June 2012, Williams announced that he would be taking over as interim director of UCOE (working with approximately ten staff members), following Greenstein's impending departure at the end of the month.[107] In the same announcement, he wrote that University of California Online anticipated rolling out an additional nineteen courses over the next nine months (which, together with the six released in spring 2012, would total twenty-five) and would begin marketing efforts to enroll non–University of California students in July. However, Williams acknowledged that cross-campus enrollment would likely not happen before 2014. In July, Williams stated that University of California, Berkeley, was beginning to look into offering more courses through Coursera in a way that would complement University of California Online.[108] This also followed an important

104. http://senate.universityofcalifornia.edu/onlineeducation.march2012.html.
105. http://senate.universityofcalifornia.edu/committees/council/Council.02.22.12.minutes.pdf.
106. http://senate.universityofcalifornia.edu/committees/ucep/ucep.4.2.2012.minutes.pdf.
107. www.ucop.edu/uconline/_files/KWilliams_UCOnline_update.pdf and www.ucop.edu/uconline/staff-and-advisors/index.html.
108. www.dailycal.org/2012/07/22/ucs-online-involvement/.

transition in the university's administration, as Aimee Dorr—who, among other roles, had previously chaired the UCLA AS—was appointed as the new university provost on July 1, 2012.[109] Nevertheless, in the same month, Wendy Brown—the outgoing chair of the Berkeley Faculty Association—blasted the way in which Edley largely "brushed aside" faculty concerns when his plan was first conceived and kept on pursuing seemingly different objectives and deferring important questions of shared governance.[110]

A total of seven hundred students took University of California Online courses in the spring and summer semesters of 2012, and—because they were all already enrolled in the University of California system—no additional revenue was generated. At the same time, UCOE spent $4.6 million developing and marketing its project in the 2011–12 school year. An eighteen-month contract with Blackboard constituted $4.3 million of this $4.6 million, and the overall program was expected to cost $7 million in 2012–13 for additional development and marketing efforts.[111] In November 2012, the blue-ribbon panel released the first iteration of its evaluation of UCOE, painting quite a disappointing picture of the initiative.[112] The panel was dissatisfied with the program's unclear goals and narrow-mindedness and was also concerned about UCOE's inability to provide timely progress reports of suitable scholarly quality (all while continuing to tap loan funds). It recommended that the UCOE program be delayed until a fuller evaluation of results could be performed for all online courses offered. In a February 2013 revision, the blue-ribbon panel put forth an updated report in response to additional data reported by UCOE, largely reiterating the original points in its November report while acknowledging UCOE's recent data analyses. The University of California Education Evaluation Center at the University of California–Santa Barbara carried out these data evaluations, which

109. http://newsroom.ucla.edu/portal/ucla/dean-aim-e-dorr-named-provost-235494.aspx.
110. http://keepcaliforniaspromise.org/2714/wheres-uc-online-now-and-how-will-we-get-our-7-million-back.
111. http://chronicle.com/article/UC-Online-Faces-Challenges-in/134778/.
112. http://senate.universityofcalifornia.edu/committees/brp/RP2Dorr_Blue RibbonPanelReport_Transmittal021313.pdf.

found generally positive attitudinal results among students and faculty involved with University of California Online.[113]

As of spring 2013, University of California Online offered fourteen courses (with twenty-one additional UCOE-supported courses in development), having enrolled—up to that point—1,700 University of California students (who took University of California Online courses primarily as offerings from their home campuses) and only 11 non–University of California students.[114] These non-degree students paid between $1,400 and $2,160 in tuition for each class, depending on the number of credits offered and the length of each course. As a result, by the end of the 2012–13 academic year, University of California Online had generated no more than $23,100 in tuition revenue from non–University of California students in an effort to repay the loan.[115] University of California Online is now looking at other ways to bring in much-needed revenue to pay back the loan, including offering its course development services (perhaps through licensing) to other outside programs interested in developing online courses and actively targeting both community college students hoping to transfer to a University of California institution and California residents who meet the University of California eligibility criteria.[116] In January 2013, with strong support from Governor Jerry Brown, the university received a $10 million earmark from the state of California to develop online undergraduate courses. Although the $10 million was not expressly designated to pay off the $7 million loan, it has clearly been helpful in reducing the tensions surrounding the loan.[117]

Edley, who no longer leads the effort and is listed only as a member of the initiative's Faculty Oversight Committee, now acknowledges that the dream of a virtual University of California campus is

113. www.ucop.edu/uconline/about/uc-online-education-faqs.html#evaluation.

114. http://mfeldstein.wpengine.netdna-cdn.com/wp-content/uploads/2013/05/The-Right-to-Educational-Access-Final.pdf.

115. www.ucop.edu/uconline/_files/uc_online_fact_sheet.pdf.

116. http://dailybruin.com/2013/01/17/uc-may-increase-online-courses/ and www.ucop.edu/uconline/_files/uc_online_fact_sheet.pdf.

117. See Carl Straumsheim, "A Changing Economy Changes Online Education Priorities at the U. of California," *Inside Higher Ed,* August 13, 2014, available at www.insidehighered.com/news/2014/08/13/changing-economy-changes-online-education-priorities-u-california.

all but over. Edley had thought that the pilot project was intended to serve as a first step in the natural transition to a virtual campus. However, once problems began arising with the pilot, various parties sought to preclude such a transition from happening, instead viewing the pilot project as an end in itself.

Today the university has largely shifted gears from UCOE's top-down strategy to a campus-by-campus innovation system (which places more emphasis on cultivating the creativity of individual faculty members in devising approaches that incorporate online and blended learning).[118] In the meantime, individual campuses and the University of California system have made concerted efforts to broaden and diversify their online learning efforts. Individual experiments too numerous to list abound, but two examples include (1) the University of California, Berkeley's joining the edX consortium and conducting substantive research on MOOCs (massive open online courses) through BRCOE's MOOCLab and (2) a system-wide Innovative Learning Technology Initiative (ILTI) that seeks to—among other things—create both a pilot cross-campus enrollment webpage and a formal approval process for cross-campus course credit.[119] University campuses also continue to offer more than two thousand online courses through University of California Extension, most of which cannot be formally used for credit toward University of California degrees (unless they are designated as "concurrent enrollment" courses).[120]

As for University of California Online, it is now trying to integrate itself into the University of California's overall online learning strategy—which includes initiatives at individual campuses, fully online master's degrees, ILTI, and MOOCs—rather than setting itself apart (as it had previously tried to do) as the "premier" University of California online education program.[121]

118. www.thenation.com/article/176037/tech-mania-goes-college?page=3 D0,1#.

119. www.dailycal.org/2014/01/27/uc-officials-announce-initiatives-improve-online-education-systemwide/ and http://mooclab.berkeley.edu/.

120. http://extension.berkeley.edu/static/studentservices/concurrent/ and http://regents.universityofcalifornia.edu/regmeet/jan13/e2.pdf.

121. www.ucop.edu/uconline/_files/uc_online_fact_sheet.pdf.

Princeton University

William G. Bowen

University Context and General Faculty Mindset

Princeton is a research university focused on the arts and sciences, including engineering, without professional schools of law, medicine, business, or education. From a governance standpoint, this means that there is a single faculty, which is a tremendous advantage from many points of view—it simplifies many things. The faculty acts as a single body; there is no faculty senate. Also, the administration of the university is highly centralized, with much power in the Office of the President.

Princeton is both highly selective and highly endowed. The university's strong resource base means that many of the most difficult

The reader should know that Bowen was a graduate student in economics at Princeton from 1955 to 1958 (PhD in that year). He then joined the economics department as a faculty member. He was provost, under President Goheen, from 1967 to 1972, and then president from 1972 to 1988. As provost, Bowen was the first chairman of the Priorities Committee, was actively involved in the work of the Patterson Committee on coeducation (overseeing the analytical research behind it and drafting parts of the report), and was also an active participant in the work of the Kelley Committee. These involvements may, of course, color some of his observations. This case study is based mainly on four sources: (1) James Axtell's history of Princeton, *The Making of Princeton University: From Woodrow Wilson to the Present* (Princeton, NJ: Princeton University Press, 2006); (2) the Kelley Report, cited above; (3) interviews conducted by Bowen at Princeton—especially with Robert Durkee (vice president and secretary) and David Dobkin (dean of the faculty); and (4) materials from the Princeton Archive.

and controversial decisions facing many other colleges and universities (such as which courses or departments to close, and how to respond to substantial budget cuts) are not front and center at Princeton today, though there have certainly been "tough days" in the past, including in the 1970s (see various President's Reports) and 2008 (as a result of stock market corrections), never mind the Great Depression of the 1930s. Still, governance arrangements that work well for Princeton today might not work as well at institutions that lack either the financial and other resources that Princeton possesses or its relatively simple organizational structure.[1]

In general, there is, and has been for many years, an exceptionally good working relationship between the administration and the faculty—with most academic administrators coming directly from the faculty ranks. There is very little "we–they" thinking. As Dean of the Faculty David Dobkin put it, "This excellent relationship is built on trust, which has been developed over many years."[2]

The faculty generally think of themselves as "all-rounders"— teachers of both undergraduates and graduate students, and serious scholars. Very little use is made of adjuncts; TAs teach sections of

---

1. Larry Bacow comments (February 18, 2014, in personal correspondence): "I think I have said this before to you but I am once again struck by how similar Princeton and MIT are in terms of governance structure—a unitary faculty, no senate, and a strong president who controls most resources either directly or indirectly. By the way, one useful lens to examine how colleges and universities are organized is to ask how they make decisions to allocate the three scarce resources one needs to get anything done on a college campus: money, space and slots. The latter being faculty slots, student slots, and staff headcount. At MIT, all these resources (with the exception of graduate student enrollment) are managed centrally. By contrast, at Harvard, all are managed within the schools. Of course, the ad hoc process at Harvard gives the president final say on tenure decisions but not on the number of tenure track slots within individual schools."

2. Dean Dobkin has just announced that he will retire from the position of dean of the faculty after a distinguished tenure. In responding to a note from me, congratulating him on his service, he sent me this message (February 20, 2014, personal e-mail): "I have fond memories of a dinner at Lowrie house [the President's residence] in 1981 when you welcomed me to Princeton as a new member of the faculty. There is a tone to this place that I learned at that dinner that has served me well ever since." It is possible, in a university as relatively small and cohesive as Princeton, to have such dinners and thus inculcate an attitude toward "academic community" that discourages skepticism if not downright hostility between faculty and administration.

some large courses, but not more than that. Also, there is a history of heavy involvement of the most respected faculty in governance, including service on the most important committees. A key question for the future is whether the extensive involvement of senior faculty in governance will be affected by the ever-increasing specialization within disciplines and the tendency of the Internet to encourage extra-institutional collaborations and loyalties. There is also the question of whether the increasing fragmentation of higher education (with growing gaps in pay and resources between comparatively wealthy schools like Princeton and most other institutions) will lead to tensions that can have unpredictable effects. Pressures on doctoral education nationwide could also have local ramifications.

The tumultuous events of the late 1960s led to the work of a special committee, the "Kelley Committee" (named for its chairman, Stanley Kelley, a widely respected professor of politics), which in turn caused the trustees to issue a formal *Statement of Policy on Delegation of Authority* (found in the appendix to this case study), which has had lasting value. See my discussion in *Lessons Learned*.[3] The *Statement on Delegation* distinguishes among matters where the trustees exercise only "general review" (e.g., faculty appointment processes, curricular decisions, and other academic matters), matters where trustees exercise "prior review" (when there is a claim on funds, or the setting of budgets), and matters where there is "authority directly exercised" by the trustees (investments, real estate transactions, and so on).[4] When authority in some areas is del-

3. See William G. Bowen, *Lessons Learned: Reflections of a University President* (Princeton, NJ: Princeton University Press, 2011), pp. 9–10. The *Statement of Policy on Delegation of Authority* is reprinted as appendix 11 of the Kelley Report, pp. 161–63; it is also reprinted here as an appendix to this case study.

4. Robert Durkee thinks that the role of the Faculty Committee on Admissions could be reviewed and may need clarification, consistent with policies on delegation. There is now ongoing discussion by trustees and others as to whether the faculty should in fact have full authority over admissions policy because it affects alumni relations, fundraising, athletics, and so on, not just academic qualifications. As Durkee explained (in an interview by Bowen, paraphrased here): At issue here is a broad question of delegation and how shared governance should work. What is being discussed is admission "policy," or, in the terms we have been using recently, admission "philosophy." The key document we use in orientating new trustees, and a key document in our most recent review of governance policy

egated by the trustees to the faculty, it is always delegated through the president.

Choosing the Faculty Whose Voices Are to Be Heard

Although the faculty may, from time to time, speak as a collective body, "the faculty" are generally consulted and heard through individual faculty members serving on committees; thus this discussion begins with the question of how such individuals are chosen.

Today there is a faculty "Committee on Committees," which both sets slates of candidates (for faculty-wide votes) for the most important committee positions and selects faculty for non-elected spots on committees. There is substantial administrative involvement in this process, with the dean of the faculty having oversight of it; the president is also eligible to meet with the committee ex officio. Prospective members of the Committee on Committees are suggested by the Faculty Advisory Committee on Appointments and Advancements (the "Committee of Three"); the dean of the faculty, acting for the president, selects members and brings the slate to the full faculty for approval. When the committee presents its own proposed slates to the faculty for ratification (with individuals who are candidates for elected positions to be chosen subsequently by secret ballot), there is

and practice, is the *Statement of Policy on Delegation of Authority* first adopted in 1969. In describing areas where the trustees provide "oversight and general review," the Statement says that "procedures for recruiting undergraduate students, including criteria for admission, are the responsibility of the President, the Dean of the College, and the Dean of Admission, acting pursuant to policies determined with the advice of faculty committees on admission, subject to the general review of the trustees." In its next section, the Statement says: "It is assumed that major changes in policy . . . will be brought to the trustees for review and approval before final decisions or commitments are made." In citing examples of situations where trustees would exercise prior review and approval, the Statement includes "changes in admissions policies affecting sizeable categories of potential students." So I'm not sure it's a matter of "whether faculty should in fact have full authority over admissions policy since it affects alumni relations, fundraising, athletics, etc., not just academic qualifications" so much as an attempt to respect the delegation regarding recruitment procedures and criteria for admission, while also exercising prior review and approval of potentially significant changes that could affect sizeable categories of potential students.

an opportunity for the faculty to make additional nominations from the floor. This opportunity is a useful "escape valve." In practice, however, additional nominations are rarely made. Faculty concurrence with the recommendations of the Committee on Committees basically ratifies the legitimacy of the nomination process.

Faculty involvement in choosing members to serve on committees has a long history at Princeton. According to the archivist (Daniel J. Linke), the faculty Committee on Committees (formerly the Committee on the Constitution of Faculty Committees) dates to at least 1935, the year of the earliest record of it within the archives. (Axtell's history, referenced below, indicates that the committee actually dates back to John Grier Hibben's years as president—the second decade of the twentieth century.) In 1935 the committee was composed of the president and three faculty members. By 1964 it had four faculty members, one from each academic division (humanities, sciences, social sciences, and engineering). By 1971 the committee had eight faculty members, one tenured and one non-tenured from each of the four academic divisions. It is worth noting the active involvement of administrative officers, including the president, from Princeton's early days.

Faculty are appointed to ad hoc committees by either the president or the dean of the faculty, depending in part on the visibility and scope of the committee. Recent examples include the ad hoc committee on grading policy and search committees for the deans of the graduate school and the faculty; another recent example is the committee on online learning. Of course the faculty could always challenge the use of the appointment process if they wished to do so. The fact that it has never been challenged (to my recollection) is an indication that the process seems to work and to be regarded as legitimate.

The highly influential Kelley Committee on the governance of Princeton, which produced several interim reports in the late 1960s and then a final report in 1970 (see earlier reference), is an exception in that almost all members, except those appointed ex officio, were elected by various constituencies (the faculty, the undergraduates, and the graduate students). This was essential to demonstrate the "legitimacy" of the committee, which was, after all, created precisely because major questions were raised at that time about "legitimacy" in all its forms.

Selecting Administration and Faculty

Selecting the President

The trustees have the responsibility for selecting the president, setting the terms of the president's compensation, reviewing his or her performance on a regular basis, and, if need be, making a change. There is a long history of using advisory committees with heavy faculty representation in selecting a president, and in the last two presidential searches, faculty served directly on the Trustee Search Committee, as did students and staff members. No president could survive for long without clear faculty support.

Selecting Other Senior Academic Officers

The president recommends such appointments to the trustees for formal action. Generally speaking, there is faculty consultation in the appointment process.

Selecting Chairs of Departments

Chairs of departments are tremendously important, because most academic matters of consequence originate in departments—including both faculty appointments/advancements and curricular matters—and the chairs are often influential in shaping recommendations. Here is the response of David Dobkin, dean of the faculty, when asked how chairs are selected (given in an interview on November 26, 2013, and paraphrased): The dean of the faculty writes to all members of the department, asking for their confidential advice, and letters are shared with the president/provost. Letters are often very informative about departmental matters of all kinds. The dean of the faculty then appoints chairs, sending formal letters, but only after close consultation with the president and usually with the provost. Chairs are certainly not elected and serve varying amounts of time. There is definitely no presumption that the responsibility of chairing the department will be rotated among all members. This same process has been used for many years (with minor modifications). Lawrence Bacow (in an interview on February 19, 2014) noted: "So much of shared governance (when it works well) follows this form. It would be difficult to codify this process of informal consultation that is taken very seriously, but it is very important."

Selecting and Advancing Faculty

The president makes recommendations for appointments of tenure-track faculty to the trustees, who invariably approve these recommendations.[5] There have been very occasional "rumbles," such as when one trustee objected publicly to the appointment of Professor Peter Singer because he disagreed with his views (and also threatened to withhold personal financial support); but attempted interventions of this kind have not succeeded—at least not in recent years. And in this case the trustees issued a public rebuke of the trustee in question.

Today there is a highly regularized process for faculty peer review and advice to the president before such recommendations are made. This review process applies to all new appointments at the tenure ranks, to all promotions to and through the tenure ranks, to the reappointment of assistant professors and senior lecturers, and to all salary actions affecting these faculty members. The key faculty committee providing this advice is the previously mentioned Faculty Advisory Committee on Appointments and Advancements, known informally as the Committee of Three because for many years it had three elected faculty members (chosen originally from among the chairs of departments in what were then the three divisions of the faculty—sciences, humanities, and social sciences). The president has chaired the committee for many years, and it never meets without the president. The president participates actively in the work of the committee. The dean of the faculty is the secretary of the committee and the organizer of its work, and the senior academic deans meet with the committee. The faculty membership of the committee has evolved over the years and today "consists of six members of the Faculty, all of whom shall be full professors. There shall be at least one from each division, three from

---

5. Once, when I was president, a prospective faculty member whose appointment was going to the trustees for approval asked me: "What happens if the trustees turn down your recommendation?" My answer: "Both of us will be looking for jobs!"

Divisions I and II [humanities and social sciences], and three from Divisions III and IV [sciences and engineering], not more than one shall be from any department, and at least two shall be current departmental chairs."[6] The committee is clearly understood to be advisory to the president. But it is rare indeed (almost unheard of) for the faculty members of the committee, who are the only voting members, to make a recommendation to the president that he or she does not accept. There is a determined effort to reach consensus. The committee itself does not hesitate, however, to turn back recommendations from departments or to adjust salary recommendations from departments or departmental chairs. In considering tenure recommendations, the committee consults outside experts whom it chooses, almost always on the advice of the dean of the faculty. This process, which is anything but routine, can become acrimonious—but the decisions of the committee are generally accepted with good grace.

There is also a Faculty Committee on Conference and Faculty Appeal, which serves as a review board to handle faculty grievances and particularly situations in which a faculty member thinks that he or she was wrongly disciplined or dismissed. The committee has direct access to the Board of Trustees, and the committee's "charter" refers to trustee minutes going back as far as 1918 (when John Grier Hibben was president).

This strong role of the president and the faculty in the appointment process has not always been the rule. In the university's history, trustees played a large role in faculty appointments prior to Woodrow Wilson's presidency (1902–10).

In trying to deal with the "inadequate faculty" of his time, President James McCosh (1868–88) had to overcome obstacles. One was that, in these years, "the Trustees jealously guarded their prerogative of appointing faculty members. At best, McCosh could send them two or three nominations . . . but they chose in the end" (Axtell, p. 37).

The election of Francis Patton to succeed McCosh in 1888 was a hopeful sign to the younger faculty, who wanted to transform Prince-

6. *Rules and Procedures of the Faculty of Princeton University and Other Provisions of Concern to the Faculty,* last printed June 1994, updated November 2012, www.princeton.edu/dof/policies/publ/fac/rules_toc/chaper2/, accessed October 1, 2014.

ton into a true university (Axtell, p. 41). Patton said all the right things, but turned out to be lazy and unwilling to do what needed to be done to change things. Patton characterized college administration as "a business in which Trustees are partners, professors the salesmen, and students the customers" (42). The appointment process was inconsistent and often marked by favoritism and "outrageous nepotism" (44). Retiring chairs often selected their own successors. And, in the end, "particularly with the president's abdication in faculty development, the trustees were responsible for all appointments in fact as well as in law" (47). Dissatisfaction with Patton mounted, and he was persuaded to retire in June 1902. Woodrow Wilson was elected to succeed him.

In the early 1900s, Wilson took power from the trustees. He prepared the way for major reform by "reordering key faculty committees, making important administrative appointments, and receiving—and taking—from the trustees effective authority over academic and faculty affairs" (Axtell, p. 48). (Note the similarity to the role played by Benjamin Ide Wheeler at the University of California at almost exactly the same time.) In 1902 "the trustees acceded to Wilson's request for unpublicized power to fire faculty, even tenured and chaired professors" (49). Also, Wilson simply went ahead and made key faculty appointments ahead of trustee approval—the trustees had to approve as a matter of law, but de facto authority was exercised by the president (50).

Wilson shared power with faculty—when he chose to do so. In spite of his autocratic tendencies, he delegated considerable authority to his chosen department heads and counted on them to "enforce the higher new standards" (Axtell, p. 58). (This is a good reminder that grants of authority are not all-or-nothing—the president can consult and delegate and yet retain final authority.) Wilson kept real control in the president's office until his resignation in 1910.

As one of Wilson's young faculty supporters put it, he became "an autocrat up to the limit. In [appointments] he hardly left anything to the faculty"—or to the trustees (Axtell, p. 50). Wilson asked for resignations of three key faculty members, whom he regarded as "dead wood." This was before the founding of the American Association of University Professors (AAUP) and the establishment of national standards for tenure (52). Official records don't reveal what really happened. Axtell, however, tells the full story of these "resignations" in gory detail (52–59).

Axtell goes on to say that Wilson not only fired faculty, he hired them—"always with the active collaboration and often at the initiative of his department chairmen and his astute dean of the faculty, Henry Fine" (Axtell, p. 59). Wilson played a very active role in faculty recruitment but also used faculty whom he trusted. In hiring his "preceptors," he involved the departments. "Some departments, such as English, voted as a whole; in others, the chairman and Wilson made the final decision" (65).

"The abrupt and acrimonious end of Wilson's presidency in 1910—his forced resignation by the Trustees as he ran for the governorship of New Jersey—could easily have slowed or reversed his curricular reforms and faculty development" (Axtell, p. 72). However, Hibben was elected Wilson's successor, and Hibben saw that progress was not interrupted. "According to Wilson's key lieutenant, Henry Fine, Hibben upon election called a meeting of Wilson's faculty leaders and begged them to join him in 'continuing and furthering the great instructional and University work that Wilson had begun'" (73). The transition was seamless.

The increasing curricular demands put extraordinary pressures on the Princeton faculty. "To enable them to perform and compensate them for these heavy duties, Hibben (and his successors) sought to give them maximum autonomy and competitive economic rewards. . . . Hibben believed that the time was right to fully enfranchise the faculty. At the first faculty meeting after he assumed office, Hibben 'turned over to the Faculty the appointment of all its committees'" (Axtell, p. 76). Dean Henry Burchard Fine applauded this step and called it "a thing wholly unprecedented and of the first importance" (76–77). (Note, however, the earlier discussion that emphasizes the continuing role, up to the present day, of heavy administrative involvement in the appointment of faculty committees.)

Hibben did more: "He created a faculty-elected advisory committee to meet regularly with the trustees' curriculum committee. . . . He appointed three faculty each year to the trustees' honorary degrees committee. . . . And most important of all, he established a Faculty

Advisory Committee on Appointments and Advancements, whose three elected members, all full professors and often department chairmen, met with the president to decide all nominations for tenure, retention, and promotion. This hardworking, powerful 'Committee of Three' (as it is still known . . .) gave the faculty major authority over its own development as it dealt with departmental recommendations" (Axtell, p. 77). Hibben also put in place new safeguards to protect the rights of individual faculty who were dismissed (77).

On Hibben's retirement, the faculty recognized that "'from the first, he chose [unlike his predecessor] to be primus inter pares, taking the faculty into his confidence, entrusting to it a full measure of responsibility, steadily safeguarding its privileges and dignity.' In short, he had completed the foundation of the modern Princeton faculty" (Axtell, pp. 77–78).

There are many lessons in this history. One is that what needs to be done (in Wilson's time, a major upgrading of the faculty) clearly has a major impact on the power the president needs to exert. A second lesson is that when the faculty is better, it is easier to give them authority—as Hibben did. A third lesson is that the timing of grants of authority to the faculty is often closely related to the need to alleviate pressures on the faculty and the need to recruit able faculty—that is, the market power of the faculty. All of these factors were present during the early years of Hibben's presidency, from 1912 on. This was of course the period when many universities were strengthening their faculties, and it is probably no coincidence that this was the time when key committee structures of today (The Committee on Committees, Committee of Three, and Conference Committee to handle appeals) were established. A fourth lesson is that it is possible for the president to exert power even when there is extensive delegation of authority to the faculty, as Wilson demonstrated and as I did at Princeton via my work with the Committee of Three in the 1970s and 1980s (Axtell, p. 98). Exerting this power is relatively easy with new appointments and with promotions (especially when faculty in the affected departments welcome the president's active involvement in faculty recruitment and when, as in the case of the life sciences at Princeton, aggressive recruitment from "on high" was essential to get results because substantial commitments of resources were required. There are situations like this one in which faculty recruitment is possible only when the university—through the president—must offer new space, commitments to recruit more faculty, and so on. Of course trustee support for aggressive commitments is also essential in such situations, but this does not mean trustee control over actual appointments. Exerting power on faculty staffing is harder, but not impossible, when there is a need to send people away—the president can freeze salaries, speak candidly with individuals about their dire prospects, and so on. But the president today could not just dismiss faculty, as Wilson did when he was president. Procedures of the faculty and national standards provide for a careful process and for appeals—see again the example of the University of California, as recounted in Taylor's history of the AS. Of course I agree with essentially everyone in academia that the fact that presidents cannot exercise unilateral power to dismiss is, as my colleague Michael McPherson put it, "a good thing." Some presidents, as history teaches us, may want to claim excessive authority to dismiss, especially in the face of severe pressures.

Making Curricular Decisions

General Decisions

Of course there are many academic areas in which the faculty is expected to act: the calendar is one of these. But in this section we focus on curricular matters.

In the normal course of events, departments make recommendations concerning new courses and major course revisions to the faculty's Committee on the Course of Study, which in turn reviews the proposals and, presumably, makes a recommendation for action to the faculty as a whole. When the faculty votes, this is almost always the end of the matter, because this is an instance in which the trustees normally exercise only "general review." However, if a curricular proposal were to be so sweeping that it required substantial new resources, it would need to be taken by the president to the trustees for "prior approval." Recent examples include the building of the new Andlinger Center for Energy and the Environment and the building of the new Neurosciences Institute.

There is no general requirement that the faculty must vote to approve the closing or even the suspension of programs, as seems to be the case at Macalester (see that case study). The clearest case in point is the action taken by President Robert F. Goheen in 1971 to suspend the graduate program in Slavic Studies. No faculty action was involved. As Dean of the Faculty Dobkin explained, when it is necessary to reduce the scale of a program, or even to suspend one (as in the case of the graduate program in Slavic Studies), the administration simply reduces the approved number of graduate student "slots."[7]

When a new Department of Molecular Biology was created in the 1980s after a prolonged search for new leadership and for funding for new space and new appointments, various faculty committees and then the faculty as a whole voted for the creation of the new department—and in the process eliminated the old Department of Biochemistry. This was a major action, which was led by the president and provost; the trustees were also heavily involved because very large commitments of funds were required.[8]

In 1985 the Department of Statistics merged with Civil Engineering and Operations Research and thus ceased existence as a separate department. Because a merger was involved, faculty action was required, but this was pro forma because all parties (including the chairman of the Department of Statistics, Geoffrey Watson) were in favor of the merger. Statistics was just too small to function on its own after the retirement of its most famous member, John Tukey.

Decisions about Teaching Methods for Online Learning

Individual faculty members have near-total control of the content of courses; the role of departments in overseeing both the content of courses and teaching methods varies widely.

In the case of technology and online offerings, Princeton is in an avowedly "experimental" mode. The university is a participant in the Coursera program and has now joined another platform, NovoEd. To

7. Dobkin, interview by Bowen, November 26, 2013.
8. For a full discussion of the process leading to this major reinvigoration of the life sciences at Princeton, see Bowen (2011), pp. 73–76.

date, faculty with an interest have just "done their own thing." There is no policy as to how online teaching and the use of technology affect teaching loads. Faculty have been encouraged to experiment, and there has been no inclination at Princeton, as there has been at schools such as Amherst and Duke, to have a general faculty "policy" on such matters. Approximately $250,000 has been spent on the first phase of course development (covering about seven courses). These funds came from general budgetary appropriations to the Office of the Dean of the College, and their outlay has been coordinated by this office in consultation with the Office of the Provost. Recognizing that there are many issues here that need to be considered, the university established an ad hoc "Committee on Online Courses," which was chaired by Gideon Rosen, a professor of philosophy and chairman of the Humanities Council, and which included an administration member from the Office of the Dean of the College. Members were appointed by the dean of the faculty, acting with the president. The ad hoc committee issued its report on June 24, 2013. President Christopher L. Eisgruber is interested in this issue and has encouraged general faculty discussion. (But, unlike the situation at the University of California, the president's office at Princeton has not tried to "drive" the creation of online offerings and has not focused on revenue generation possibilities; instead, activity has been allowed, even encouraged, to "rise up" from the faculty. Of course financial pressures at the University of California are quite different from those at Princeton. Princeton has been able to afford, in recent years, to "let a hundred flowers bloom.")

There is no need to summarize the conclusions of the report here. In the main, the committee takes a rather cautious approach that leaves open many important questions about ultimate control over the use and distribution of online materials. As of now, the report recommends: "The copyright in digital materials produced for on-line courses should belong to the instructor." (Note that this recommendation differs from the Stanford policy, which vests ownership rights in the university—and apparently some at Princeton have raised questions about the wisdom of the Princeton approach.) The report does not deal with the issue of whether there should be an institutional policy regarding, or institutional responsibility for, the "sustainability" of online courses produced by Princeton faculty that may be used by other institutions. The report does recommend both continued experimentation in this area (without giving Princeton "credit" to non-Princeton students for successfully completing Princeton-originated MOOCs) and the "establishment of a new Committee for On-Line Courses tasked with vetting proposals for on-line courses, allocating funds for course development, and more generally with overseeing and assessing Princeton's experiment with on-line courses." The faculty approved the establishment of such a standing committee in the spring of 2014.

Oversight of Research

In the aftermath of the extraordinary growth of federally sponsored research at Princeton (as at other research universities) during and after World War II, the faculty voted to establish the University Research Board (URB) in December of 1958. The URB continues to have important responsibilities, perhaps more of them than in the past, but it is no longer seen as advisory to the president (its initial responsibility). That role is now played by the dean for research, a relatively recent position that grew out of recognition that the kind of faculty leadership necessary with respect to oversight of research could not be provided on a part-time basis by the chair of the URB. In its early days, the URB spent a great deal of time on the complicated issue of indirect cost recovery and on the contentious issue of classified research. The URB has always been chaired by a prominent faculty member, and its first chairman was the distinguished scientist Professor Henry DeWolf Smyth. The URB was very important in developing and overseeing (with the Office of the Dean of the Faculty) elaborate policies governing professional research staff, including those associated with two huge projects, the Plasma Physics Laboratory and the Princeton–Penn Accelerator.[9] Dean Dobkin raised the important question (in an interview with me) of whether there is a

9. Bowen was asked by President Robert F. Goheen to carry out a study of this area, which resulted in a report titled "The Federal Government and Princeton University: A Report on the Effects of Princeton's Involvements with the Federal Government on the Operations of the University," Princeton University, 1962.

possible analog here with the evolving need at some institutions for a more regularized set of policies for professional teaching staff.

Student Discipline

The faculty has long had responsibility for student discipline. The trustees have delegated responsibility in this area to the president, who in turn has delegated it to certain administrative officers (e.g., the dean of students) and to the faculty. As the general history of higher education demonstrates, unruly students have long been a problem, and the trustees/president have had to look to the faculty for help in dealing with it. Axtell (37) notes that an obstacle faced by Woodrow Wilson in seeking to improve the academic quality of Princeton was the "attitude and behavior of unruly, badly prepared students." Faculty, who should have dealt with the situation, were often, in Axtell's words, "complicit."

There continues to be a Committee on Discipline (for undergraduates), which has faculty members, a dean, and student members. This committee, and the faculty at large, have to approve all suspensions and disciplinary actions above some threshold. Apparently at some places the faculty role in student discipline (and student life generally) has been replaced by a cadre of student-life professionals; this has not happened at Princeton. The university also continues to have a student-run Honor Committee for undergraduates.

In the aftermath of the establishment of the Kelley Committee in the late 1960s, and the turbulent times that led to the creation of this committee, the faculty and other university bodies approved the establishment of the Council of the Princeton University Community (see next section), which has responsibility for setting rules of conduct "applicable to all members of the resident University Community," and thus for policies about protests and demonstrations (what is permissible and what is not); the council also has a Judicial Committee, with faculty as well as student and staff members, which is responsible for hearing charges of violations of such policies and for imposing penalties, and which also has an appeal function.[10]

10. See the Kelley Report, especially pp. 42–47 and the appendix material.

Faculty Advice on General Policies

Machinery for General Consultation

From the early days, presidents of Princeton have consulted with faculty on a wide range of matters. The method of consultation was generally informal (with the president deciding whom to consult, and on what subjects) until the time of President Hibben, who "created a faculty-elected advisory committee to meet regularly with the trustees' curriculum committee" (Axtell, p. 77). This was the predecessor to the faculty Conference Committee of today, which was used for years by presidents for general advice, as well as serving as both a vehicle for communication between the trustees and the faculty and an appeal body for aggrieved faculty.

A change in consultative machinery was made in 1957. At that time, Dean of the Faculty J. Douglas Brown wrote to President Goheen recommending that a new faculty committee, called the Faculty Advisory Committee on Policy (FACP), be created to free up the Faculty Conference Committee to focus on its main work of serving as a channel of communication with the Board of Trustees.[11] There is no reliable record of the issues on which presidents consulted the Conference Committee prior to the establishment of the FACP, but it is safe to assume that they covered a wide gamut, including issues related to World War II and its effects on Princeton.

We do have records of the work of the FACP from 1957 forward, and the archives show that the matters considered by the committee in the years prior to the mid-1960s included advising on changes to the Rules and Procedures of the Faculty and governance of faculty committees; rules for sponsored research; student discipline policy; academic policy (broadly conceived—topics include the course of study, university lectures as part of the curriculum, suggested distribution of special funds, promoting faculty scholarship, travel to professional conferences, leave policy, and the creation of a law school); and general university policy (library issues, nepotism, conflict of interest, and retirement age).

11. The Princeton University Archives contain Dean Brown's memo as well as a great deal of material about the activities of the Conference Committee. I am indebted to the archivist, Daniel J. Linke, for finding these materials.

The next wave of changes in faculty roles occurred in the late 1960s and early 1970s at the time of the Kelley Report, "The Governing of Princeton University" (Final Report, April 1970, cited earlier). The Kelley Report mainly provided a good rationale for governance procedures already in place, tweaked the procedures in fairly modest ways, and introduced a broader system of campus governance in which faculty participated, along with students, staff, and others.[12] One major innovation was the establishment of a campus-wide consultative body, the Council of the Princeton University Community (CPUC), which had faculty members, undergraduates and graduate students, officers and staff members, and a modest alumni representation. The president was (and is) the chair.

In his 1970 President's Report, President Goheen described the changes resulting from the report of the Kelley Committee as making for "a broader and more regular inclusion of representatives of the faculty, the student body, and the staff in the consideration of issues that affect them" (Axtell, p. 21). President Goheen applauded the creation of the CPUC and its early work as a major contribution to the deliberative process, "especially when contentious issues such as the war in Vietnam roil the waters."

But President Goheen also noted that on one important question, the voting of the General Motors proxies in April 1970 (on environmental issues), the trustees declined, after careful deliberation, to follow the recommendation of the CPUC and voted against the proposals advocated by the "GM Campaign" (Axtell, p. 22). This is important, because the action demonstrated that the trustees retained the power to act on such matters, and that the CPUC was advisory in fact and not just in name.

Goheen also applauded the good work of the Executive Committee of the CPUC (which included all the members of the FACP, as well as students and others) in drafting various resolutions. He also paid special attention to the good work of the newly created Judicial Committee (which handled skillfully the hearings that led to disciplinary actions following the heckling of Secretary Hickel in March 1970).

12. See Axtell (pp. 348–58) for a description of the events at Princeton in the 1960s, the setting in which the Kelley Report was prepared, and its major conclusions, as summarized in the text.

One of the most important of the other committees of the CPUC was the Priorities Committee—which to this day recommends budget actions to the president (including actions on tuition/financial aid) and resource allocation decisions of many kinds. This committee contains faculty, student, and staff members; is chaired by the provost; and issues public reports of its recommendations to the president—who in turn makes recommendations to the trustees.[13] This is an area in which "prior review" by the trustees is required.

In reflecting on the CPUC, President Goheen expressed this concern in his last annual report (for 1969–70): "My [broadest] concern is of longer range and has no easy solution. Active participation in the affairs of the Council and its committees puts inordinate demands upon the time of the senior University officers, faculty members, students, staff and alumni involved" (Axtell, p. 18). "The price of such service to the University can be high" (18). "How long such participation can be sustained . . . is uncertain" (18). Goheen then added, in concluding his report, "Of course, should the University be entering calmer, easier seas, and should that respite last, the demands placed upon the Council and its members will lessen. . . . In such periods, the CPUC perhaps might serve the community best by meeting only occasionally. . . . But in times when the winds of change blow hard . . . the Council will always be confronting fresh tasks, and election to it will be no sinecure" (18). At that time, when I served as provost and then president, I tried to convince various deans that it was better to spend time in meetings in order to avoid crises than to spend even more time cleaning up a mess afterward. My efforts along this line were not always successful, and the issue of how much process is the right amount will always be a live issue. Michael McPherson adds: "I think this is a point of general importance. One application is in thinking carefully about ground rules on IP in early stages, rather than later undoing commitments made without careful anticipation of future possibilities."[14]

---

13. Service on the Priorities Committee has proven to be a good training ground for faculty who later become administrators. David S. Lee, who has recently been named provost, was a faculty representative on the Priorities Committee, and there are many other similar examples.

14. McPherson to the authors, December 17, 2013, personal conversation.

A clear consequence of the advent of the CPUC is that most discussion of broad issues now goes there. A good example is the recent controversy in the town of Princeton over the relocation of the Dinky (train) station. Robert Durkee reported, in an interview, that he briefed the CPUC several times on this issue; in earlier days, such a discussion would presumably have occurred with the FACP.

There have been other changes in the use made of the FACP. For a time, when I was president, the FACP continued to function as it had in the past. But then (according to Robert Durkee, in an interview, paraphrased): At some point after you left office, this committee ceased to play the broad and senior-level advisory role it had played in earlier times. It still serves as a filter through which changes in the Rules and Procedures of the Faculty are vetted before they go to the full faculty for adoption, but this is almost always done by e-mail exchange, not in-person meetings. This committee also may be asked to advise on other "policy" questions that relate to things like benefits policy and retirement incentive programs as they affect the faculty. But with respect to broader questions of University policy, the consultation would be either with the Committee of Three or with an ad hoc committee constituted for the specified purpose. There may be several reasons why this change in the role and stature of the committee occurred, but surely one reason was the requirement that the [FACP] committee members serve on the Executive Committee of the CPUC. This made service on the FACP both potentially more time-consuming and perhaps less interesting.

In an interview, I asked Dean David Dobkin: "Has the faculty's Advisory Committee on Policy atrophied over time?" His answer: "Yes. The committee now meets almost entirely by e-mail and handles only housekeeping functions. The president and other administrators turn to other bodies, or informal sources." Dobkin continued: "We all know where to go for advice." Much use has been made of ad hoc committees (see below). In 2008, when there were significant financial issues, the president turned to the Committee of Three for advice as to what to do about faculty salaries; the Priorities Committee was also involved. Dobkin said: "We go where there is expertise."

President Harold T. Shapiro, who succeeded me, said, when I asked him about this: "Frankly the faculty committee I trusted most was 'the

Committee of Three,' and I often took issues to them on an informal basis to supplement what the Executive Committee of the CPUC could provide." My impression is that President Shirley Tilghman continued the Shapiro practice, no doubt for the reason he gives—and perhaps also in part because it was simply more convenient for the president than summoning another committee to meet.

There is an even more recent development. President Eisgruber has indicated that he intends to "resuscitate" the FACP as he contemplates future policies/plans. The main reason is that he wishes to use the FACP for the purpose for which it was established and not to ask the Committee of Three to do more than it was established to do. A side benefit may be to lessen somewhat the heavy burden on the Committee of Three.

There is an important lesson here: the mode of consultation used will depend on a variety of factors—the issues at hand, which faculty the president/deans trust the most, and the preferences of the president as to how he or she prefers to get advice; presidential "style," if you will, clearly matters, as it should. The formal structure may be less important than how the president chooses to use it.

Ad Hoc Committees

In terms of major impact on the university, the role of the faculty in serving on high-profile ad hoc committees may well be more important than anything else, save only the faculty's role in the faculty appointment and advancement process (the Committee of Three) and perhaps in the ongoing work of the Priorities Committee.

Perusal of the archives reveals, just in the years since World War II, a mind-bending list of ad hoc or special committees, including committees on student/faculty relations, on computing, on Far Eastern studies, and on indirect cost policies, to provide only a small sample.

As recently as the fall of 2013, President Eisgruber was quoted as announcing the establishment of a new special faculty committee to consider student evaluations and grading. And of course the ad hoc Committee on Online Courses (discussed earlier) is another example of the use of this approach. Ad hoc committees have the important advantage of allowing the membership to be tailored to the issue at hand and thus to include individuals with the requisite knowledge/skills. A second advantage is that ad hoc committees disappear into the night when their work is done.

In the period of Princeton's history that I know best from personal experience (the mid-1960s through most of the 1980s), five uses of ad hoc committees stand out:

- First was the critically important work of the Kelley Committee on the governance of the university in the late 1960s, which has already been discussed at length. Many of the contributions of this committee are now deeply embedded in the governing structure of the university.

- Then there was the Committee on the Education of Women at Princeton, which played *the* crucial role in advising the president and then the trustees on the "desirability and feasibility" of educating women at the undergraduate level. Known as the "Patterson Committee" after its chairman, Professor Gardner Patterson, a distinguished professor of economics and international affairs, this committee had roughly equal numbers of faculty and administration members, all of whom were appointed by the president. Patterson himself described this as a "faculty–administration" committee, and it exemplified the way in which faculty and administrators, confronted with an issue of overriding importance, worked closely together. Professor Patterson, not the committee itself, was given full responsibility for preparing what turned out to be a 198-page report (the "Patterson Report," July 12, 1968) that presented a massive amount of data on the feasibility of coeducation, not just its desirability. The provost's office played the critical role in assembling the data and carrying out much of the research—so this was a real partnership between faculty and administration. The report provided the rationale and the evidence that President Goheen used in recommending full coeducation (not a coordinate college) to the trustees. One especially noteworthy feature of the work of this committee is that one strong opponent of coeducation, from the beginning to the end, was on the committee: Jerry Horton from the Development Office. (Horton alone voted against the recommendation for coeducation.) Having a vocal and determined dissenter proved very valuable in both raising important questions and convincing skeptical alumni that all points of view had been heard by the committee. Patterson was a highly respected faculty member, which also made a great difference to the trustees—many of whom were reluctant to go against the views of the faculty, as well as the administration, on what many came to see as an issue of educational policy. The faculty voted overwhelmingly to support the recommendation of the committee.

The Committee on the Future of the College, chaired by Professor Marvin Bressler, in the years immediately following the adoption of coeducation, urged the trustees (successfully) to back away from their original commitment to maintain the number of men students in each undergraduate class and instead adopt a policy of "equal access." Here again, the committee's work was a blend of careful analysis and equally careful exposition of the rationale for the proposed change in policy.

The Committee on Undergraduate Residential Life, chaired by J. Anderson Brown, who was then Dean of Students, played a critical role in moving the university to a system of residential colleges, thereby correcting in a major way a problem that had beset the university since at least the days of Woodrow Wilson. Neil Rudenstine, then the provost of the university, played a leading role in the work of this committee.

The Committee on the Chapel, led by Professor John Marks and Thomas Wright, secretary of the university, had a diverse group of faculty members with a variety of religious persuasions; it reported on May 18, 1979. This committee worked closely with a parallel Trustees' Advisory Committee on the Roles of the Chapel and the Dean of the Chapel, which was led by Trustee John Coburn, a bishop of the Episcopal Church, and which submitted its own report to the trustees on September 28, 1979. (It is worth noting that the Trustees' Committee, like the Patterson Committee on Coeducation, had a dissenting member—which again gave greater credibility to its recommendations.) These two committees came to very similar conclusions and were instrumental in making Princeton a much more welcoming place for Jewish students and students from all religious persuasions; they also paved the way for the selection of a new dean of religious life, Frederick Borsch.[15]

It is entirely possible that greater and greater use will be made of ad hoc committees, because the traditional standing committee structures are not well suited to address many contemporary issues that cut across traditional committee jurisdictions. The future of online learning is a good example—but in this instance an ad hoc committee recommended that a new standing committee on the subject be created (see the earlier discussion of online learning)!

In addition to the work done by these (and other) ad hoc committees, the university has benefited enormously for many years from the tireless work of other faculty in considering the divisive issue of divestment and the politically charged issue of the place of the Reserve Officer Training Corps (ROTC) on the campus.

• In dealing with the issue of divestment from companies doing business in South Africa, the faculty understood that it had only an advisory role, albeit an important advisory role. As the president at the time, I took the lead in working with the trustees to craft a statement explaining why the university did not, in general, favor the divestment approach.[16] Not surprisingly, there was some disagreement with the university's position, especially among students, but the faculty never voted in favor of general divestment from companies doing business in South Africa—though they certainly had the authority to make such a recommendation to the trustees if they had chosen to do so.

• The ROTC case is especially interesting from a shared governance perspective. A clear distinction was drawn between aspects of the

15. For accounts of the work of these committees, see William G. Bowen (2011), pp. 112–15, and Frederick Houk Borsch, *Keeping Faith at Princeton: A Brief History of Religious Pluralism at Princeton and Other Universities* (Princeton, NJ: Princeton University Press, 2012).

16. See William G. Bowen, "The Case against Divestiture," *PAW*, May 22, 1985, pp. 24–26 (reprinted in *Ever the Teacher: William G. Bowen's Writings as President of Princeton* [Princeton, NJ: Princeton University Press, 1987], pp. 29–36).

ROTC issue that fell squarely within the faculty's purview (who should get course credit for what, and what criteria should determine who did and did not enjoy faculty status) and broader issues of relations between the university and the government, which were for the trustees to decide.[17]

Conclusion

In general, Princeton's small size (a single faculty), widely shared agreement on its mission, excellent faculty leadership, history of effective collaboration between faculty and administration, generous financial resources, strong and thoughtful support from trustees and alumni (in most cases), and the tradition of "open doors" to the offices of the president, provost, and deans have contributed to an effective system of governance. It is widely understood that any faculty member concerned about any issue can get a hearing. In forming committees, the general pattern has been to mix faculty members with key members of the administration (and with students and others, in some situations). Even more generally, there has been a reluctance to "compartmentalize" roles by assigning either faculty or administrators sole involvement in deciding most things (though the locus of final responsibility for "deciding" has been clearly understood). The practice of establishing ad hoc committees composed of individuals with competence in an area, and of individuals with diverse perspectives, has also been helpful.

Informal procedures (and a willingness to tolerate some limited degree of ambiguity) have worked in part because of the university's size and history. Also relevant is the fact that Princeton is wealthy enough to have avoided the need for dramatic reductions in staff and closing of programs—actions that have had to be considered at many other institutions. But the history of governance at Princeton also illustrates that when there are really contentious issues (as in the late 1960s), it is important to have in place governance structures that are widely seen as legitimate.

17. See Bowen (2011), pp. 21–23.

There are forces at work nationally (such as growing specialization of faculty, the impact of technology on teaching methods and perhaps on the "unbundling" of faculty roles, growing gaps between "have" and "have-not" institutions, the rise of adjunct faculty, concerns over inequality in America and the role of education in promoting social mobility, and issues confronting doctoral education) that could create pressures of unknown kinds on governance at all institutions of higher education, including even highly advantaged ones like Princeton. There is certainly nothing to be said for complacency.

APPENDIX: STATEMENT OF POLICY ON DELEGATION OF AUTHORITY, ADOPTED BY THE BOARD OF TRUSTEES OF PRINCETON UNIVERSITY

October 24, 1969

In order to clarify the actual practice and procedures followed in the governance of the University, the Board of Trustees declares its intent, in matters of policy as well as of operations, to continue to delegate broad authority to the President and, through him, to the Officers of the Administration, the Faculty, and the Students as more specifically set forth below. While the Trustees may and do delegate authority in wide areas, they cannot either delegate it irrevocably or consign to any other parties their final responsibilities under the law and the terms of the Princeton Charter.

Policy initiative in almost all areas rests with the President and various members of the resident University community. Beyond this there have evolved, generally speaking, three modes by which Trustees share or delegate, normally through standing or special committees, powers and responsibilities in University operations and decision making.

General Review

In electing members of the Faculty, the Trustees are guided almost entirely by the recommendations of the President and the Advisory

Committee on Appointments and Advancements and exercise their responsibility through a continuing review of the quality of the President's leadership in the maintenance of a highly qualified faculty and by a periodic check of the integrity and efficiency of the procedures followed in the appointment and advancement of faculty members. In matters of curriculum, the creation and abolition of courses, the establishment of requirements for degrees, the prescription of academic procedures, and in most matters within the purview of the University Research Board, the Trustees have delegated their authority to the President and Faculty to be exercised through the appropriate bodies and officers of the University. Procedures for recruiting new students, criteria for admissions, and continuing relations with the leadership of schools are the responsibility of the President, the Dean of the College, and the Director of Admission acting pursuant to policies determined with the advice of faculty and student committees on admission, subject to the general review of the Trustees. Oversight of student life and discipline, including the formulation of rules of conduct and dormitory regulations, has been delegated to the President and Faculty to be exercised through various faculty and student groups in accordance with duly constituted procedures.

The functioning of the Library is supervised by the Librarian under the direction of the central administration, with the advice of faculty and student committees, the Trustees' concern being directed to the overall quality of the Library and the effectiveness of its operations. Likewise, in the areas of health and athletics the Trustees exercise general oversight, together with occasional professional advice in matters of health and medical care. Requirements for physical space and services are formulated by the several departments in collaboration with the central administration and subject to general review by the Trustees. Plant operations are entirely in the hands of administrative officers. The preparation of the annual budget proceeds through a complex process under the direction and supervision of the central administration, with detailed review by the Trustees, largely through their Committee on Finance, in the light of available funds and previously established priorities.

Prior Review

It is assumed that major changes in policy and any substantial new claims on funds will be brought to the Trustees for review before final decisions or commitments are made. The Trustees thus exercise a prior and general review in such matters as the allocation of a significant proportion of the University's resources, the setting of priorities for development, changes in instructional method of broad bearing for the institution, the determination of tuition and fees, steps to be taken to improve the social and living conditions of students, plans calling for new construction, the establishment or abolition of departments or schools, changes in admissions policies affecting sizeable categories of potential students, and changes in relations with outside educational and social institutions and governmental agencies.

Authority Directly Exercised

In matters concerning financial health and physical properties the Trustees participate directly in the formulation of policy and the conduct of the business of the University. The Trustee Committee on Finance directs the investment of University funds and supervises the management of the off-campus real estate of the Corporation. The Trustees establish fundraising policies, approve major development programs, help to identify important sources of potential financial support, and raise funds. Through the Committee on Grounds and Buildings, and with the advice of the President, the Faculty Advisory Committee on Architecture, and other resident members of the University with relevant interests and competence, the Trustees actively supervise long-range physical planning, the determination of architectural styling and landscaping, and the general condition of the University's physical plant.

In addition to what has been indicated above, it is understood more generally that the Board may contribute advice and criticism to the shaping of academic programs and the conduct of affairs in the University. If the Board is to assess general policies wisely, it must be fully and currently informed and be alert and sensitive to particular conditions and requirements. Members of the Board often have expe-

rience and competence that can be helpful to the University in its dealing with specific problems, and their advice is most valuable in the
early consideration of new policies.

It is the stated intent of the Trustees to continue the general
arrangements described above. Modifications of these arrangements
may from time to time be adopted in order to improve the University's pursuit of its essential missions and to give the Trustees the benefit of wider points of view in the exercise of the power and authority
vested in the Board by the law and the Charter of the University.

Macalester College

Jack E. Rossmann

This case study provides an overview of significant issues affecting institutional governance at Macalester. The narrative encompasses a broad examination of events that have taken place primarily since 1950 and comments on the roles that faculty have played in the decision-making process right up to the present. Special attention is accorded the role of technology in the teaching and learning process, particularly its impact on faculty engagement in decision-making.[1]

Jack E. Rossmann is professor of psychology (emeritus) at Macalester College. He joined the faculty in 1964 as coordinator of educational research and assistant professor of psychology. In 1967–68 he was director of research in the Counseling Center at the University of California, Berkeley, and in 1971–72 he was a research associate at the American Council on Education. Rossmann served as Macalester's vice president for academic affairs during 1978–86, and in 1986–2007 he was a professor of psychology.

1. The ideas expressed in this report were generated by reviewing materials in the Macalester archives, as well as the Macalester *Fact Book* and *Faculty Handbook,* and from conversations with both current and retired Macalester faculty members, several staff members, and President Brian Rosenberg and Provost Kathleen M. Murray. Of the twenty-two faculty members with whom I had conversations, ten are retired and twelve are still teaching full-time. The departmental homes of those faculty members included biology, chemistry, communication studies, economics, educational studies, geography, mathematics, physics, political science, psychology, religious studies, and sociology. Faculty conversations took place in August, September, October, and November 2013.

The Early Years

Macalester was founded in 1874 and chartered by the state of Minnesota. Its founder, the Reverend Edward Duffield Neill, served as a Union Army chaplain in the Civil War and subsequently held positions in three US presidential administrations. Journeying to the Minnesota Territory in 1849 to do missionary work, he founded two churches and served as the state's first superintendent of public education and first chancellor of the University of Minnesota. Neill believed that only a private college could offer both the academic quality and the values needed to prepare citizens for leadership. He planned a college that would be equal in academic strength to the best colleges in the East. It would be Presbyterian-affiliated but nonsectarian, making it inclusive by the standards of the times. Although Neill served as president during the first ten years of Macalester's existence (1874–84), the first president who had responsibility for both students and faculty was the Reverend Thomas A. McCurdy (also a Presbyterian minister), who served from 1884 to 1890.

The gift establishing the college was made by Charles Macalester, a prominent Philadelphia businessman and philanthropist. With additional funding from the Presbyterian Church and from the new college's trustees, Macalester officially opened in the fall of 1885 with five professors, six freshmen, and fifty-two preparatory students. Early faculty appointments, including James Wallace, a professor of classics who would later serve as dean and the college's fifth president (1894–1906), were made by the Board of Trustees, upon recommendation of the president.[2] During these early years, the small number of faculty (fewer than ten until the turn of the twentieth century) met weekly (7:30 each Friday evening for several years) and made decisions about student life as well as the course of instruction. In May 1886, the faculty established the following "rule of government": "Any student known to frequent any place where intoxicating drinks of any kind are sold shall be expelled from college." On May 23, 1891, the faculty meeting minutes noted: "The Dean was instructed to inform the trustees that the cleansing of the privies is necessary

2. Macalester College *Catalog*, 2013, http://catalog.macalester.edu/content.php?catoid=8&navoid=821, accessed April 3, 2014.

for the health of the students." One month later (June 18, 1891), the minutes recorded that "the Dean reported that the privies had been cleaned at the expense of the board."[3]

During the first five or six decades of its existence, Macalester evolved into a good regional liberal arts college associated with the Presbyterian Church. In 1950, the college gained some visibility as the first college in the country to fly the UN flag along with the US flag. By the 1950s, James Wallace's son, DeWitt (who had attended Macalester from 1907 to 1909), and his wife, Lila Acheson Wallace, the owners and publishers of the *Reader's Digest,* had begun making large gifts to the college. Their philanthropy was an important factor in the rising ambition represented in the Stillwater Conference and would have a substantial impact on Macalester's future development.

The Stillwater Conference

In January 1961, Macalester's Board of Trustees created a Long-Range Planning Commission to study and make recommendations regarding the college's future purposes and goals, curriculum and instruction, faculty, student body, facilities, and administrative organization. The thirty-one-member commission, which was composed of fourteen trustees, six administrators, nine faculty members, and two "friends of the college," met periodically from April through July and presented its report to the board on September 8–9, 1961, at the Lowell Inn in Stillwater, Minnesota.

The Purpose and Goals Committee recommended that Macalester should be "Christian in spirit and Presbyterian in background but sectarian in outlook." The Curriculum and Instruction Committee, which was chaired by President Harvey Rice (1958–68) and included two trustees, the dean, and one faculty member, recommended that the college offer only the BA and MEd degrees and that the MEd degree be reviewed in three years (the MEd degree was dropped in 1968). The BS degree and related programs would be phased out (e.g., elementary education, physical education, journalism, nursing,

3. Faculty Meeting Minutes, May 23, 1891, and June 18, 1891.

secretarial courses, 3–2 engineering, and medical technology). (Prior to 1949, only the BA degree had been awarded.) It was noted that, if this recommendation was adopted by the board, it would not be reviewed by the faculty but would be implemented by the faculty and administration. This appears to be the only instance (since 1960) in which the trustees made the final decision about a curriculum issue.

The Faculty Committee, which was also chaired by the president and included trustee, faculty, and administrative representation, recommended that the percentage of faculty with PhDs should move from approximately one-third to one-half as soon as possible and eventually to two-thirds. Faculty salaries should be increased significantly (to a rating of "good" when compared with the "best colleges"). Fringe benefits should be increased. Teaching loads should be adjusted to encourage research. A regular sabbatical leave program should be implemented. Secretarial assistance should be provided for faculty, and consideration should be given to hiring graduate students as teaching assistants. Exchange professorships should be developed, and faculty should be encouraged to seek foundation grants.

The Student Committee made a number of important recommendations: the size of the student body should be 1,500–1,700; at least 20 percent of the students should come from outside the region; there should be equal numbers of men and women; the rate of retention should be increased; students should come from varied economic, social, cultural, and geographical backgrounds; 3–5 percent of the students should be international; a "lack of finances should not prevent students eligible for admission from pursuing their education at Macalester"; at least 75 percent of the students should live on campus, and the athletics facilities should be improved.

The Facilities Committee recommended that construction should begin immediately on a number of new projects, and within a few years the campus witnessed a "building boom" with construction of a fine arts center (housing the music, art, speech and drama, and humanities departments), a science building (housing the chemistry, physics, and mathematics departments), a stadium, a dining hall, two residence halls, and a new power plant. All of these buildings were

1964

completed by the fall of 1964. A second science building opened in the fall of 1969.[4]

The Committee on Administrative Organization recommended that there should be four administrative divisions: curriculum and instruction, student life, business operations, and development; and the academic departments should be organized into divisions: arts, humanities, behavioral sciences, social sciences, and physical sciences.

At the meeting of the Board of Trustees on September 8–9, 1961, virtually all of these recommendations were adopted. Three important points should be noted: these recommendations provided a framework for major decisions for many years; there were more faculty members than administrators on the commission's committees; and decisions related to phasing out programs had faculty input, but the final decisions were made by the board.

A National Liberal Arts College (1960s)

In the spring of 1969, Wilbur Elston, a Macalester trustee and editorial writer for the *Minneapolis Tribune,* published this opinion piece:

> Liberal arts colleges which limit their enrollment ought to become more selective. With more and more youngsters wishing to go to college, they can raise their standards and attract as many applicants as they do now—and probably more—depending on the level to which their standards are raised. As their standards and excellence increase, they can also attract students from a wider geographical area and those from more diverse social backgrounds—if this is what the colleges wish to do. If they follow this course, such colleges also can reduce their purely vocational

4. Since the 1960s, a new library, residence hall, campus center, and athletics building and the Institute for Global Citizenship have been added, and major upgrades have taken place in the science buildings and fine arts complex. Faculty members played an active role at the macro level (on the Resource and Planning Committee) and in working with the architects as new and improved academic buildings were being designed.

courses, their community service programming, their "peripheral" activities, and lay greater stress on purely liberal arts courses. They may be able to broaden the base of their financial support if they attain greater excellence.

Elston's statement touches on several of the key points from the Stillwater plan and represents a reasonable approximation of what Macalester attempted to achieve for the rest of the twentieth century.

With the Stillwater Conference decisions as the guide, Macalester moved toward implementing many of the recommendations. Among these was the movement toward becoming a national liberal arts college. For several years, high school students from around the country who had achieved "finalist" status in the National Merit Scholarship competition were offered very attractive financial aid packages as "*Reader's Digest* Merit Scholars." In the mid- to late 1960s, Macalester was among the top ten colleges in the country in the number of National Merit Scholars, and the percentage of new students from outside Minnesota and the Midwest began to increase significantly.

Recruitment of Senior Faculty

Following through on the Stillwater recommendations to increase the percentage of faculty members with PhDs and strengthen academic departments, the college undertook a major recruitment effort. Between 1963 and 1968, 20–25 new faculty members were hired at the associate or full professor level in sixteen different departments. (The total number of full-time faculty at the college at that time was approximately 125.) Many new PhDs were also hired at the assistant professor level during this same period. The response of continuing faculty to this flurry of hiring was mixed. While most departments were pleased to add positions, many senior faculty were less than enthusiastic about bringing in "senior" colleagues. Although continuing faculty participated in the hiring process, Dean of the College Lucius Garvin was the primary decision-maker, and his goal was the establishment of "pillars of excellence" among the departments.

Adoption of the 4-1-4 Academic Calendar (1963)

Following the Stillwater Conference, Macalester faculty began to consider a variety of new curricular and calendar options. In 1961–62, the college was operating with a traditional semester calendar (the first semester ended in January) and a traditional semester-credit-hour system for awarding academic credit. During the 1962–63 academic year, the faculty approved significant changes in the calendar and the awarding of credit.

Effective with the 1963–64 academic year, Macalester adopted a 4-1-4 calendar. The numbers indicated both months in each term and the typical number of courses taken each term. The fall term was four months long (September through December), the interim term was one month long (January), and the spring term was four months long (February–May). The standard course load for each student during the fall and spring terms was four courses, and each course was regarded as a four semester-credit-hour course (i.e., a student taking the standard four courses during a term would receive the equivalent of sixteen semester credit hours for completion of those courses). Completion of thirty-one fall- and spring-term courses and four interim-term courses was required for graduation. The move to the 4-1-4 calendar grew out of the work of a faculty committee, and was approved by the faculty and supported by the administration. Thirty years later (1993–94), the faculty voted to reinstate the "semester-credit-hour" concept. Subject to certain restrictions, a course can now receive between one and eight semester credit hours. Five years after the return of the semester credit hour, the faculty voted to eliminate the January (interim/intersession) term.

Faculty Governance and the Curriculum

By the mid- to late 1960s, with tacit and later explicit trustee approval, the faculty assumed responsibility for curricular decisions, academic performance, graduation requirements, and the academic calendar. In the language of the current *Faculty Handbook*:

> The Faculty recognizes the Board of Trustees as the final institutional authority and, at the same time, emphasizes the inescapable

interdependence among governing board, administration, faculty, staff, and students, the importance of adequate communication among these components and full opportunity for appropriate joint planning and effort. . . . In the government of Macalester College, the Board of Trustees, in certain areas, delegates primary responsibility to the faculty and, in others, involves the faculty before making final decisions. In every area it is imperative that all parties should seek agreement before decisions are made. Where the faculty has primary responsibility, it is expected that other parties will concur with the faculty judgment except in rare instances and for compelling reasons.[5]

Dropping Mandatory Chapel Requirement (1966)

Soon after the 4–1–4 calendar was adopted, the influx of new faculty began to occur, and many other changes began to be considered. These changes related to both the curriculum and out-of-class activities. Throughout most of its history before the 1960s, Macalester students were required to attend chapel and a separate convocation on a weekly basis. Beginning in the 1950s, students had the option of attending a less religious "confrontation" event instead of chapel. During the 1960s, questions were raised by students and faculty members about the value of these requirements. In April of 1966, the faculty took action to eliminate the requirement of chapel/confrontation and convocation without the need for or expectation of trustee action.

Expanding Faculty Roles and Prerogatives (1960s)

Throughout most of Macalester's early history, faculty meetings were chaired by the president of the college. In the fall of 1968, the president and the chief academic officer (holding the titles of executive vice

5. Macalester College *Faculty Handbook, 2013–2014*, www.macalester .edu/provost/facultyhandbook/01facultyconstitution/faculty-constitution-20130319 .pdf, p. 1, accessed April 14, 2014. Note the rather close congruence between this statement of delegation and the one adopted by the Princeton trustees at about the same time; see the Princeton case study.

president and provost) had decided that the latter would chair the meetings. In November 1968, the faculty approved a motion that "the presiding officer of the faculty should be elected by a majority vote of the faculty." This proposed change in the Faculty Constitution was subsequently approved by the board of trustees, and the first elected presiding officer took office in the spring of 1969. That process continues to the present time and has been adopted by a number of other liberal arts colleges.

The first official mention of a faculty role in faculty personnel matters appears in the 1958 *Faculty Handbook,* which states that among the additional functions of the faculty would be "recommendation to the administration of the principles governing appointment, promotion, and rank of faculty members." A 1962 amendment to the Faculty Constitution created a Committee on Faculty Personnel to advise the president and dean. The first Faculty Personnel Committee was elected to serve in 1962–63. In April 1966, the Education Committee of the Board of Trustees decided that responsibility for/consultation on amendment to the Faculty Constitution regarding faculty appointment, promotion, and salary should be between the faculty and administration. Final decisions regarding tenure, however, were to be made by the board (based upon a recommendation from the Faculty Personnel Committee), and the annual budget (which requires board approval) includes a recommendation for a salary improvement pool for both faculty and staff. Individual salary decisions for faculty members are made by the provost, based upon department chair recommendations. Faculty hiring decisions are made by the provost based upon Search Committee recommendations. In May 1967, the faculty adopted these changes to the Faculty Constitution and by-laws.

One of the most significant expansions of faculty authority occurred approximately a decade later. Based upon the recommendation of an ad hoc faculty committee, the faculty decided in 1976 (with administration approval) that "faculty shall have primary responsibility for the implementation of faculty personnel policies (including) the awarding of tenure to members of the faculty." Around 1990, the faculty by-laws were changed so that the president and provost became members of the Faculty Personnel Committee, and promotion and tenure decisions were to be made by committee consensus.

Expanding Educational Opportunity (1968–69)

In the fall of 1968, a new president, former Health, Education, and Welfare Secretary Arthur S. Flemming, arrived at Macalester with a strong commitment to issues of social justice. In December, the chair of the Faculty Advisory Council entered into the record of the faculty meeting that a "program to expand educational opportunities" was being developed. The president worked closely with the Advisory Council, and by the spring of 1969, a Program to Expand Educational Opportunities had been approved by the faculty and was launched. EEO, as it came to be known, had three major components: student recruitment, staff and faculty recruitment, and the development of support systems for students of color. These admission and faculty recruitment policies were approved by the Board of Trustees. For the student cohorts entering in the fall of 1969 and the fall of 1970, 10–15 percent of the enrollees were students of color (African American, Native American, Hispanic, and Puerto Rican) who were awarded attractive financial aid packages. For each of these four groups, a full-time program director was hired, and a learning skills center was developed to provide support in writing and mathematics. In addition to these staff members, a significant number of faculty members of color were hired in various academic departments, and new staff members of color were hired throughout the college.

Student Activism (1968–74)

During the latter part of the 1960s, Macalester students, like their peers across the United States, actively participated in political and social movements. Motivated partially by their concern about America's involvement in Vietnam, student deaths at Kent State University, and other national events, students participated in several protest activities. Among these was the occupation of former Vice President Hubert Humphrey's campus office in the spring of 1969. By the fall of 1969, in response to student pressure, residence hall policy had been changed so that students could opt to live in residence halls that were co-ed by floor. At this same time, the faculty voted to give responsibility for student conduct to the Office of Student Services. In the fall of

1974, in the wake of an economic downturn (discussed below), students occupied an administrative building to protest trustee-approved cutbacks in the EEO program.

Financial Crisis, Low Enrollment, and Tight Budgets (1970–84)

Following the rapid change in the nature of the student body, faculty personnel, and curriculum (revision of general education and approval of internships) that occurred during the 1960s, the college experienced a period of financial turmoil during the first half of the 1970s. Less than three years after he took office, and without any formal consultation with the faculty, the board asked President Flemming to resign. Unfortunately, conditions were about to go from bad to worse. Shortly before Flemming's resignation, DeWitt Wallace, the college's principal benefactor, announced that he and his wife were withdrawing their financial support.[6] In April 1971, the faculty minutes recorded that "a special committee was created to deal with faculty reductions for 1972–73." This committee was composed of three faculty members and three administrators. Ultimately, twelve full-time (non-tenured) faculty members (approximately 10 percent of the full-time faculty) were "let go," and about the same number of administrative staff members left the college. A new president, James Robinson, former provost at Ohio State University, arrived in the fall of 1971, but three years later (November 1974) he abruptly left to accept the presidency of the University of West Florida.

6. The withdrawal of Wallace's support may have been connected to an unpleasant experience that Tricia Nixon, one of President Richard M. Nixon's daughters, had while visiting Macalester. According to the *Papers of the Nixon White House*, part 5, H. R. Haldeman, *Notes of White House Meetings, 1969–1973*, Nixon's chief of staff, Bob Haldeman, recorded this entry on the evening of October 15, 1970: "Called tonight all cranked up because Macalester College kids gave Tricia a bad time with obscene signs. Wants DeWitt Wallace, who funds the place, to put the screws on them." See H. R. Haldeman, *The Haldeman Diaries: Inside the Nixon White House* (New York: Berkley Books, 1995), p. 242. The telephone log entry can be found in Joan Hoff Wilson, ed., *Papers of the Nixon White House* (Bethesda, MD: University Publications of America, 1993), available at http://roosevelt.nl/topics/papers_nixon.pdf.

In the summer of 1975, President John B. Davis Jr. arrived on campus during a particularly difficult time. During most of the years of his presidency (1975–84), Macalester's enrollment was 10–20 percent below what was perceived as the optimum enrollment, and 70–80 percent of the applicants were being admitted. During this period the budget was balanced, and no academic programs were eliminated. Except for major grants from the National Endowment for the Humanities (for an innovative faculty development program titled Ways of Knowing), the National Science Foundation (a faculty development grant to enhance computer skills), and the Fund for the Improvement of Postsecondary Education (for a faculty renewal program), tight institutional budgets did not allow for many "bold" changes at the college.

Recruiting and Supporting International Students (1970s)

Following the decision of the faculty in 1970 to eliminate the foreign language requirement for graduation, the chair of one of the language departments proposed that the tenured faculty in the language departments (Spanish, German, French, and Russian) should combine their efforts and develop an English as a second language (ESL) program. This proposal met with the approval of the rest of the faculty, and the program was launched. Large numbers of "full-pay" students from Malaysia (tuition paid by the Malaysian government) and Saudi Arabia (tuition paid by family members and/or the government) began to enroll at Macalester. It quickly became apparent that full-time faculty members with a strong background in teaching ESL would be needed to ensure the success of the program. Thus a "linguistics" department was established. By the mid-1970s, four full-time NTT faculty members had been hired, the program gained a positive international reputation, and 10–15 percent of the college's entering students were from countries outside the United States. This strong presence of "no-need" international students played an important role in helping Macalester survive the financial difficulties of the 1970s. By 1990, the ESL program had been phased out by the administration and faculty (a more traditional linguistics program replaced it), but 12 percent of the students continue to be international students, and they now come from 70–80 different countries.

NTT = Non Tenure Track

Macalester's Changing Relationship with the Presbyterian Church (1960s–90s)

Jeanne Kilde's *Nature and Revelation: A History of Macalester College* (2010) outlines the long-term, and somewhat complex and evolving, relationship between the college and the Presbyterian Church. From the school's close ties to the church at the time of its founding (with Presbyterians as presidents and a large proportion of Presbyterians on the board of trustees), the religious orientation of college leaders has changed dramatically; the religious backgrounds of the four most recent presidents have been Unitarian, Catholic, Lutheran, and Jewish. By the 1990s, as Kilde notes, "the identity of the college itself as Presbyterian . . . had all but disappeared. Most enrolled students, it is safe to say, know little if anything about the historical Presbyterian roots of the college, much less its current relationship with the church."[7] This assertion is supported by survey data collected from incoming Macalester students in the fall of 2013. Among these students, only 2 percent identified themselves as Presbyterian. In 1973 (the first year for which comparable data are available) this figure was 10 percent.

It should also be noted, however, that the college maintains a covenant with the Synod of the Lakes and Prairies of the Presbyterian Church (U.S.A.). This covenant, which was renewed by the college and the synod in 2011, affirms: "The Presbyterian Church (U.S.A.) and Macalester College freely covenant together to support education that leads to growth in scholarship, faithfulness in character, and preparation to serve the common good. This is an historic and continuing relationship that both the church and college value, dating from the launch of our common history in 1880."[8] From the perspective of faculty members, a key moment occurred at the May 1969 faculty meeting, when the faculty decided that meetings would no longer begin with a prayer.

7. Jean Kilde, *Nature and Revelation: A History of Macalester College* (Minneapolis: University of Minnesota Press, 2010), p. 320.
8. Macalester College *Catalog*, www.macalester.edu/religiouslife/about/, accessed April 3, 2014.

Reader's Digest Stock and Initial Public Offering
(1980s-90s)

Shortly after John Davis assumed the presidency in 1975, he and a key member of the board of trustees paid a visit to DeWitt Wallace in New York City. One of the eventual outcomes of this meeting was a decision by the Wallaces to put more than 500,000 shares of *Reader's Digest* stock into a State of New York Support Organization for Macalester. Before the Wallaces died (DeWitt in 1981 and Lila in 1984), they made a significant gift of 513,550 shares of *Reader's Digest* common stock to Macalester. Dividends from this stock contributed about $1 million annually to the college's operating budget. In February 1990, there was an initial public offering (IPO) of the Macalester stock and that of several other support organizations, and the stock was split twenty-fold. This meant that Macalester held 10,270,000 shares of *Reader's Digest* stock. The initial offering was for $20 per share, so on the day of the IPO, the Macalester stock was valued at more than $200.5 million. During subsequent months, the stock rose to more than $50 per share, then "retreated" over the next several years. Today Macalester is totally divested of *Reader's Digest* stock, but the gift of that stock has played a key role in increasing the size of Macalester's endowment from $37 million in 1985 (before the receipt of the stock) to its June 30, 2013, value of $689 million.

Former Macalester president Michael S. McPherson has important observations about the history of the Wallaces' gift and its relationship to institutional governance:

> Although Mac had limited control over the endowment overseen by the Support Organization (SO), whose chair was the CEO/Board Chair of the company Reader's Digest Association (RDA), the sole purpose of the SO was to benefit Macalester College, so the funds were included in the endowment. The large valuation of the endowment when RDA went public expanded the college's horizons, but President [Robert M. "Bob"] Gavin, Jr. (1984–96) wisely put relatively little of that money into ongoing, hard-to-reverse program expansion, and put most of the money into a fund for capital improvement. As RDA's stock performance

304   Case Studies

declined (roughly coinciding with McPherson's assuming the Presidency) this decision to restrain growth in operations was crucial. Still the sharp decline in the endowment was considerable as the value of the stock that provided the majority of Mac's endowment fell by half over three years.

The challenge facing the College was to restrain spending in the near term to reflect the substantial decline in income from the (now reduced) endowment, while not cutting spending so severely as to undermine in a lasting way the investments in improving the College that were underway. To accomplish these twin goals, the Trustees needed to spend a larger annual percentage of the (now diminished) endowment than was the norm, and the faculty and staff needed to accept more restraint in salary gain and funds for innovation than was habitual.[9]

McPherson attributes the success of this strategy to several factors. First, the college's wealth was a recent phenomenon. Unlike at institutions whose faculties had become accustomed to abundant resources, the Macalester faculty's "sense of entitlement" was much more limited. Second, the administration created a Long-Range Planning and Budget Committee, and its strong faculty and staff representatives, who were widely respected by the college's leadership, recognized that pressing for short-term spending might imply consuming the "seed corn." Third, as McPherson observes, "The Board recognized that its responsibilities were broader than maximizing the value of the endowment and appreciated that one role of endowment is to provide a resource to be drawn on when times demanded it." At one point, as he notes, "the faculty were demanding more severe cuts in program and salaries while Trustees urged an increase in spending from the endowment"—a combination McPherson regarded as "remarkable." Finally, administrators wisely followed a practice of being open with both the Trustees and the on-campus community about the college's financial situation and possible ways to respond.[10] The crisis on

9. Michael S. McPherson to Jack E. Rossmann, William G. Bowen, and Eugene M. Tobin, April 8, 2014, private correspondence.
10. McPherson, April 8, 2014.

campus eased when the attorney general of New York (Eliot Spitzer) persuaded the CEO of RDA that dissolving the SOs and providing opportunity for their beneficiaries (including Macalester) to divest their holdings would be prudent, whereas failure to do so might have unpleasant consequences.

Strengthening and "Globalizing" the College (1980s–90s)

From the 1960s, when Macalester became a member of the Associated Colleges of the Midwest (ACM), a consortium of liberal arts colleges in Minnesota, Iowa, Wisconsin, and Illinois, the college used ACM schools as the point of comparison for most important variables such as faculty salaries, proportion of the annual budget going to "educational and general" expenses, size of endowment, and so on. With the increase in the size of the endowment as a result of the Wallaces' gifts, it became possible for the college to think beyond the Midwest and to begin to compare itself with the top twenty-five liberal arts colleges in the country.

The increased endowment made it possible to make two simultaneous changes—increase the size of the faculty and decrease the teaching load. Both changes were made with strong faculty support and with approval of the board of trustees and president. From 1963 through 1996–97, the official teaching load had been six courses (e.g., three courses in the fall, two courses in the spring, plus one course during three of four interim terms). In the fall of 1997, the January term was dropped, and the teaching load was changed to five courses (2–0–3, or 3–0–2). What made the decreased teaching load possible was an increase in the number of tenured/tenure-track faculty. Between 1985 and 2013, this number went from 108 to 153 (an increase of 42 percent), while the enrollment grew from 1,613 full-time students to 2,020 full-time students (a 25 percent increase).

In 1994, a dean of international studies was appointed, and the International Studies major was strengthened. With significant support from a donor, the Institute for Global Citizenship was created in 2005, and the institute moved into a new building in 2009. The institute, coupled with a large percentage of international students, majors in six languages, and a strong study-abroad program, ensured the strength of the college's emphasis on internationalism.

Interdisciplinary Programs: Addition/Subtraction (1990–2010)

During the period of faculty expansion (from 1990 to 2010), when there was an increase of approximately thirty tenured/tenure-track faculty members, some significant changes also occurred in the structure of the curriculum. One department (communication studies) was phased out, one new department came into existence (media and cultural studies), and one interdepartmental concentration became a department (linguistics). Most of the change, however, took place with the addition of interdepartmental concentrations. In the 1990–92 catalog, ten interdepartmental concentrations were identified. In the 2013–14 catalog, all of those concentrations still exist (one is now a department—linguistics—and two have merged), but nine new interdepartmental concentrations have been added.

The elimination of the communication studies department (and the creation of the linguistics and media and cultural studies departments) required approval by the entire faculty. The addition of inter-departmental concentrations was based upon recommendations from the faculty's Education Policy and Governance committee (EPAG), and the approval of the faculty. Because faculty members traditionally address the creation and elimination of instructional programs with great seriousness, the *Faculty Handbook* offers the clearest understanding of how the process works. The handbook states that EPAG's responsibility includes "consideration and recommendation to the general faculty of changes in the organization of academic departments including their creation, significant modification, or elimination." A subsequent section of the handbook outlines the procedure for "Discontinuance of a Department, Major and/or Minor." The procedure includes the following statement:

> EPAG shall make a written report and recommendation to the faculty regarding the proposed discontinuance. . . . If EPAG recommends discontinuing a department, it shall provide its full report

to the faculty a minimum of ten days before the next faculty meeting, at which its recommendation may be discussed. A voting member of the faculty at that meeting may present a motion to reject EPAG's recommendation, and such a motion may be discussed, but a vote on the motion shall be postponed until the next regular meeting of the faculty. In order to be adopted, such a motion to overturn EPAG's recommendation shall require the support of at least two-thirds of the members of the faculty voting, a quorum being present. The recommendation of EPAG shall become effective in the absence or failure of such a motion.[11]

During the 2012–13 academic year, in the wake of falling enrollments in Russian and a small number of majors, EPAG recommended discontinuing the Russian Studies major. One of the tenured faculty members was retiring, the other tenured faculty member was assured of a position in another department, and the number of students and majors was among the smallest of the language departments. Therefore, EPAG recommended that the major be phased out. A faculty member moved to reject the committee's recommendation, and the faculty voted 100–47 against EPAG's motion to discontinue, barely meeting the two-thirds majority needed to pass.

Movement Away from Need-Blind Admissions (2005–06)

Prior to the cohort of students who enrolled at Macalester in the fall of 2006, admissions decisions did not consider a family's ability to pay. Following a major review of this policy, it was recommended that the college join most other private colleges and universities and become a "need-aware" institution. This recommendation was approved by the faculty and Board of Trustees with the understanding that the college would maintain its long-standing commitment to social and economic diversity, meet the full need of admitted students, and establish a financial aid budget to maintain financial equilibrium.

11. Macalester College *Faculty Handbook, 2013–2014*, section 4, "Curriculum and Procedures," p. 13.

Changing Roles and Faculty Involvement in Decision-Making

Virtually without exception, both current and retired faculty interviewed for this case study expressed the view that members of the faculty have played a key role in most of the significant events that have taken place at the college during the past fifty years. It can be asserted that the faculty had little responsibility for creating the financial difficulties of the early 1970s, but many would say that the faculty helped develop important strategies to make it possible for the college to get through the "tough years" and emerge as a stronger institution.

As noted earlier, during Michael McPherson's term as Macalester's president (1996–2003), the college had to cope with a decline of about 25–30 percent in the value of the endowment because of a drastic decline in the value of the *Reader's Digest* stock. Looking back on those years, McPherson acknowledged that it is easier to work with faculty to economize, and so on, when faculty have not had time to become used to affluence:

> The lesson I want to draw . . . is this: it was so much easier to manage through this strenuous situation at Macalester than it . . . would have been at Williams [where McPherson had been dean of faculty] or a similarly long established place. At Mac, major wealth was quite a new experience, and there were still faculty around who had experienced the earlier rollercoaster years of the late 60s and early 70s. The faculty at Macalester . . . were far more willing to make sacrifices like pay freezes, postponement or cancellation of planned physical improvements, faculty expansion plans, etc. Indeed, I actually had to struggle with a faculty committee on priorities that wanted to make cuts that I thought would do lasting damage. I am not sure what practical lessons to draw from this but it seems significant.[12]

Today, one of the major concerns among faculty is the difficulty of convincing their colleagues to stand for election to major committees. This appears, in part, to reflect the increasing specialization and

12. Michael S. McPherson to Jack E. Rossmann, November 27, 2013, personal correspondence.

professionalization of faculty that has taken place across many sectors of higher education and the increasing demands on faculty time. At liberal arts colleges like Macalester, faculty have also become increasingly wary of investing substantial amounts of time in standing committees when their recommendations are rejected at faculty meetings.[13]

Exemplifying this dilemma is a recent change in the faculty by-laws that makes it possible for nominations for major faculty committees to be based upon $x + 1$ nominations (e.g., if a committee needs three new members, the election can be based upon four nominees for that committee), whereas for more than forty years it was required that there be $2x$ nominees (e.g., six nominees for three openings). There is speculation that the hesitance to serve on major committees is based on at least two issues: (1) a perception that service to the college is not valued significantly in decisions related to promotion, tenure, and salary improvement, (2) a perception that when dealing with some recent issues (such as the proposed discontinuation of the concentration in Russian Studies), the faculty as a whole did not support the recommendation of a committee that had worked very hard to bring that recommendation to the faculty.

One current faculty member felt that faculty involvement in the budgeting process has been getting weaker. Another colleague commented that the faculty have a lot of power, but now there seems to be a lot of distrust across academic divisions and between the faculty and the administration. Smaller departments worry about the future of their departments, and the allocation of resources is increasingly seen as a zero-sum game. If a faculty position is to be added to Department X, it will probably be taken from Department Y.

Adjunct Faculty Seeking to Organize (2014)

In April 2014 Macalester's adjunct faculty members filed a petition with the National Labor Relations Board seeking the right to orga-

---

13. Note the earlier discussion of the decision by the faculty at large to reject the recommendation of the faculty committee in the case of the proposed closing out of the Russian Studies major. As Michael McPherson notes in private correspondence with the authors, "It may be significant that in the Reader's Digest of America episode in the late 1990s, when the faculty governance system worked, I think, well, votes in faculty meeting did not play an important role."

nize as a collective bargaining unit of the Service Employees International Union (SEIU). Although the reallocation of resources from tenure-track to contingent faculty has been most evident at research universities, comprehensive institutions, and community colleges, liberal arts colleges like Macalester, which are located in large metropolitan areas, have not been immune from such trends. Forty-four percent of Macalester's approximately 275 faculty members are adjuncts, and they teach one-third of the college's courses. Many adjunct faculty serve as sabbatical-leave replacements. Full-time NTT faculty are eligible for sabbaticals and maternity leave, but there are understandable concerns among part-time faculty about job security, compensation, and their role in campus governance. In June 2014, SEIU leaders withdrew the petition for an election on the day before it was scheduled to begin. Although unionization issues are new to liberal arts colleges, they are likely to become increasingly familiar in the near future.[14]

The Role of Technology in Teaching/Learning

One faculty member recalled Macalester's "communications system" of the 1950s and early 1960s, which revolved around Agnes, the telephone operator who knew almost everything that was going on at the college. At that time, there was also one secretary to provide "typing" support for all the members of the faculty. In contrast, there are now twenty-eight full-time staff members who work in instructional technology (IT) at the college, many of whom are providing direct support to the faculty, and all academic departments have at least a part-time department coordinator.

In the October 25, 2013, issue of the *Chronicle of Higher Education,* data from the 2013 Campus Computing Survey report responses from approximately 450 chief information officers and other senior IT officials at two-year and four-year public and private colleges and

14. See http://themacweekly.com/2014/05/macalester-opposed-to-adjunct
-faculty-union/, www.mprnews.org/story/2014/04/24/adjunct-faculty-macalester
-hamline-unionization-vote), and www.startribune.com/local/stpaul/256584971
.html, all accessed May 9, 2014. See also http://themacweekly.com/2014/06/
contingent-faculty-union-vote-cancelled/.

universities across the United States. When asked what tasks they considered "very important" in IT at their institutions, the number-one response (identified by eight out of ten respondents as "very important") was "Help faculty members integrate technology into teaching." Interviews with current Macalester faculty members support this perception of IT staff members. A very high percentage of current faculty indicate that they and their colleagues find value in new technologies and are pleased with the support they are receiving from IT staff members.

The Campus Computing Survey also indicated that two-thirds of the survey respondents said that "providing online education" was very important. This is not the case at Macalester. In the summer of 2013, a faculty member in mathematics partnered with a colleague from St. Olaf (supported by IT staff members from their institutions) to offer an online version of Applied Calculus to sixteen students from eight of the twelve colleges in the ACM. The results of this pilot program are in the process of being evaluated, but the anecdotal comments suggest that the students were satisfied, and the instructors found it to be a positive but labor-intensive endeavor. Although this course may be offered again, it is unlikely that there will be a significant increase in the number of online courses at Macalester in the near future.

A senior staff member in IT noted that "technology is a tool" that can be put to good use—but it can also be a distraction. He noted that several faculty members are making excellent use of video conferencing to bring speakers from around the world to the Macalester classroom.

Faculty Perceptions of the Future Role of Technology

A sampling of observations drawn from interviews conducted for the case study offer a range of opinion. One faculty member observed that a potential advantage of online education is that it would make it possible for students studying abroad to take a required course. He also noted that there is some possible ambiguity about the ownership of the IP for an online course. Another colleague expressed the hope that whatever the college does in the development of online education, that information will be used to help other faculty members and other institutions. A faculty member suggested that "technology is changing the way we teach," but "Macalester is selling an experience in addition to content. We can deliver online education, but I don't think we should. We don't have the support system to do the 'tech stuff.'" And another colleague indicated that students are beginning to ask about the possibility of taking online courses from other colleges. Macalester's current policy is that eight semester credit hours of such courses can be counted toward graduation. This faculty member does not see major technology-related changes at Macalester during the next four or five years. Another faculty member commented that "in educational technology, we are seeing two hundred flowers blooming, but Macalester's bread and butter is the residential model. It is an elite model, but America demands it. There will always be an Oxford and a Cambridge." Another faculty member said, "I'm in awe of technology, but I don't know what will happen in the future." Another commented, "Online education is not a product we sell. MOOCs are not likely to be our bag."

One faculty member commented that he thinks that faculty members who are good at technology are becoming campus leaders. He feels that technology empowers faculty governance and will change the nature of promotion and tenure. Another faculty member expressed concern that "technology could push faculty further into independent/entrepreneurial/self-promotion behavior." According to another faculty member, "Faculty governance is not likely to change because of new technologies." Another faculty member said, "There is not much evidence that technology is influencing governance. There is no ongoing faculty discussion about technology."[15]

Concluding Thoughts

Three key points emerge from the preceding analysis. First, the strategic planning decisions made by the Board of Trustees in 1961 (at the

15. Small, selective liberal arts colleges like Macalester are less likely than either major public universities or smaller, more endangered, colleges to feel that technology will affect faculty roles or change governance. One reason is that there is less inclination at schools like Macalester to substitute adjuncts or TAs for regular faculty. Another reason is that institutions like Macalester are less likely than large research universities to be exporters of online courses or new technologies.

Stillwater Conference) laid the groundwork for Macalester to become one of the top liberal arts colleges in the United States. Second, since the 1960s, faculty members have played a key role in shaping virtually every significant change that has taken place at Macalester, and most faculty feel that the increasing presence of technology in the classroom is not likely to have a significant impact on the role that faculty play in future decision-making at the college. Many Macalester faculty are making creative use of the new technologies in on-campus courses, but there doesn't seem to be much enthusiasm among the faculty for using the new technologies to export courses via online education or MOOCs. Third, financial support received from DeWitt and Lila Acheson Wallace has been crucial to the development of Macalester's current strengths.

The City University of New York

Martin A. Kurzweil

The City University of New York (CUNY) is a system of twenty-four community and senior colleges and graduate schools located on campuses throughout the five boroughs of New York City.[1] CUNY is the largest metropolitan university in the United

Martin A. Kurzweil is director of policy at Ithaka S+R, where he focuses on education governance and on evidence-based strategies to improve student learning. He teaches a course on education organizations at Columbia Law School, where he is a lecturer in law and was previously an academic fellow. Kurzweil served as senior executive director for research, accountability, and data at the New York City Department of Education until 2012. He has also worked as a corporate litigator at Wachtell, Lipton, Rosen & Katz and as a researcher at the Andrew W. Mellon Foundation. Kurzweil's publications include *Equity and Excellence in American Higher Education,* winner of the 2006 Outstanding Book Award of the American Educational Research Association.

1. CUNY's twenty-four institutions include eleven senior colleges that offer baccalaureate programs (Baruch College, Brooklyn College, City College, the College of Staten Island, Hunter College, John Jay College, Lehman College, Medgar Evers College, New York City College of Technology, Queens College, and York College); seven community colleges that offer associate but not baccalaureate programs (the Borough of Manhattan Community College, Bronx Community College, Guttmann Community College, Hostos Community College, Kingsborough Community College, LaGuardia Community College, and Queensborough Community College); the William E. Macaulay Honors College; the Graduate School and University Center; the CUNY Graduate School of Journalism; the CUNY School of Law; the CUNY School of Professional Studies; and the CUNY School of Public Health. See *Investing*

States and the third-largest university system,[2] serving more than 270,000 students in credit-bearing programs and 200,000 students in continuing and professional programs.[3] Its more than 7,100 full-time and more than 11,200 adjunct faculty are represented by one of the largest university faculty unions in the country.[4]

Governing and administering a system of CUNY's size would be complex regardless of the structures in place. For much of its fifty-year history, the task of managing the university was rendered more challenging by a structurally weak central administration and a generalist board of trustees more focused on particular campuses than on the university as a whole. Moreover, the administration and the board had to contend with state and city politics and politicians from above and with cross-cutting lines of authority below.

The consequence was a lack of coordination across the university, rendering CUNY a "confederation" of largely independent institutions rather than a coherent university system.[5] From the late 1960s through the 1980s, a series of severe fiscal strains and politically fraught policy decisions, such as opening admission to virtually any city high school graduate, were exacerbated by the decentralized governance structure, yielding a sharp decline in CUNY's academic standing.

---

in Our Future: The City University of New York's Master Plan, 2012–2016 (hereafter Master Plan, 2012–2016), p. 3, available at www.cuny.edu/news/publications/masterplan.pdf.

2. The State University of New York and the California State University System are thought to serve more students. If the enrollment reported at their websites is accurate, however, CUNY may now be the largest university system in the country. Compare http://en.wikipedia.org/wiki/City_University_of_New_York with http://en.wikipedia.org/wiki/List_of_the_largest_United_States_colleges_and_universities_by_enrollment.

3. Master Plan, 2012–2016, p. 3.

4. Ibid., p. 16, and CUNY Office of Human Resources Management, Staff Facts: Fall 2010 Edition, p. 4, available at www.cuny.edu/about/administration/offices/ira/ir/additional/StaffFacts2010.pdf.

5. See Brian P. Gill, "The Governance of the City University of New York: A System at Odds with Itself," RAND DRR-2053-1, 1999, p. 14, available at www.nyc.gov/html/records/rwg/cuny/pdf/randdrr-2053-1.pdf. Gill wrote: "Both college presidents and faculty regard CUNY as a loose confederation rather than a unified system."

Since the mid-1990s—and accelerating under the chancellorship of Matthew Goldstein from 1999 to 2013—there has been a shift toward more centralized governance of CUNY, with the primary aim of shoring up academic standards. Although day-to-day management is still in the hands of the presidents and faculty of individual campuses, Goldstein and his allies on the board consolidated authority for university-wide policy-making through several structural and management changes. They used this authority to raise academic standards, stabilize finances, promote hiring in key disciplines, develop innovative programming (including online degrees), and more closely integrate the university.

A number of Goldstein's central initiatives generated frustration and resistance among faculty leaders and the faculty union, the Professional Staff Congress (PSC), who argued that they infringed on core areas of faculty governance, among other concerns. In addition to protests, faculty votes opposing initiatives, and boycotts of central task forces, the PSC has sued CUNY several times over these reforms. The leaders of the University Faculty Senate (UFS), the university-wide faculty governance body, joined two of those suits as plaintiffs.

In each case, however, the courts ruled that the Board of Trustees was the sole body authorized by state law to "govern" and "administer" the university, including its academic policies, and that its bylaws did not bindingly delegate any of that authority to the faculty.[6] Although most public university systems—such as the University of California system—formally vest authority in a central board, much of that authority is delegated to the faculty. The CUNY Board of Trustees' *retention* of final authority over academic policy is unusual, and it is the baseline condition that has facilitated the recent moves toward greater centralization.

The remainder of this case study describes the structure and dynamics of CUNY's governance. The first section provides a

---

6. N.Y. Educ. Law, sec. 6204; ibid., sec. 6206; *Professional Staff Congress v. City Univ. of N.Y.* (Sup. Ct., N.Y. County, no. 151021, February 25, 2014) (Singh, J.) (slip. op. pp. 13–16); *Matter of Polishook v. City Univ. of N.Y.,* 234 A.D.2d 165 (App. Div., 1st Dep't, 1996).

historical overview—starting with CUNY's predecessor institutions and going through the 1990s—with a particular emphasis on system governance. In the second section, the study describes the governance structure that has been in place since 1999, including the key actors and their responsibilities. To illustrate the dynamics of this governance structure in action, the third section details some of the signature policy initiatives of the Goldstein chancellorship: (1) the elimination of remedial education at senior colleges, (2) online instruction and the CUNY School of Professional Studies, (3) cluster hiring and promotion of faculty research, (4) a major capital campaign and the CUNY Compact state financing plan, and (5) the Pathways Initiative to align transfer credit and general education requirements across campuses.

Sources for this study are discussed in the footnotes. In addition to CUNY administrative and board materials, state laws, public reports, and a handful of academic resources, the study relies on information gathered through personal interviews with current and former CUNY administrators and faculty, to whom I am deeply grateful for their time, insight, and institutional knowledge.[7]

Historical Overview

Predecessor Institutions

CUNY is a relatively recent invention, created in 1961 by an act of the New York State Legislature. Unlike the State University of New York (SUNY), established a few years earlier, however, CUNY was not formed out of whole cloth. Instead, it brought together seven

7. I conducted interviews with Counsel to the Chancellor Dave Fields (January 6, 2014); Chancellor Emeritus Matthew Goldstein (February 18, 2014); Senior Vice Chancellor Jay Hershenson (February 20, 2014); former executive vice chancellor and provost Alexandra Logue (January 30, 2014, and February 27, 2014); Professor and University Faculty Senate Chair Terrence Martell (April 30, 2014); University Dean for Academic Affairs John Mogulescu (February 18, 2014); University Dean for Academic Technology George Otte (February 18, 2014); and Senior Vice Chancellor and General Counsel Frederick Schaffer (February 6, 2014).

pre-existing and independently managed institutions. Indeed, its two oldest colleges were founded in the nineteenth century.

The Free Academy was founded in 1847 by an act of the State Legislature and passage of a referendum submitted to the voters of New York City, and it opened its doors to students in 1849.[8] Originally a high school and polytechnic for boys, the academy was authorized by the State Legislature to offer postsecondary degrees in 1854, and the legislature renamed it the College of the City of New York (or City College) in 1866.[9] In 1870, to support the expanding public school system, the legislature authorized the School for Female Monitors to award postsecondary degrees to teachers and renamed it the Female Normal and High School. (It was renamed Hunter College in 1914.)[10]

Students at both institutions were educated free of charge, but admission was limited: initially, to young men (at City College) and women (at Hunter) who passed an entrance exam and later to those who met high school grade-point-average (GPA) thresholds and course requirements.[11] The requirement of a minimum GPA persisted at City College and Hunter, and was extended to new city institutions (including evening divisions and community colleges) through the 1960s.[12]

Both City College and Hunter were governed initially by the city's Board of Education. When the five boroughs merged in 1900, the

---

8. James Traub, *City on a Hill: Testing the American Dream at City College* (Reading, MA: Addison Wesley, 1994), pp. 21–26.

9. Traub, pp. 21–26; Sheila C. Gordon, "The Transformation of the City University of New York, 1945–1970" (doctoral dissertation, Columbia University, 1975), p. 15.

10. Gordon, p. 16.

11. Between 1900, when New York City's high school system was beginning to be established, and 1924, any student who earned a regents diploma was eligible to enroll. By 1924, city high schools were graduating more students than City College and Hunter could accommodate, and the boards of both colleges instituted grade-point-average and course requirements that limited admission to roughly the top 20 percent of city high school graduates. Traub, pp. 32–33 and 46.

12. Sally Renfro and Allison Armour-Garb, "Open Admissions and Remedial Education at the City University of New York," report prepared for the Mayor's Advisory Task Force on CUNY, New York, 1999, pp. 14–16, table 2, available at www.nyc.gov/html/records/rwg/cuny/pdf/history.pdf.

Board of Education, overwhelmed with its expanded scope of responsibility for elementary and secondary schools, relinquished its trusteeship of City College to a new, nine-member City College Board of Trustees created by the legislature. Hunter separated from the Board of Education and received its own board in 1915.[13]

The consolidation of the five boroughs also brought pressure for City College to expand its offerings outside Manhattan, particularly to populous Brooklyn. To meet this demand, City College opened an evening division for men in Brooklyn in 1909, which was joined by a women's evening division operated by Hunter in 1917.[14] The evening divisions, in contrast to the "day sessions," charged tuition.[15]

Brooklyn continued to advocate for its own day college, and had support in the State Legislature. After several false starts, the legislature in 1926 consolidated the City College and Hunter boards into the Board of Higher Education, composed of mayoral appointees. In addition to being given authority over existing higher education institutions in New York City, it had a mandate to create new institutions to meet demand (with a special directive to establish a college in Brooklyn).[16] Within a decade, the board established Brooklyn College (1930) and Queens College (1937).

The Board of Higher Education appointed a president to administer each institution, but initially created no central administration. In its first few decades, the board itself routinely interfered in management of the colleges—including in faculty appointments, where the board notoriously rewarded political loyalty over academic qualifications.[17] Until 1938, for example, the Board of Higher Education chose department chairs at its sole discretion; one result was a City College math department chairman who referred to himself as "the LaGuardia Professor" in honor of his patron, Mayor Fiorella LaGuardia.[18]

13. Gordon, p. 20.

14. Ibid., pp. 20–21.

15. CUNY Matters, "When Tuition Was Free, Sort Of," CUNY, New York, October 12, 2011, available at http://www1.cuny.edu/mu/forum/2011/10/12/when-tuition-at-cuny-was-free-sort-of/.

16. Gordon, pp. 21–22.

17. Traub, p. 37.

18. Ibid.

Notwithstanding his namesake department chair, LaGuardia took several steps to professionalize the Board of Higher Education. He appointed distinguished members and encouraged a shift from operational details to broad strategy. His appointees, in turn, created an Administrative Council of presidents and appointed staff members to coordinate the central functions of the university.[19]

The shift to a more hands-off board accelerated as a result of increasing organization by the faculty of the various institutions. The faculty at City College began to form associations in the 1920s, focused on academic freedom and faculty rights. In 1935, the New York College Teachers Union was founded and began to recruit across campuses. In 1938, the faculty at City, Hunter, Brooklyn, and Queens Colleges formed the Legislative Conference as a representative organ.[20] By the end of 1939, the associations and the unions had secured eligibility for tenure after three years, statutory tenure protections, the right to elect department chairs, a leading role in curricular development and faculty appointment and dismissal, and creation of a representative faculty governing council on each campus.[21] The board retained approval authority, and the college president retained significant executive and budgetary control of the campus, but the faculty gained a powerful voice in academic and personnel decisions.

Unlike LaGuardia, his mayoral successors tended to appoint machine politicians to the board, such as long-serving board member and chair Gustave Rosenberg, who had little expertise in higher education and instead used their positions to consolidate political power.[22] Disagreements between the LaGuardia appointees and these later appointees continued through the 1950s, delaying several important developments. For example, legislation in 1948 creating SUNY also authorized local governments to establish two-year community colleges, supported by a mix of state and local funds and

19. Gordon, pp. 25–32.
20. Irwin Yellowitz, "Academic Governance and Collective Bargaining in the City University of New York," *Academe* 73, no. 6 (1987): 8.
21. Carol Smith, "The Dress Rehearsal for McCarthyism," *Academe* 97 (July–August 2011), available at www.aaup.org/article/dress-rehearsal-mccarthyism#.UzSMrPldXTo.
22. Gordon, pp. 56–58.

tuition.[23] Despite clear demand for such institutions, the Board of Higher Education did not act until reformist Mayor Robert Wagner came into office and made two-year programs a priority. The board then established Staten Island Community College (1955), Bronx Community College (1957), and Queensborough Community College (1958) in rapid succession.[24] Another example of board gridlock is the long gap between its creation of the post of chancellor in 1955 and its filling of that position for the first time in 1960.[25]

CUNY's Founding and the Turbulent 1960s

Several national and state developments led to the transformation of the affiliated city colleges into the City University of New York in 1961. Following the Soviet Union's launch of Sputnik in 1957, there was national momentum to increase the supply of PhDs, particularly in science and engineering. (CUNY's predecessor institutions were not authorized to award doctoral degrees.) Furthermore, California's Master Plan, introduced in 1960, set the standard for coordinated state systems of higher education. Every ambitious governor in the country—including New York's Governor Nelson Rockefeller, who came into office in 1959 promising to bolster higher education in the state—sought to catch up to California.[26]

In 1961, the New York State Legislature united City, Hunter, Brooklyn, and Queens Colleges and Staten Island, Bronx, and Queensborough Community Colleges into the City University of New York. The state law authorized the Board of Higher Education to oversee CUNY, but reconstituted it to include twenty-four members, all appointed by the mayor.[27] As a way for the state to retain some oversight, the authorizing act required CUNY to submit a Master Plan to the State Board of Regents every four years addressing, among other things, new curricula, facilities, and changes in admission policies.[28]

23. Ibid., pp. 49–50.
24. Renfro and Armour-Garb, pp. 14–15, table 2; Gordon, p. 36.
25. Gordon, pp. 33–36.
26. Ibid., pp. 81–82.
27. New York State Higher Education Act of 1961.
28. N.Y. Educ. Law, secs. 237 and 6206.

Furthermore, any new degree program had to be registered with the regents.[29] There was also the prospect that the state could exercise the power of the purse, though it allocated no funding to CUNY after authorization.[30]

The 1961 Higher Education Act also created the office of University Chancellor, who would act as the "chief educational and administrative officer of the city university" and would be appointed by and "serve at the pleasure of" the board.[31] The campus presidents, however, continued to be appointed and supervised directly by the Board of Higher Education.[32] The bylaws further limited the authority of the chancellor over the presidents, declaring that "the authority, functions, and appellate powers of the presidents with regard to the educational administration and disciplinary affairs in their several colleges will not be abridged."[33] This unusual arrangement reflected the many political compromises that went into the Higher Education Act. As one commentator noted, Governor Nelson Rockefeller sought to ensure that the legislation was "acceptable to the Regents, SUNY's Board of Trustees, and the Board of Higher Education (BHE) in New York City, the presidents of major private universities, and Catholic, Protestant, and Jewish groups concerned about the church–state issue as it related to student aid proposals."[34] In short, the unification of CUNY accommodated the pre-existing influence of local interest groups.

Decentralized governance was reinforced by the next few generations of mayoral appointees to the board. From the late 1960s through the 1980s, board appointees typically did not have knowledge or standing in higher education, but were instead political figures with some affiliation with particular campuses. In the view of some observers, those affiliated board members played an outsized role in

29. Ibid., sec. 210; Regulations of the Commissioner of Education, sec. 52.1.
30. Gordon, p. 146.
31. N.Y. Educ. Law, sec. 6206.
32. Gill, p. 14 (citing former Board Bylaws, sec. 4.2).
33. Ibid. (quoting former Board Bylaws, sec. 11.2).
34. Judith S. Glazer, *Nelson Rockefeller and the Politics of Higher Education in New York State* (New York: Nelson A. Rockefeller Institute of Government, May 1989), p. 7, available at http://files.eric.ed.gov/fulltext/ED319271.pdf.

determining policy for their campuses—the full board would not act with respect to a campus without those affiliated board members' support. Thus campus presidents effectively reported to the handful of board members most interested in their campus. Furthermore, because the campus presidents had more knowledge and expertise than their board supervisors, they typically had loose rein to manage their campuses. Strong presidents took advantage of this, whereas weaker ones deferred more to their campus faculties. But in either case, decisions were made with a campus focus, not a university focus.

The new CUNY board did undertake two significant central initiatives in its first two decades. The first was a rapid increase in the number of campuses (which, though not its intention, further diluted central authority). By 1970, the university had more than doubled the number of campuses, from seven to eighteen. The new campuses were Borough of Manhattan Community College (1963), Kingsborough Community College (1963), John Jay College of Criminal Justice (1964), Richmond College (1965), York College (1966), Baruch College (1967), LaGuardia Community College (1967), Lehman College (1967), Medgar Evers College (1967), and Hostos Community College (1970).[35] In 1964, CUNY also assumed responsibility for the New York City Technical Institute, which had previously been managed by the now-defunct Board of Estimate, and renamed it New York City Community College.[36]

The second significant central initiative by the CUNY board was a university-wide change in admissions policies. As noted above, since the early 1900s, all CUNY institutions had limited admission to students achieving a threshold high school GPA. By 1960, the threshold was 85 for senior colleges and 77 for community colleges, both high standards for the time.[37] Although the new campuses met some of the pent-up demand for seats, the high admissions standards continued to have distributional consequences. In particular, New York City's growing African American and Puerto Rican pop-

35. Renfro and Armour-Garb, pp. 14–15, table 2.
36. Gordon, p. 88n2. Interestingly, the Board of Higher Education did not seek to acquire New York City Technical Institute (NYCTI); the transfer was prompted by the NYCTI faculty.
37. Gordon, p. 160.

ulations were underrepresented at CUNY, particularly in the more selective senior colleges.[38]

From 1965 to 1967, debates over admissions—and the related policies for tuition (which still was not charged for day students at senior colleges) and state funding—divided the board and pitted the board chair, Gustave Rosenberg, against the university chancellor, Albert Bowker. Rosenberg was a "traditionalist" who viewed CUNY's high admission standards and free tuition as critical to its status. Bowker preferred a more open admissions policy, and viewed charging tuition as a way to facilitate expansion and entice more funding from the state. Both sides lobbied the governor, state legislatures, and the new mayor, John Lindsay, for their cause.[39]

Bowker eventually emerged in a better position, and, with allies in the State Legislature (including an increasingly powerful African American and Hispanic caucus), pursued an incremental path to expanding access. The first effort was a well-funded program to increase minority enrollment known as SEEK (Search for Education, Elevation, and Knowledge). SEEK offered conditional admission to senior colleges and academic and financial assistance to students from impoverished neighborhoods.[40] In 1968, Bowker proposed and the board adopted a resolution to take a number of additional steps, including offering unconditional admission to SEEK students and instituting some quotas, with the goal of eventually achieving proportional representation for minority groups in the university as a whole.[41] Accordingly, the 1968 Master Plan included a proposal to transition by 1975 to a multi-tiered system of admission similar to that employed in California.[42]

Bowker's incremental central plans were derailed, however, by increasing tensions on the individual campuses. In 1969 cuts in the

38. Between 1960 and 1970, African Americans increased from 14 to 20 percent of the city's population, and Puerto Ricans increased from 8 to 11 percent. Nathan Glazer and Daniel Patrick Moynihan, *Beyond the Melting Pot,* 2nd ed. (Cambridge, MA: MIT Press, 1970), p. xxxi; Gordon, pp. 161–63.

39. Ibid., pp. 178–98.

40. Ibid., pp. 196 and 199. CUNY also created a community college version of SEEK called College Discovery. Ibid., pp. 196 and 199.

41. Ibid., pp. 208–9.

42. Ibid., p. 223.

budget were looming, and many anticipated a decline in freshman enrollment the following year. In April, a faculty group at City College passed a resolution calling for the college to maintain the proportion of African American and Puerto Rican students in the freshman class in the event of such a cut. A group of African American and Puerto Rican student activists reacted to this resolution by taking over part of the City College campus. The students' list of demands included racially proportional representation and ethnic studies programs. The president of City College closed the campus for more than a month, refusing to negotiate with the students. When the college was reopened by court order, the students resisted and the police were called in. Protests spread to other campuses, and City College's president resigned as a result.[43]

Not long after the violence, negotiations began among City College officials, the students, and prominent African American and Puerto Rican politicians. This group produced a proposal to admit half of CUNY's students using traditional academic criteria, and the other half from impoverished high schools without regard to grades. The proposal was rejected by City College's Faculty Senate and publicly opposed by New York's major politicians and unions, who were concerned that such a proposal would squeeze out middle-class students.[44]

With both the incremental approach and the quota approach rejected, support for fully open admissions began to build. In July 1969, the Board of Higher Education voted to admit any New York City high school graduate who applied beginning in 1970.[45] A board-appointed Commission on Admissions—composed of faculty, students, administrators, alumni, and representatives of community organizations—produced an implementation plan that depended heavily on class rank and the SEEK program and generated significant dissent.[46] Bowker and his administration crafted an alternative that the board approved: all students with a GPA of 80 or higher, or who were in the top 50 percent of their high school class, would be

43. Ibid., pp. 215–17.
44. Ibid., pp. 217–20.
45. Ibid., p. 222.
46. Ibid., pp. 227 and 231–32.

admitted to a senior college. In addition, the SEEK program would be expanded by 85 percent.[47] All other city high school graduates would be eligible for admission to a community college. In 1970, CUNY also eliminated tuition at community colleges and night divisions.[48] Less than a decade after its founding, CUNY had become a free and virtually open-access university.

The Development of Collective Bargaining and Governance Plans

Another important change that occurred in the 1960s was the advent of collective bargaining over the terms and conditions of faculty employment. In the early 1960s, the Legislative Conference (LC) began to demand recognition as the collective bargaining agent for CUNY. In 1963, the United Federation of College Teachers (UFCT), a local of the American Federation of Teachers, also began to recruit within CUNY and challenged the LC's dominance. After New York State passed the Taylor Law in 1967, authorizing collective bargaining for public employees (including those at public colleges), tenured faculty selected the LC as their bargaining agent, while non-tenured faculty selected the UFCT. Despite their rivalry, the two unions merged in 1972 to form the PSC.[49]

In 1971, the board adopted a resolution on university governance. The official goal of the resolution was to promote a more systematic approach to managing the university as a whole, while also erecting barriers to a perceived erosion of campus authority.[50] The desire to have a counterweight to the faculty unions may also have played a role in the board's decision-making.[51] The resolution created various system-wide bodies, including the UFS, the Council of Presidents, the University Student Senate, the Council of Provosts, and others. It also

47. Ibid., p. 236.
48. CUNY Matters.
49. Yellowitz, p. 8.
50. CUNY Board of Higher Education, *Statement of Policy on the Organization and Governance of the City University of New York,* New York, February 9, 1971.
51. Yellowitz, p. 8.

required each campus to adopt a governance plan indicating which bodies have which powers and responsibilities. Most individual campuses had existing faculty committees that had evolved over the years. But because the board had to approve the campus governance plan, there was a certain degree of uniformity—for instance, each campus had a "faculty council," but the composition varied from campus to campus.

The line between faculty collective bargaining and faculty governance can be fuzzy, and indeed, in the early years of the PSC, there were disputes over whether certain aspects of governance could be collectively bargained. During its first contract negotiation in 1972–73, the PSC attempted to enshrine the existing campus governance processes in the collective bargaining agreement by including a provision that stated: "The rights, privileges, and responsibilities of the University Faculty Senate shall not be diminished during the term of this Agreement." CUNY successfully resisted the union's efforts to include the clause in the contract, notwithstanding a fact-finding panel's non-binding recommendation that governance processes were "past practices" that could be included if the parties agreed.[52] In another dispute in 1974, the PSC sought to block a board decision to add students to personnel review committees. CUNY raised the issue before the New York Public Employment Relations Board, which ruled that governance matters like the composition of personnel committees were not a mandatory subject of negotiation.[53] The union had somewhat more success when it sought to influence academic policy outside the negotiation process. For example, in 1973 CUNY sought to introduce caps on the number of professors who could be tenured. The PSC organized protests and a boycott of meetings with the chancellor, and in 1974 the board reversed course.[54]

52. Larry G. Gerber, *The Rise and Decline of Faculty Governance* (Baltimore: Johns Hopkins University Press, 2014), pp. 114–15; Irwin H. Polishook, "Unions and Governance—The CUNY Experience," *Academe* 68, no. 1 (1982): 16–17; and Yellowitz, p. 9.

53. In re Board of Higher Education of the City of New York and Professional Staff Congress/CUNY, No. U-0904 (Public Employment Relations Board, April 29, 1974), available at http://digitalcommons.ilr.cornell.edu/cgi/viewcontent.cgi?article=1008&context=perbdecisions; Yellowitz, pp. 9–10.

54. Ibid., p. 10.

The state legislature also adjusted the organization of the Board of Higher Education in the early 1970s, partly in response to faculty and student activism. In 1974, the legislature reduced the number of appointed board members from twenty-four to ten, with seven appointed by the mayor and three appointed by the governor. Jay Hershenson, who was a Queens College student at the time and is now CUNY's senior vice chancellor, successfully lobbied the state legislature to include the chair of the University Student Senate (Hershenson, at the time) as an ex-officio voting member of the Board of Higher Education. The legislation also gave the chair of the UFS a non-voting position on the board.

The Fiscal Crisis of the 1970s and the Shift to State Control

In 1976, New York City was on the brink of bankruptcy, and it announced quite suddenly that funding for CUNY would be cut by a third. This unexpected and significant decrease in funding forced the entire university to close for two weeks in June. Over the next several years, CUNY had to lay off hundreds of faculty and staff.[55]

In 1979, the city and New York State reached an agreement under which the state would assume financial responsibility for the senior colleges and continue to share responsibility for the community colleges. The agreement also required all institutions to begin charging tuition and raised entrance standards for senior colleges (from high school students in the top 50 percent of their classes to students in the top 35 percent of their classes). This change brought CUNY's funding formula and tuition practices into alignment with all other public colleges and community colleges in the state.[56]

The 1979 CUNY Financing and Governance Act, which implemented these changes in financing, also reorganized the Board of Higher Education into the Board of Trustees. Instead of seven members appointed by the mayor and three appointed by the governor, the Board of Trustees would have fifteen appointed members, with

55. Traub, p. 77.
56. N.Y. Educ. Law, sec. 6221; Patricia J. Gumport and Michael N. Bastedo, "Academic Stratification and Endemic Conflict: Remedial Education Policy at CUNY," *Review of Higher Education* 24, no. 4 (Summer 2001): 339.

ten appointed by the governor and five appointed by the mayor. The board members would serve a seven-year term, with the option of reappointment to a second term, and would stay in the position beyond their term if the governor or mayor did not appoint a replacement.[57] The new Board of Trustees retained both ex-officio positions.[58]

The 1979 legislation explained that the university "must remain responsive to the needs of its urban setting and maintain its close articulation between senior and community college units." In other words, the legislature sought "an integrated system" that would "facilitate articulation between units."[59]

An Institution Adrift

Although the state takeover provided a certain degree of stability, throughout the 1980s CUNY continued to struggle with funding issues, declining enrollments, and perceptions of poor academic quality. The change in board structure following the shift to state control did not lead to an effective system-wide response to this crisis of confidence in CUNY. The board was still populated by affiliates of one campus or another, the chancellor did not have authority over presidents or the unified support of the board, and individual campuses accordingly continued to operate essentially independently. Furthermore, the open-admissions policy was strongly supported by the board. Some individual campuses, such as Baruch and Hunter, were able to bolster their academic standing through subtle end-runs around the open-admissions policy, such as increasing course requirements and requiring skills tests to deter less serious students from attending. But on the whole, the academic reputation of CUNY was in decline.

In response to the diminished public funding and elected officials' calls for more efficient use of resources, Ann Reynolds, appointed chancellor in 1990, pursued a more centralized approach to CUNY's academic offerings. Reynolds first created an Advisory Commit-

57. N.Y. Educ. Law, sec. 6204.
58. Ibid.
59. N.Y. Educ. Law, sec. 6201.

tee on Academic Program Planning consisting of campus presidents and distinguished faculty and chaired by Leon Goldstein, president of Kingsborough Community College. She tasked the committee with developing a "central planning effort" to increase collaboration across colleges, protect core missions and academic quality, increase efficiency, and preserve student access.[60]

The committee's report, released in 1992, was focused on consolidating programs that were considered unnecessarily duplicative. A hundred pages of the report were devoted to specific recommendations for the abolition or consolidation of degree programs at individual campuses across the university, in dozens of fields. The committee believed these changes would "enhance the vitality and the quality of each of the colleges and, at the same time . . . allocate program resources more effectively to meet the educational needs of the City and the State."[61] The changes also would involve central coordination, meant to ensure that the university as a whole continued to offer a wide variety of programs, even if each college offered fewer.[62]

Faculty leaders and the union vociferously criticized the Goldstein Report, and Reynolds and the board quickly backed down. The critics objected to the "autocratic decision process" as well as the specific recommendations, which were derided as based on simplistic analysis, inconsiderate of student needs, and anti–liberal arts. In the background was the prospect that the recommendations would eliminate a large number of faculty positions.[63]

Reynolds and the board retreated to the Academic Program Planning process, which required campus-based, rather than central, review of programming. Each program was required to be reviewed every ten years, "under the leadership of the College President and in accordance with the College governance plan." The reviews would "depend upon campus initiatives within established governance procedures," although

60. City University of New York, Chancellor's Advisory Committee on Academic Program Planning, "A Report to the Chancellor" (New York, 1992), p. 2; Gill, p. 16.
61. Chancellor's Advisory Committee on Academic Program Planning (1992), p. 3; Gill, p. 16.
62. Gill, pp. 16–17.
63. Ibid., pp. 17–18.

the board resolution did specify certain factors that individual campuses should consider in their reviews.[64]

Reynolds's next step was to propose a series of board resolutions in 1995 and 1996 that would require standardization of several academic requirements across individual campuses. The most significant change was to reduce the number of credits required to graduate, from 128 to 120 in senior colleges and from 64 to 60 in community colleges, which brought credit requirements into greater alignment with national norms. The UFS opposed these changes and voted against them, but the board passed the resolutions anyway. The chair of the UFS sued CUNY to block the change, and was joined by the faculty union, the PSC. The suit alleged that the resolution on graduation requirements violated a board bylaw that gave faculty authority, "subject to guidelines, if any, as established by the board, for the formulation of policy relating to the admission and retention of students including health and scholarship standards therefor, student attendance including leaves of absence, curriculum, awarding of college credit, granting of degrees."[65] The suit further charged that the resolution was arbitrary and capricious because there was no factual basis for the change in graduation requirements.[66]

In the *Polishook* case, as it has come to be called after the leader of the union at the time, the trial judge ruled for the plaintiffs on both grounds. On appeal, the court held that the Board of Trustees was not required "to consult with the senior college faculties prior to implementing . . . [r]esolutions[,] as the Board of Trustees is charged with 'govern[ing] and administer[ing] the city university'" pursuant to state law.[67] It nevertheless upheld the lower court's arbitrary and capricious decision. After the New York Court of Appeals granted leave to CUNY to appeal the arbitrary and capricious ruling, but not to the petitioners to appeal the faculty governance ruling, the parties

64. Ibid., p. 18. The review factors specified by the board included assessment of student outcomes, courses offered and enrollments, resources, faculty activity, satisfaction of students and alumni, and external recognition. Gordon, p. 18.

65. Board Bylaws, sec. 8.5.

66. *Professional Staff Congress* v. *City Univ. of N.Y.* (slip. op. p. 7).

67. *Matter of Polishook* v. *City Univ. of N.Y.*

reached a settlement. The UFS chair and the PSC agreed to drop the suit if the board of trustees passed a resolution clarifying a process for allowing professional programs to seek waivers from the credit reduction (which had been a sticking point), and reaffirmed the bylaw regarding faculty responsibility for curriculum, *subject to board guidelines*.[68]

Although the college-based program planning and efforts to adjust credit requirements did address some low-hanging fruit, they were insufficient to slow the rise of public criticism of CUNY's academic quality. In 1997, for example, Matthew Goldstein, then president of Baruch College, gave an attention-grabbing speech at the Center for Education Innovation calling for an increase in admission standards and limitations on remediation. Although Baruch had taken some steps to improve its students' academic standing, Goldstein saw limits to what any individual campus could do in the face of general board policy, and wanted to see the whole university operating as a coherent, integrated institution.

Many members of the board, as well as Chancellor Ann Reynolds, were committed to the open-admissions policy, and disagreed with Goldstein's focus on tightening admissions and remediation as a pathway to a better reputation. Mayor Rudolph Giuliani and Governor George Pataki, however, latched onto these concerns, and began to advocate for higher standards at CUNY. Disputes over standards between legacy board members and those appointed by Giuliani and Pataki may have contributed to the chancellor position's remaining open for two years after Reynolds departed for the University of Alabama in 1997.

In May 1998, the mayor formed the Advisory Task Force on the City University of New York, chaired by former Yale University president Benno Schmidt, to examine and make recommendations regarding CUNY's budgeting, funding, and financial management; the university's governance processes; and its open-admissions policies and remedial education programs. The task force issued a series of reports in 1999—with a lead report titled *The City University of New York: An Institution Adrift*—that criticized CUNY for its poor

---

68. *Professional Staff Congress* v. *City Univ. of N.Y.* (slip. op. p. 7).

academic standing and uncoordinated approach to governance, and recommended a long list of reforms.[69]

In the part of the task force report most relevant to this study, prepared by a researcher from the RAND Institute, the author attributed many of CUNY's academic problems to "a dysfunctional system of governance."[70] As the RAND report elaborated: "Battles for leadership among CUNY's stakeholders have become increasingly rancorous. Lines of responsibility are tangled and poorly defined. CUNY colleges often act more like independent institutions than complementary members of a system."[71] The RAND report detailed a lack of oversight by the board and the state regents, a chancellor without authority over campus presidents, entrenched faculty, and multiple veto points within faculty governance, all of which made system-wide coordination and change of any kind difficult.[72]

By 1999, the board had largely turned over to reform-oriented Giuliani and Pataki appointees. (Benno Schmidt joined the board in August 1999 and would become chair in 2003, after Herman Badillo resigned as chair to run for mayor.) In the summer of 1999, the board recruited Matthew Goldstein—who had left Baruch to become president of Adelphi University a year earlier—as university chancellor, and tasked him with implementing the recommendations in *An Institution Adrift*. As a condition of his appointment, Goldstein insisted that the campus presidents report to him, rather than the board. The board assented, passing a resolution making the change.[73]

An Overview of the Current Governance Structure

The 1999 change in the reporting structure of campus presidents was the final major piece of the current governance structure to come into place, making this an appropriate point in the timeline to review

69. Mayor's Advisory Task Force on the City University of New York, *CUNY: An Institution Adrift*, New York, 1999, available at www.nyc.gov/html/records/rwg/cuny/pdf/adrift.pdf.

70. Gill, p. 1.

71. Ibid.

72. Ibid., passim.

73. Board Bylaws, sec. 4.2.

the offices and bodies that manage CUNY today, the scope of their authority, and their relationship to one another.

The Board of Trustees

Under CUNY's authorizing legislation, the Board of Trustees has broad authority over policy for CUNY. According to Section 6204 of the Education Law, "The board of trustees shall govern and administer the city university. The control of the educational work of the city university shall rest solely in the board of trustees which shall govern and administer all educational units of the city university."[74] The law further enumerates the board's particular responsibility for facilities, faculty appointments, budgets, degrees, programs, and courses.[75]

However, the board's authority is hedged from above by the State Legislature and the governor of New York, who have joint power to amend CUNY's authorizing legislation and set CUNY's budget. The governor and the mayor of New York City also have the power to appoint the majority of the board's members: of its seventeen members, ten are appointed by the governor, and five are appointed by the mayor. The other members are a student representative elected by the University Student Senate, and a non-voting faculty member elected by the University Faculty Senate. Board members, other than the student and faculty members, serve seven-year terms, renewable for seven years. Board members may be removed from the board by the authority that appointed them only for misconduct, neglect of duties, or mental or physical incapacity. The chair and vice chair of the board, however, serve in those positions at the pleasure of the governor.[76]

Additionally, the State Board of Regents, whose members are elected by the legislature, must approve certain foundational policies, encapsulated in the Master Plan submitted by CUNY every four years. For most of CUNY's history, the Master Plans were a collection of vague goals organized by central office or college. Chancellor Goldstein sought to make the process more meaningful by tying the Master Plan to the

74. N.Y. Educ. Law, sec. 6204.
75. Ibid., sec. 6206.
76. Ibid., sec. 6204.

university budget. Executive Vice Chancellor Alexandra Logue further refined the process by developing a mission statement and broad, forward-looking objectives based on CUNY's authorizing legislation and organizing specific, budget-connected goals around those themes.

The board's policies are collected in its bylaws and in the *Manual on General Policy*. Until 2002, the manual was available to the public only in hard copy in campus libraries, and it was rarely updated. In 2002, the central administration, under Special Counsel to the Chancellor Dave Fields, began to consolidate all decisions of the Board of Trustees, identifying and reconciling superseded policies and publishing the policies online. This process clarified the extensiveness of board pronouncements on policies and has made the individual campuses more aware of university-wide policy.[77]

The reconciled *Manual on General Policy* lays out broad guidelines on everything from academic freedom (incorporating the 1940 AAUP *Statement of Principles*) to admissions, program elimination to treatment of laboratory animals, and facilities management to pre-tenure review.[78] Although there is still significant flexibility for individual campuses, nearly everything they do is within a framework set out by the board.

The University Chancellor and Central Administration

The board appoints the university chancellor, who is "the chief executive, educational and administrative officer of the city university of New York and the chief educational and administrative officer of the senior and community colleges and other educational units and divisions for which the board acts as trustees."[79] At the university level, the chancellor is responsible for "institutional strategy and policy on all educational and administrative issues affecting the university, including . . . a comprehensive overall academic plan for the university," with a goal of "unify[ing] and coordinat[ing] college educational planning, operating systems, business and financial procedures and

77. CUNY *Manual on General Policy*, available at http://policy.cuny.edu/manual_of_general_policy/#Navigation_Location.

78. Ibid., secs. 1.02, 1.07, 1.04; art. IV; sec. 5.151.

79. Board Bylaws, sec. 11.2; N.Y. Educ. Law, sec. 6206.

management."[80] With respect to individual campuses, the chancellor "oversee[s] . . . campus leadership, including by setting goals and academic and financial performance standards for each campus," "recommends to the board the appointment of the college president and senior campus staff," and presents to the board "all important reports, recommendations, and plans submitted by a college president, faculty or governance body with his/her recommendations, if any."[81]

As noted, upon Matthew Goldstein's appointment, the campus presidents began reporting to the chancellor, rather than the board. This shift made clear that the board would accept policy proposals only through the chancellor. It consolidated the agenda and made it much less likely that presidents could circumvent the chancellor and appeal directly to the board. (Indeed, Goldstein had done this himself while at Baruch.) It also reduced or eliminated the special influence of particular board members over the policies of individual campuses with which they were affiliated. On the other hand, critics of the change have warned that diminished presidential autonomy has made it more difficult to recruit talented and ambitious presidents.

Campus Presidents and Administrators

The Board of Trustees appoints the president of each campus, based on recommendations by the chancellor.[82] Since 1999, the presidents are formally "advisor[s] and executive agent[s] of the chancellor" (before that time, they were "advisors and executive agents" of the board). Nevertheless, they have "full discretionary power to carry into effect the bylaws, resolutions, and policies of the board . . . and policies, programs, and lawful resolutions of the several faculties and students."[83] Presidential responsibilities include "general superintendence over the facilities, concerns, officers, employees, and students of his/her college" in accordance with a "college master plan"; acting as "chairperson of the faculty, faculty council, and the committee on faculty personnel and budget," consistent with the campus governance plan; "transmit[ting]

80. Board Bylaws, sec. 11.2.
81. Ibid.
82. Board Bylaws, sec. 11.2.
83. Ibid., sec. 11.4.

to the chancellor recommendations of his/her faculty or faculty council on matters of curriculum and other matters falling under faculty jurisdiction"; recommending to the chancellor an annual campus budget; and consulting with departmental and faculty committees and making recommendations concerning appointments and tenure.[84] In carrying out their duties, the presidents are charged with "the affirmative responsibility of conserving and enhancing the educational standards and general academic excellence of the college under his/her jurisdiction."[85] (CUNY's professional schools have deans, rather than presidents, but they function similarly.)

All campus presidents and professional school deans are members of the Council of Presidents, which meets regularly to "advise the chancellor" on the Master Plan and the operating and capital budgets of the university, and to "recommend to the chancellor procedures and policies that affect more than one of the constituent colleges" and "plans for the development of physical properties."[86]

When he assumed management of the presidents, Goldstein instituted a Performance Management Process (PMP). Under the process, the chancellor releases goals for the year in January. Campus presidents are responsible for developing specific campus goals aligned to the university goals. Although they are supposed to consult with their faculty on the goals, only some presidents do so. By June of the following academic year, the campus presidents prepare a report covering their progress with regard to each goal, plus a president's letter summarizing and explaining the results. Some presidents share the report broadly on their campuses, but others do not. The central office compiles a report for the chancellor on each campus that includes the campus's report and analysis by the central office of data relevant to each goal. The chancellor meets with each president during the early summer to go over results, and follows up with a private letter to the president summarizing the discussion and seeking more information on some topics.[87]

84. Ibid.
85. Ibid.
86. Ibid., sec. 4.2.
87. CUNY, "CUNY's Performance Management Process: A Key Tool in the Integrated University," New York, http://www1.cuny.edu/resources/performancetargets/2006_07/cunype.pdf, accessed October 30, 2014.

Some financial benefits for presidents and campuses are tied to results in the PMP, though their impact has been limited. Presidents' annual raises were based in part on the results. However, as a matter of propriety, administrators have gone without raises since the most recent faculty contract expired in 2010 (see below), which has diminished some of the impact of the PMP. When Alexandra Logue took over the PMP in 2006, she also introduced a fund to be distributed to the programs on campus that most contributed to a positive PMP result, but campus administrations had difficulty distributing the funding in a targeted way.[88]

Although many presidents tried to keep PMP results close to the vest, the PMP did generate some additional transparency. For example, until Alexandra Logue took over the process in 2006, centrally collected data on retention, graduation rates, and other campus quality indicators were not available publicly. Prompted by Logue, Goldstein decided to make the data public. This decision—which required no faculty input and no board approval—made the individual campuses accountable for their students' outcomes in a way that they had never been before.

Vice presidents, provosts, and deans (specific positions vary from campus to campus) serve at the pleasure of the president, but must be approved by the board. Department heads, by contrast, are elected by departmental faculty for renewable three-year terms, though they may be removed by the president (see below for more details).[89]

Faculty Governance

Faculty governance plays a role at both the campus and university levels. At the university level, the UFS is "responsible, subject to the board, for the formulation of policy relating to the academic status, role, rights, and freedoms of the faculty, university level educational and instructional matters, and research and scholarly activities of university-wide import."[90] Members of the UFS serve two-year terms,

88. Ibid.
89. Board Bylaws, sec. 9.1. The exception to this rule of departmental election is the Graduate School, where the heads of each doctoral program are appointed by the president of the Graduate School. Board Bylaws, sec. 9.4.
90. Board Bylaws, sec. 8.10.

and many members are reelected repeatedly. Although the chair of the UFS changes regularly, the members of its executive committee have remained largely the same for many years.

Each campus has a formal governance plan approved by the board, which must include a faculty or academic council.[91] As noted above, the faculty councils are "responsible, subject to guidelines, if any, as established by the board, for the formulation of policy relating to the admission and retention of students including health and scholarship standards therefor, student attendance including leaves of absence, curriculum, awarding of college credit, granting of degrees," as well as other "educational affairs customarily cared for by a college faculty."[92]

Although there is some variation in the specifics from campus to campus, the faculty councils typically consist of department heads, additional faculty representatives from each department, and additional at-large delegates.[93] Most but not all individual campuses include the president and deans in the faculty council. Some include student representatives in the faculty council. Queens College, for example, has an Academic Senate that includes faculty and students, but not the president or other administrators.[94] At small campuses, the whole faculty is on the faculty council. At larger campuses, faculty representatives (or student representatives) are elected. For example, at Queens College, faculty elect representatives within departments, divisions, and college-wide; students elect representatives by class year and college-wide.[95]

The campus faculty councils are independent of the UFS, although there is some coordinated action. The bylaws state explicitly that "the powers and duties of the university faculty senate shall not extend to areas or interests which fall exclusively within the domain of the fac-

91. Board Bylaws, sec. 8.6.

92. Ibid., sec. 8.5.

93. The bylaws provide some guidelines for faculty governance, but also note that a duly approved campus governance plan can supersede those guidelines. Board Bylaws, sec. 8.11.

94. CUNY, "Academic Senate Charter: Queens College of the City University of New York," New York, available at www.cuny.edu/about/administration/offices/la/governance-plans/queens.pdf.

95. *Academic Senate Charter: Queens College.*

ulty councils of the constituent units of the university."[96] But the chair of the UFS has regular, informal meetings with the chairs of each campus council. Occasionally the UFS circulates a recommended resolution to campus councils. The campus faculty councils are not obliged to take up any UFS resolution, however, and many do not.

Departments also play a substantial role in day-to-day decision-making at the campus, though their structure and specific role are determined by the campus faculty council and therefore vary from campus to campus.[97] Under the bylaws, departments "have control of the educational policies of the department through the vote of all of its members who have faculty rank or faculty status," though these decisions are subject to policies of the board and campus faculty councils.[98] Department chairs are elected by the members of the department to a three-year term, but the campus president may recommend (through the chancellor) that the board vote to remove an elected chair if, after careful consideration and conferral with the department, the president determines that that person lacks the capacity "to act effectively as the departmental administrator and spokesperson and as a participant in the formation, development, and interpretation of college-wide interest and policy."[99] The Board Bylaws also specify certain departmental committees and procedures with respect to personnel and budget decisions, but all of these (as well as the duties of the departments) may be superseded by a campus governance plan approved by the board.[100]

Formally, the UFS, campus faculty councils, and departments are advisory bodies—they recommend policies to the Board of Trustees, which has final authority. The policies voted for by the campus faculty councils become recommendations that the campus president takes to the chancellor. Although the bylaws state that the chancellor "shall" present the proposals to the board, in practice the policies are reviewed by vice chancellors and other administrators—especially the Office of Academic Affairs, the Office of Human Resources

96. Board Bylaws, sec. 8.10.
97. Board Bylaws, sec. 9.1.
98. Ibid.
99. Ibid.
100. Board Bylaws, secs. 9.1–9.6 and 9.9.

Management, and the General Counsel—who negotiate with the individual campuses. Nevertheless, in the words of Senior Vice Chancellor Jay Hershenson, the decisions of the governance bodies frequently carry "moral weight" and are usually put forward and adopted by the board. In fact, the board's *Manual of General Policy* declares that "the focus of major decision-making is properly at the college level."[101]

Most policies generated by the UFS, campus faculty councils, and departments are presented to the board in the Chancellor's University Report (CUR), in which the chancellor compiles resolutions from individual campuses and the central administration that the board addresses with a single vote.[102] If a board member has a question about a particular decision that is part of the CUR, it will be pulled out and discussed and voted on separately. The CUR includes nearly all financial and personnel decisions at the campus level. Appointments at the level of campus vice president or lower are considered as part of the CUR; appointments of campus presidents (or, in the central administration, appointments at the level of vice chancellor or above) are calendared separately.[103] Significant academic policies are not included in the CUR, but are instead considered by a committee of the board focused on academic policy, programs, and research before going to the full board.

In addition to their policy creation function, faculty governance bodies can be an important site of opposition. At the campus level, policies generally must be approved by the faculty council, although campus presidents have significant leverage because they control the budget. Still, it is rare for a campus president to seek to push through a campus policy over faculty opposition.

Although most central policies are not controversial, there have been flare-ups over the years (such as over the program review and graduation credits initiatives described above, and several of the initia-

101. *Manual of General Policy*, sec. 2.08.

102. CUNY, "Guidelines for the Presentation of Academic Matters in the Chancellor's University Report," New York, available at www.cuny.edu/academics/programs/resources/CUR/ChancellorsUniversityReportGuidetoRevisedAugust2012.doc.

103. CUNY, "Guidelines for the Presentation of Academic Matters in the Chancellor's University Report."

tives described in the next section). Typically, these flashpoints involve policies that faculty see as being within their prerogative, usually related to academics. To oppose a central policy, the UFS and some campus faculty councils have taken votes opposing the policies, protested, and demanded explanations from the central administration, but they have no formal authority to block the initiatives.[104] On two occasions, the leaders of the UFS sued CUNY. As described above, in 1997 the UFS chair sued CUNY to block the resolution to lower the number of credits required for graduation, and, as explained below, in 2011 the chair and vice chair sued to block the Pathways Initiative. In both cases, the courts ruled for the university.[105] Interestingly, both suits were filed by the same UFS chair, Sandi Cooper, who held the position in 1997 and had cycled back into it by 2011.

The Faculty Union

CUNY's faculty is unionized, and its representative body is the PSC. Terms and conditions of employment, such as pay scales and maximum course loads, are governed by a collective bargaining agreement negotiated between the central administration and the PSC. The most recent collective bargaining agreement was entered into in 2007 and covered the period through 2010.[106] Under the Triborough Amendment to the Taylor Law, the terms of the labor contract remain in effect until a new one is entered.[107]

Although the PSC's scope of authority is limited to terms and conditions of employment, the leadership has tried to involve the union

104. See, for example, the UFS's webpage listing actions in opposition to the Pathways Initiative. CUNY, UFS, "Resolutions, Letters & Statements on General Education, Articulation & the Pathways Process," New York, https://sites.google.com/site/universityfacultysenatecuny/senate-action/resolutions-on-pathways, accessed October 30, 2014.

105. *Professional Staff Congress* v. *City Univ. of N.Y.* (Sup. Ct., N.Y. County, no. 151021, February 25, 2014) (Singh, J.) (slip. op. pp. 13–16); *Matter of Polishook* v. *City Univ. of N.Y.*, 234 A.D.2d 165 (App. Div., 1st Dep't, 1996).

106. CUNY, "Memorandum of Agreement for a Successor Collective Bargaining Agreement between the City University of New York and the Professional Staff Congress/CUNY," New York, September 20, 2007, available at https://cuny.edu/about/administration/offices/lr/lr-contracts/PSCMOA2007-10.pdf.

107. N.Y. Civil Law, sec. 209-a(1)(e).

in many other issues that affect the faculty, including academic policies. The PSC has been especially aggressive in this regard since 2000, when Barbara Bowen took over the leadership of the union.[108] Generously funded by a salary check-off, the PSC has the ability to finance publicity, lobbying, and legal actions. It is also able to garner support from the AAUP and other local and national unions. All of this has given the PSC a powerful voice, and its efforts to influence system-wide academic policy have created occasional tension with the UFS. At the campus level, however, the PSC representatives tend to focus more on individual members' grievances and leave academic policy to the faculty councils.

CUNY's Governance in Action

The current governance structure has made it possible for a unified board and chancellor to carry out significant central initiatives. Chancellor Goldstein and Board Chair Benno Schmidt used that authority to implement a number of plans designed to restore CUNY's academic reputation and promote greater integration of the university's individual campuses, many drawn from Schmidt's report *An Institution Adrift*.

The UFS, campus faculty councils, and the PSC have objected to a number of these initiatives, often vehemently. Citing the primacy of individual campuses in instruction, the different needs and priorities of each campus, and the importance of faculty buy-in and ownership of academic policy, faculty leaders and the union fought the central policy initiatives through all the means at their disposal. This repeated oppositional dynamic generated significant animosity between faculty leaders and the Goldstein administration, making cooperation less likely with each new initiative. But the structure of decision-making, especially after the change in reporting structure, and the close relationship between Goldstein and the board, allowed the administration to push its policies through despite the resistance.

This section discusses five of the most significant central initiatives of the Goldstein chancellorship, with special reference to the governance issues involved. The five initiatives—eliminating remedial course-

108. www.psc-cuny.org/about-us/president-barbara-bowen.

work at senior colleges, instituting online courses and the creation of the CUNY School of Professional Studies, cluster hiring and the promotion of faculty research, the capital campaign and CUNY Compact, and the Pathways Initiative—were selected for their substantive diversity and for the unique aspects of governance they illustrate.

Eliminating Remedial Courses at Senior Colleges

In May 1998, the board passed a resolution implementing one of *An Institution Adrift*'s most controversial recommendations: eliminating remedial courses at senior colleges and requiring a demonstration of readiness for credit-bearing courses for admission.[109] This recommendation had been the target of extensive public criticism from the PSC, the UFS, and many individual faculty, as well as politicians and the press, who asserted that the change would make CUNY less accessible, in general, and would prevent African American and Latino students from attending senior colleges, in particular.[110] In the background, too, were potential cuts in faculty positions due to the presumed decline in enrollment.

The remediation change became a bellwether for CUNY's ability to change, and Mayor Giuliani and Governor Pataki applied significant pressure on the board to make it happen. Perhaps spurred by this political pressure, the board passed the remediation resolution without formal consultation with the faculty and over opposition from the UFS and the PSC. After a successful faculty challenge to the resolution under the open meetings law, the board passed it again, in front of a large and angry crowd of opponents, in January 1999.[111]

109. CUNY, "City University of New York Trustees Approve Resolution to End Remediation in Senior Colleges," New York, June 4, 1998, http://www1.cuny .edu/events/press/june4_98.html, accessed October 30, 2014.

110. Allison Gendar, "CUNY Board Scraps Remedial Classes," *New York Daily News*, January 26, 1999, available at www.nydailynews.com/archives/ news/cuny-board-scraps-remedial-classes-article-1.831403; Sara Hebel, "N.Y. Board of Regents Approves CUNY Plan to Limit Remedial Education," *Chronicle of Higher Education*, December 3, 1999, available at http://chronicle.com/ article/NY-Board-of-Regents-Approves/9457.

111. Minutes of the CUNY Board of Trustees, January 25, 1999, p. 30, available at http://policy.cuny.edu/board_meeting_minutes/1999/01-25/pdf/; Gendar.

Unlike most other decisions regarding CUNY academic policy, the board vote on remediation was not the final decision. The CUNY Master Plan, approved by the Board of Regents, included the open-admissions policy as well as a provision requiring every campus to offer any remedial instruction required by its students. Although there was some debate over whether amendment of the Master Plan was required by law, the regents claimed the authority to review the change, and CUNY acquiesced.[112] Accordingly, after the board resolution, the fight over remediation shifted to the closely divided Board of Regents, with both sides aggressively lobbying its members.

Goldstein was installed as chancellor after the board resolution on remediation but before the Board of Regents vote. As soon as he was installed, Goldstein began personally lobbying the members of the Board of Regents to pass the Master Plan Amendment. On the Friday night before a Monday vote, he met for several hours with one of the regents who was leaning toward a "no" vote, and convinced him to change his mind. The final vote of the regents was 9–6 in favor of the policy change, with one abstention.[113]

According to Goldstein, in retrospect, winning the remediation battle was "pivotal" to the success of future central initiatives. Beyond the substance of the change, the board's unilateral resolution and the political "trench warfare" in the regents' vote demonstrated the power and determination of the board and chancellor. The episode gave Goldstein and the board credibility to take on other academic reforms and institution building. It was also held out as evidence of renewed seriousness about academics that became the basis for a major fundraising campaign.

Despite its earlier opposition, the UFS did not try to disrupt implementation of the remediation change. The regents' approval of the change in admissions and remediation was contingent on review of the policy and re-approval after a period of time. When it came time for the review, CUNY reported that, since the remediation change, enrollment at senior colleges, including black and His-

112. Karen W. Arenson, "CUNY Review by Regents Is Questioned by Governor," *New York Times*, August 14, 1998, available at www.nytimes.com/1998/08/14/nyregion/cuny-review-by-regents-is-questioned-by-governor.html.

113. Hebel.

panic enrollment, had increased substantially. The policy was unanimously reapproved.[114]

Instituting the CUNY School of Professional Studies and Online Instruction

The percentage of CUNY courses with online components is extremely low compared to that at peer institutions. The exception to this general pattern is the CUNY School of Professional Studies (CUNY SPS), founded in 2003 as a unit within the Graduate School and University Center, with a mix of adjuncts and consortial faculty from other CUNY campuses. CUNY SPS initially offered continuing education programs but soon expanded its portfolio to a broad range of certificate and degree programs, many offered entirely online. The structure and development of CUNY SPS is interesting both as a model of governance related to online instruction and as an example of a process that the Goldstein administration used to create several new, streamlined, and demand-sensitive institutions that might have been held up if they had been pursued through more traditional means.

According to University Director of Academic Technology and CUNY SPS Associate Dean of Academic Affairs George Otte, there are a number of ardent and innovative practitioners of online instruction at CUNY, but online instruction has had limited impact on the university as a whole. After some forays into message boards and course management software in the 1990s, CUNY obtained grants from the Sloan Foundation in the early 2000s to train faculty in creating course websites and eventually building online courses. Interested faculty from across the university participated, but involvement was limited. There was little incentive to provide distance education when students were all geographically close, and campus provosts, who had to give permission to participate, were often leery of online instruction. Because of this, the online instruction work tended to be

114. Sara Hebel, "New York Regents Approve CUNY's Remediation Plan after 3 Years of Monitoring," *Chronicle of Higher Education*, December 13, 2002, available at www.thechronicle.info/article/New-York-Regents-Approve/117083/.

under the radar, and to focus on online solutions to specific instructional problems (such as time-shifting for working students).

The obstacles to online degree programs were even more imposing than the obstacles to more general uses of online instruction. A faculty task force in the early 2000s considered options for online degrees but could not reach consensus on how to pursue them. Some members of the leadership of the UFS were opposed to online instruction as a matter of principle, viewing it as a pathway to "automating faculty out of existence." But for the most part, online degrees and online instruction were simply not priorities for most faculty leaders.

Executive Vice Chancellor for Academic Affairs Selma Botman decided to concentrate online degrees at CUNY SPS. Doing so had the advantage of consolidating administration and support. The CUNY SPS governance structure also had the advantage of streamlining program development, avoiding the multiple veto points typical of the governance structures at other individual campuses.

CUNY SPS was one of the first new campuses created using a governance model that became a hallmark of the Goldstein administration's significant institution-building effort. General Counsel Frederick Schaffer began by amending the governance plans of the Graduate School and University Center. The University Center was established as a separate entity, and was recast as an umbrella for new entities, each of which would have its own "radically simple" governance plan. The new entities would have a streamlined faculty council initially composed mostly of appointees of the chancellor and the president of the Graduate School. The faculty of most new entities would primarily be adjunct or consortial—meaning that they have appointments at other CUNY campuses and are released by their provost to do work at the new entity. Rather than departments, most of the new entities would have program committees with appointed academic directors, which would focus primarily on program development. Although they vary in mission, structure, and timing of creation, CUNY SPS, the CUNY School of Public Health, the Macaulay Honors College, and the CUNY Graduate School of Journalism all employ features of this governance model.[115]

115. All CUNY governance plans are available at www.cuny.edu/about/administration/offices/la/governance-plans.html.

CUNY SPS opened in 2003, offering a single certificate program. It was managed by a nine-member governing council that included three members appointed by the UFS, three appointed by the chancellor, and three appointed by the president of CUNY Graduate School. The Governing Council's primary role was (and is) to approve programs prior to their going to the board for approval. At most individual campuses, program creation is difficult because departmental and faculty approval are required, and there are inevitably disagreements. Although it has since added more layers of decision-making, at its origin, the Governing Council was the sole body at CUNY SPS that made decisions about program creation, and six of the Governing Council's votes were provided by appointees of the administration who reliably approved new programs the administration supported.[116]

Over time, the CUNY SPS Governing Council expanded by including the academic director of each program, additional faculty representatives from large programs, and student representatives. There are currently thirty-four members, a majority of them faculty working in the programs. The Governing Council has formed separate curriculum and personnel committees that do a first review of program proposals and faculty, respectively.

Program formation typically begins with the chief academic officer convening a program committee, usually four to five interested faculty from around the university. Some program ideas start with CUNY SPS administrators, who seek out appropriate faculty; some are proposed by faculty looking for an outlet for new ideas. The program committee designs the program and presents it to the Curriculum Committee, which reviews the proposal and, if it approves, sends it to the Governing Council. If the Governing Council approves, it goes to the university's Office of Academic Affairs for review. If that review is successful, the executive vice chancellor for academic affairs presents the proposed program to the Board of Trustees' Committee on Academic Policy, Programs, and Research, which votes on sending it to the full board. With Board of Trustees

116. CUNY, "School of Professional Studies Governance Plan," New York, www.cuny.edu/about/administration/offices/la/governance-plans/sps.pdf, accessed October 30, 2014.

approval the program proposal is sent to the New York State Education Department for final review.[117]

Once a program is approved, a program director is selected and begins to operate. Typically the program director is one of the faculty on the original program committee. Occasionally, an outside director is hired. Each program also has a program committee that includes the consortial faculty who teach in the program. Perhaps because the consortial faculty have self-selected into the program and may have been part of its creation, the program committees tend to operate harmoniously. As an added incentive for consortial faculty to help build their programs, consortial faculty are paid for program and course development as well as teaching.[118]

With this structure, the number of programs offered by CUNY SPS increased rapidly; after 2008, most of the new programs were online. Initially, CUNY SPS's governance documents prohibited it from offering any degrees that were duplicative of degrees offered elsewhere in the university. Eventually, *non-duplicative* was interpreted to allow CUNY SPS to offer an online version of degrees offered at other individual campuses. With demand high for the initial set of degree programs, the rule was amended to permit any type of degree program. As of fall 2014, CUNY SPS serves almost 2,600 students through ten bachelor's degree programs (eight of which are online) and six master's degree programs (two of which are online).[119]

According to University Dean for Academic Affairs and CUNY SPS Dean John Mogulescu, CUNY SPS was not designed to promote online instruction, but it became a magnet for enthusiasts of online courses around the university. Because CUNY SPS is able to cherry-pick among these interested faculty, those who create the programs are highly motivated to do something new and innovative, and

117. City University of New York, "Academic Program Resources: Flow Charts," www.cuny.edu/academics/programs/resources/flow-charts.html, accessed October 30, 2014.
118. CUNY Graduate Center, Provost's Office, "Allocation System," www.gc.cuny.edu/About-the-GC/Provost-s-Office/Governance,-Policies-Procedures/Detail?id=4360, accessed October 30, 2014.
119. CUNY School of Professional Studies, "About Us," http://sps.cuny.edu/about/, accessed October 30, 2014.

there are no faculty that are being forced to change their ways. This has allowed CUNY SPS to offer online instruction that is designed, in the words of George Otte, "soup to nuts." Instead of relying on an instructional tech team whose role is to "web-ify" a faculty member's existing course, CUNY SPS provides seminars to faculty on how to build courses specifically for an online format.

With some notable exceptions, such as the John Jay College of Criminal Justice's online program, CUNY SPS is CUNY's main site for online instruction.[120] Although it is less robust than in the past, opposition to online instruction still exists because of concerns about the effect on department culture, resistance to change (including resistance to the additional work that would be required to change a course's format), conviction that less is learned online, or discomfort with technology. It may simply be easier for campus administrators not to try to overcome that resistance, and the outlet of CUNY SPS is an additional excuse not to rock the boat.

Several factors suggest that expansion of online instruction at CUNY may be imminent. First, CUNY SPS has offered an online instruction workshop to faculty of other individual campuses, and it has drawn about seven hundred participants (albeit out of a full-time and adjunct faculty of more than eighteen thousand). Second, on some individual campuses as many as 50 percent of full-time faculty have been hired in the past ten years, and many of them have taken an online course at some point. Finally, the Pathways Initiative (described below) should make it easier for students from other individual campuses to enroll in CUNY SPS online courses and bring the credit back to their home institutions. In the past, the student demand was there, but enrollment was inhibited by the need for students to obtain a permit from the provost's office of their home institution to take a course offered by another CUNY campus, and those officials were often reluctant to approve those permits. Permitting changes initiated by Executive Vice Chancellor Alexandra Logue in 2013 make it easier for students to take online

---

120. John Jay College of Criminal Justice, "John Jay College of Criminal Justice—Online," http://johnjayonline.com/, accessed October 30, 2014.

courses at CUNY SPS, which might also generate pressure on other individual campuses to offer online instruction.

Cluster Hiring and the Promotion of Faculty Research

Although decisions on individual faculty hires have generally been left to the faculty of individual campuses, Chancellor Goldstein introduced a policy of cluster hiring early in his tenure. Under this policy, individual campuses were incentivized to hire in particular areas, "targeted for their importance to society and the economy, their relation to existing CUNY strengths, and their relevance to educational need."[121] Science, technology, engineering, and mathematics fields were a special focus, aligned to the chancellor's Decade of Science initiative.[122] Other areas included U.S. history, teacher education, demography, art history, visual art, and foreign languages.[123] Incentives included dedicated funding lines and consortial appointments in new institutions, especially the Macaulay Honors College.[124]

The PSC—though not the UFS—objected to the cluster hiring initiative as an intrusion on faculty governance. An underlying issue was that the initiative, although it increased faculty numbers, allocated funding in a way that sacrificed quantity for disciplinary focus. As a membership organization, the union cared more about quantity. Goldstein persisted, however, and because it was not an area covered by collective bargaining, there was little the union could do to stop it. The efficacy of the cluster hiring initiative remains to be seen; UFS Chair Terrence Martell, who favors aggregating resources to create areas of strength on individual campuses, does not believe it was sufficient to disrupt the culture of spreading resources thinly across too many fields.

Another effort to develop faculty was an amendment to CUNY's IP policy to incentivize faculty research. There was a sense that faculty research output was too low for a university of CUNY's size. The

121. *CUNY 2008–2012 Master Plan*, pp. 2–3, available at www.cuny.edu/about/administration/chancellor/masterplan_08_12.pdf.
122. *CUNY 2008–2012 Master Plan*, pp. 2–3.
123. Ibid., pp. 2–3.
124. Ibid., pp. 15–16.

IP policy was out of date, and Goldstein instructed General Counsel Frederick Schaffer to amend it in a way that would motivate more research. For example, one amendment granted faculty 50 percent of royalties, the highest rate in the country.[125]

The IP policy change never went through the UFS for approval. Instead, the chancellor formed a task force and invited the UFS to appoint representatives, which it did. Every change to the policy was positive or neutral for faculty, so there was little opposition. But after the work was complete, the PSC complained that the policy should have been collectively bargained and brought a grievance. In a ruling ultimately upheld by the New York Court of Appeals, the Public Employment Relations Board confirmed that, as long as it did not conflict with a provision of the collective bargaining agreement, the Board of Trustees can make or amend policy (even one relating to the terms and conditions of employment) as long as it provides the PSC with a copy of the proposal and "consults" the union.[126]

The Capital Campaign and the CUNY Compact

Additional funding was, of course, a critical component of efforts to improve the academic standing of CUNY, and Chancellor Goldstein was effective at shoring up CUNY's finances. Goldstein increased central fundraising efforts, initiating a capital campaign that brought in about $3 billion. He also prompted more fundraising by campus presidents, incentivizing them to do so by double-counting private fundraising in the PMP and by providing central support. Some administrators and faculty objected to the increased central role in fundraising, expressing concern that it would take away campus autonomy.

Goldstein also negotiated an innovative funding relationship with New York State based on the new approach of aligning the Master Plan to CUNY's budget. Under the 2006 and 2011 CUNY Compact legislation, the state committed to maintenance of effort on funding

125. CUNY, "City University of New York Intellectual Property Policy," sec. VI(b)(3), available at www.cuny.edu/about/administration/offices/la/IP-Policy.pdf.
126. *In Re: Professional Staff Congress–City University of New York v. N.Y. State Pub. Empl. Rel. Bd.*, 7 N.Y.3d 458 (N.Y. Ct. App. 2006).

and to covering a portion of new programmatic initiatives and faculty hiring described in the Master Plan, while CUNY agreed to increase philanthropic revenues, undertake internal restructuring and efficiency measures, and institute tuition increases. The 2011 legislation enabled the board to raise undergraduate tuition by up to $300 annually through 2016. The tuition increases would track economic indicators (such as the Consumer Price Index or the Higher Education Price Index), and full financial aid for needy students would be maintained.[127]

Beyond the uses to which it was put, the revenue generated through fundraising and the CUNY Compact had an impact on governance. Specifically, by diminishing CUNY's dependence on state funding and stabilizing the amount of state funding CUNY could expect, these initiatives weakened one of the levers by which politicians in Albany could influence the board and the chancellor.

The Pathways Initiative

The final major Goldstein initiative, the Pathways to Degree Completion Initiative (Pathways Initiative), was designed to integrate the university academically; as such, it generated the most significant pushback from faculty protective of autonomous campus governance.

From 1961 until the Pathways Initiative was implemented in 2013, every campus had broad leeway to define the course requirements for general education and major fields of study. When a student transferred from one campus to another, the faculty (sometimes a single faculty member) would determine whether each of the student's courses at the sending campus matched a course at the receiving campus and therefore would count for credit. The faculty on each campus had little incentive to accept credits from other individual campuses because doing so meant less demand for courses (and instructors) and a smaller budget. At some individual campuses, the same factors created an incentive to increase the number of general education credits required for a degree to one of the highest levels in

127. CUNY 2008–2012 *Master Plan*, pp. 6–7.

the nation.[128] These two tendencies meant that CUNY students who transferred between individual campuses—an increasingly common phenomenon—were often required to earn many more than 120 credits during their academic careers in order to graduate: the average CUNY baccalaureate graduate earned 130 credits to obtain a 120-credit degree.[129] Of course, many students who might have earned a degree if they had been able to transfer their credits never earned one at all.[130]

The Pathways Initiative, developed by Executive Vice Chancellor Alexandra Logue and Chancellor Goldstein, and passed by the Board in June 2011, required the chancellor to establish a task force to develop common transfer and general education policies for the university. Chancellor Goldstein sought nominees from the UFS for the task force, but the UFS declined to put forward nominees, protesting that it was given too few spots on the task force and, more broadly, that general education policies were academic decisions that should be handled by elected campus faculty councils instead of chancellor-appointed faculty committees. Goldstein pushed ahead, appointing faculty members and administrators to the task force and selecting the dean of the CUNY School of Law as the chair.[131]

In December 2011, the task force generated recommendations for common general education distribution requirements and a process for translating credits across individual campuses, which the chancellor accepted.[132] Task force members and Logue went through an extensive consultation process before submitting the proposal to the chancellor. In addition to publicly posting and soliciting feedback on draft recommendations, central administration representatives participated

128. *Master Plan 2012–2016*, pp. 49–50.

129. Ibid., p. 49.

130. These statistics on transfer credits were disputed by the UFS. For example, UFS Chair Terrence Martell contended that the typical transfer student lost only 2.66 credits—less than one course's worth—as a result of transferring. Terrence Martell, "The Real Motivation for Pathways? It Can't Be Transfer," CUNY UFS blog post, December 5, 2012, https://sites.google.com/site/universityfacultysenatecuny/UFS-blog/pleasesendcommentstocunyufsgmailcom, accessed October 30, 2014.

131. *Master Plan 2012–2016*, p. 50.

132. Ibid.

in numerous meetings of various faculty groups to explain and solicit input on the Pathways Initiative.[133] Furthermore, the new requirements did not mandate specific courses; they set in motion a process in which each campus would submit courses to faculty review committees for qualification in the areas of the general education requirements and major fields of study.[134] On every campus, departments reviewed and submitted courses; on some, the faculty council curriculum committee approved submissions; on a few, the full faculty council voted on submissions. The general education requirements and transfer credit rules took effect in the fall semester of 2013.[135]

The Pathways Initiative was popular among most students, but very unpopular among many faculty. In addition to declining to nominate members of the task force and passing numerous resolutions opposing the initiative, the UFS chair and vice chair, along with the PSC, filed suit to block the initiative.[136] The plaintiffs alleged that the board resolution breached the settlement agreement in the *Polishook* case, which, they argued, confirmed that the faculty had authority over matters of curriculum—effectively, that the board could act only on curriculum matters first approved by the faculty. The second ground for the suit was that the state open meetings law was violated by some campus presidents submitting implementation schedules and creating course review committees without going through the faculty.[137] The plaintiffs did not seek a preliminary injunction, and by the time the case was argued in November 2013, the Pathways requirements had already gone into effect.

At the urging of the UFS and PSC, the AAUP also wrote a letter protesting the Pathways Initiative as an infringement on faculty

133. *Professional Staff Congress v. City Univ. of N.Y.*, no. 151021 (slip. op. p. 3).

134. *Master Plan 2012–2016*, p. 51.

135. "Pathways Update: Fall 2013," *CUNY Academic News*, October 10, 2013, available at http://www1.cuny.edu/mu/academic-news/2013/10/23/pathways-update-fall-2013/.

136. The UFS has created a webpage with documentation of faculty opposition to the Pathways Initiative. See CUNY, UFS, "Resolutions, Letters & Statements on General Education, Articulation & the Pathways Process."

137. Interview with Frederick Schaffer; *Professional Staff Congress v. City Univ. of N.Y.*, no. 151021.

governance.[138] In a response letter, Chancellor Goldstein pointed out that in its own governance policy, the AAUP concedes that although academic and curricular decisions should ordinarily rest with the faculty, on certain critical issues the board may act on its own and state its reasons for doing so publicly. Goldstein argued that this was such a case.[139]

In February 2014, the trial court in the suit to block the Pathways Initiative ruled for CUNY. The court reaffirmed that the Board of Trustees was the sole body authorized by state law to "govern" and "administer" the university, including its academic policies, and that neither its bylaws nor the settlement agreement in the *Polishook* case granted a veto over curricular matters to the faculty.[140] The court further ruled that the implementation process for Pathways was not intended to circumvent the open meetings law. To the contrary, the court determined that CUNY "disseminated information widely and sought input from any interested parties through meetings, websites, webinars, consultations, discussions with members of the CUNY community, and telecasts online, on cable television and on the CUNY channel."[141] The PSC and the UFS chair are appealing the ruling.[142]

The PSC also filed a grievance under the collective bargaining agreement, claiming that the Pathways Initiative circumvented the

138. Barbara Bowen, president, PSC, and Sandi Cooper, chair, UFS, to B. Robert Kreiser, associate secretary, AAUP, November 16, 2011, letter, available at http://cunyufs.org/A/N/AAUP.pdf; B. Robert Kreiser, associate secretary, AAUP, to Matthew Goldstein, chancellor, CUNY, and Benno Schmidt, chair, Board of Trustees, CUNY, January 12, 2012, letter, available at http://cunyufs .org/A/AAUPletter.pdf.

139. Matthew Goldstein, chancellor, CUNY, to B. Robert Kreiser, associate secretary, AAUP, January 23, 2012, letter, available at http://cunyufs.org/ A/012312GoldsteintoKreiser.pdf; Matthew Goldstein, chancellor, CUNY, to B. Robert Kreiser, associate secretary, AAUP, March 21, 2012, letter, available at http://cunyufs.org/A/toKreiser.pdf.

140. *Professional Staff Congress v. City Univ. of N.Y.*, no. 151021 (slip. op. pp. 15–16).

141. Ibid. (Sup. Ct., N.Y. County, no. 103414, February 27, 2014) (Singh, J.) (slip. op. p. 8).

142. PSC, CUNY, "A Statement by Barbara Bowen and Terrence Martell on Pathways Lawsuit Decision," New York, March 11, 2014, available at www .psc-cuny.org/statement-barbara-bowen-and-terrence-martell-pathways-lawsuit -decision.

Board Bylaws on curriculum development, violated academic freedom, and involved retaliation against faculty opposed to the initiative, all in violation of the collective bargaining agreement. In a decision that was a surprise to many observers, the arbitrator ruled that the grievance was subject to arbitration, although she has not yet issued a decision on the substance.[143]

The lawsuit and the grievance together highlight what is at stake in the fight over Pathways: who gets to decide academic matters at CUNY. The lawsuit claims, at base, that the faculty governing bodies must initiate policies related to academics and curriculum. The PSC grievance contends, at base, that the process of curriculum development is a term and condition of employment, and the union has a right to grieve (and eventually arbitrate) an alleged violation of the governance procedures set forth in the Board Bylaws and the college's governance plans. CUNY's administration, on the other hand, maintains that the board, as a matter of state law, retains final authority on academic and curricular matters, subject to neither a faculty veto nor collective bargaining. Although the administration won the first round in court, the fight for control of CUNY continues.

Conclusion

For much of its fifty-year history, CUNY has been defined by two characteristics. The first is its origin as a confederation of pre-existing institutions with strong traditions of self-governance and organized faculty. The second is the open-admissions policy, which, although well-intentioned, was carried out without the resources and capacity to serve the influx of under-prepared students and seriously damaged CUNY's academic reputation. Perhaps ironically, the decentralized governance of the university greatly diminished its ability to address systematically the academic challenges raised by open admissions.

For the past fifteen years, a realigned presidential reporting structure, a supportive board, dedicated central administrators, and a

143. In the Matter of Professional Staff Congress & City Univ. of N.Y., Opinion & Award on Arbitrability (Am. Arb. Assoc. Case no. 13 672 00349 13, December 12, 2013).

forceful personality have enabled Chancellor Goldstein to impose university-wide policies in a way that previous chancellors failed to do. Guided by the blueprint in *An Institution Adrift*, Goldstein sought to rebuild CUNY's academic reputation through higher standards and new institutions, put the university on more solid financial footing, and make academic policies across individual campuses more coherent for the current, highly mobile student body.

In doing so, he generated passionate opposition from the faculty governance bodies and the union. This opposition reached a crescendo with the Pathways Initiative, the most direct effort to centrally coordinate academic policy. From the perspective of faculty leaders like UFS Chair Terrence Martell, Pathways represented overreach by an administration unchecked by the Board of Trustees. The frustration among faculty leaders runs deep: in Martell's words, Pathways did more than poison the well—"there's no well left to poison." And the efforts to block the Pathways Initiative have not stopped with its implementation: the PSC and Martell have appealed the trial court's rulings,[144] a grievance filed by the union claiming that Pathways was subject to collective bargaining is pending,[145] and faculty councils and the UFS continue to issue protest resolutions.[146]

Goldstein stepped down as chancellor at the end of the 2012–13 academic year. His successor, James Milliken, installed in June 2014, inherits an institution and a position that are very different from what they were in 1999. He also inherits a faculty that is eager to reassert itself and, over time, if not immediately, a board whose membership will reflect the priorities of a new mayor and (eventually) a new governor. As UFS Chair Martell put it, although administrators and board members come and go, the "faculty" is there forever. Indeed, there are already signs of a shift in the balance of power. During a

144. "Statement by Barbara Bowen and Terrence Martell on Pathways Lawsuit Decision."

145. In the Matter of Professional Staff Congress & City Univ. of N.Y., Opinion & Award on Arbitrability.

146. PSC, CUNY, "Brooklyn College Faculty Vote to Retake Control of Curriculum Decision Making; Vote No Confidence in CUNY Board of Trustees," April 25, 2014, available at www.psc-cuny.org/our-campaigns/brooklyn-college-faculty-vote-retake-curricular-control.

review of Pathways required by the enacting resolution, the interim chancellor between Goldstein's and Milliken's terms, William Kelly, reached an agreement with the UFS to adjust some of the general education requirements and give the UFS and faculty councils a greater role in the decision-making process.[147] Although supporters of the faculty position view this as a welcome change in tone and willingness to compromise, supporters of the Goldstein administration and Pathways view it as the beginning of a slippery slope. Time will tell whether Chancellor Milliken is willing or able to continue on the path laid out by Goldstein, whether he will set CUNY on a different path, or whether the forces competing for control of this largest of urban universities will once again leave CUNY adrift.

147. "A Message from the Interim Chancellor Regarding Pathways Review," *CUNY Academic News,* February 13, 2014, http://www1.cuny.edu/mu/academic-news/2014/02/13/a-message-from-the-interim-chancellor-regarding-pathways-review, accessed October 30, 2104.

INDEX

Page numbers for entries occurring in figures are followed by an *f* and those for entries in notes, by an *n*.

Cole, Jonathan R., 46n67, 68n3

collaboration: among institutions, 187–89; in online learning programs, 173–74, 175, 176, 182–83. *See also* shared governance

collective bargaining, 91, 143, 158, 159, 327, 328, 343. *See also* unions

College of Charleston, 133–34n4, 201–2

colonial America: faculty members in, 16–17, 19–20; higher education governance in, 14, 15–16n6, 15–22

Columbia University: academic freedom controversies, 45, 46, 47n68; Butler as president, 45, 46, 47n68, 96–97; Hofstadter's commencement speech at, 88, 92; non-tenure-track faculty, 157n38

communism, 70–75. *See also* loyalty oaths

Communist Party (USA), American, 75, 239n60

community colleges: in California, 79, 227; changes in 1970s, 102n70; growth of, 78; in New York, 108, 315–16n1, 321–22, 324, 327, 329

Condliffe Lagemann, Ellen, 53–54n80

contingent faculty. *See* non-tenure-track faculty

Cook, Bryan J., 192n24

Cooke, Morris L., 55

Cooper, Sandi, 343, 357n158

Cornell University, 29

corporate decision-making, 54–56, 150, 184–85

Cosman, Ben, 104n73

costs: cutting, 5, 178, 181, 197–99, 244–45, 305; education and related expenditures per full-time-equivalent student, 193–96, 194f, 195f, 197, 197n28; importance of, 177–81, 179n3, 197, 197n28; increases in, 197. *See also* budgets

Council of the Princeton University Community (CPUC), 94, 97, 101, 149–50, 276, 278–80, 281

Coursera, 114, 116n97, 125, 170, 187, 257, 273

CPUC. *See* Council of the Princeton University Community

Cremin, Lawrence A., 10, 10n13

Cripps, Michael J., 153n32

Cross, John G., 104n73, 152n30

Crow, Michael, 106n76, 137

CSU. *See* California State University system

CUNY. *See* City University of New York

CUNY Financing and Governance Act, 108–9, 329–30

curricula: closing programs, 106–7, 167, 273; for online learning, 173, 175–76; portfolio approach to, 173

curricular control: at City University of New York, 129–30, 356–58, 360; conflicts over, 64; by faculty, 166–68, 175–76; at Macalester, 297–98; at Princeton, 97, 272–73; at University of California, 128n108, 221, 240–41, 242, 243–44

Davidson, Christina C., 170n54

Davis, Angela, 239n60

Davis, John B., Jr., 302, 304

Day, Jeremiah, 27n31

deans. *See* administrators

decision-making: corporate, 54–56, 150, 184–85; in departments, 5, 182; informal, 131–32; nimble, 185–86, 211. *See also* governance; personnel decisions

Declaration of Principles on Academic Freedom and Academic Tenure, 1915 (AAUP), 42, 43, 43n61, 47, 73

de Forest, Jennifer, 53–54n80

democracy, 149, 191

denominational colleges, 21–22, 25, 28, 30–31, 55, 63. *See also* private colleges and universities

department chairs: elected, 341; history of, 31, 57, 65n103; at Princeton, 35–36, 266–67, 269; roles of, 32, 35–36, 57, 64–65; selecting, 141, 266–67; at University of California, 237

departments: authority of, 64–65; closing, 106–7, 167, 273, 307–8; curricular control by, 166–68, 240; decision-making in, 5, 182; emergence of, 31, 33;

allocation, 151, 167–68, 182–84, 241, 262n1, 279; in student life, 246–47, 276; student performance assessment, 168; surveys on, 208–9n43; teaching, 69n6, 70, 80, 82–83n36. *See also* curricular control; governance; research; shared governance

faculty senates. *See* academic senates

faculty unions. *See* unions

Fain, Paul, 188n17

Fields, Dave, 318n7, 336

Figlio, David N., 157, 157n39

financial aid, 111, 151, 296, 300, 308, 354

Findlay, James, 22n21

Fine, Henry, 37, 39, 43n61, 270

Finkin, Matthew W., 41n57, 49–50, 49n73, 50nn74–75, 51, 61nn95–96, 76–77n22, 139, 139n13, 201, 201nn33–34, 205

Finney, Joni E., 77n23

Fishman, Rachel, 117n101, 171n59

Flaherty, Colleen, 155n35, 200n31, 202n36

Flemming, Arthur S., 300, 301

Flexner, Abraham, 56n85

Florida State University, 133–34n4

foundations: higher education and, 53–56; online learning funding, 254

fragmentation of faculty, 18, 76, 83–84, 189–93, 196–97, 230n36, 263

Free Academy, 319

freedom of expression: Free Speech Movement, Berkeley, 72, 88–89, 224, 226, 233, 236, 246; of students, 140n14, 230–31, 231n40, 232–33. *See also* academic freedom

Friedman, Milton, 146n22

Fromson, Brett D., 185n13

Gardner, David P., 72n11, 73n13, 74, 74n16, 224n18, 225n20

Garvin, Lucius, 296

Gates Foundation, 123n106, 254

Gavin, Robert M., Jr., 96, 304

Geiger, Roger L., 10, 10n13, 20–21n19, 25n26, 26, 26n28, 27n30, 30, 31n36, 37n51, 44, 44n64, 45, 45n65, 53, 53nn79–80, 54n81, 55, 55nn82–83, 56, 56n86, 57, 57n87, 61n94, 68n3, 70n8, 79n27, 217, 217n2, 220n10, 231n42

Geiser, Saul, 79n26

Gendar, Allison, 345nn110–11

General Education Board, 54

General Motors, 278

Georgia State University, 117, 171

Gerber, Larry G., 6n9, 15n5, 143nn16–17, 144n18, 150n29, 328n52

Germany, research universities in, 28, 29

GI Bill, 77

Gill, Brian P., 316n5, 323nn32–33, 331nn60–63, 332n64, 334nn70–72

Gillmor, C. Stewart, 140n15

Gilman, Daniel Coit, 29

Gitlin, Todd, 88n47, 98n63

Giuliani, Rudolph, 109, 333, 334, 345

Glazer, Judith S. *See* Glazer-Raymo, Judith

Glazer, Nathan, 325n38

Glazer-Raymo, Judith, 100n66, 323n34

Global Campus, University of Illinois, 118, 167, 254

Goheen, Robert F., 150n27; coeducation policy and, 282; Council of the Princeton University Community and, 149–50, 278, 279; federal research funding and, 70n8, 275n9; Kelley Committee and, 92, 278; personality of, 96; as Princeton president, 144–45n20, 273, 277; as provost, 95n60

Golden, Andrew, 110n84

"Golden Age" of 1960s, 77–92, 177, 179–80

Goldenberg, Edie M., 104n73, 152n30

Goldin, Claudia, 2n2, 10, 62n97, 63, 63nn98–99, 65, 65n104, 68n3, 188, 188n18

Goldstein, Leon, 331

Goldstein, Matthew, 318n7, 357n159; as Baruch president, 333, 337; capital campaign and, 353; as CUNY chancellor, 109, 119–20, 317, 334, 337, 344–45, 346, 347, 352–55, 358–59; Master Plans and, 335–36, 346, 353–54; Performance Management Process, 338, 339; personality of, 96;

National Education Association, 99
National Education Longitudinal Study of 1972 (NELS-72), 3
National Education Longitudinal Study of 1988 (NELS-88), 3
National Labor Relations Board, 310–11
National Merit Scholars, 296
Neal, Homer Alfred, 69n5
Neill, Edward Duffield, 292
NELS. *See* National Education Longitudinal Study
New America Foundation, 117
New York City: fiscal crisis of, 329; high schools in, 319n11; minority population of, 324–25, 325n38. *See also* City University of New York
New York City Board of Education, 319–20
New York City Board of Higher Education, 108–9, 320–21, 322, 323, 327–29
New York City Technical Institute (NYCTI), 324, 324n36
New York College Teachers Union, 321
New York Public Employment Relations Board, 328, 353
New York State: CUNY Compact laws, 353–54; CUNY Financing and Governance Act, 108–9, 329–30; governors of, 329–30; legislature, 320, 321–22, 325, 329, 335; Taylor Law, 91, 327, 343
New York State Board of Regents, 322–23, 335, 346
New York University, 147
Next Generation Learning Challenges, 123n106, 254
The Next Generation University, 117–18
Nixon, Tricia, 101n69, 301n6
non-tenure-track (NTT) faculty: academic freedom of, 163–64; committee participation of, 164; continuing appointments of, 163; demand for, 153–54, 157n38; full-time, 158–59, 161–64, 311; in future, 153, 160–64, 199; governance impact of, 70, 155–56, 160–64; heterogeneity of, 156–57, 157n38; increased number of, 18, 104, 141–42,

152–55, 161, 190, 199, 229; introductory courses taught by, 157–58; master teachers, 156–57, 161–64; online learning and, 159–60, 171, 256; part-time, 152, 155, 157n38, 158, 311; promotions, 158–59; revolutionary shift toward, 153; supply of, 154–55; teaching performance of, 157–58, 163; working conditions of, 162n45. *See also* unions, non-tenure-track faculty
Northwestern University, 50n75, 157–58
Novak, Steven J., 25n26
NovoEd, 273
NTT faculty. *See* non-tenure-track faculty
NYCTI. *See* New York City Technical Institute
Nygren, Thomas I., 23n23, 170n55

Obama, Barack, 2
O'Neil, Robert M., 51n76, 52n78
online learning: at City University of New York, 119–20, 347–48, 350–52; collaborative efforts in, 187–88, 188n17, 189n19; concerns about, 123–24, 125, 172, 208, 253–54, 255–56, 351; cost savings from, 127, 178, 178n1, 179n3, 181, 244–45; costs of, 178n1, 244–45, 245n67, 258; course design for, 350–51; customizable platforms for, 172, 173, 187, 188, 189n19; degree programs, 121, 251, 254n89, 317, 348, 350; effective programs, 170–71; enrollment increased by, 117–18, 171, 173n64, 256–57; evaluations of, 258–59; faculty roles in, 114–17, 116n97, 118–20, 126, 169, 172–76, 185–86, 244–45, 252–53; goals of, 127, 178n1, 199, 245; governance impact of, 112–20, 116n97, 172–73n62, 172–76, 313, 313n15, 347–48; innovative contributions of faculty, 142, 170, 172–73n62, 173n64, 245n67, 260, 274; instructors, 159–60, 171; intellectual property rights issues in, 114, 174, 274, 312; at liberal arts colleges, 312–13, 313n15; at Macalester, 312–13, 314; MOOCs

(massive open online courses), 114–16, 125, 155, 170, 172, 260, 275; at Princeton, 273–75, 284; research on, 172n61; returns on investment in, 173n64; staffing impact of, 155, 155n35; success factors in, 120–21, 127, 172–73n62; sustainability of, 274–75; top-down initiatives, 244; at University of California, 120–27, 123n106, 244–45, 251–60

Otte, George, 347, 351

Oxford University, 14

Oxtoby, David, 144n20

pacifists, 45, 46

Palmer, Iris, 117n101, 171n59

Parker, Jo Ellen, 210n45

Parry, Marc, 122n105

Pataki, George, 109, 333, 334, 345

Patel, Vimal, 162n45

Pathways Initiative, CUNY, 127–30, 186–87, 343, 351, 354–58, 359–60

Patterson, Gardner, 282–83

Patton, Francis, 35, 268–69

Pearson, 172n61

Pennington, Hilary, 117n101, 171n59

personnel decisions: academic freedom and, 41–44, 45–48, 51n76, 61, 242–43; appointments, 139–41, 237–40, 267–69, 270–72, 299; cluster hiring, 352; in colonial America, 19; controversies, 41, 47–48, 239n60, 242–43; departmental involvement, 32; faculty roles in, 33, 34–41, 47, 50, 139–42, 237–40; firings, 36, 41, 45–48, 269–70, 271, 272, 301; flexibility needed in, 163n46; issues, 140–42; presidential authority, 32, 34, 35, 220; procedures, 139; promotions, 82–83n36, 140–41, 238, 239, 267, 268; recruitment, 271–72, 294, 296, 300, 306; for research staff, 69–70; retirements, 103–4, 103n72, 141, 154; reviews, 141, 220, 238, 267; rights of individuals, 39–40, 44; trustee roles in, 35, 268. See also non-tenure-track faculty; tenure

Pichler, Susanne, 23n23, 205n40

Pitts, Lawrence, 124

Polishook, Irwin H., 328n52

Polishook case, 332–33, 343, 356, 357

politics: City University of New York and, 316; influence of, 219n8; state university funding, 201–2, 219n8; student activities, 230–31, 232–33, 246. *See also* protests

Post, Robert C., 41n57, 43n61, 49–50, 49n73, 50nn74–75, 51, 61nn95–96, 139, 139n13, 201, 201nn33–34, 205

Potts, David B., 22n21, 31n36

Powers, William C., 134, 135n6

Presbyterian Church, Macalester College and, 292, 293, 303

presidents: appointments of, 27n31, 38, 266; backgrounds of, 55–56; in colonial America, 19–21; corporate models for, 150; evaluating performance of, 138; faculty personnel decisions by, 32, 220; firings, 133–35, 137–38, 211n47; future roles of, 208–9; hiring, 133–35, 137–38; intermediary roles of, 26; as leaders, x, 96, 135, 136–37, 208–9, 209n44; political figures as, 133–34n4; power of, 19–20, 29, 31–32, 35–41, 135; relations with faculty, 135–36, 135n7, 140–41, 142, 148–49n25; of research universities, 29, 31–32; roles and responsibilities of, 35–41, 63–64, 208–9, 208–9n43; selection of, 19–20, 133–34n4, 133–36, 137–38. *See also individual institutions*

Princeton University: ad hoc committees of, 281–85; admissions policies of, 263–64n4; coeducation at, 282–83; Committee of Three, 34, 39, 41, 264, 267–68, 271, 280–81; Committee on Committees, 41, 264–65; committee structure of, 94, 264, 268, 270–71, 272, 276, 277–78, 280–85; comparisons to University of California, 221–22nn11–12; Conference Committee, 41, 60, 271, 277; Council of the Princeton University Community, 94, 97, 101, 149–50, 276, 278–80, 281;

Princeton University (*continued*)
culture of, 95–96, 95n61; curricular
decisions at, 97, 272–73; department
chairs, 35–36, 266–67, 269; endowment of, 110n84, 261–62, 285; faculty-
administration relationships, 60, 262,
262n2, 269, 270–72, 277, 280–81, 282,
285; Faculty Advisory Committee on
Policy, 277, 278, 280, 281; faculty committees, 60, 221n11; faculty roles at, 39,
40–41, 47, 95, 97, 221–22n12, 263–65,
267–68, 270–85; federal research funds,
69–70, 70n8, 275; financial challenges
of, 110n84, 262, 280; governance history, 101n68, 221–22n12, 265, 268–
72, 277–79; governance structure of,
93–96, 261–68, 262n1, 285–86; graduate programs of, 273; Hiss controversy at, 74–75; online learning at,
273–75, 284; personnel decisions at,
34–36, 37, 39–41, 47, 267–72; Priorities Committee, 94, 151, 261n, 279,
279n13; protests in 1960s and 1970s,
92–93, 94–95, 97–98, 98n63; research
oversight at, 275; residential colleges at,
283; ROTC issue, 97–98, 284–85; Special Committee on the Structure of the
University (Kelley Committee), 92–94,
97, 236n56, 261n, 263, 265, 278, 282;
teaching assistants at, 262–63; tuition
increases at, 101; University Research
Board, 69–70, 275; wrestling program
of, 146n23
Princeton University Board of Trustees:
academic freedom controversies and,
75; advisory committees of, 283–84;
faculty appointments by, 267, 268;
faculty committees and, 268, 277–78,
283; members of, 75, 97n62, 146n23;
relations with presidents, 35; roles of,
97–98, 263–64, 266, 272, 273, 278;
*Statement of Policy on Delegation of
Authority*, 93–94, 97, 263, 263–64n4,
286–89; Wilson and, 37, 269
Princeton University presidents: academic freedom controversies and, 46,

75; evolution of roles of, 268–72; faculty personnel decisions by, 34, 35,
36, 39–41, 267–68, 269–71; power of,
261, 266; relations with faculty, 40–41,
60, 221–22n12, 270–71; relations with
trustees, 35; selection of, 266. *See also*
Goheen, Robert F.; Hibben, John Grier
"Jack"; Wilson, Woodrow
Pritchett, Henry, 55
private colleges and universities: admissions policies of, 165; denominational,
21–22, 25, 28, 30–31, 55, 63; education and related expenditures per
full-time-equivalent student of, 194–
95, 194f, 196, 197n28; financial sustainability of, 198n29; tuition increases
at, 197. *See also* liberal arts colleges;
individual institutions
private sector: corporate decision-making, 54–56, 150, 184–85; foundations,
53–56, 254; higher education and, 21
Professional Staff Congress (PSC), City
University of New York: on cluster hiring, 352; collective bargaining, 328,
343; formation of, 91, 327; grievances,
353, 357–58; lawsuits, 317, 332–33,
357; leaders of, 343–44; opposition to
board initiatives, 317, 344, 345; Pathways Initiative and, 356–58, 359; roles
of, 343–44
Progressive Era, 43
Proposition 209 (California Civil Rights
Initiative), 148, 148n24, 250
protests, 1960s and 1970s: antiwar, 88,
92, 94–95, 97–98, 98n63, 230; at
Berkeley, 230–31; Berkeley Free Speech
Movement, 72, 88–89, 224, 226, 233,
236, 246; campus regulations, 230–31,
232–33; at City College of New York,
326; civil disobedience, 232, 246; disciplinary responses to, 246; impact
of, 91–92; at Macalester, 300–301;
at Princeton, 92–93, 94–95, 97–98,
98n63
provosts. *See* administrators
PSC. *See* Professional Staff Congress

public universities. *See* land-grant universities; state universities

Queens College, 320, 321, 322, 340

Rabban, David M., 52n78
race relations: affirmative action issues, 148, 148n24, 249–50, 300, 325–27; civil rights movement, 88; faculty of color, 92
Radcliffe, Evan, 150n28
Radner, Roy, 85n39
RAND Institute, 334
Reader's Digest, 105, 293, 304–6, 309
Reader's Digest Merit Scholars, 296
Reagan, Ronald, 234
real estate development, 147
regents. *See* trustees; University of California Board of Regents
religious denominations. *See* denominational colleges; Presbyterian Church
Renfro, Sally, 82n34, 319n12, 322n24, 324n35
representative governance, 191
research: defense-related, 78, 226; federal funding of, 68–69, 69n5, 78, 82, 100, 275; foundation support of, 56; intellectual property policies and, 352–53; oversight of, 275; professional staff, 69–70, 70n8, 80, 103, 161, 228–29; status of, 83; undergraduate training in, 162, 162n44
research universities: bureaucracy in, 33; in China, 49; emergence of, 27–33; establishment dates of, 24f, 28, 28n33; faculty of, 29, 31, 32–33, 80, 161–62, 162n44; faculty roles at, 56–57, 68–69, 103; features of, 28, 30; future of, 199; graduate teaching assistants at, 57; growth of, 82, 226; land-grant universities, 23, 24f, 28, 165; non-tenure-track faculty, 154; presidents of, 29, 31–32; women faculty at, 99. *See also* Association of American Universities; *individual institutions*
Reserve Officer Training Corps (ROTC): at Princeton, 97–98, 284–85; protests

against, 91–92, 98n63; at University of California, 230n37
resource allocation: administrator and trustee roles in, 167–68; constraints on, 181; faculty roles in, 151, 167–68, 182–84, 241, 262n1, 279
retirement: incentives for, 141; mandatory, 103–4, 103n72, 141, 154
Reuther, Walter, ix–x
Reveley, Taylor, 198n30
Reviewing the Academic Presidency, 150
Reynolds, Ann, 330–32, 333
Rice, Andrew, 113n89
Rice, Harvey, 293
Riesman, David, 10, 32n40, 63–64, 64nn101–2, 69, 69n6, 82–83n36, 91n53, 138n10
Rivard, Ry, 115n95, 116nn97–98, 133–34n4
Robinson, James (American Express chairman/CEO), 185n13
Robinson, James (Macalester president), 301
Rockefeller, John D., 54
Rockefeller, Nelson, 322, 323
Rosen, Gideon, 274
Rosenberg, Brian, 191, 191nn21–22, 208–9n43, 210, 210n45, 212, 212n49, 291n1
Rosenberg, Gustave, 321, 325
Rosenthal, Michael, 46n66, 47n68
Ross, Edward A., 41–42
Rossiter, Margaret R., 99, 99n64
Rossmann, Jack E., 291n
ROTC. *See* Reserve Officer Training Corps
Rothblatt, Sheldon, 80n28, 87n44, 231n42
Rudenstine, Neil L., 48n71, 97n62, 190, 190n20, 283
Rudolph, Frederick, 10, 10n13, 16, 16n8, 17n10, 20n17, 24n24, 26, 27n30
Rule 17, 230–31
Ruml, Beardsley, 180n4
Rumsfeld, Donald, 146n23
Russell, Bertrand, 48n71
Rutgers University, 146n22, 158
Ruthven, Alexander Grant, 61

St. Olaf College, 312

Sandel, Michael, 116

San Jose State University, 115, 116

Savio, Mario, 88. *See also* Free Speech Movement

Schaffer, Frederick P., 203, 203n38, 204, 204n39, 205n41, 318n7, 348, 353, 356n137

Schapiro, Morton O., 153, 153n31, 157n39

Schmidt, Benno C., Jr., 90, 333, 334, 344

Schmidt, Peter, 51n76, 76–77n22, 133–34n4, 156n37, 202n37

Schonfeld, Roger C., 175n66

school districts, 188–89

School of Professional Studies (SPS), City University of New York, 119–20

Schrecker, Ellen W., 74, 74n17

science: departmental organization, 241–42; division from humanities, 83–84, 229–30. *See also* research

SEIU. *See* Service Employees International Union

Selingo, Jeff, 117n101, 171n59

Service Employees International Union (SEIU), 156, 156n36, 311

sexual harassment and assault, 133n3

Shapiro, Harold T., 146n23, 280–81

Shapiro, Judith, 138–39n12

shared governance: "Berkeley Revolution of 1919–1920," 38–39, 220–21, 221n11; consultation, 101n68, 185–86, 266–67, 277; faculty market power and, 84–86; meaning of, 6, 9, 210–11; for online learning, 172–74, 175–76; resource allocation, 151, 167–68, 241; rethinking, 205–12; students included in, 101, 101n68; support for, 6, 59, 144; at University of California, 72, 235, 238, 239, 241–42, 244; use of term, 205, 205n40

Shulman, James L., 146n23

Simmons, Daniel, 124, 255–56

Singer, Peter, 267

Slemrod, Joel, 159n41

Sloan, Douglas, 14–15n4

Sloan Foundation, 347

Smelser, Neil J., 87, 87n44, 88n47, 211–12, 212n48, 230n37

Smith, Carol, 321n21

Smith, Tobin, 69n5

Smith, Wilson, 91n53, 92nn54–55

Smyth, Henry DeWolf, 69, 275

SNHU. *See* Southern New Hampshire University

Snow, C. P., 83

Snyder, Susan, 145n21

socioeconomic status, higher education and, 3–4

Soter, Kevin B., 157n39

South Africa divestment issue, 284

South Carolina legislature, 201–2

Southern New Hampshire University (SNHU), 159–60, 171

Soviet Union, Sputnik launch by, 69n5, 78, 226, 322

specialization of faculty, 18, 33, 63, 84, 107, 189–90, 250–51, 309–10

Spencer, Herbert, 41

Spencer Foundation, xii

Spies, Richard, 170–71n56, 187n16

Spitzer, Eliot, 306

sports. *See* athletics

Sproul, Robert: Academic Senate and, 38n53, 60, 73, 221n11; career, 222, 222n15; Kerr and, 87n43; loyalty oath controversy and, 71, 223, 224, 225; relations with faculty, 60, 101n68, 142, 247–48; staff of, 225n23; as UC president, 87n43, 222–23, 225n23, 226

Sproul Directives, 230–31, 232

Sputnik launch, 69n5, 78, 226, 322

Stadtman, Verne A., 37n51, 220n10, 228n32

Stanford, Mrs. Leland, 41

Stanford University: administrators of, 140n15; divestment from coal companies, 144n20; faculty members, 41–42; Highwire Press and, 185n13; online learning at, 274; presidents of, 29

Statement of Policy on Delegation of Authority (Princeton), 93–94, 97, 263, 263–64n4, 286–89

Tressel, Jim, 133–34n4
Trow, Martin, 87n44
trustee roles: activism, 6n9; clarifying, 6; disciplinary, 25–26; faculty appointments, 35; historical evolution of, 15–16n6, 16, 17, 19, 21, 25–27, 33; legal, 19; linkage with broader society, 75n18, 97–98; relations with faculty, 25, 26–27, 63–64; resource allocation, 167–68
trustees: academic freedom defenders, 75; alumni as, 26; backgrounds of, 22, 55–56, 97n62, 138; personalities of, 97n62; politicians as, 323, 334. *See also* boards of trustees
Tukey, John, 273
Turner, Sarah E., 4n5, 23n23, 156–57, 157n38, 230n36

UCEP. *See* University Committee on Education Policy
UCLA. *See* University of California, Los Angeles
UCOE. *See* University of California Online Education Initiative
Udacity, 115
UFCT. *See* United Federation of College Teachers
UMassOnline, 117
unions: collective bargaining, 91, 143, 158, 159, 327, 328, 343; faculty, 90, 91, 102n70, 129–30, 321; power of, 344; of teaching staff, 251
unions, non-tenure-track faculty: collective bargaining agreements, 158, 159, 328; at Macalester, 310–11; opposition to, 156; organization efforts of, 155–56, 156n36, 327; at University of California, 256. *See also* Professional Staff Congress
United Federation of College Teachers (UFCT), 91, 327
US Department of Education: Institute of Education Sciences, National Center for Education Statistics, 154n34; National Center for Education Statis-

tics, Integrated Postsecondary Education Data System, 3n3, 152n30
University Committee on Education Policy (UCEP), University of California, 121–22, 121n104, 124, 247–48, 252, 253, 255–56
University Council–Academic Federation of Teachers, 256
University Innovation Alliance, 188n17
University of California: admissions policies of, 165n48, 220, 227, 249–50; campuses of, 223; chancellor selection at, 237; changes in 1960s, 78–80, 87n43, 226–33, 230n37; comparisons to Princeton, 221–22nn11–12; degree requirements of, 243–44, 244n66; department chairs at, 237; enrollments of, 226–27, 248; expansion of, 78–79, 222–23, 227; faculty committees of, 235–36; faculty personnel decisions at, 36–39, 47, 220; faculty quality at, 79, 80; faculty roles at, 36, 47, 166, 219, 234–51; financial challenges of, 123–24, 219–20, 255; governance structure of, 87n43, 217, 218–33; graduate programs of, 79; Innovative Learning Teaching Initiative of, 126; loyalty oath controversy at, 41, 52, 71–74, 223–25; Master Plan of, 78–79, 79n26, 226–27, 228, 322; as multiversity, 18; non-tenure-track faculty at, 251, 256; politicization of faculty of, 72–73; post-tenure reviews at, 141; as research university, 80, 228–29; shared governance at, 72, 235, 238, 239, 241–42, 244; student activities at, 230–31, 232–33; "Wheeler–Sproul–Academic Senate model," 222–23
University of California Academic Senate (AS): Academic Assembly, 232n43, 248; Academic Council, 38n53, 122–23, 124, 221n11, 233n49, 236, 239n60, 242–43, 247, 248, 249, 253, 255–56, 257; admissions policies and, 165n48; advisory role of, 247–49; affirmative action issues